YOU LOOK LIKE DEATH

TALES FROM THE UMBRELLA ACADEMY™

GERARD WAY   SHAUN SIMON   I.N.J. CULBARD   NATE PIEKOS

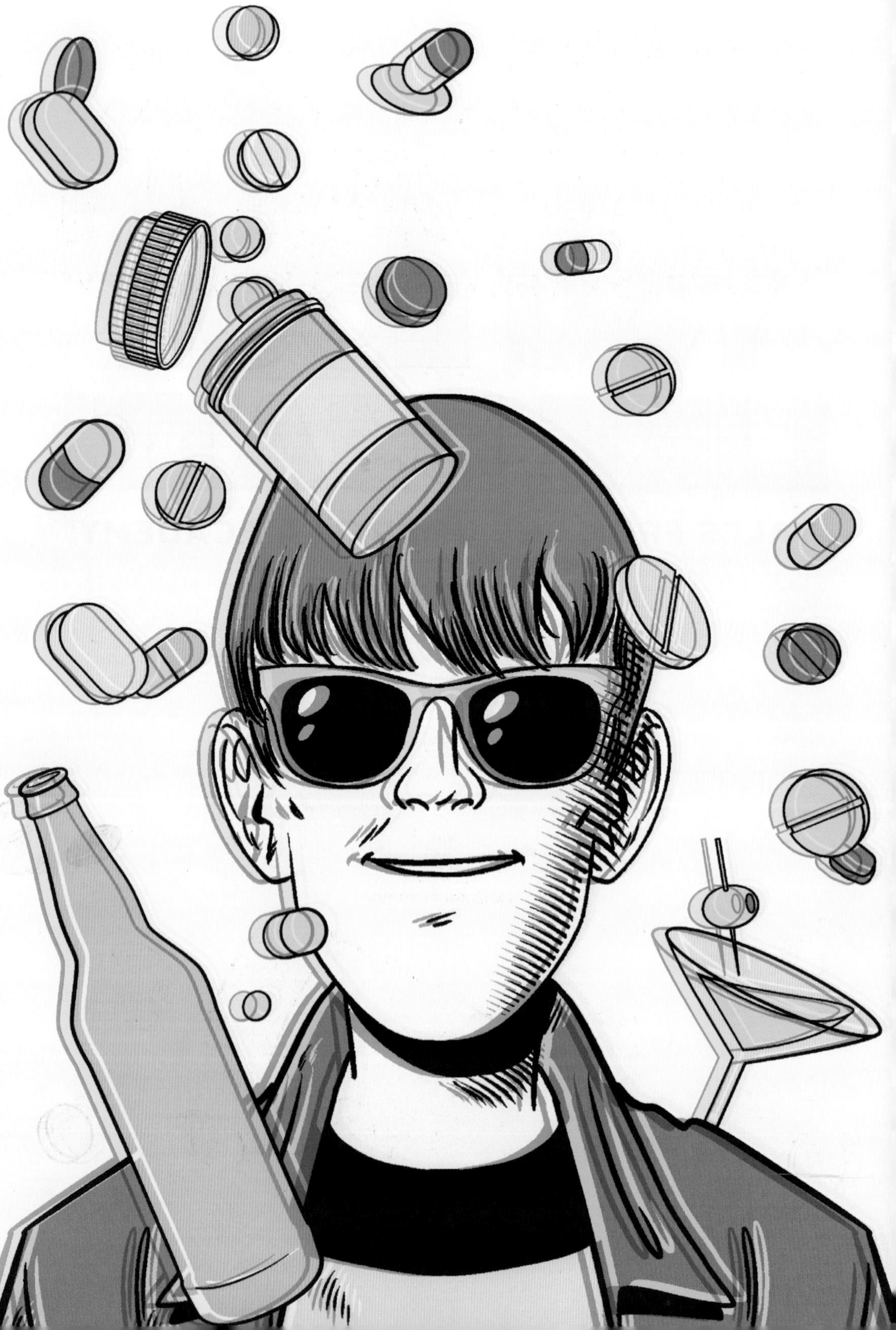

YOU LOOK LIKE DEATH

TALES FROM THE UMBRELLA ACADEMY™

STORY
GERARD WAY AND SHAUN SIMON

ART & COLORS
I.N.J. CULBARD

LETTERS
NATE PIEKOS OF BLAMBOT®

COVER AND CHAPTER BREAKS BY
GABRIEL BÁ

***UMBRELLA ACADEMY* CREATED BY**
GERARD WAY AND GABRIEL BÁ

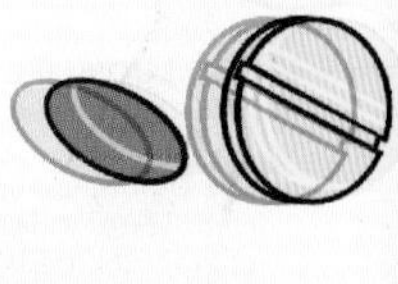

DARK HORSE BOOKS

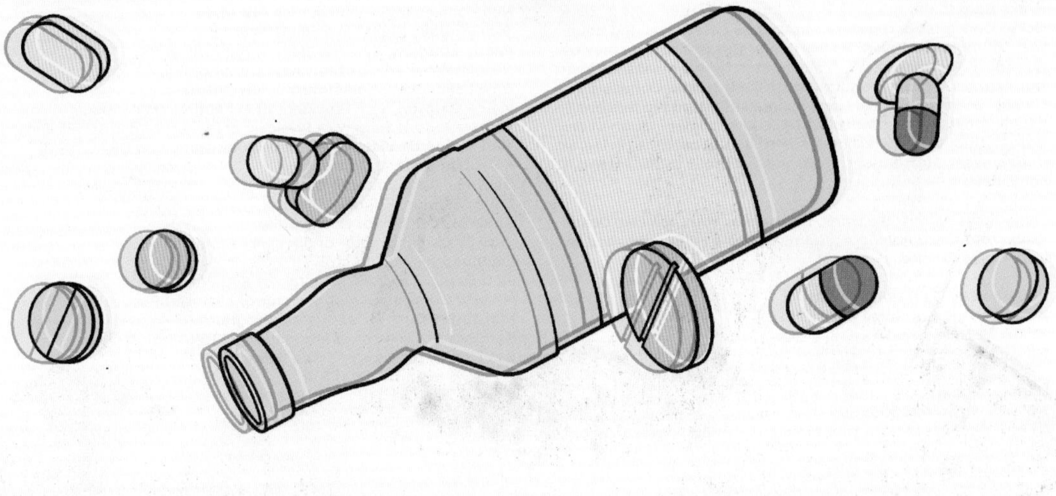

"To Robert, for elevating, levitating,
and activating our Klaus."—GERARD WAY

"To Christine."—SHAUN SIMON

"To K, J, and B."—I.N.J. CULBARD

"To Concetta."—NATE PIEKOS

PRESIDENT & PUBLISHER MIKE RICHARDSON **EDITOR** DANIEL CHABON

ASSISTANT EDITOR CHUCK HOWITT **COLLECTION DESIGNER** ETHAN KIMBERLING

DIGITAL ART TECHNICIAN ALLYSON HALLER

YOU LOOK LIKE DEATH
THE UMBRELLA ACADEMY™

First Edition: March 2021
Ebook ISBN 978-1-50671-909-2
Trade Paperback ISBN 978-1-50671-910-8
10 9 8 7 6 5 4 3 2 1
Printed in China

This volume reprints the comic-book series *You Look Like Death:
Tales from the Umbrella Academy* issues #1–#6, published by
Dark Horse Comics.

Published by Dark Horse Books
A division of Dark Horse Comics LLC
10956 SE Main Street
Milwaukie, OR 97222

DarkHorse.com
Advertising Sales: (503) 905-2315
To find a comics shop in your area, visit comicshoplocator.com

FOREWORD

BY ROBERT SHEEHAN

I swallowed a comic. Inhaled the bastard. Called *The Umbrella Academy*. Then got to be possessed of the guy who floats out of Gerard and Gabriel's combino-brain.

Floats, with such ennui. Who levitates lusciously. Who self-destructs ooh! with such cool you can't help but egg him on, toward oblivion.

This guy called Klaus. In a baggy stripey sweater. Who flirts with the darkness. That oool' endless abysssss, on either side of usss, that ol' sliver of light we've agreed to call life. Klaus is your passing, made flesh (ink). Albeit pale, but definitely still chic flesh (ink).

Who sniffs at death like turned milk. Who pats it on its little bumbum. He wet-willies (Wet-Willy Instructions–suck finger. Insert finger in ear of another person ((living or dead)). Repeat same ad infinitum.)
all of our fundamental fears. He nipple cripples our sense of calm, collected grown-upedness.
'Excuse me, Waiter, I was just in control, having rare banter with my wife, until this rude skinny man levitated up and twisted me right on the nipple. How did he judge so accurately where it was under my polo shirt?!'

To Klaus, the sun doesn't shine per se. Not even in LA. It illuminates the dark.
Annoyingly, for eight, nine, even up to sixteen hours some days.
He wishes some spectre would give him some dirt on the sun, so he could drift up there and blackmail him to stop shining altogether, forever.

Who leaves the picture, begging to be coloured in according to the numbers, devoid. Colourless. Because it is. All on its own. And if you want to colour it in, kid, that's completely up to you.

To whom life is as equally empty as death. So finds it equally as drab, because he realises they're one and the same. And both, for him, come with the same inescapable wailing shackles.
He knows that life ought not be given the level of reverence it gets. Giving it that much only declares all-out war on death.

Klaus is at war, and losing, naturally. Pitted from day dot by Reggie against what ghosts cause his ceaseless haunting. The undead chickens are chattering. And if emotions are the expression of thought in the body, then relax the emotions and you can relax the thoughts, right? And what's a great body relaxant? Heroin, honey!

Heroin. And more heroine...

And Klaus's defences are dwindling–and that's right about where we drop in. With our binoculars. Like Jimmy Stewart. To *You Look Like Death* Klaus.

What is it about you humans that makes you such eager voyeurs of your own destruction? That compulsion very same that makes you double cautious around safety hazards? Like cliff edges.

Klaus is a cliff edge.

And edging closer confronts you with the possibility of your own death. Klaus is not a cliff edge. He's just dangling out over the side of the cliff edge in a hammock, smoking and being disturbed by you, sweating and nervously peering over, from reading Poe's *Tales of Mystery & Imagination*.

And as you edge closer you catch a glimpse of what Klaus can't escape seeing all the sunny day long. Death, you look her square in the face, on the precipice. And it's not the instant death part that scares you and makes you recoil, it's that it's already here. The absolute certainty of your death, which will happen 100% so what are you so scared about? Relaaax. And how little equipment/language/real ritual we have to really deal with it. We have no negotiation tactics in this match. Except, maybe Klaus?

Death ain't really death, not for Klaus. Can't be, it's just an interval. It's just a stop and a change-over at a busy railroad junction. The journey is to be continued. And continued. And continued. And continuuuued... And continued.
So go on then, son, destroy yourself. Remind us all...

And where better to do it than Tinseltown! The city of dreams. Dreams and unfinished business.

My understanding of the Hindu god Hanuman, is this fiercely devoted but very cheeky white monkey god who, even in appearance, is a contradiction. He once mistook the sun for a fruit and climbed up there and came back with a dislocated jaw. He spends his time tying folks' shoelaces together and Saran wrapping the toilet bowl. Making prank calls. Throwing fireworks at the fringes of your cassock.

Destruction is far from off Hanuman's dessert menu. Klaus, I've often pondered, is the hauntingly fashionable reoccurrence of Hanuman.

This time incarnated as the guy who wouldn't look out of place as an extra in the back of an Ingmar Bergman movie. Until he gets fired for making incessant snorting sounds over the Swedish dialogue.

Klaus is from the same source of what the Hindus understand, that by characterising/embracing an awareness of your own Hanuman, there occurs in you access to *infinite* founts of creative power. Behind the destruction, the silly, the unease, beyond the stupid, the painful, the surreal childish, the total head-thrown-back Hanuman abandon, lies a thousand comic books worth. Of Klaus. Looking like Death, and how would Gerard know unless he's really looked.

Is there no greater proof that destruction is creation (and t'other way round) than Klaus? They're two sides of the same coin, no? If you asked me, Klaus stems from a ghost who haunted Gerard once upon a time. Who was Gerard once upon a time.

The face of his shadow. Lucky devil.
These days, Gerard clearly doesn't mind haunting back. He'd be killing Klaus for company, killing him with kindness, incessantly inviting him to the candlelit writing table. For supper and sweet mince and sherry afters. In the sanctum of his sunny studio in Eagle Rock.
Both of them, negotiating terms long into the quiet night. What parts Klaus is willing to put on the table, and permit Gerard to reveal.

I imagine Gerard, writing Klaus late at night. He is listening. To the rustling of the yew and the camphor tree. He can detect fierce silence between the loud crickets outside.
His wife and daughter are sound asleep.

He thinks back. To when Klaus was less a concept, more a poltergeist. To that relief of permitting his self-control to sliiiide, to the thrill of sawing through the tether of his own life, while peering down into the abyssss, and seeing no bottom. Surely nothing is off their table?

Conquer the ghost. That Gerard breaks his own down to all its composite parts, whisks them all into a larger-than-life bowl and then publishes his findings to the world in the form of a comic book character, is a feat of self-love. And what does he really find when he looks? Beyond the pain of its groping, strangulating tentacles?
A reward. Of a seemingly bottomless well of Klaus. Who pours out of Gerard in abundance, flowing like torrent water onto Gabriel's work-station.

Klaus and *The Umbrella Academy* are the chicken and the egg. I think, and I don't even know which of them came first or why we differentiated them. And maybe I'm biased, but maybe Gerard's mischief sprite that sprouted into ink as Klaus might be the one and the same, about same as chicken and egg same, as *The Umbrella Academy*.
That he is at the source. Or is the source. Of the universal human impulse. Which fuels the whole *Umbrella* world into its existent darkness and macabre.

Klaus is Gerard's haunting. Klaus is the last song you'll ever hear on the radio. Klaus is what you end up with when you have no choice but to unplug the ceaseless beast.
You could say Gerard inflicted Klaus with what Klaus inflicted on him. Spiteful Gerard! He gave Klaus a haunting.

He gave Klaus a Klaus. He gave him ghosts to conquer. And he gave Klaus enormous power. And now, there's no end to the amount of punishment he can take and no matter how much he endures, he always leaves me wanting more! What is that.

Klaus looks like death.

But I think it would be closer (and much less catchy) to say Klaus looks like Death is killing him. He's a thousand deaths all rolled into one. Ol' Grim Reaper's got him under siege, and his fortress walls are crumbling. And inside he's dying with a thirst that no opiate water can quench. Poor thing. He doesn't know he's making his war and has the power to unmake it. No one ever told him. Poor thing.

Reggie was too busy forcing his super-skills to grow that he left to rot the neglected soul beneath. A soul that, as Jesus wittily dubbed it, is 'as a branch cut off from the vine.'
Not Reggie the space alien nor Grace the robot possess the human gift, to teach him that you can't run away from yourself. And if you surrender and let all the ghosts squat in your house then expect the invitation to be extended to lots more, until before long you can barely move around your own kitchen without screaming. Without being possessed by the fearful impulse to fight, flight, freeze, or go limp. The latter option being Klaus's preferred.

The ghosts of memory that make such pain in his body, have become his milestones of Self. Because no one ever told him otherwise... I want to hug him. I want to take his pale, crumbling skeletal form in my arms and cuddle him, to try and free him from his wailing shackles if even for just a while (though it may make him less entertaining).

Because I am a bit Klaus too. I love Klaus. We love Klaus.
Thank you, Gerard and Gabriel and Dark Horse. For Klaus.

Yours, in this life,
ROBERT SHEEHAN

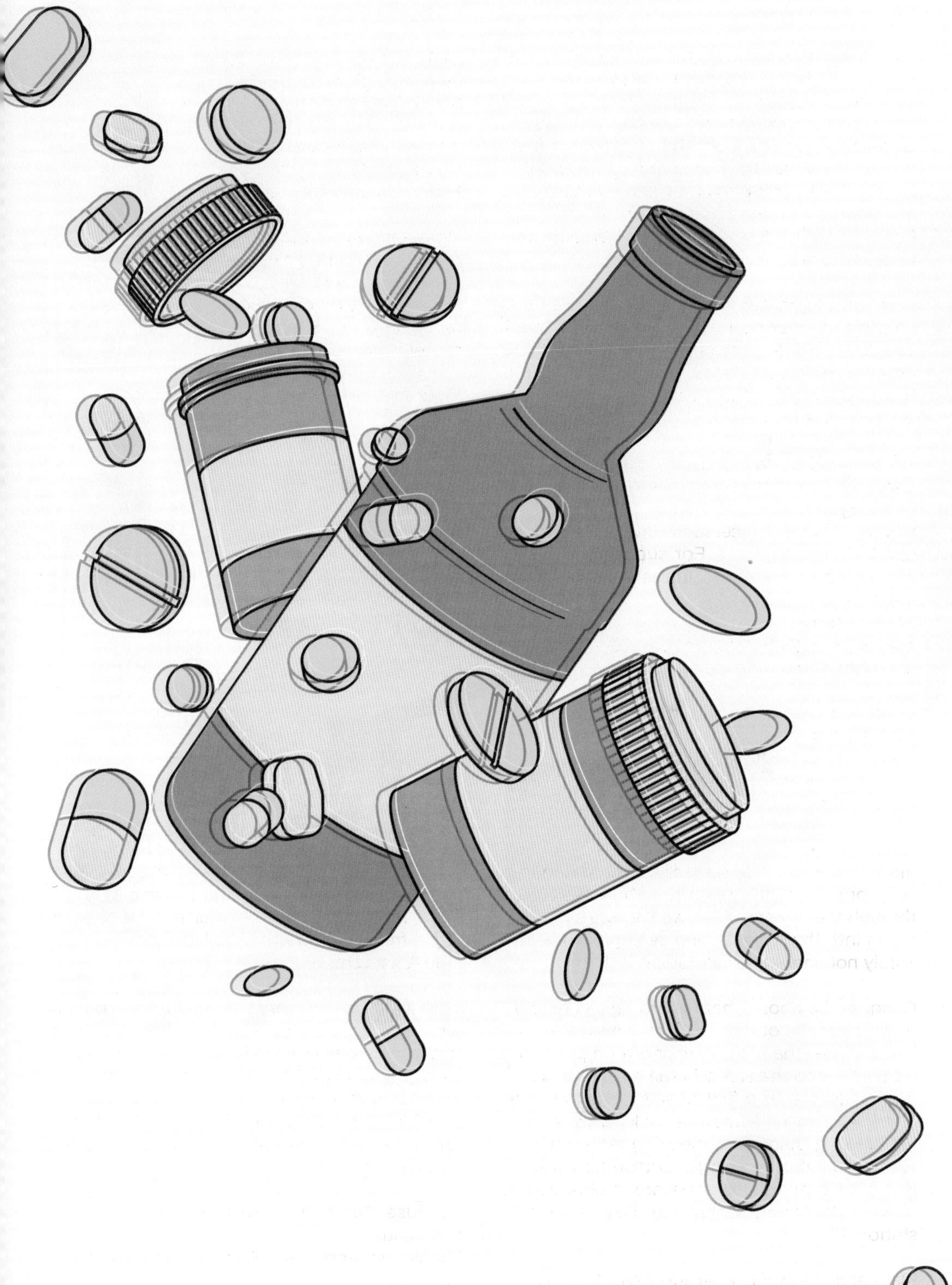

CHAPTER ONE

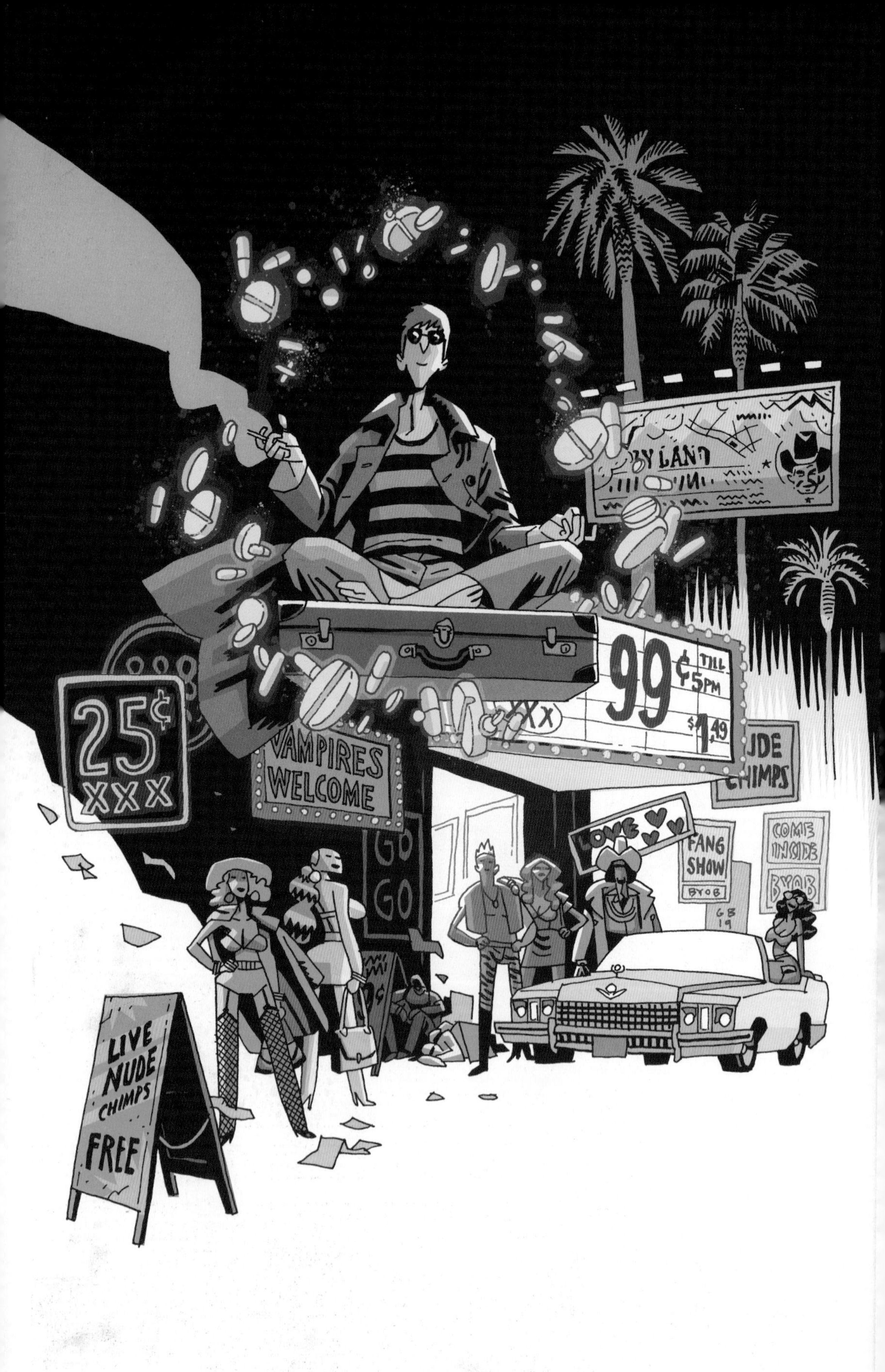
25¢
XXX
VAMPIRES WELCOME
99¢ TILL 5PM
$1.49
XXX
GO GO
LOVE
FANG SHOW
BYOB
COME INSIDE
BYOB
LIVE NUDE CHIMPS
FREE

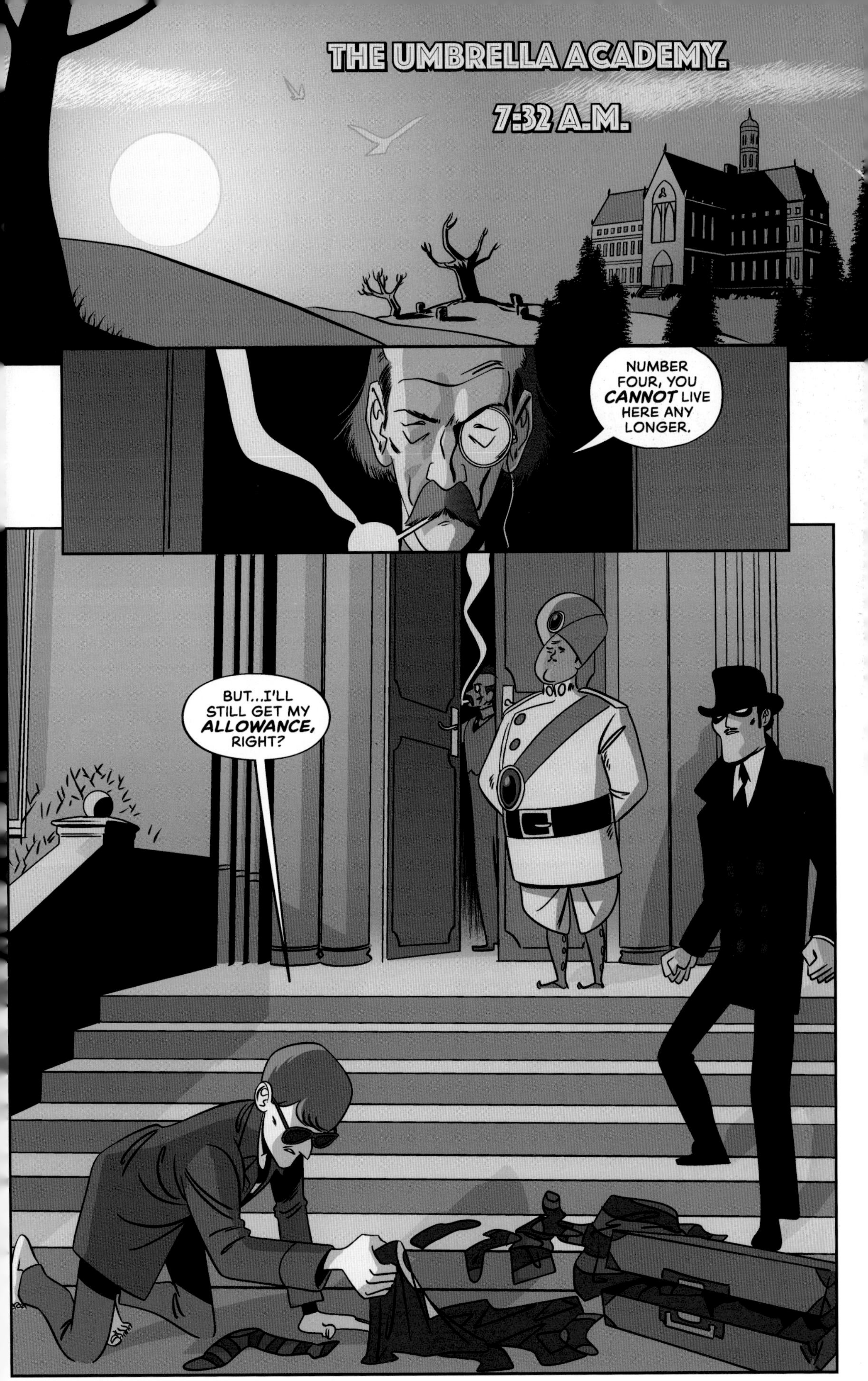
THE UMBRELLA ACADEMY.
7:32 A.M.
NUMBER FOUR, YOU CANNOT LIVE HERE ANY LONGER.
BUT...I'LL STILL GET MY ALLOWANCE, RIGHT?

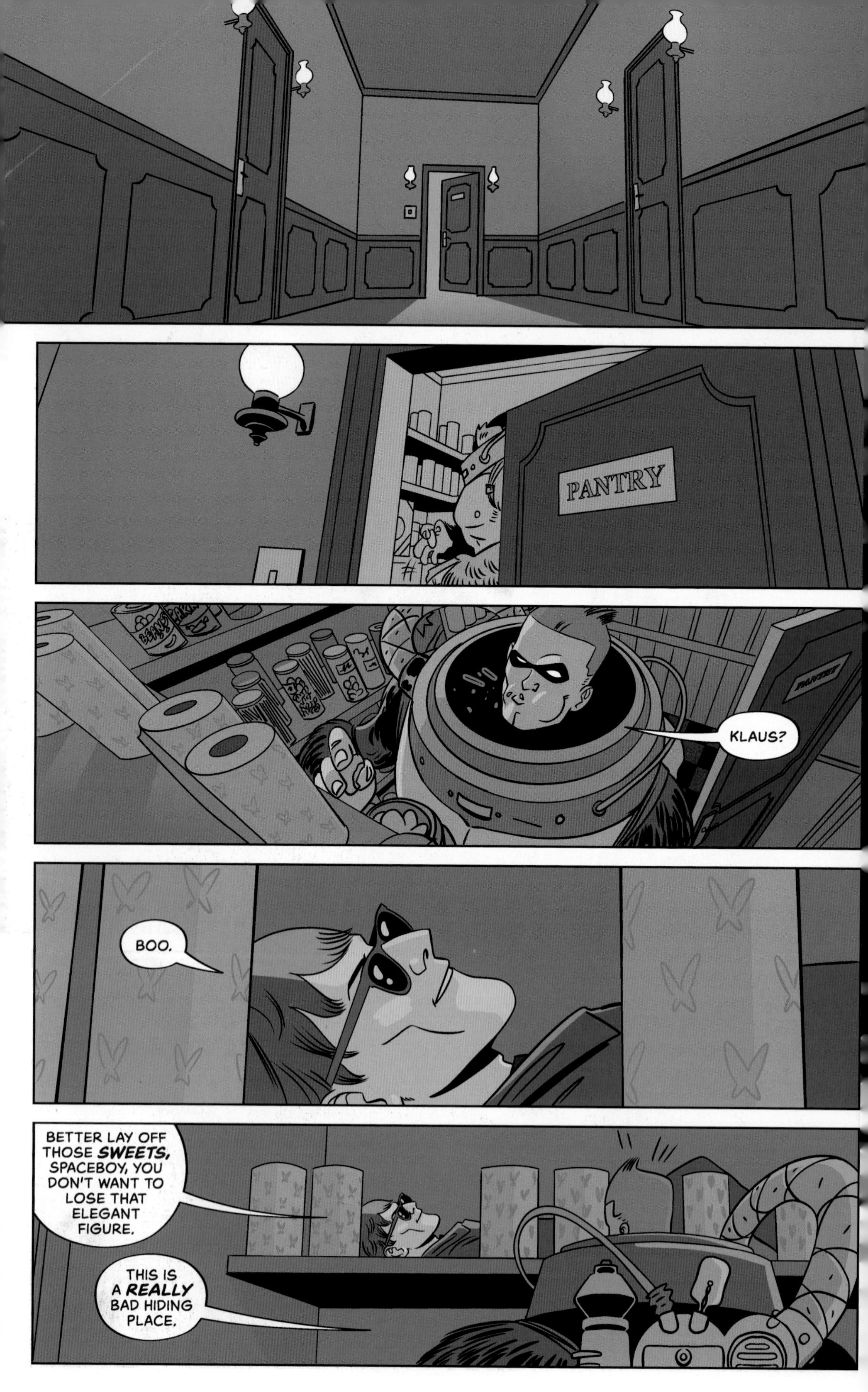
PANTRY
KLAUS?
BOO.
BETTER LAY OFF THOSE **SWEETS,** SPACEBOY, YOU DON'T WANT TO LOSE THAT ELEGANT FIGURE.
THIS IS A **REALLY** BAD HIDING PLACE.

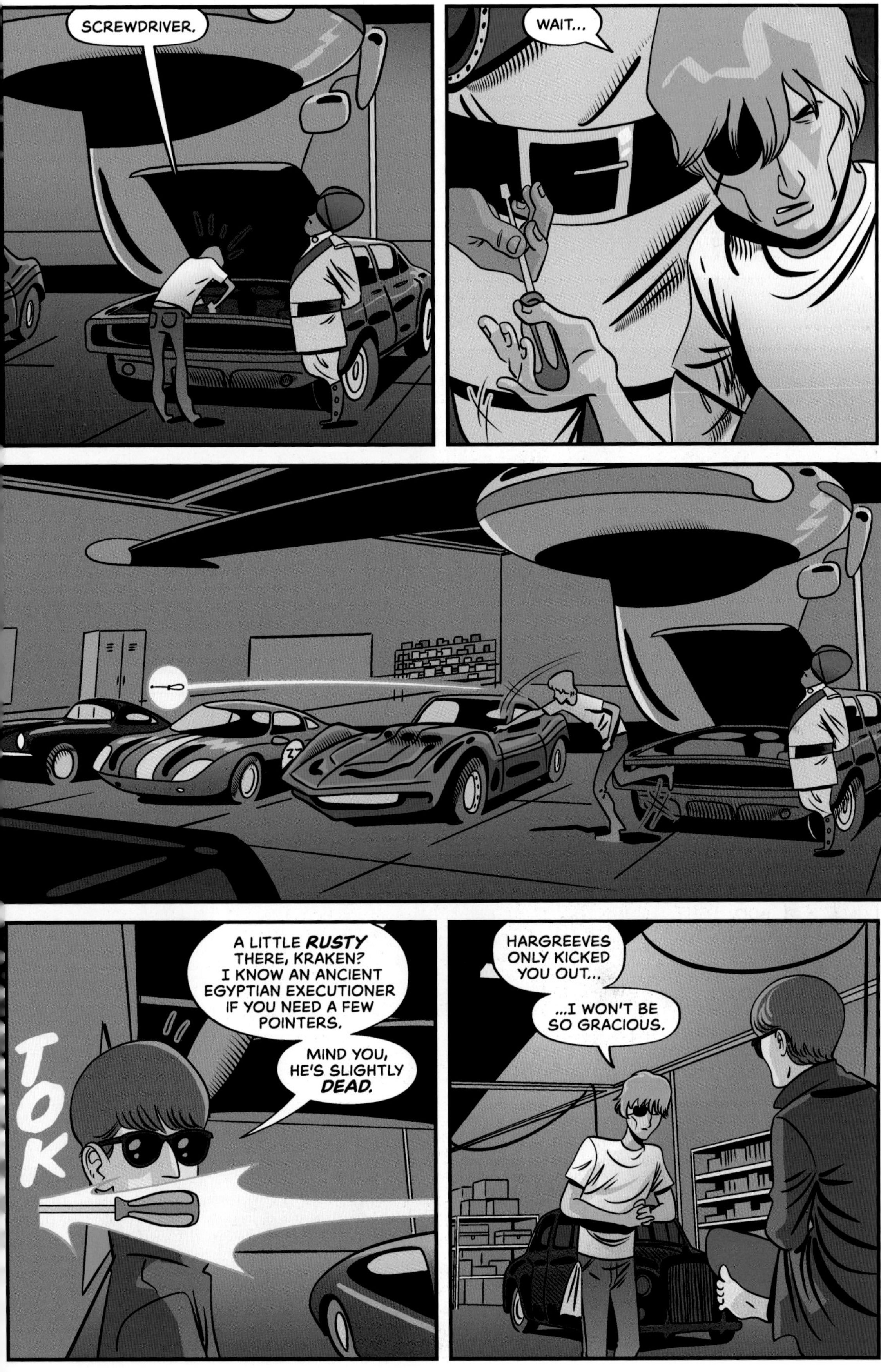
SCREWDRIVER.
WAIT...
A LITTLE RUSTY THERE, KRAKEN? I KNOW AN ANCIENT EGYPTIAN EXECUTIONER IF YOU NEED A FEW POINTERS.
MIND YOU, HE'S SLIGHTLY DEAD.
TOK
HARGREEVES ONLY KICKED YOU OUT...
...I WON'T BE SO GRACIOUS.

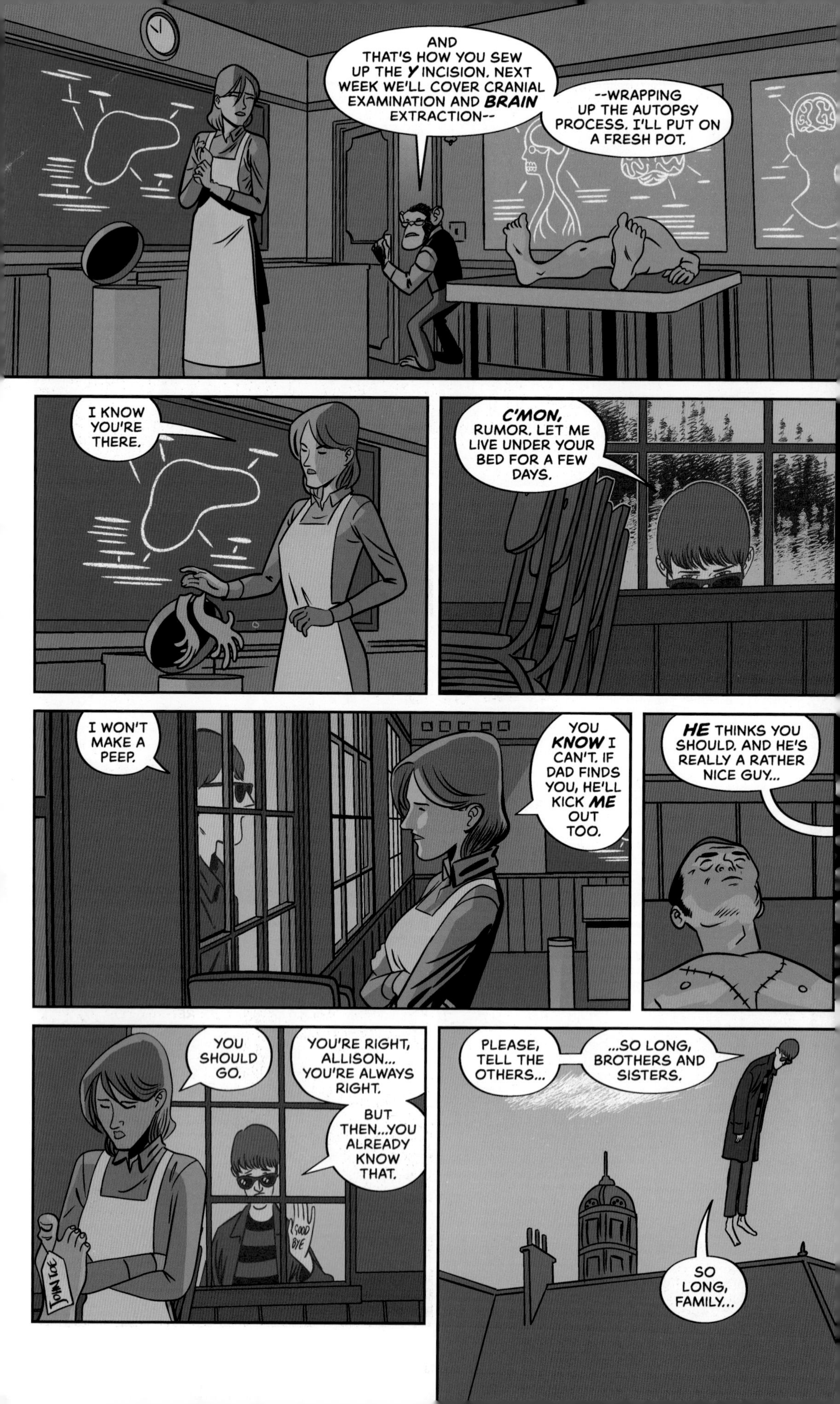
AND THAT'S HOW YOU SEW UP THE Y INCISION. NEXT WEEK WE'LL COVER CRANIAL EXAMINATION AND BRAIN EXTRACTION--
--WRAPPING UP THE AUTOPSY PROCESS. I'LL PUT ON A FRESH POT.
I KNOW YOU'RE THERE.
C'MON, RUMOR. LET ME LIVE UNDER YOUR BED FOR A FEW DAYS.
I WON'T MAKE A PEEP.
YOU KNOW I CAN'T. IF DAD FINDS YOU, HE'LL KICK ME OUT TOO.
HE THINKS YOU SHOULD. AND HE'S REALLY A RATHER NICE GUY...
YOU SHOULD GO.
YOU'RE RIGHT, ALLISON... YOU'RE ALWAYS RIGHT.
BUT THEN...YOU ALREADY KNOW THAT.
GOOD BYE
JOHN DOE
PLEASE, TELL THE OTHERS...
...SO LONG, BROTHERS AND SISTERS.
SO LONG, FAMILY...

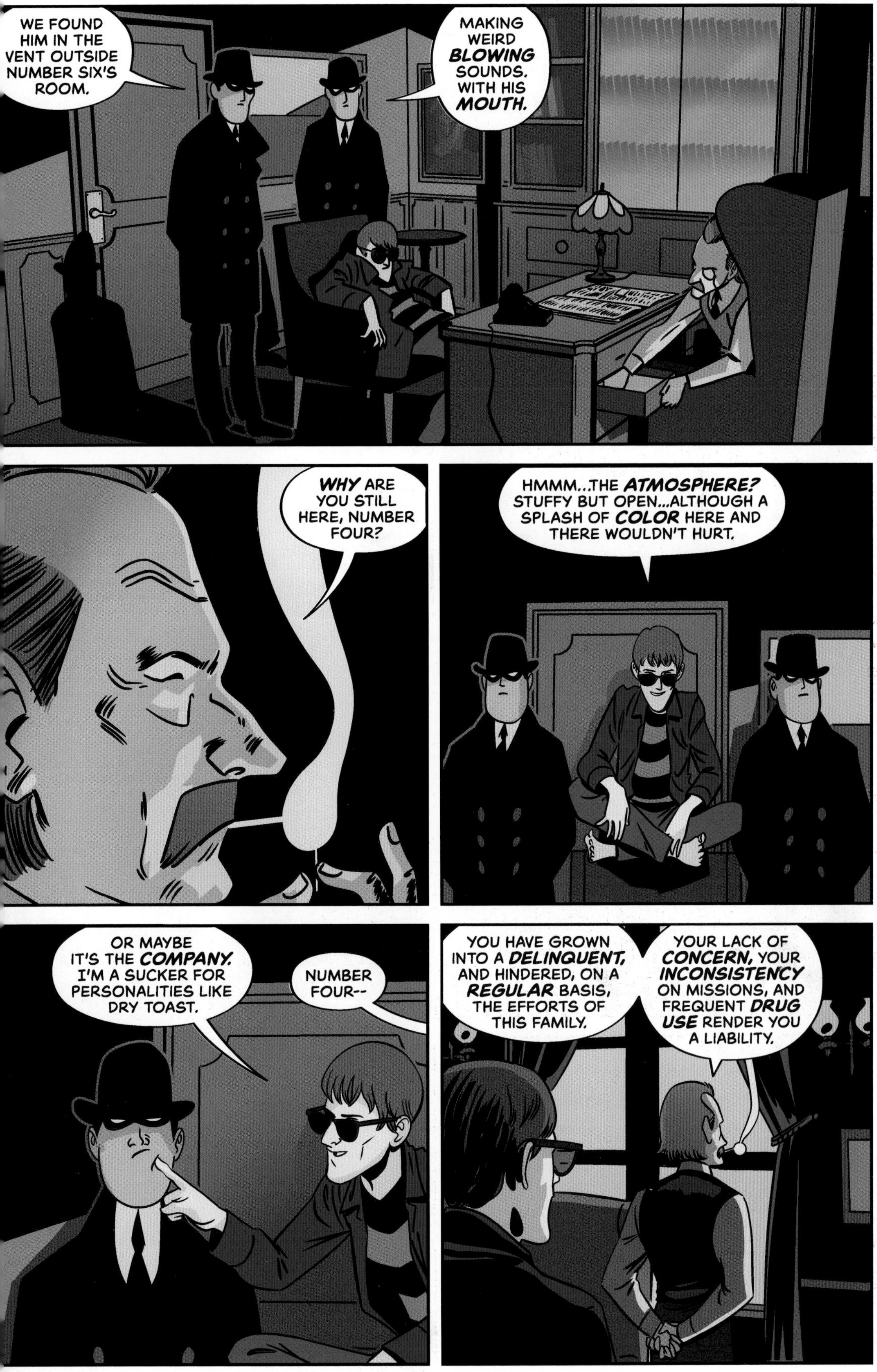
WE FOUND HIM IN THE VENT OUTSIDE NUMBER SIX'S ROOM.
MAKING WEIRD BLOWING SOUNDS. WITH HIS MOUTH.
WHY ARE YOU STILL HERE, NUMBER FOUR?
HMMM...THE ATMOSPHERE? STUFFY BUT OPEN...ALTHOUGH A SPLASH OF COLOR HERE AND THERE WOULDN'T HURT.
OR MAYBE IT'S THE COMPANY. I'M A SUCKER FOR PERSONALITIES LIKE DRY TOAST.
NUMBER FOUR--
YOU HAVE GROWN INTO A DELINQUENT, AND HINDERED, ON A REGULAR BASIS, THE EFFORTS OF THIS FAMILY.
YOUR LACK OF CONCERN, YOUR INCONSISTENCY ON MISSIONS, AND FREQUENT DRUG USE RENDER YOU A LIABILITY.

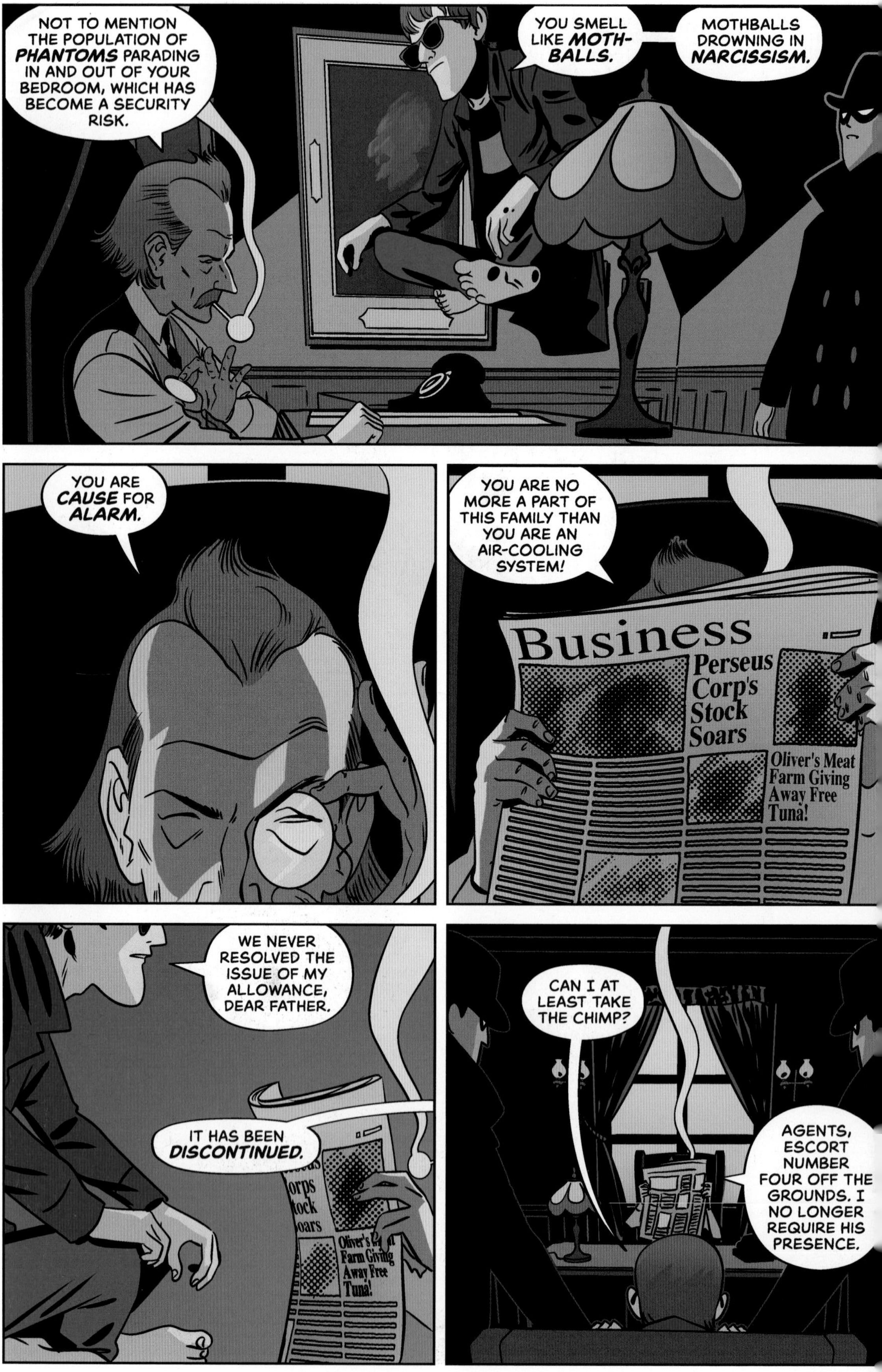
NOT TO MENTION THE POPULATION OF *PHANTOMS* PARADING IN AND OUT OF YOUR BEDROOM, WHICH HAS BECOME A SECURITY RISK.
YOU SMELL LIKE *MOTH-BALLS.*
MOTHBALLS DROWNING IN *NARCISSISM.*
YOU ARE *CAUSE* FOR *ALARM.*
YOU ARE NO MORE A PART OF THIS FAMILY THAN YOU ARE AN AIR-COOLING SYSTEM!
Business
Perseus Corp's Stock Soars
Oliver's Meat Farm Giving Away Free Tuna!
WE NEVER RESOLVED THE ISSUE OF MY ALLOWANCE, DEAR FATHER.
IT HAS BEEN *DISCONTINUED.*
CAN I AT LEAST TAKE THE CHIMP?
AGENTS, ESCORT NUMBER FOUR OFF THE GROUNDS. I NO LONGER REQUIRE HIS PRESENCE.

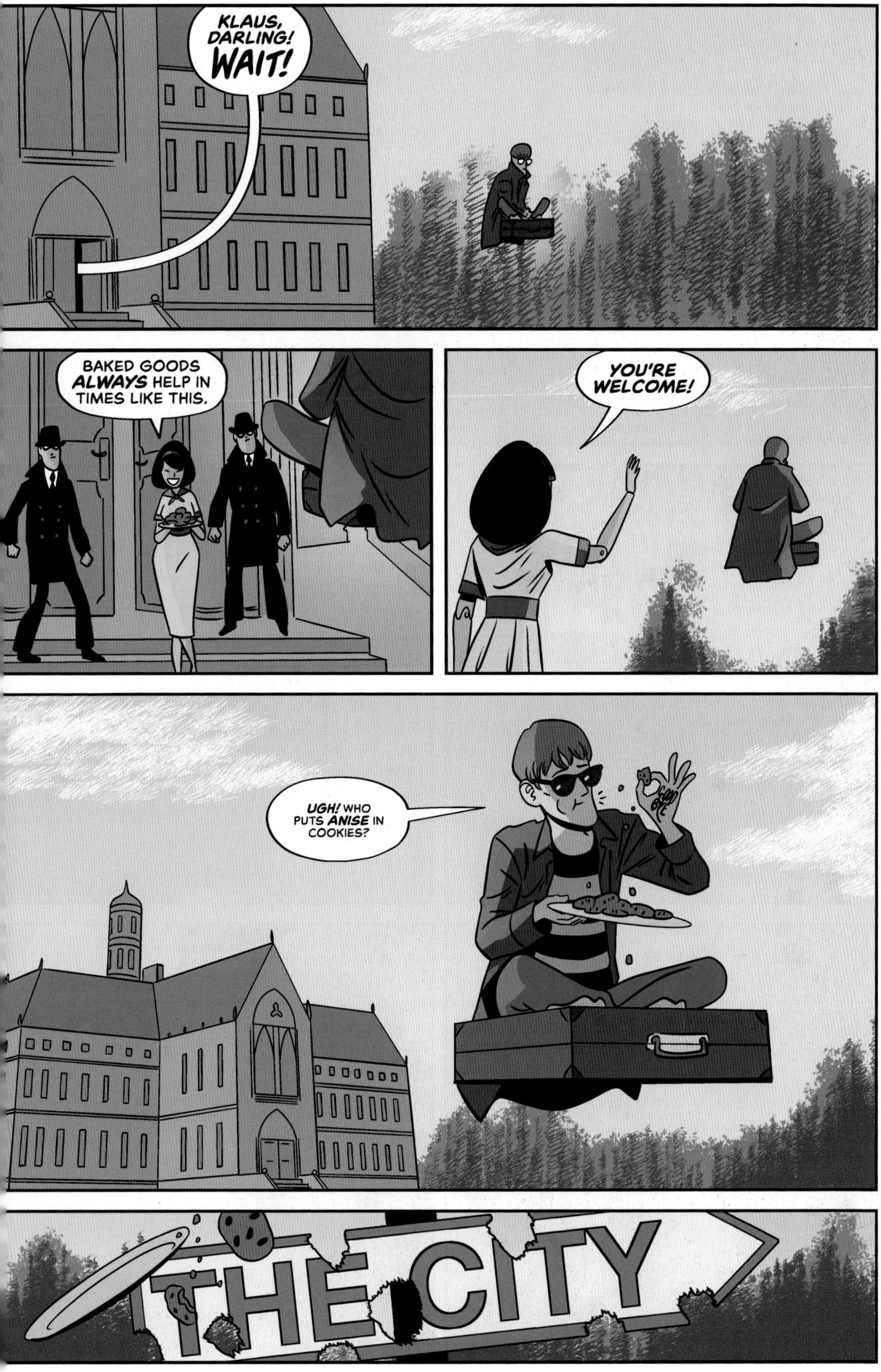
KLAUS, DARLING! WAIT!
BAKED GOODS ALWAYS HELP IN TIMES LIKE THIS.
YOU'RE WELCOME!
UGH! WHO PUTS ANISE IN COOKIES?
GOOD BYE
THE CITY

THE CITY.

WILL YOU PUT THAT THING AWAY?

AND DON'T START WITH THOSE *WILDLIFE* IMPRESSIONS EITHER.

MILDRED STOCKTON ORPHANAGE

WE AREN'T TRYING TO *SCARE* THE LITTLE GUY.

OKAY, FINE.

I JUST WANT HIM TO *LIKE* US.

THE FUTURE LIES IN THEIR HANDS

MR. AND MRS. DONAHUE--

--ARE YOU READY TO MEET YOUR LITTLE *BUNDLE OF JOY?*

OH...

MY GOD.

PARENTS ARE TRAVEL AGENTS TO LIFE'S DESTINA...

EN ARE ERRIES

odern nting

I *KNOW!* ISN'T HE JUST THE *CUTEST?*

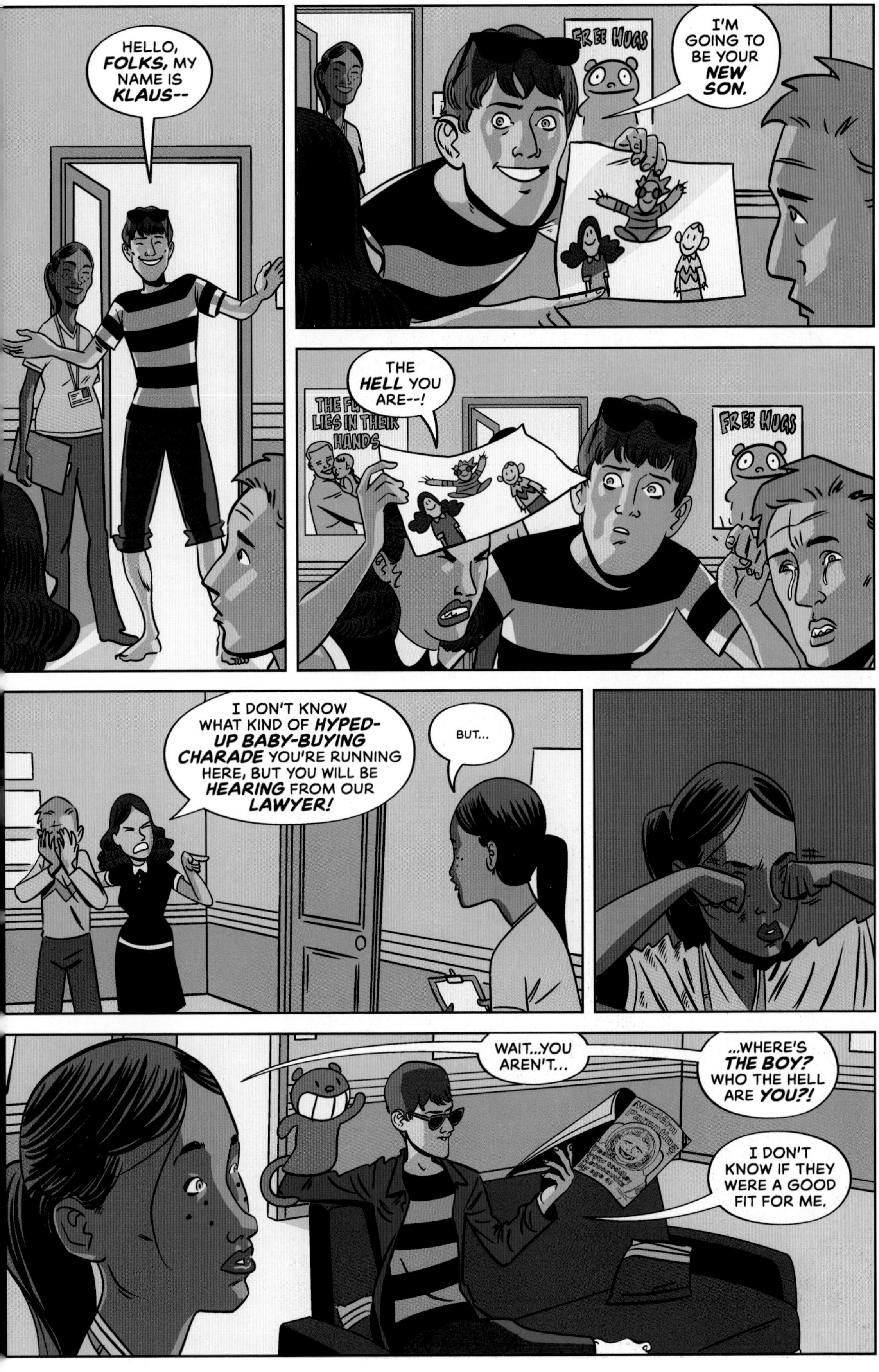

HELLO, FOLKS, MY NAME IS KLAUS--
FREE HUGS
I'M GOING TO BE YOUR NEW SON.
THE HELL YOU ARE--!
FREE HUGS
I DON'T KNOW WHAT KIND OF HYPED-UP BABY-BUYING CHARADE YOU'RE RUNNING HERE, BUT YOU WILL BE HEARING FROM OUR LAWYER!
BUT...
WAIT...YOU AREN'T...
...WHERE'S THE BOY? WHO THE HELL ARE YOU?!
I DON'T KNOW IF THEY WERE A GOOD FIT FOR ME.

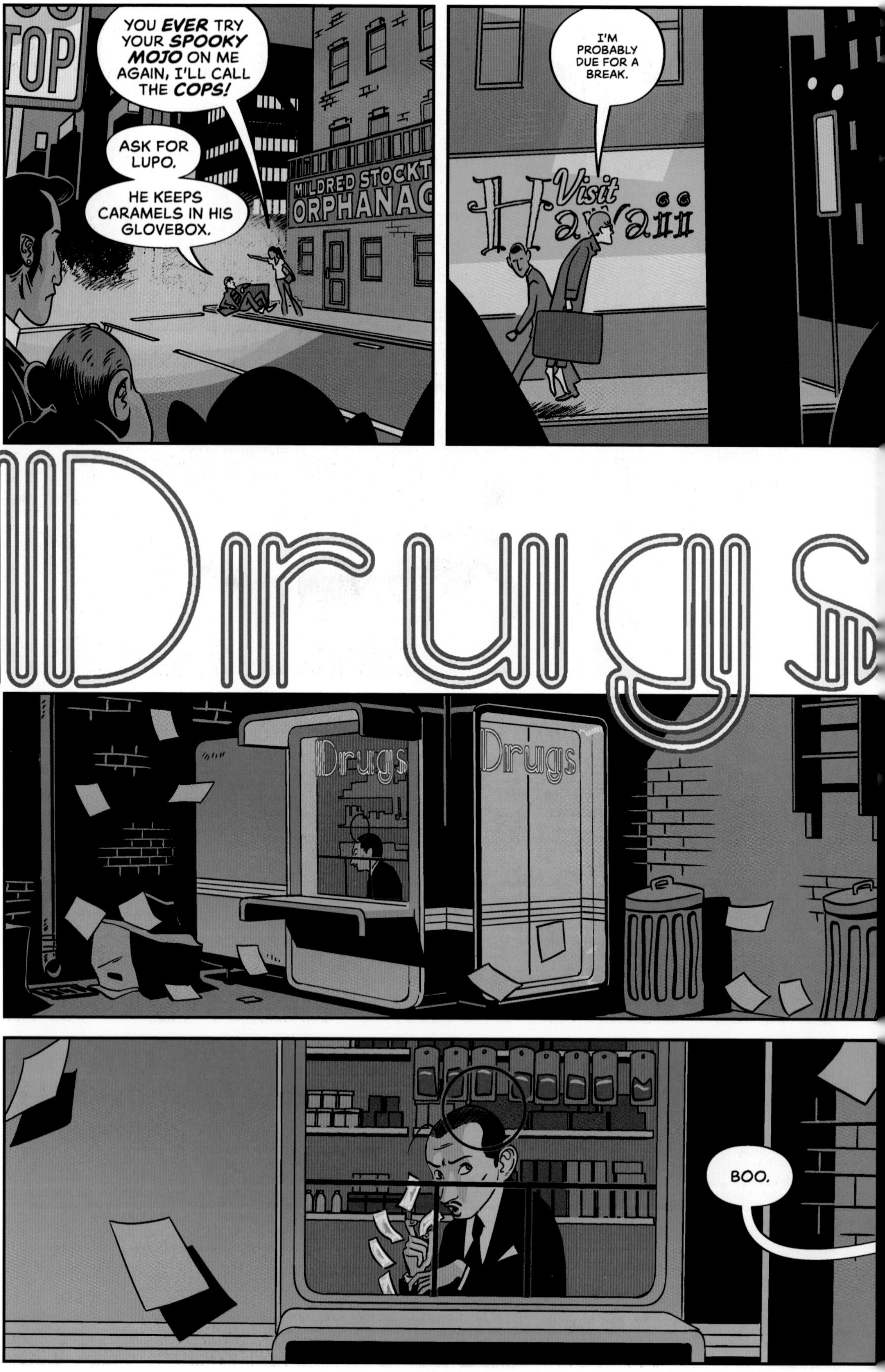
TOP
YOU EVER TRY YOUR SPOOKY MOJO ON ME AGAIN, I'LL CALL THE COPS!
ASK FOR LUPO.
HE KEEPS CARAMELS IN HIS GLOVEBOX.
MILDRED STOCKT
ORPHANAG
I'M PROBABLY DUE FOR A BREAK.
Visit Hawaii
Drugs
Drugs
Drugs
BOO.

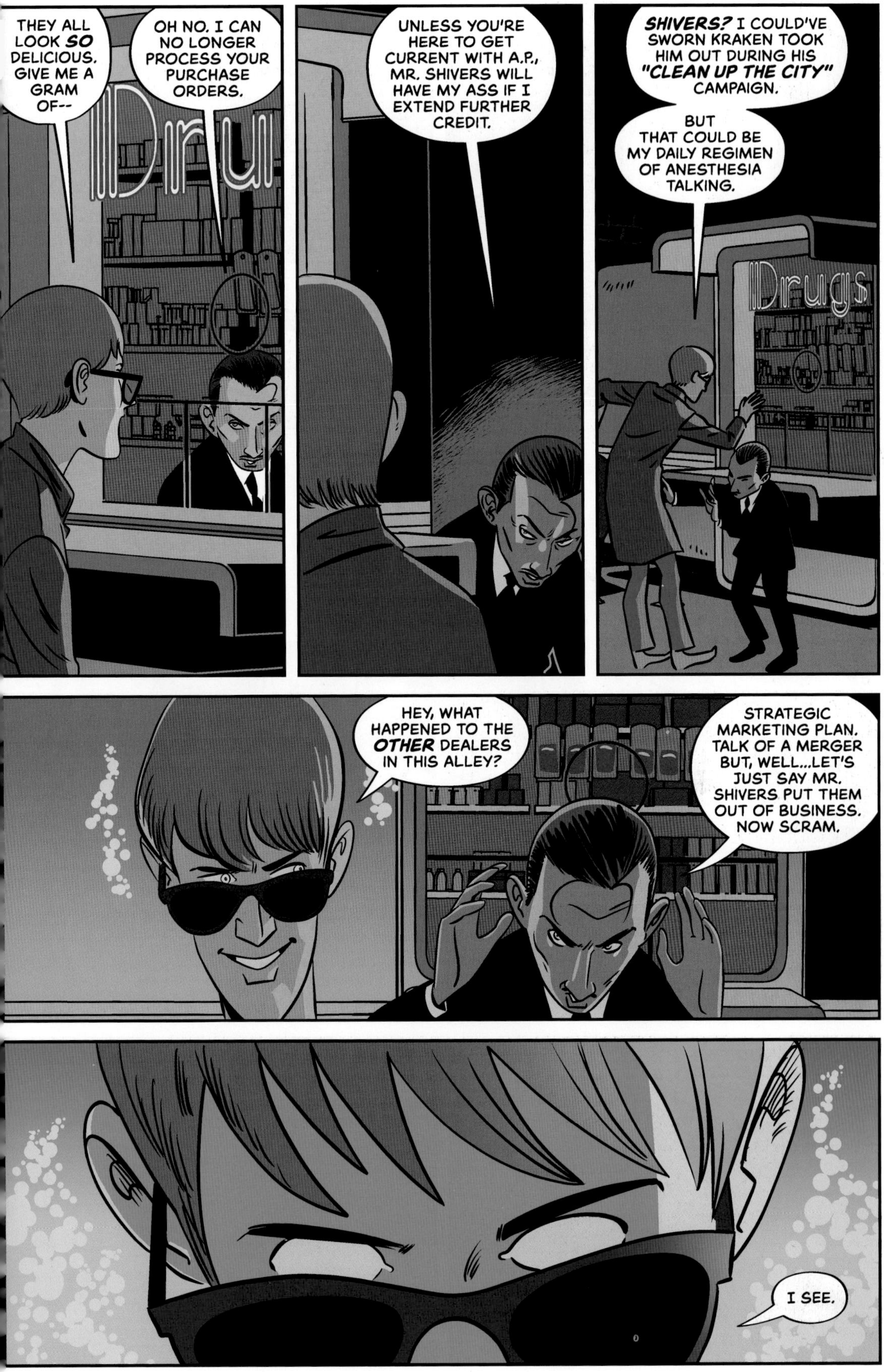
THEY ALL LOOK SO DELICIOUS. GIVE ME A GRAM OF--
OH NO. I CAN NO LONGER PROCESS YOUR PURCHASE ORDERS.
Dru
UNLESS YOU'RE HERE TO GET CURRENT WITH A.P., MR. SHIVERS WILL HAVE MY ASS IF I EXTEND FURTHER CREDIT.
SHIVERS? I COULD'VE SWORN KRAKEN TOOK HIM OUT DURING HIS "CLEAN UP THE CITY" CAMPAIGN.
BUT THAT COULD BE MY DAILY REGIMEN OF ANESTHESIA TALKING.
Drugs
HEY, WHAT HAPPENED TO THE OTHER DEALERS IN THIS ALLEY?
STRATEGIC MARKETING PLAN. TALK OF A MERGER BUT, WELL...LET'S JUST SAY MR. SHIVERS PUT THEM OUT OF BUSINESS. NOW SCRAM.
I SEE.

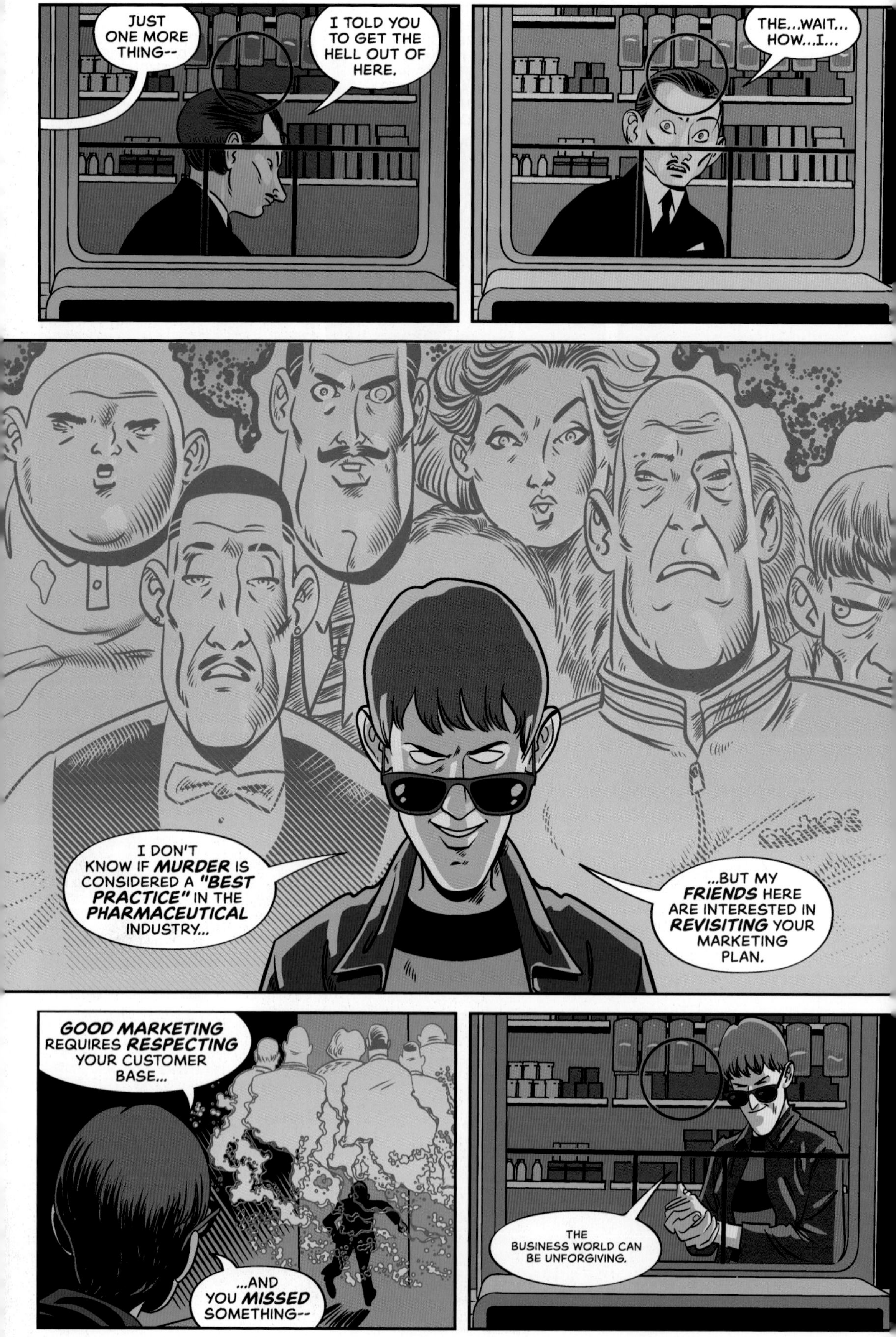

JUST ONE MORE THING--
I TOLD YOU TO GET THE HELL OUT OF HERE.
THE...WAIT... HOW...I...
I DON'T KNOW IF MURDER IS CONSIDERED A "BEST PRACTICE" IN THE PHARMACEUTICAL INDUSTRY...
...BUT MY FRIENDS HERE ARE INTERESTED IN REVISITING YOUR MARKETING PLAN.
GOOD MARKETING REQUIRES RESPECTING YOUR CUSTOMER BASE...
...AND YOU MISSED SOMETHING--
THE BUSINESS WORLD CAN BE UNFORGIVING.

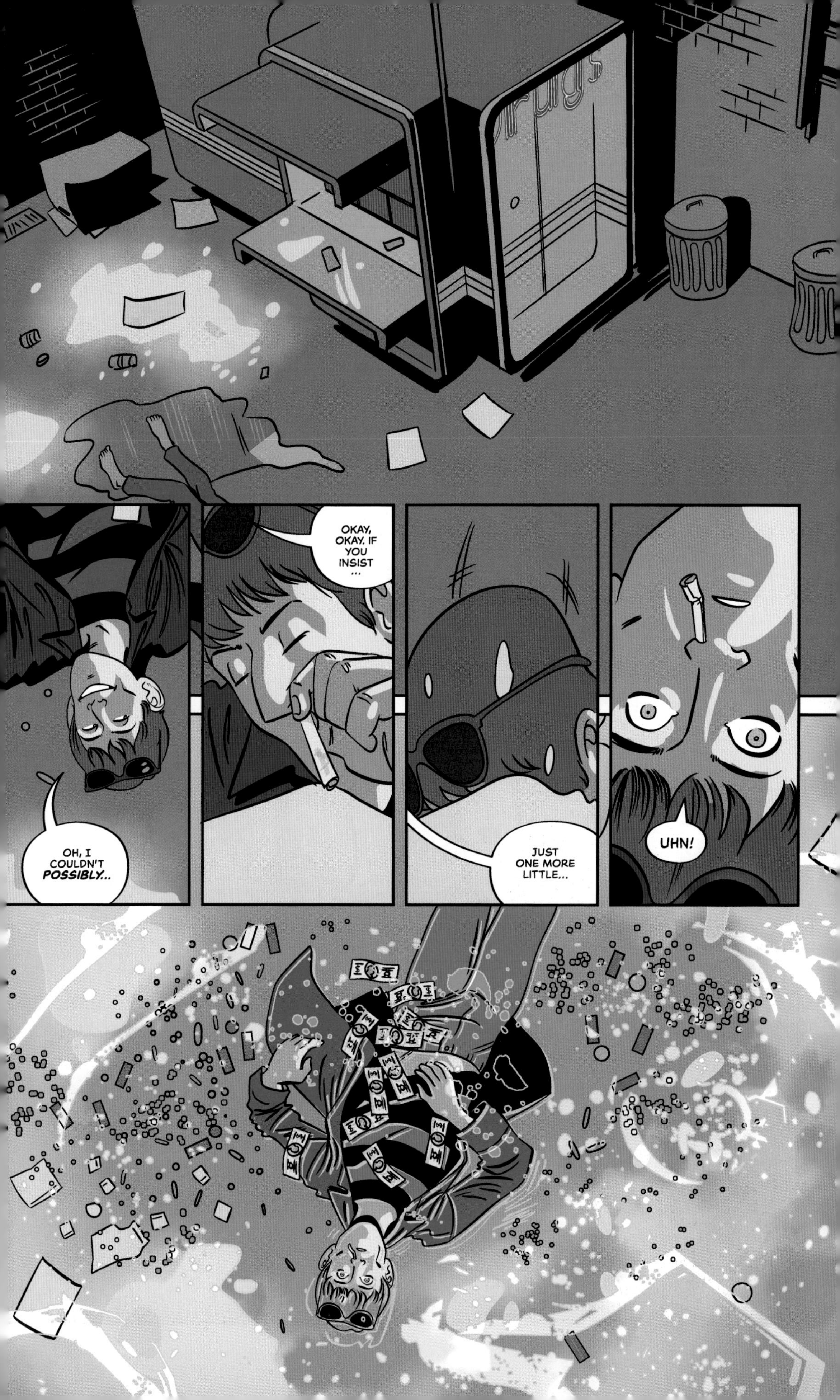
OH, I COULDN'T POSSIBLY...
OKAY, OKAY. IF YOU INSIST ...
JUST ONE MORE LITTLE...
UHN!

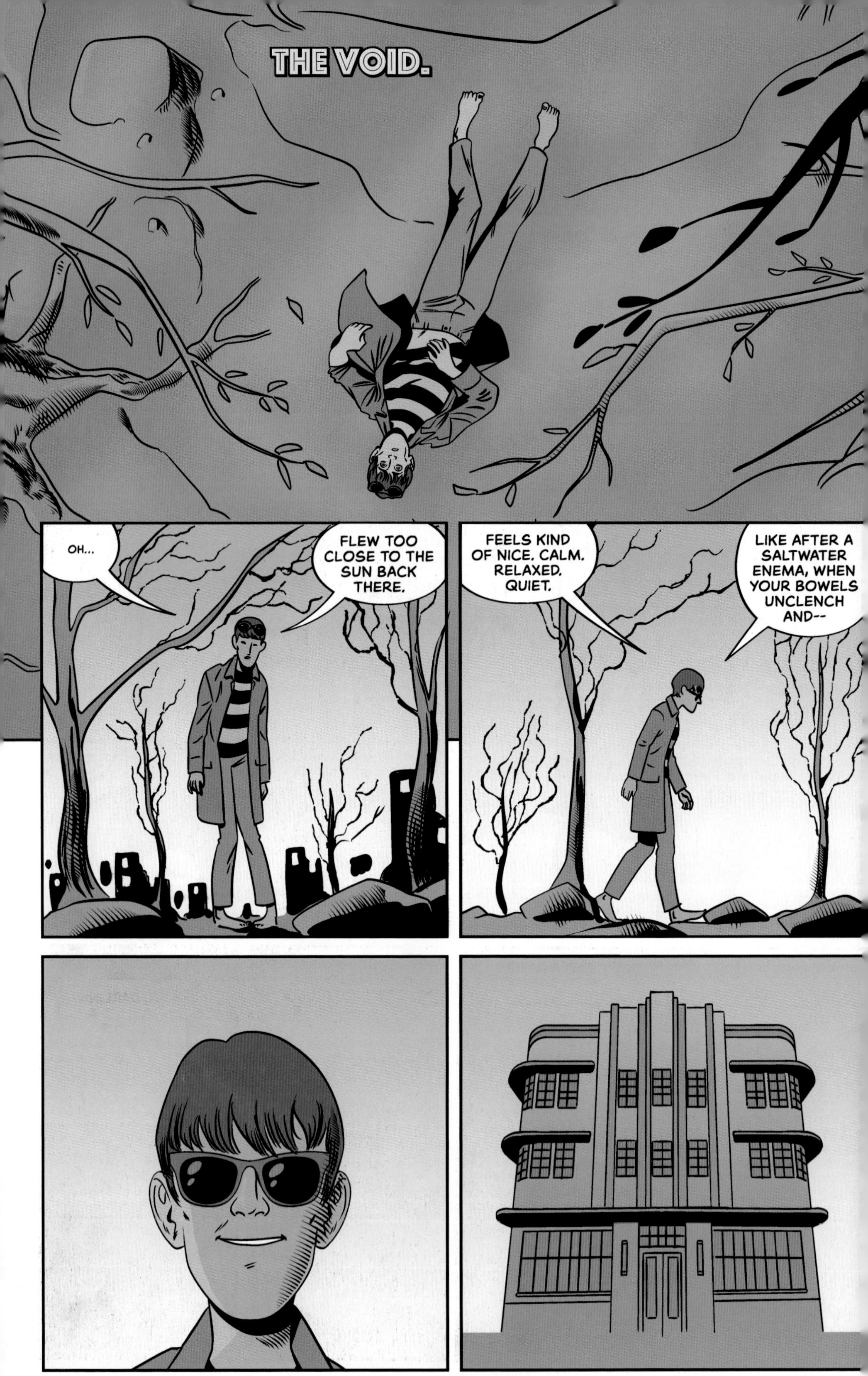
THE VOID.
OH...
FLEW TOO CLOSE TO THE SUN BACK THERE.
FEELS KIND OF NICE. CALM. RELAXED. QUIET.
LIKE AFTER A SALTWATER ENEMA, WHEN YOUR BOWELS UNCLENCH AND--

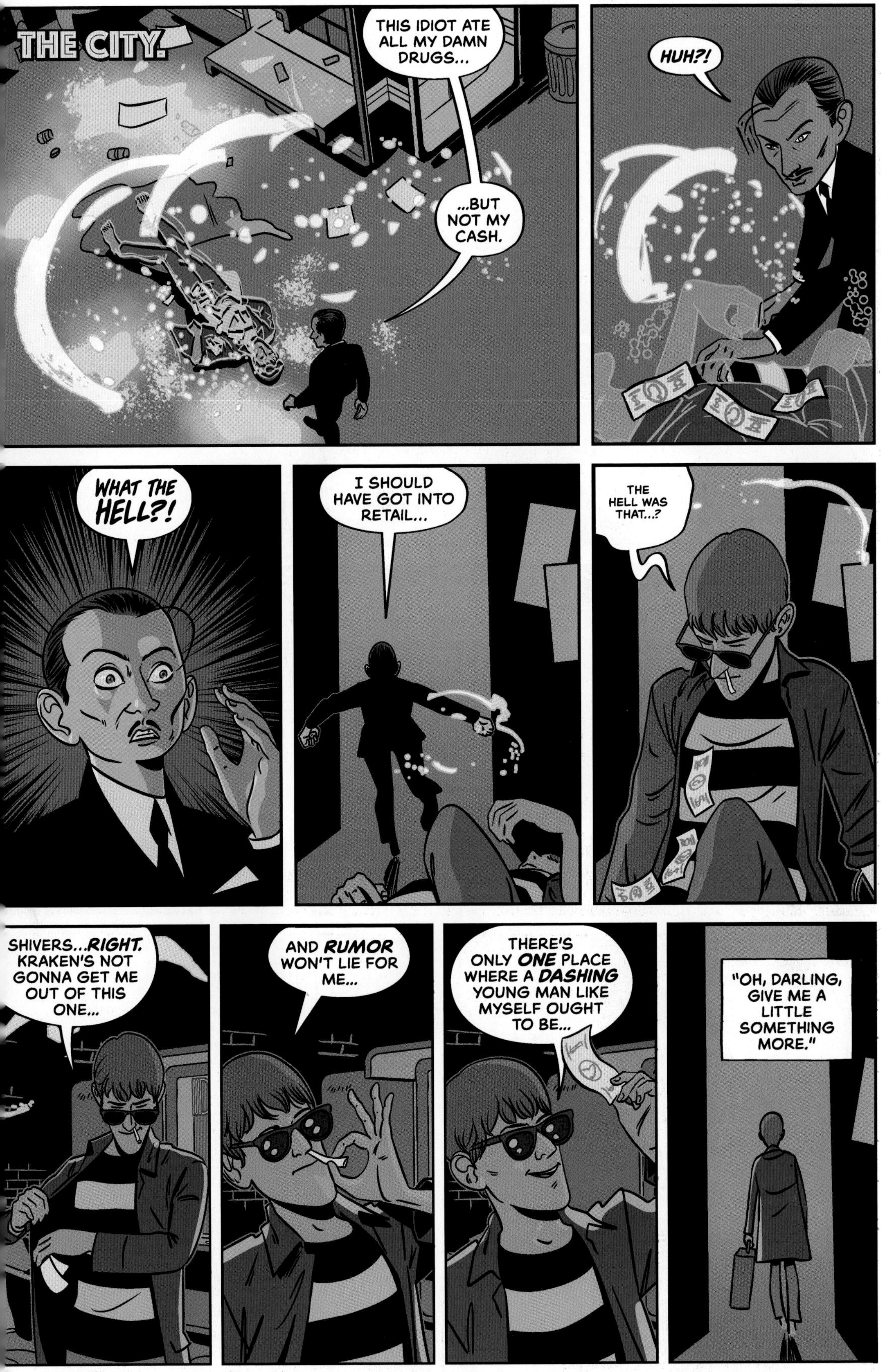
THE CITY.
THIS IDIOT ATE ALL MY DAMN DRUGS...
...BUT NOT MY CASH.
HUH?!
WHAT THE HELL?!
I SHOULD HAVE GOT INTO RETAIL...
THE HELL WAS THAT...?
SHIVERS...RIGHT. KRAKEN'S NOT GONNA GET ME OUT OF THIS ONE...
AND RUMOR WON'T LIE FOR ME...
THERE'S ONLY ONE PLACE WHERE A DASHING YOUNG MAN LIKE MYSELF OUGHT TO BE...
"OH, DARLING, GIVE ME A LITTLE SOMETHING MORE."

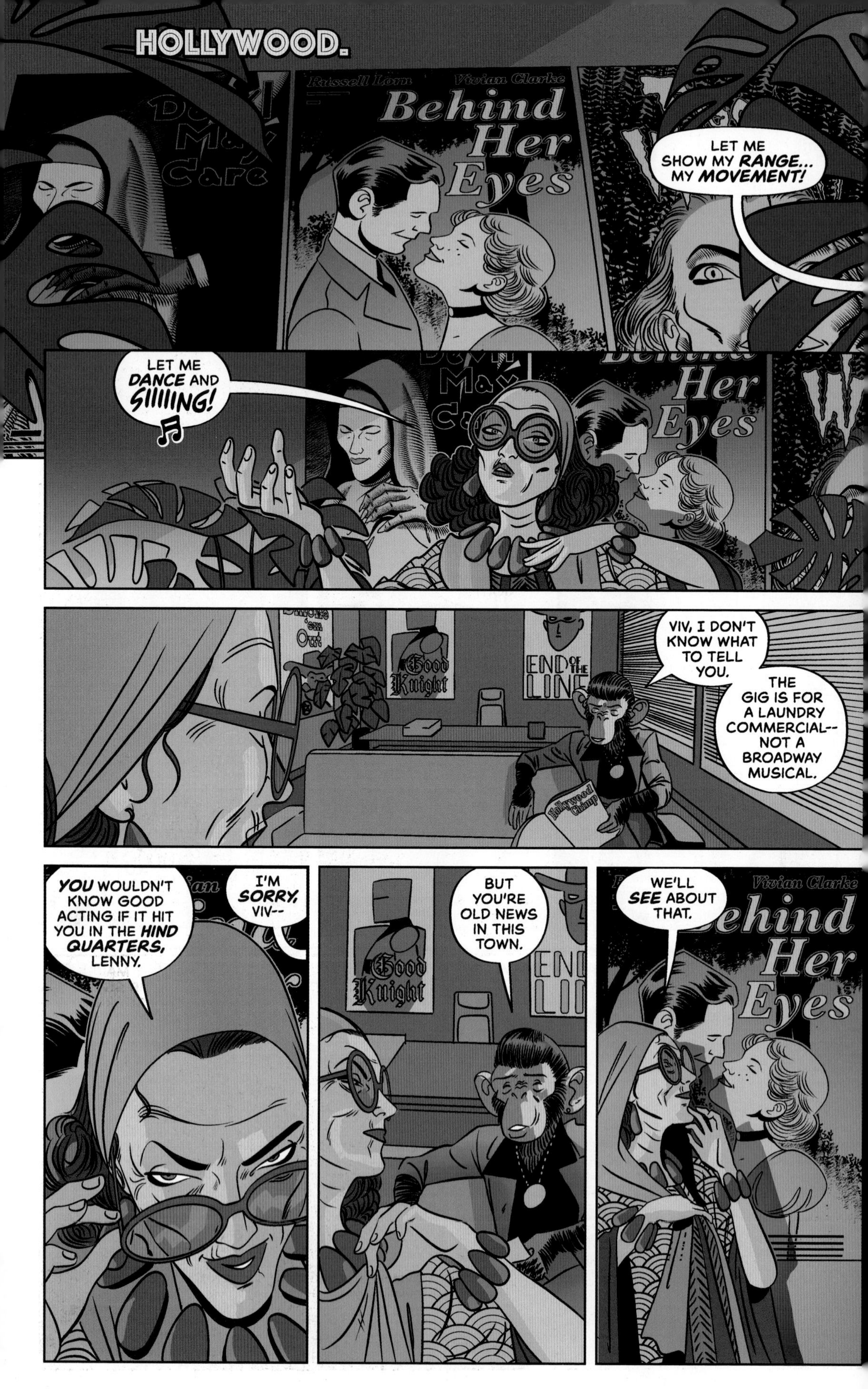
HOLLYWOOD.
Russell Lorn
Vivian Clarke
Behind Her Eyes
LET ME SHOW MY RANGE... MY MOVEMENT!
LET ME DANCE AND SIIIING!
VIV, I DON'T KNOW WHAT TO TELL YOU.
THE GIG IS FOR A LAUNDRY COMMERCIAL-- NOT A BROADWAY MUSICAL.
YOU WOULDN'T KNOW GOOD ACTING IF IT HIT YOU IN THE HIND QUARTERS, LENNY.
I'M SORRY, VIV--
BUT YOU'RE OLD NEWS IN THIS TOWN.
WE'LL SEE ABOUT THAT.

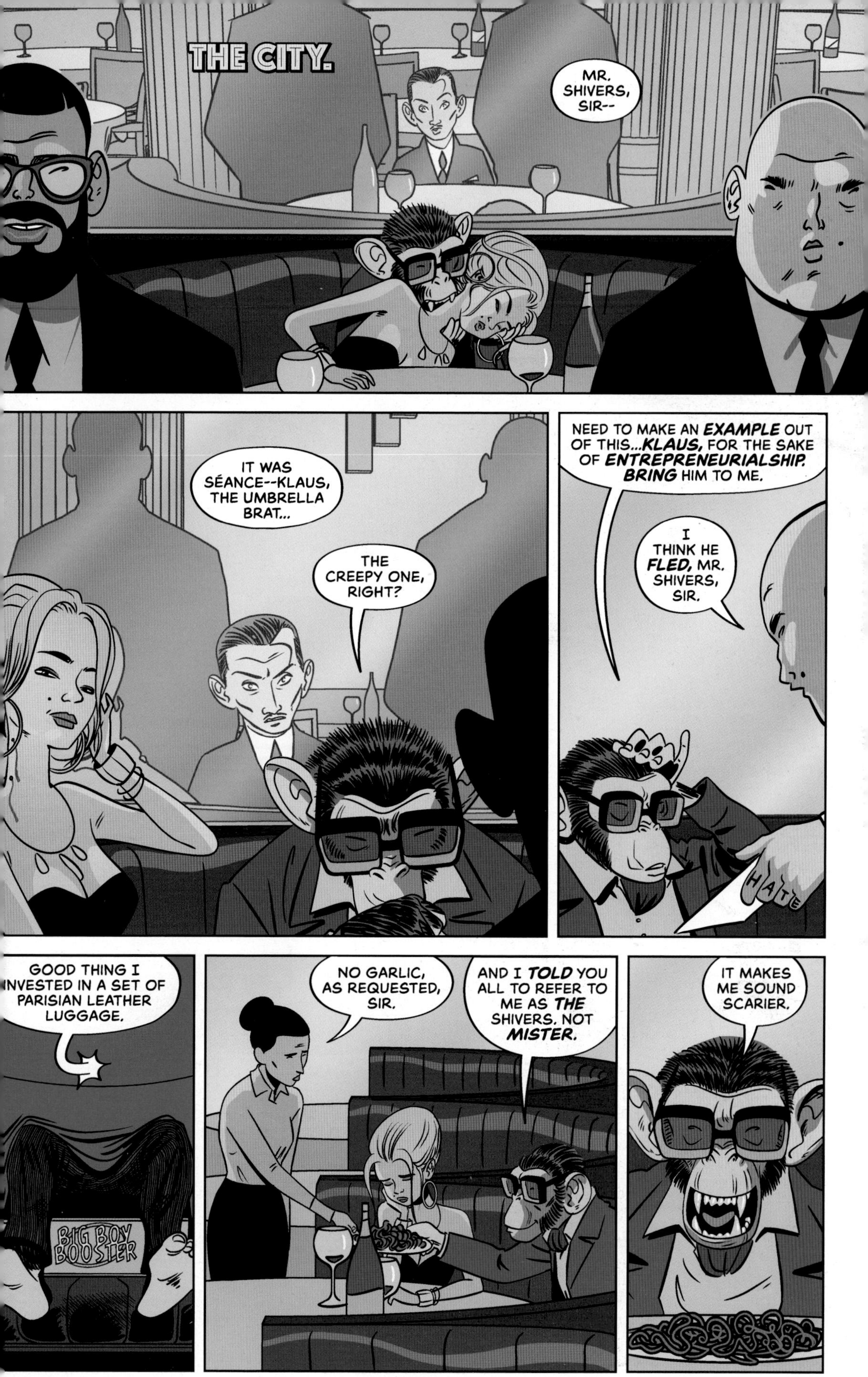
THE CITY.
MR. SHIVERS, SIR--
IT WAS SÉANCE--KLAUS, THE UMBRELLA BRAT...
THE CREEPY ONE, RIGHT?
NEED TO MAKE AN EXAMPLE OUT OF THIS...KLAUS, FOR THE SAKE OF ENTREPRENEURIALSHIP. BRING HIM TO ME.
I THINK HE FLED, MR. SHIVERS, SIR.
HATE
GOOD THING I INVESTED IN A SET OF PARISIAN LEATHER LUGGAGE.
BIG BOY BOOSTER
NO GARLIC, AS REQUESTED, SIR.
AND I TOLD YOU ALL TO REFER TO ME AS THE SHIVERS. NOT MISTER.
IT MAKES ME SOUND SCARIER.

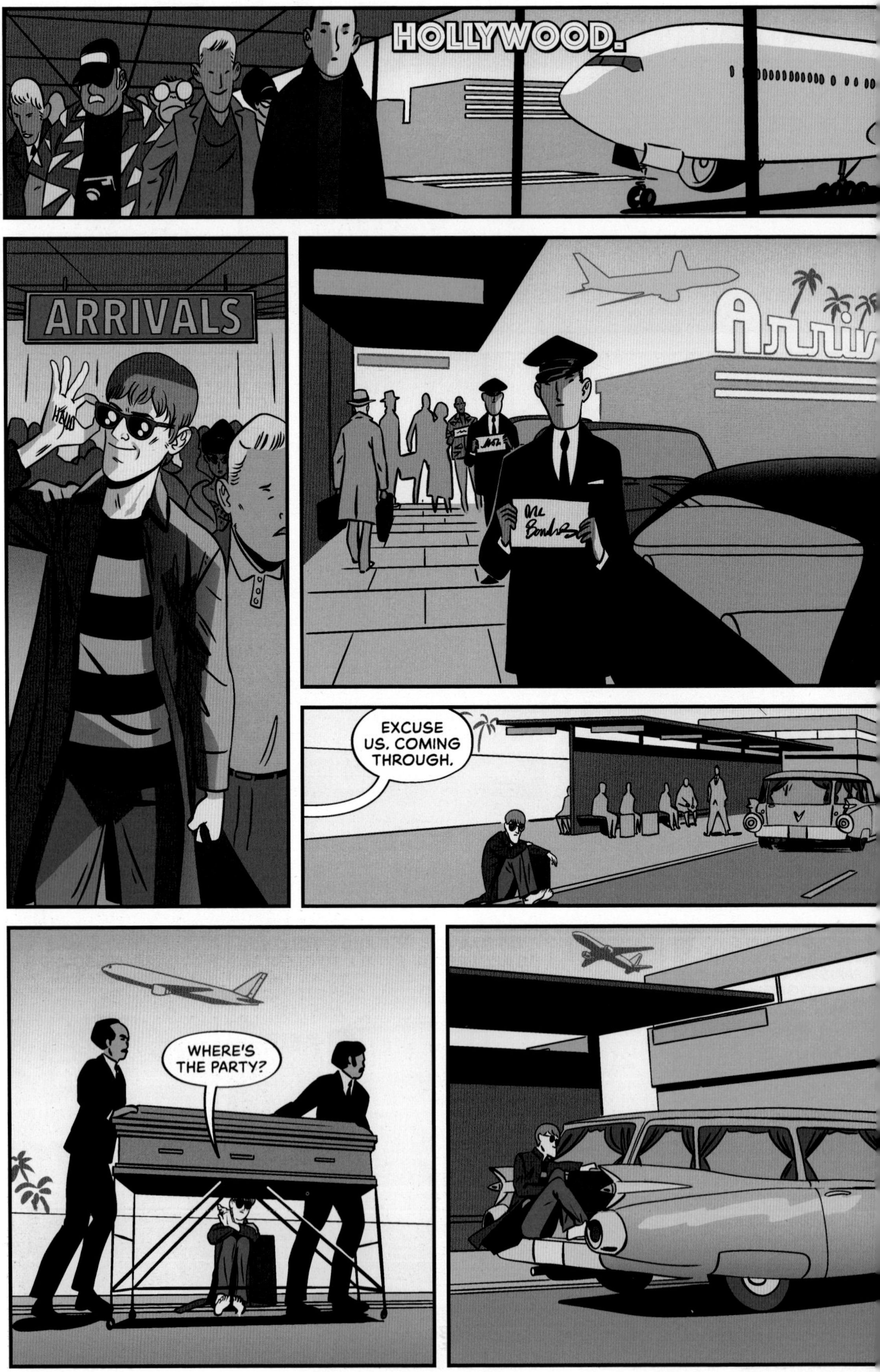
HOLLYWOOD.
ARRIVALS
EXCUSE US. COMING THROUGH.
WHERE'S THE PARTY?

FUNERAL PARLOR

...BUT I COULD NEVER TELL BRUCE OR MARY THAT.

YOU **ALWAYS** HAVE A FAVORITE, BUT UNLESS YOU'RE LOOKING TO SUBJECT YOUR KIDS TO YEARS OF THERAPY--

YEAH, YEAH.

YOU HAVEN'T SEEN A BAR IN A **GRAY** SORT OF PLACE, THAT ISN'T QUITE HELL OR HEAVEN...?

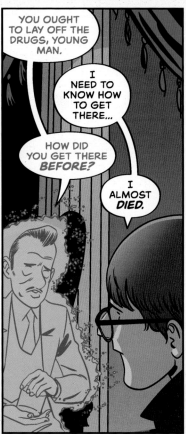

YOU OUGHT TO LAY OFF THE DRUGS, YOUNG MAN.

I NEED TO KNOW HOW TO GET THERE...

HOW DID YOU GET THERE **BEFORE?**

I ALMOST **DIED.**

SORRY ABOUT THIS...NOTHING PERSONAL.

HEY-- **TOMMY** WAS YOUR DAD'S FAVORITE!

THE OLD CORPSE **ALSO** SNORTED THE FAMILY VACATION MONEY **UP HIS NOSE.**

BUT YOU GUYS HAD A COOL **ABOVE-GROUND POOL,** RIGHT?

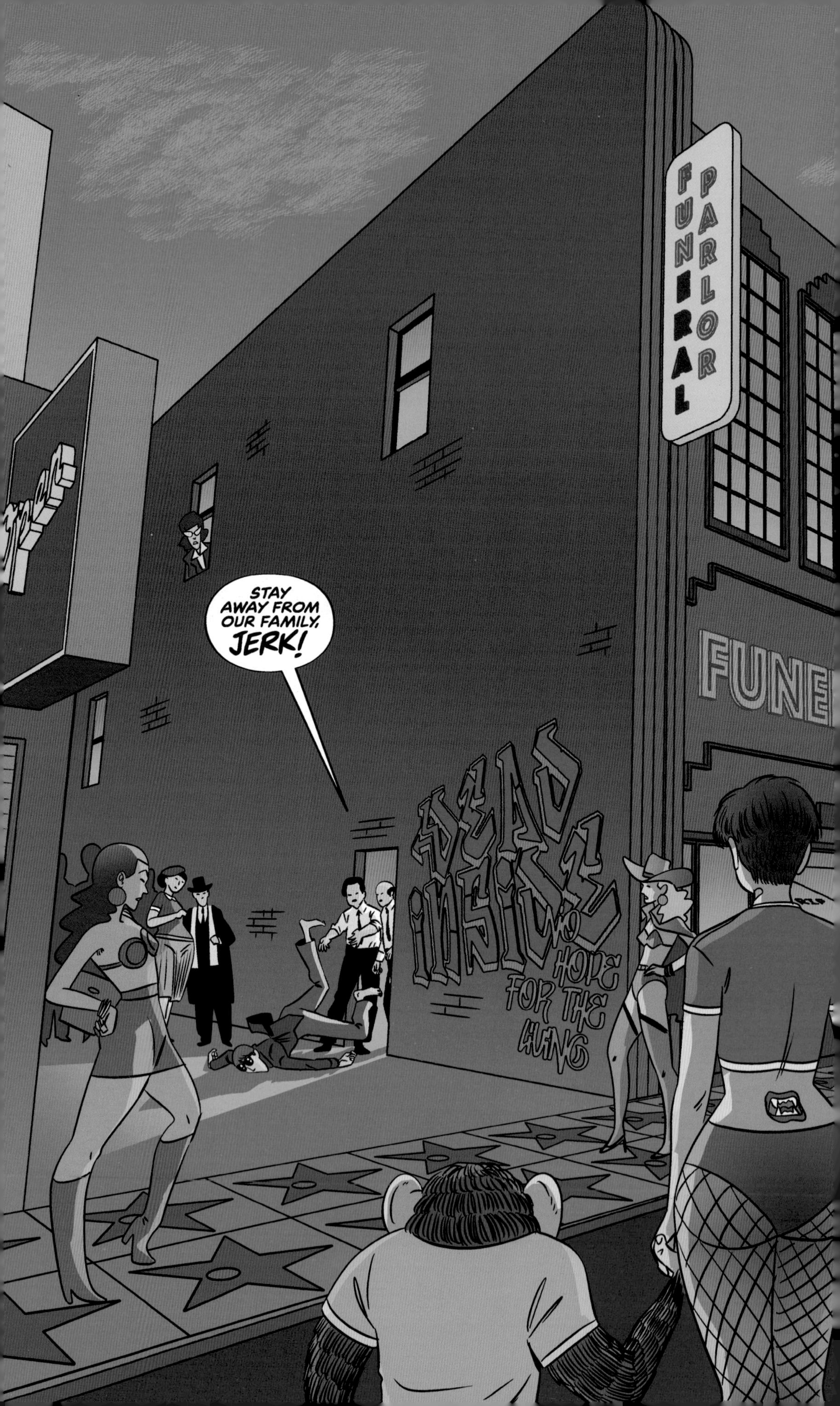
FUNERAL PARLOR
STAY AWAY FROM OUR FAMILY, JERK!
FUNE
DEAD INSIDE
NO HOPE FOR THE LIVING

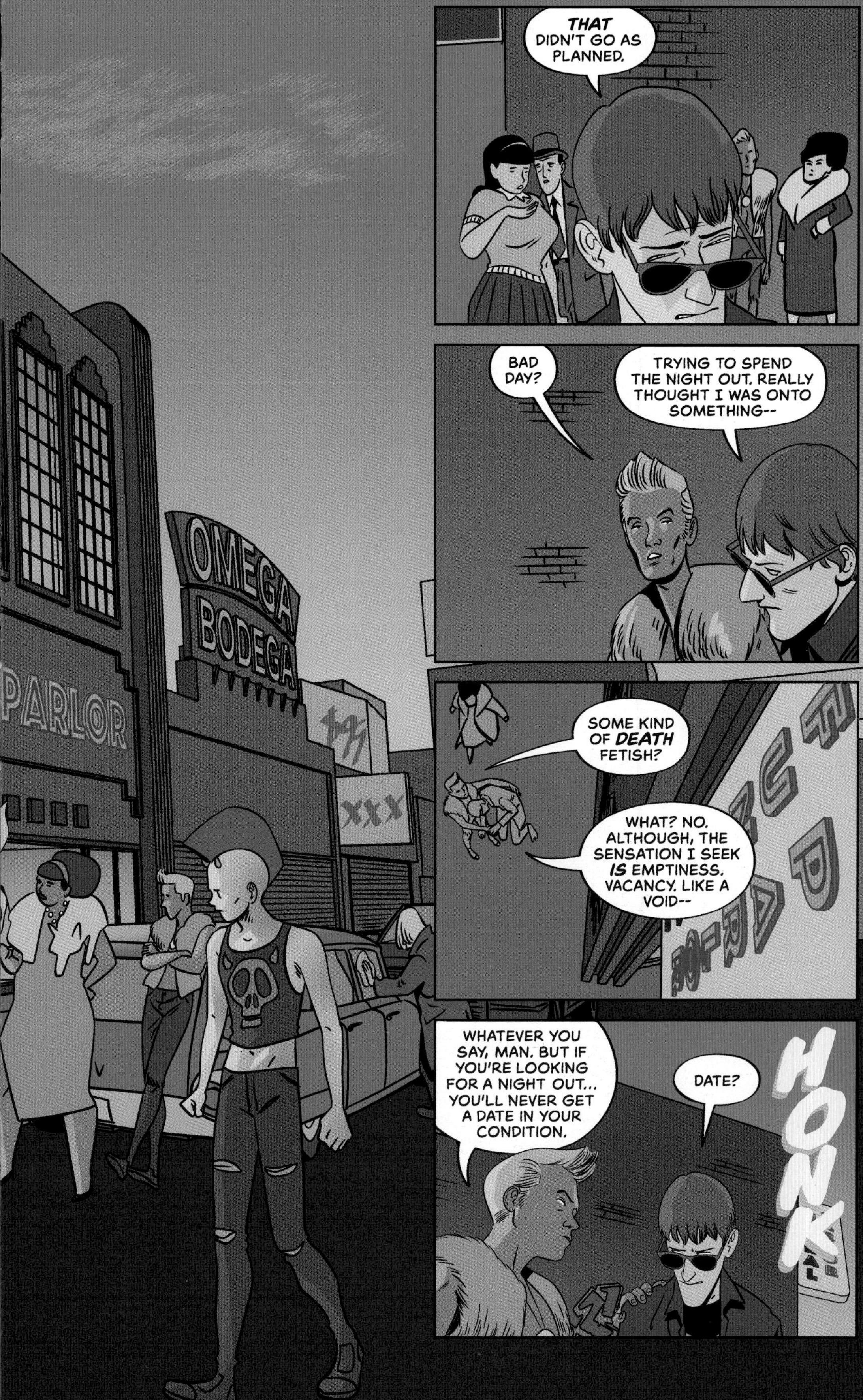
PARLOR
OMEGA BODEGA
XXX
THAT DIDN'T GO AS PLANNED.
BAD DAY?
TRYING TO SPEND THE NIGHT OUT. REALLY THOUGHT I WAS ONTO SOMETHING--
SOME KIND OF DEATH FETISH?
WHAT? NO. ALTHOUGH, THE SENSATION I SEEK IS EMPTINESS. VACANCY. LIKE A VOID--
WHATEVER YOU SAY, MAN. BUT IF YOU'RE LOOKING FOR A NIGHT OUT... YOU'LL NEVER GET A DATE IN YOUR CONDITION.
DATE?
HONK

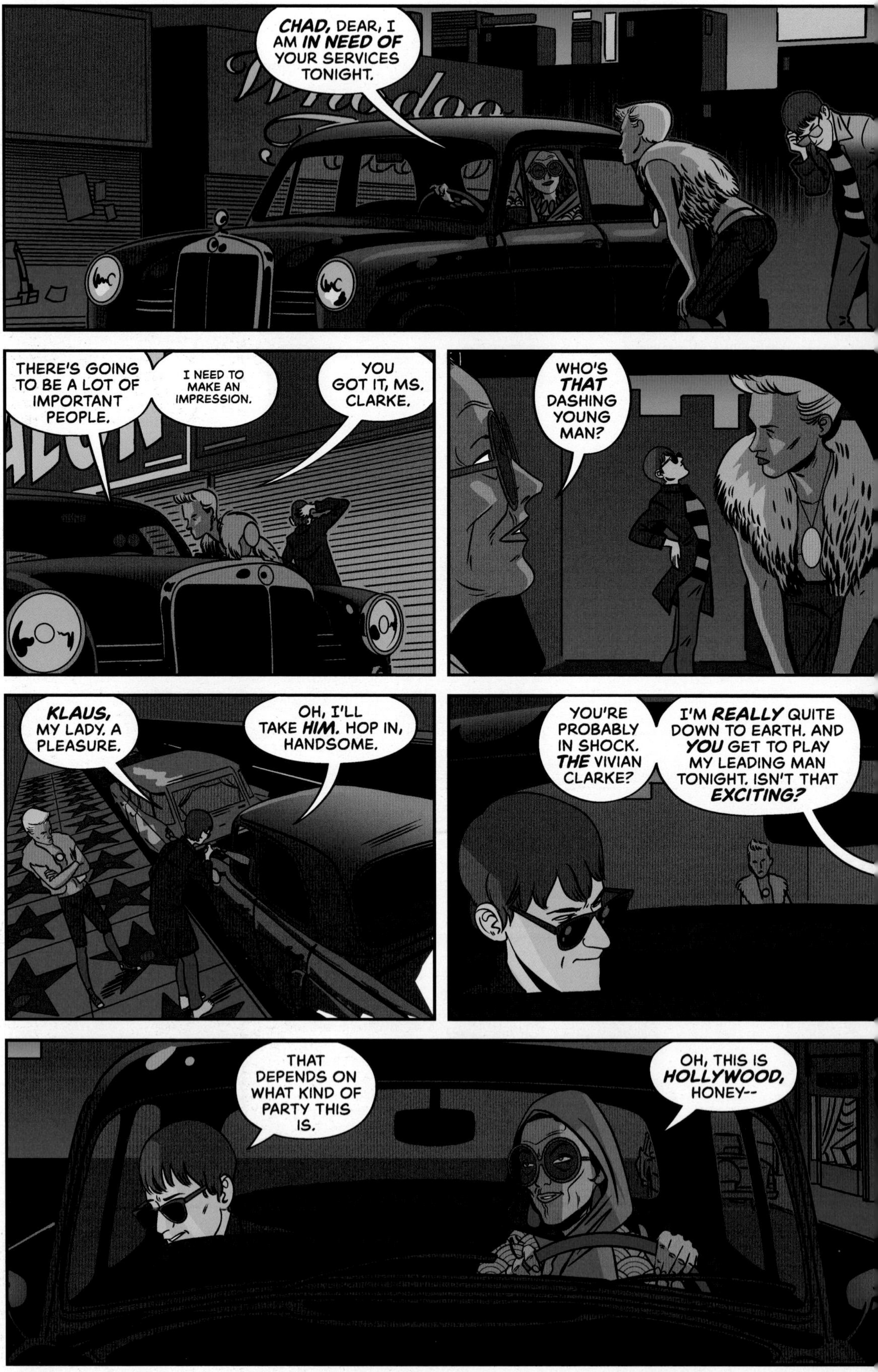
CHAD, DEAR, I AM IN NEED OF YOUR SERVICES TONIGHT.
THERE'S GOING TO BE A LOT OF IMPORTANT PEOPLE.
I NEED TO MAKE AN IMPRESSION.
YOU GOT IT, MS. CLARKE.
WHO'S THAT DASHING YOUNG MAN?
KLAUS, MY LADY. A PLEASURE.
OH, I'LL TAKE HIM. HOP IN, HANDSOME.
YOU'RE PROBABLY IN SHOCK. THE VIVIAN CLARKE?
I'M REALLY QUITE DOWN TO EARTH. AND YOU GET TO PLAY MY LEADING MAN TONIGHT. ISN'T THAT EXCITING?
THAT DEPENDS ON WHAT KIND OF PARTY THIS IS.
OH, THIS IS HOLLYWOOD, HONEY--

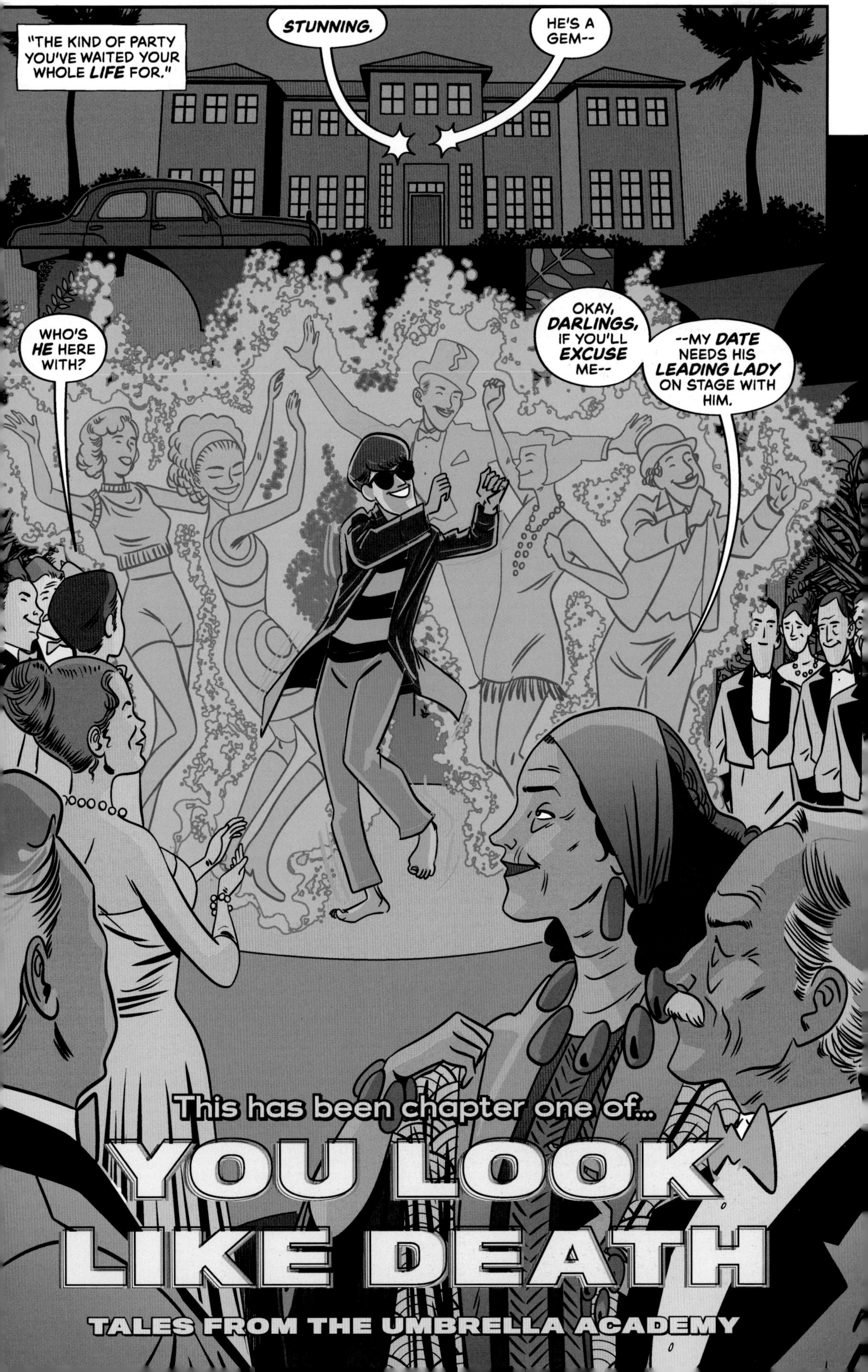
"THE KIND OF PARTY YOU'VE WAITED YOUR WHOLE LIFE FOR."
STUNNING.
HE'S A GEM--
WHO'S HE HERE WITH?
OKAY, DARLINGS, IF YOU'LL EXCUSE ME--
--MY DATE NEEDS HIS LEADING LADY ON STAGE WITH HIM.
This has been chapter one of...
YOU LOOK LIKE DEATH
TALES FROM THE UMBRELLA ACADEMY

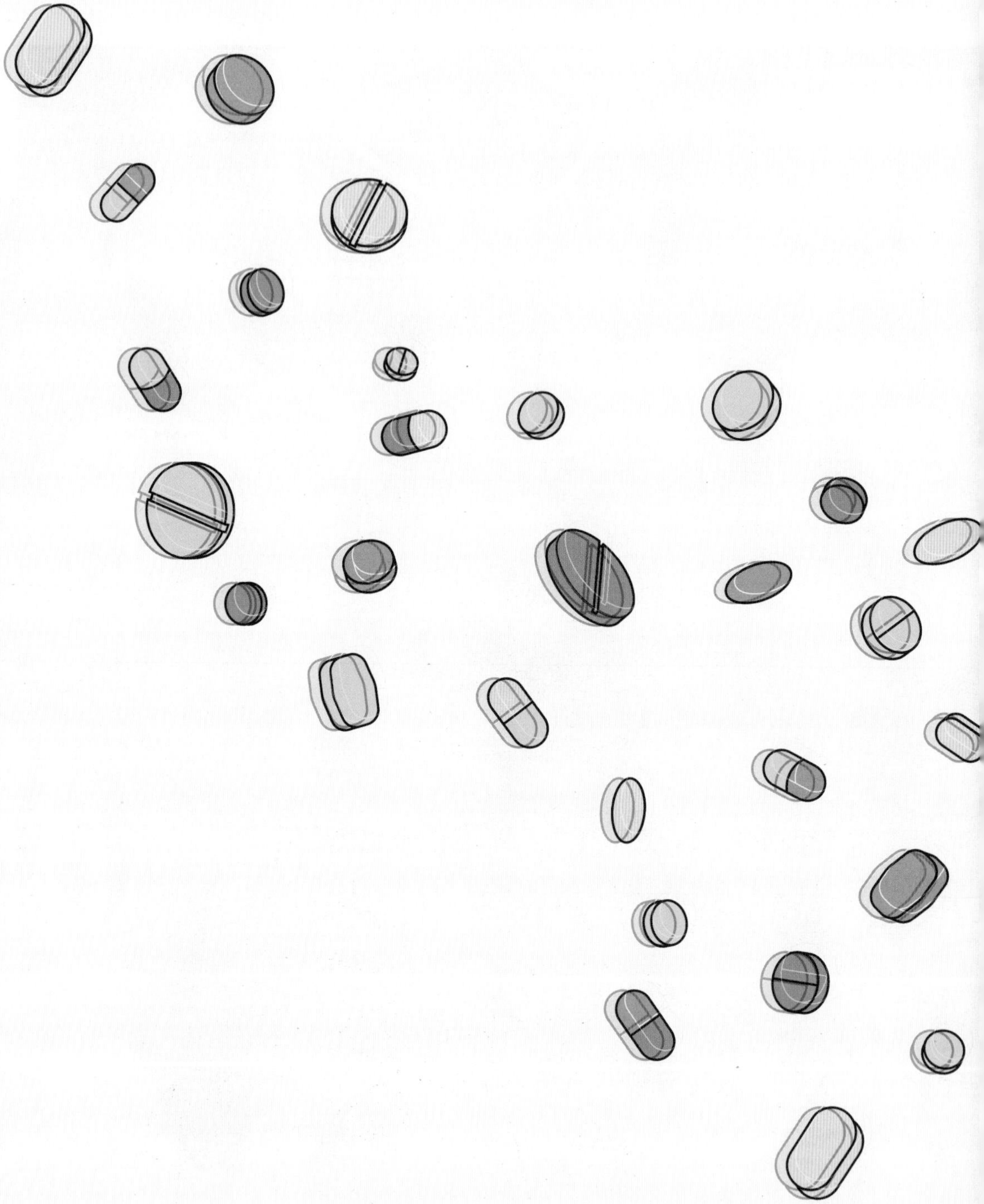

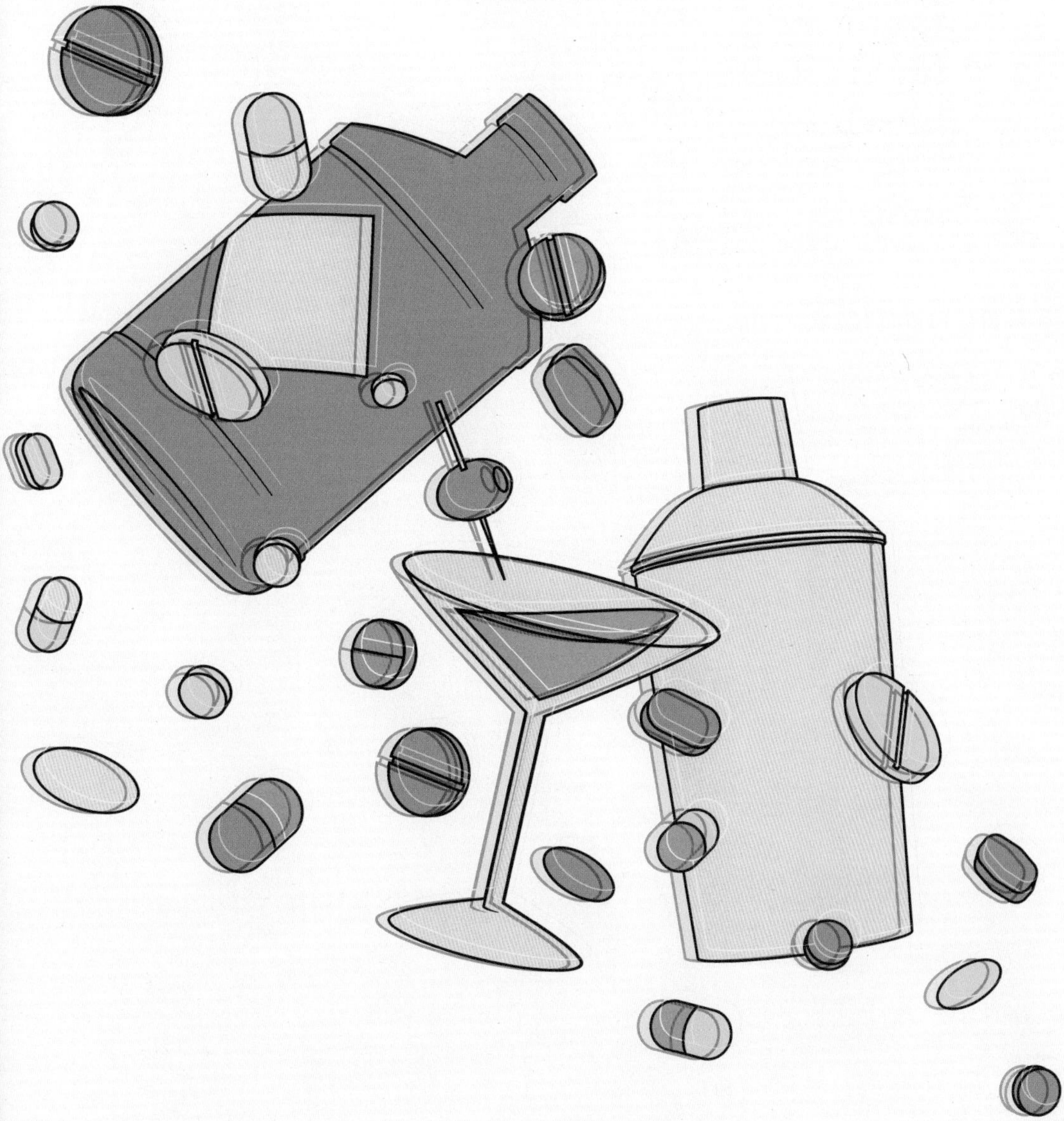

CHAPTER TWO

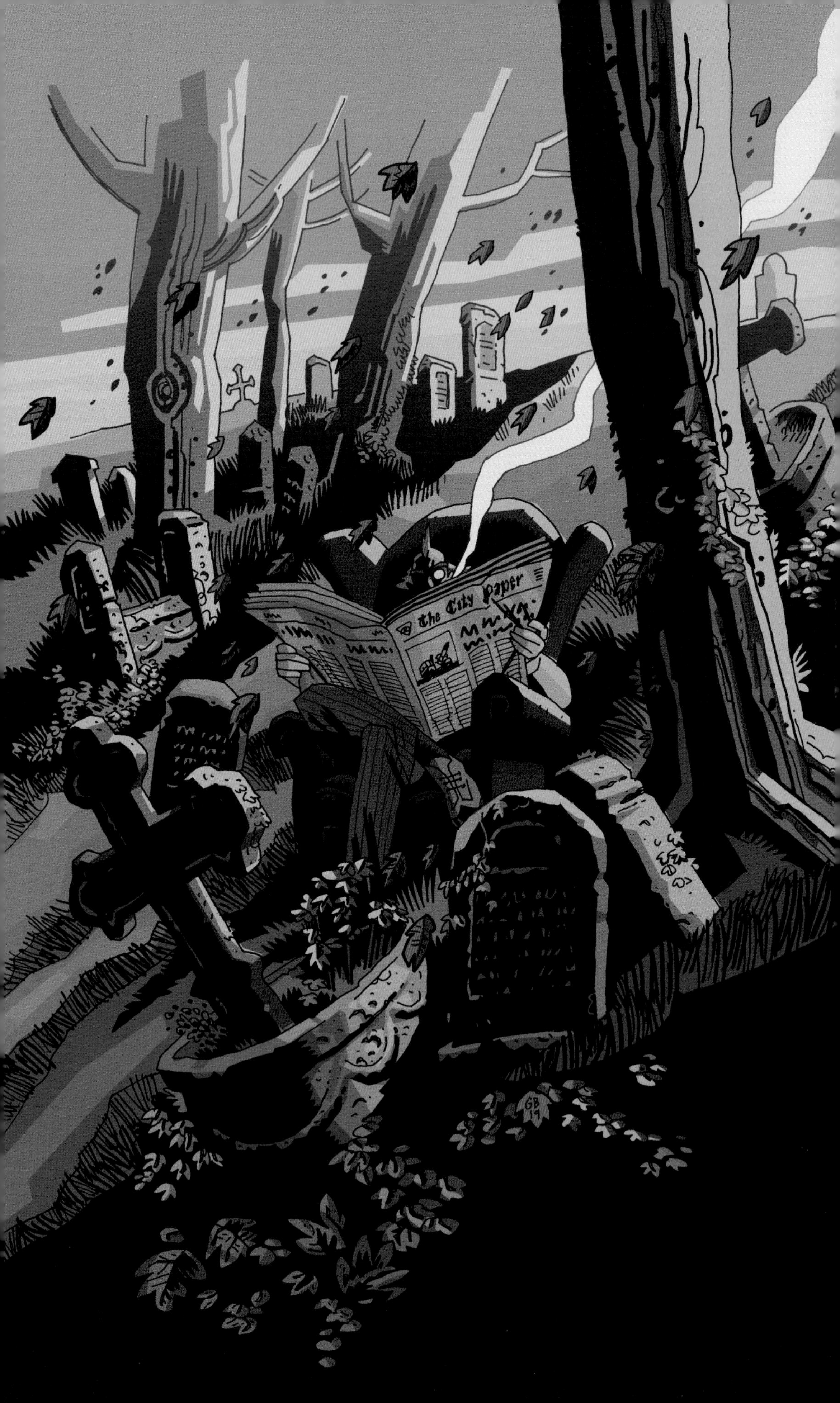
the City Paper

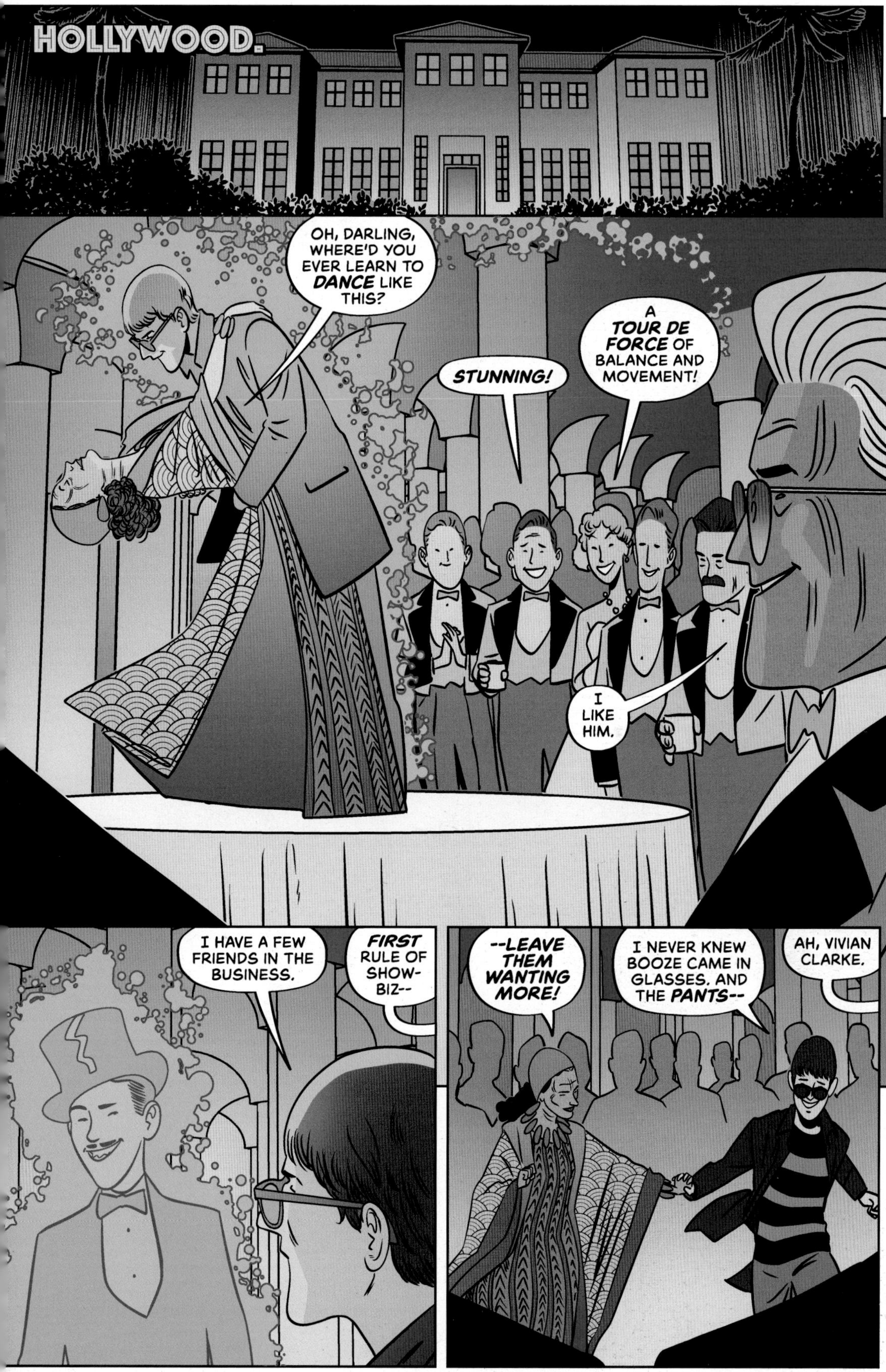
HOLLYWOOD.
OH, DARLING, WHERE'D YOU EVER LEARN TO DANCE LIKE THIS?
STUNNING!
A TOUR DE FORCE OF BALANCE AND MOVEMENT!
I LIKE HIM.
I HAVE A FEW FRIENDS IN THE BUSINESS.
FIRST RULE OF SHOW-BIZ--
--LEAVE THEM WANTING MORE!
I NEVER KNEW BOOZE CAME IN GLASSES. AND THE PANTS--
AH, VIVIAN CLARKE.

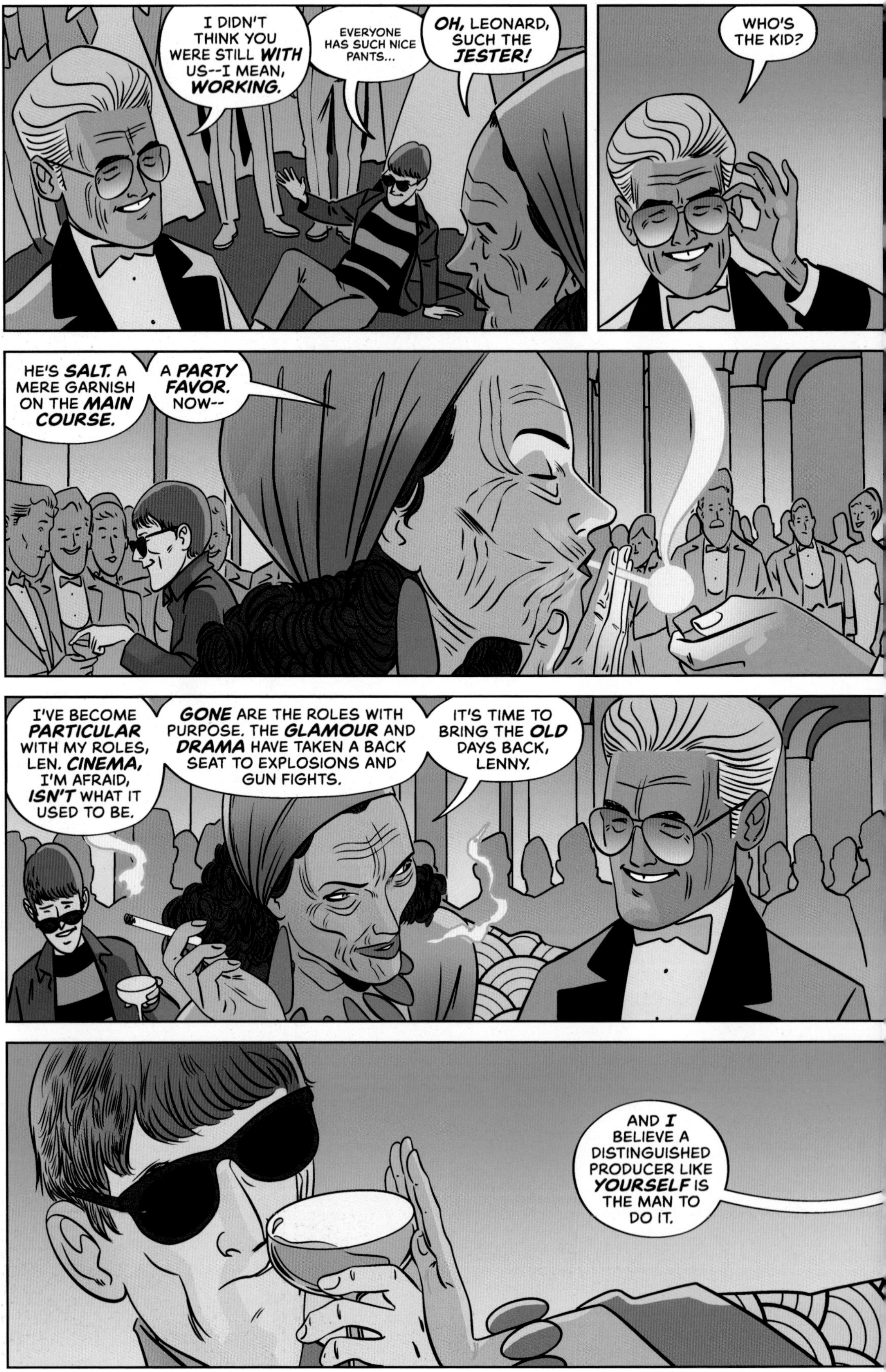

I DIDN'T THINK YOU WERE STILL WITH US--I MEAN, WORKING.
EVERYONE HAS SUCH NICE PANTS...
OH, LEONARD, SUCH THE JESTER!
WHO'S THE KID?
HE'S SALT. A MERE GARNISH ON THE MAIN COURSE.
A PARTY FAVOR. NOW--
I'VE BECOME PARTICULAR WITH MY ROLES, LEN. CINEMA, I'M AFRAID, ISN'T WHAT IT USED TO BE.
GONE ARE THE ROLES WITH PURPOSE. THE GLAMOUR AND DRAMA HAVE TAKEN A BACK SEAT TO EXPLOSIONS AND GUN FIGHTS.
IT'S TIME TO BRING THE OLD DAYS BACK, LENNY.
AND I BELIEVE A DISTINGUISHED PRODUCER LIKE YOURSELF IS THE MAN TO DO IT.

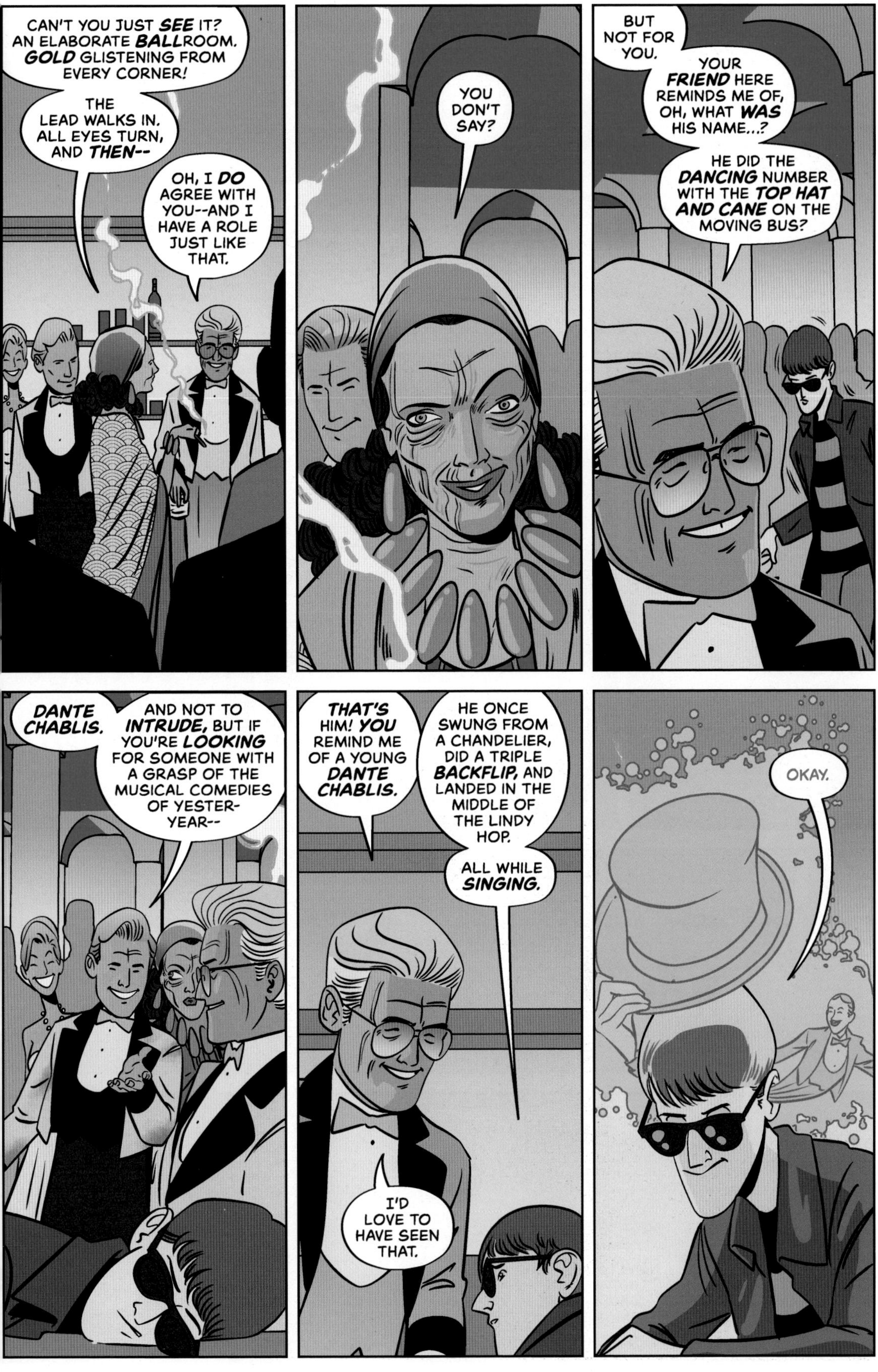
CAN'T YOU JUST SEE IT? AN ELABORATE BALLROOM. GOLD GLISTENING FROM EVERY CORNER!
THE LEAD WALKS IN. ALL EYES TURN, AND THEN--
OH, I DO AGREE WITH YOU--AND I HAVE A ROLE JUST LIKE THAT.
YOU DON'T SAY?
BUT NOT FOR YOU.
YOUR FRIEND HERE REMINDS ME OF, OH, WHAT WAS HIS NAME...?
HE DID THE DANCING NUMBER WITH THE TOP HAT AND CANE ON THE MOVING BUS?
DANTE CHABLIS.
AND NOT TO INTRUDE, BUT IF YOU'RE LOOKING FOR SOMEONE WITH A GRASP OF THE MUSICAL COMEDIES OF YESTER-YEAR--
THAT'S HIM! YOU REMIND ME OF A YOUNG DANTE CHABLIS.
HE ONCE SWUNG FROM A CHANDELIER, DID A TRIPLE BACKFLIP, AND LANDED IN THE MIDDLE OF THE LINDY HOP.
ALL WHILE SINGING.
I'D LOVE TO HAVE SEEN THAT.
OKAY.

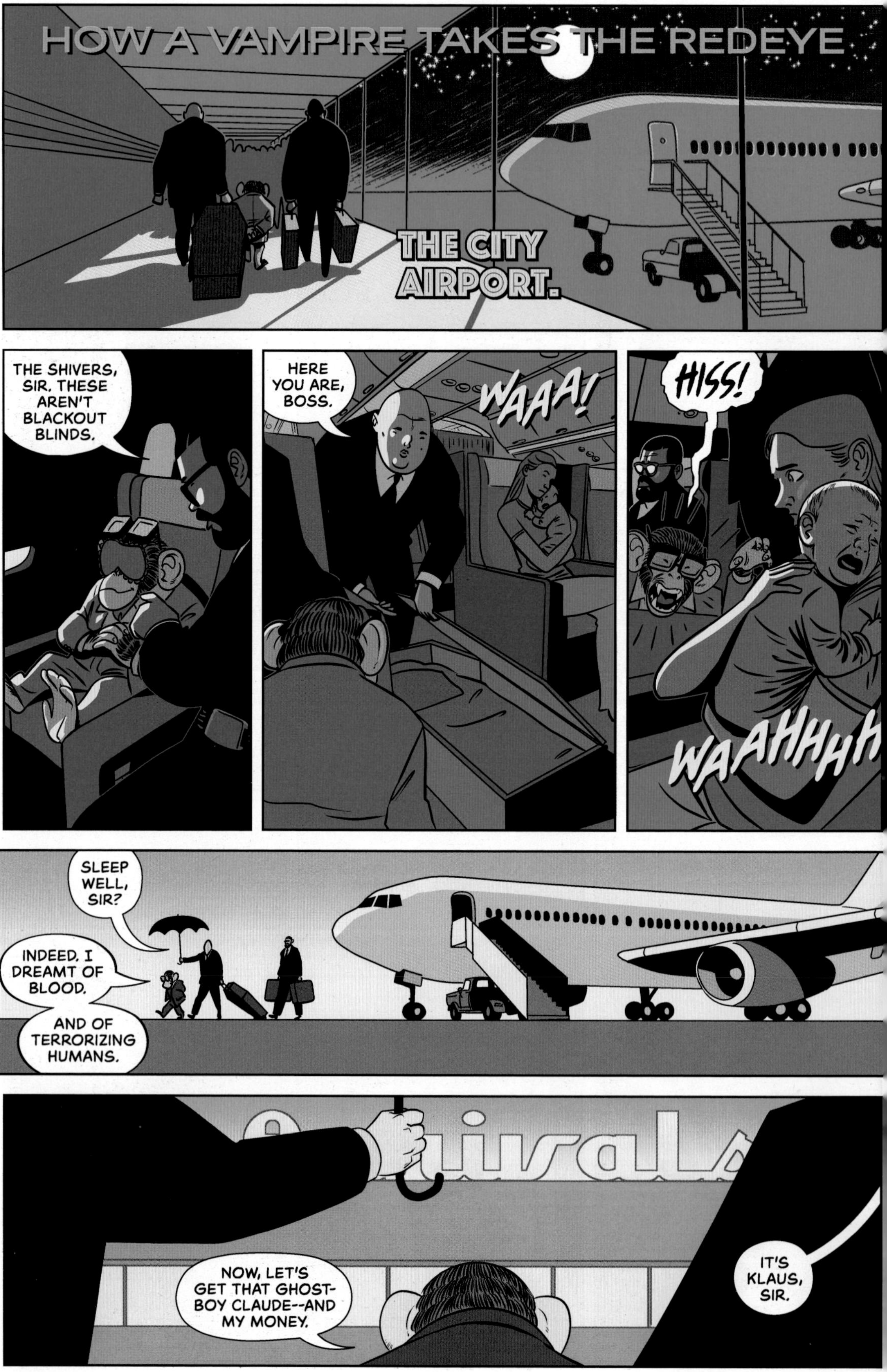
HOW A VAMPIRE TAKES THE REDEYE
THE CITY AIRPORT.
THE SHIVERS, SIR. THESE AREN'T BLACKOUT BLINDS.
HERE YOU ARE, BOSS.
WAAA!
HISS!
WAAHHHH
SLEEP WELL, SIR?
INDEED. I DREAMT OF BLOOD.
AND OF TERRORIZING HUMANS.
NOW, LET'S GET THAT GHOST-BOY CLAUDE--AND MY MONEY.
IT'S KLAUS, SIR.

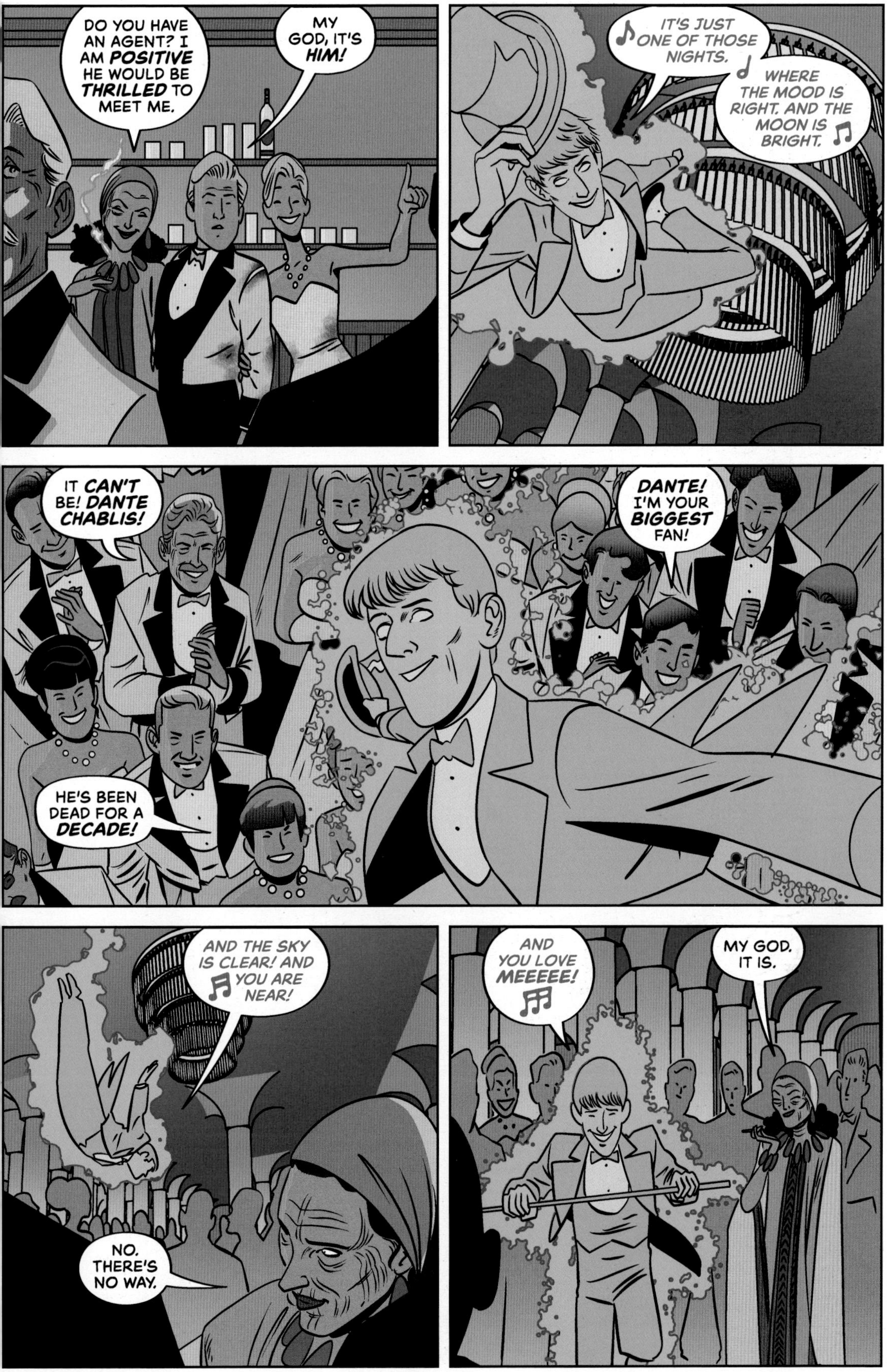
DO YOU HAVE AN AGENT? I AM **POSITIVE** HE WOULD BE **THRILLED** TO MEET ME.
MY GOD, IT'S **HIM!**
IT'S JUST ONE OF THOSE NIGHTS.
WHERE THE MOOD IS RIGHT. AND THE MOON IS BRIGHT.
IT **CAN'T** BE! **DANTE CHABLIS!**
DANTE! I'M YOUR **BIGGEST** FAN!
HE'S BEEN DEAD FOR A **DECADE!**
AND THE SKY IS CLEAR! AND YOU ARE NEAR!
NO. THERE'S NO WAY.
*AND YOU LOVE **MEEEEE!***
MY GOD. IT IS.

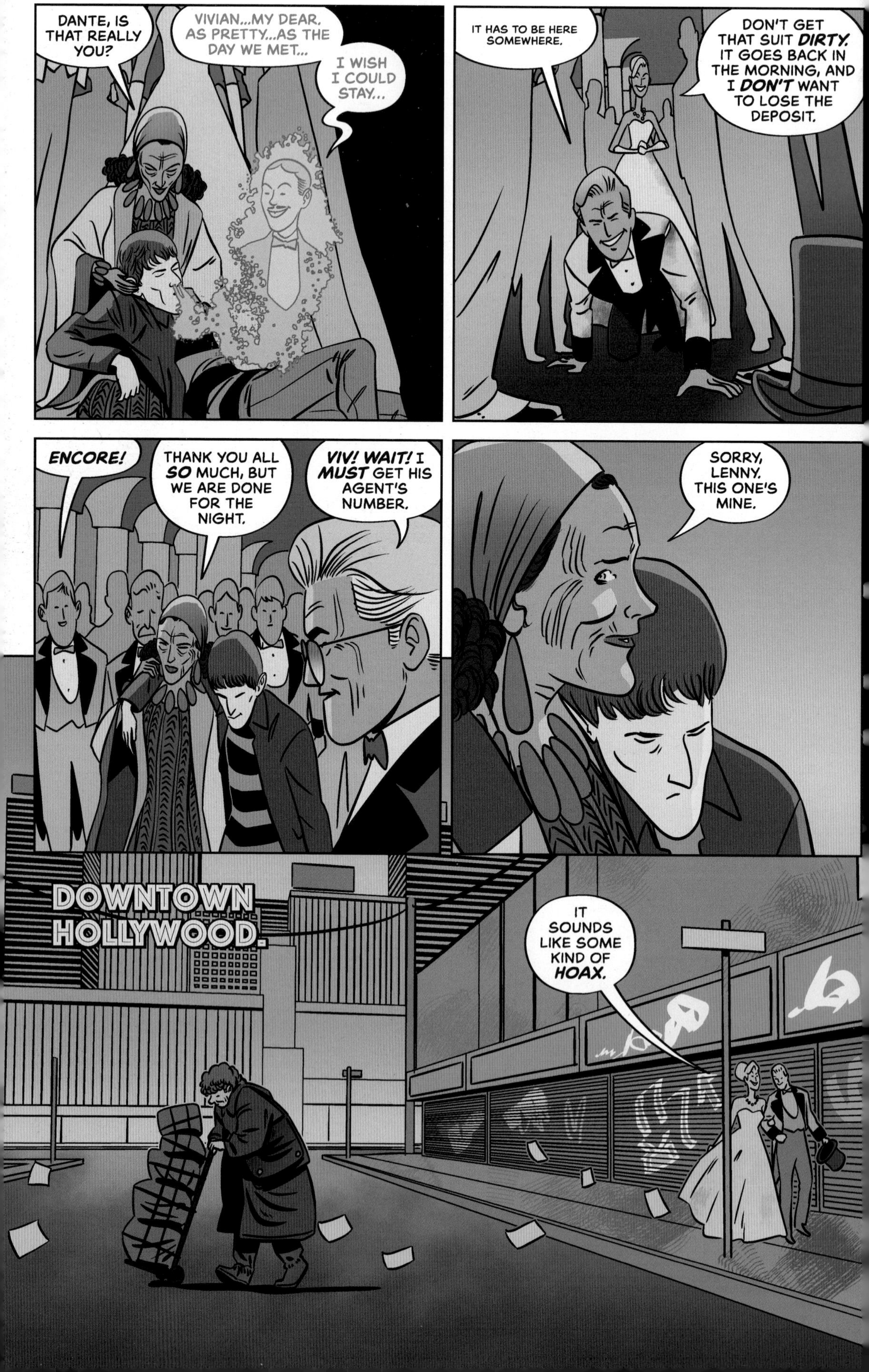
DANTE, IS THAT REALLY YOU?
VIVIAN...MY DEAR. AS PRETTY...AS THE DAY WE MET...
I WISH I COULD STAY...
IT HAS TO BE HERE SOMEWHERE.
DON'T GET THAT SUIT DIRTY. IT GOES BACK IN THE MORNING, AND I DON'T WANT TO LOSE THE DEPOSIT.
ENCORE!
THANK YOU ALL SO MUCH, BUT WE ARE DONE FOR THE NIGHT.
VIV! WAIT! I MUST GET HIS AGENT'S NUMBER.
SORRY, LENNY. THIS ONE'S MINE.
DOWNTOWN HOLLYWOOD.
IT SOUNDS LIKE SOME KIND OF HOAX.

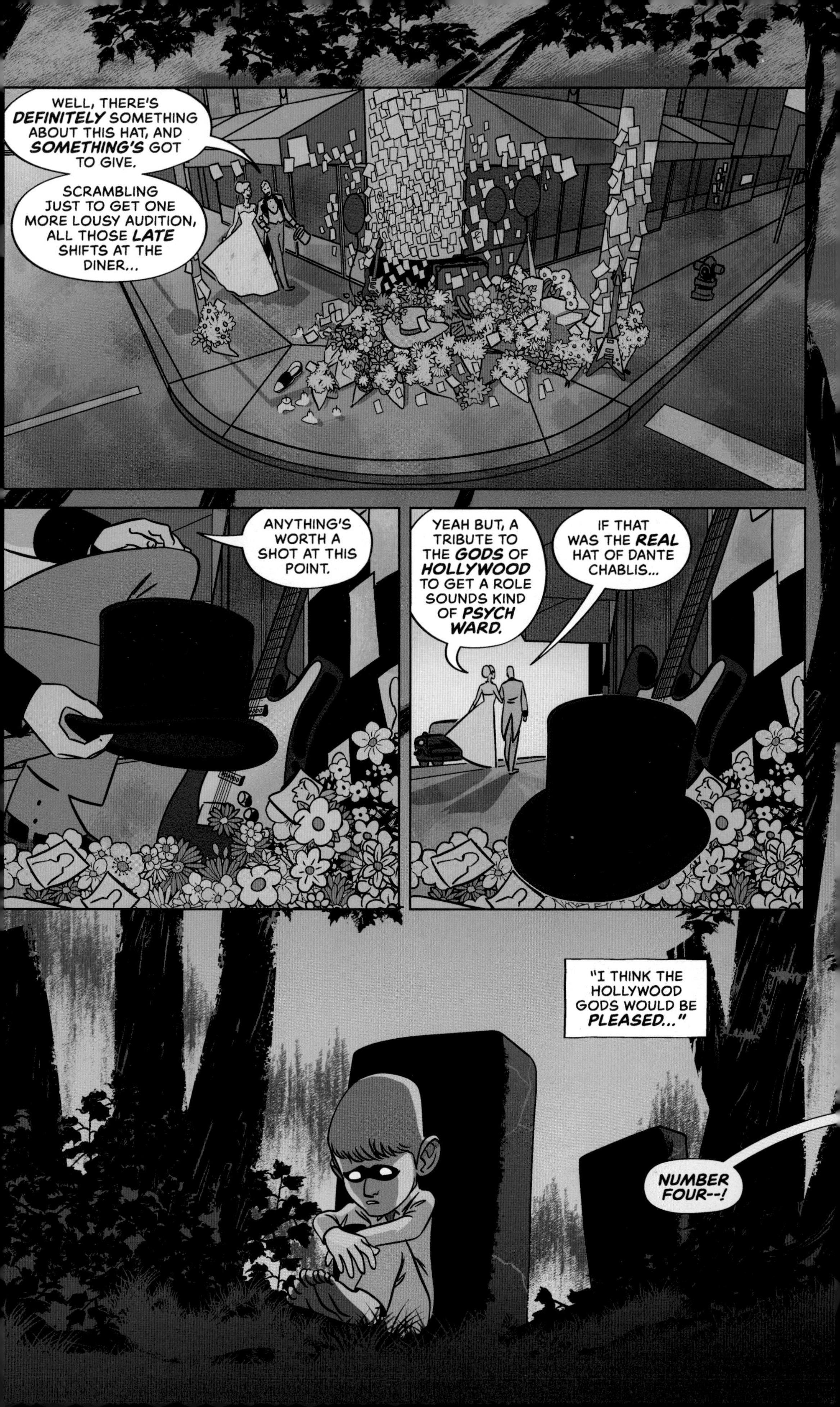

WELL, THERE'S DEFINITELY SOMETHING ABOUT THIS HAT, AND SOMETHING'S GOT TO GIVE.
SCRAMBLING JUST TO GET ONE MORE LOUSY AUDITION, ALL THOSE LATE SHIFTS AT THE DINER...
ANYTHING'S WORTH A SHOT AT THIS POINT.
YEAH BUT, A TRIBUTE TO THE GODS OF HOLLYWOOD TO GET A ROLE SOUNDS KIND OF PSYCH WARD.
IF THAT WAS THE REAL HAT OF DANTE CHABLIS...
"I THINK THE HOLLYWOOD GODS WOULD BE PLEASED..."
NUMBER FOUR--!

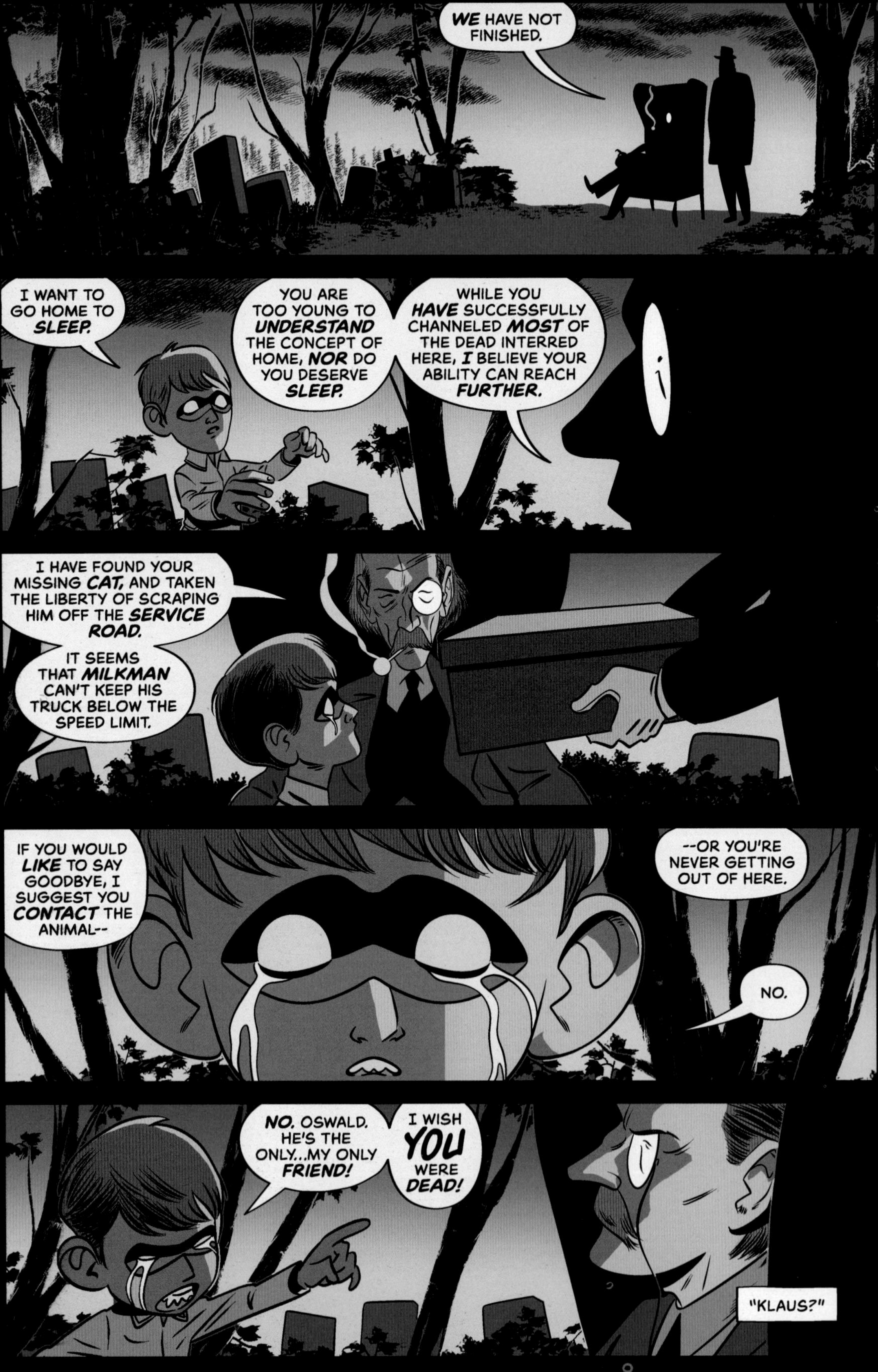
WE HAVE NOT FINISHED.
I WANT TO GO HOME TO SLEEP.
YOU ARE TOO YOUNG TO UNDERSTAND THE CONCEPT OF HOME, NOR DO YOU DESERVE SLEEP.
WHILE YOU HAVE SUCCESSFULLY CHANNELED MOST OF THE DEAD INTERRED HERE, I BELIEVE YOUR ABILITY CAN REACH FURTHER.
I HAVE FOUND YOUR MISSING CAT, AND TAKEN THE LIBERTY OF SCRAPING HIM OFF THE SERVICE ROAD.
IT SEEMS THAT MILKMAN CAN'T KEEP HIS TRUCK BELOW THE SPEED LIMIT.
IF YOU WOULD LIKE TO SAY GOODBYE, I SUGGEST YOU CONTACT THE ANIMAL--
--OR YOU'RE NEVER GETTING OUT OF HERE.
NO.
NO. OSWALD. HE'S THE ONLY...MY ONLY FRIEND!
I WISH YOU WERE DEAD!
"KLAUS?"

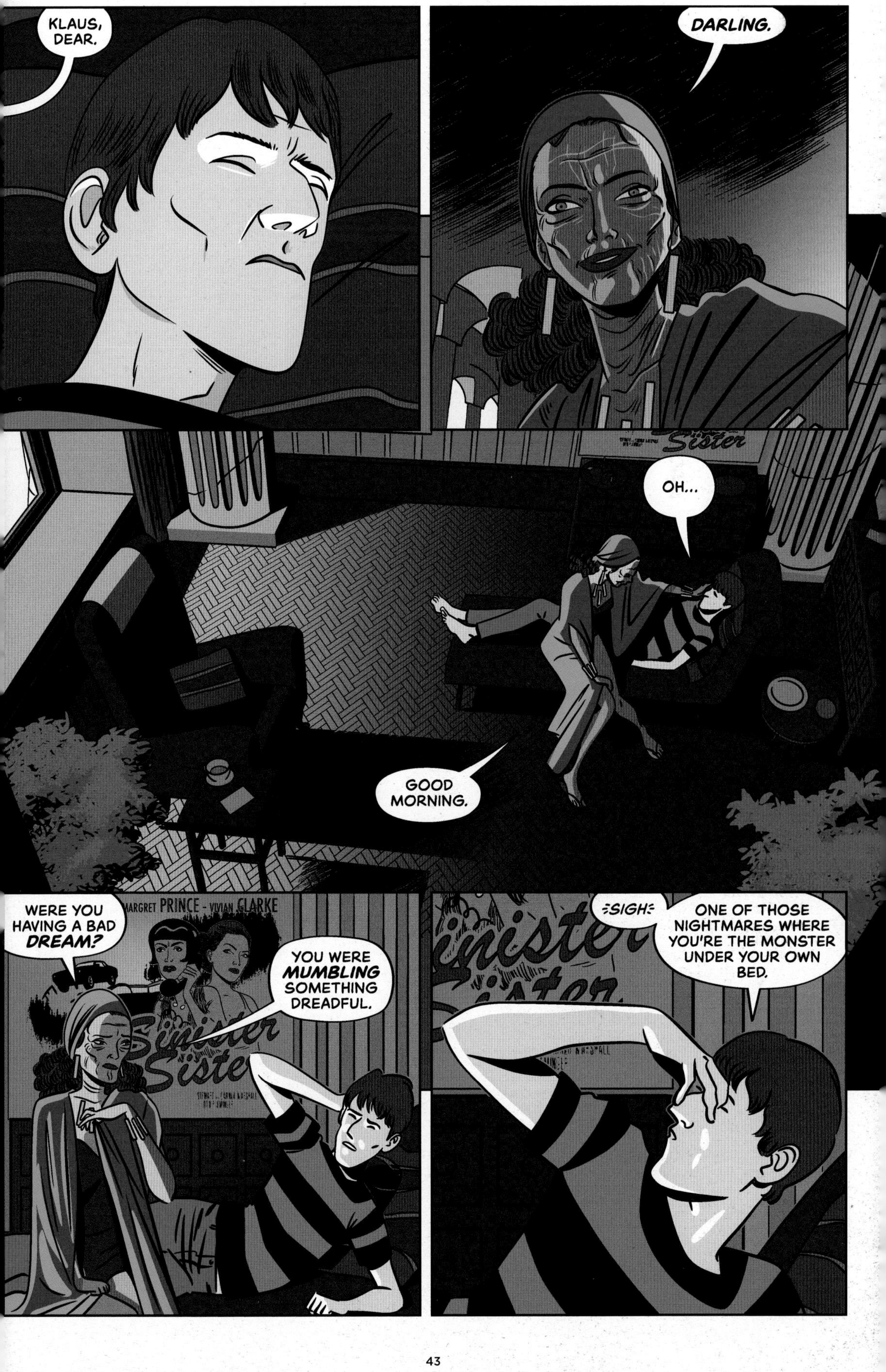
KLAUS, DEAR.
DARLING.
Sister
OH...
GOOD MORNING.
MARGRET PRINCE - VIVIAN CLARKE
WERE YOU HAVING A BAD *DREAM?*
YOU WERE *MUMBLING* SOMETHING DREADFUL.
Sinister Sister
SIGH
ONE OF THOSE NIGHTMARES WHERE YOU'RE THE MONSTER UNDER YOUR OWN BED.

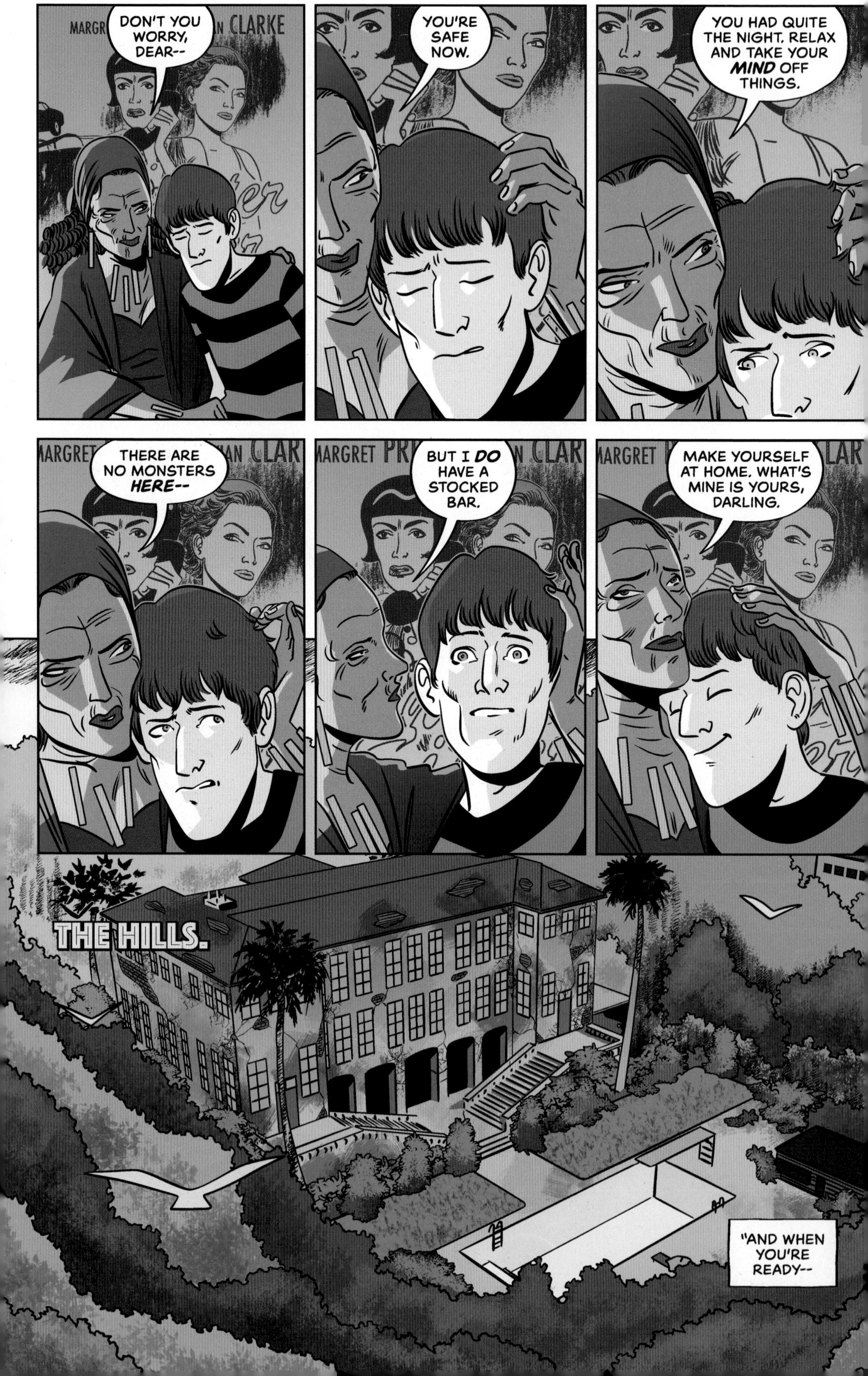

DON'T YOU WORRY, DEAR--
YOU'RE SAFE NOW.
YOU HAD QUITE THE NIGHT. RELAX AND TAKE YOUR MIND OFF THINGS.
THERE ARE NO MONSTERS HERE--
BUT I DO HAVE A STOCKED BAR.
MAKE YOURSELF AT HOME. WHAT'S MINE IS YOURS, DARLING.
THE HILLS.
"AND WHEN YOU'RE READY--

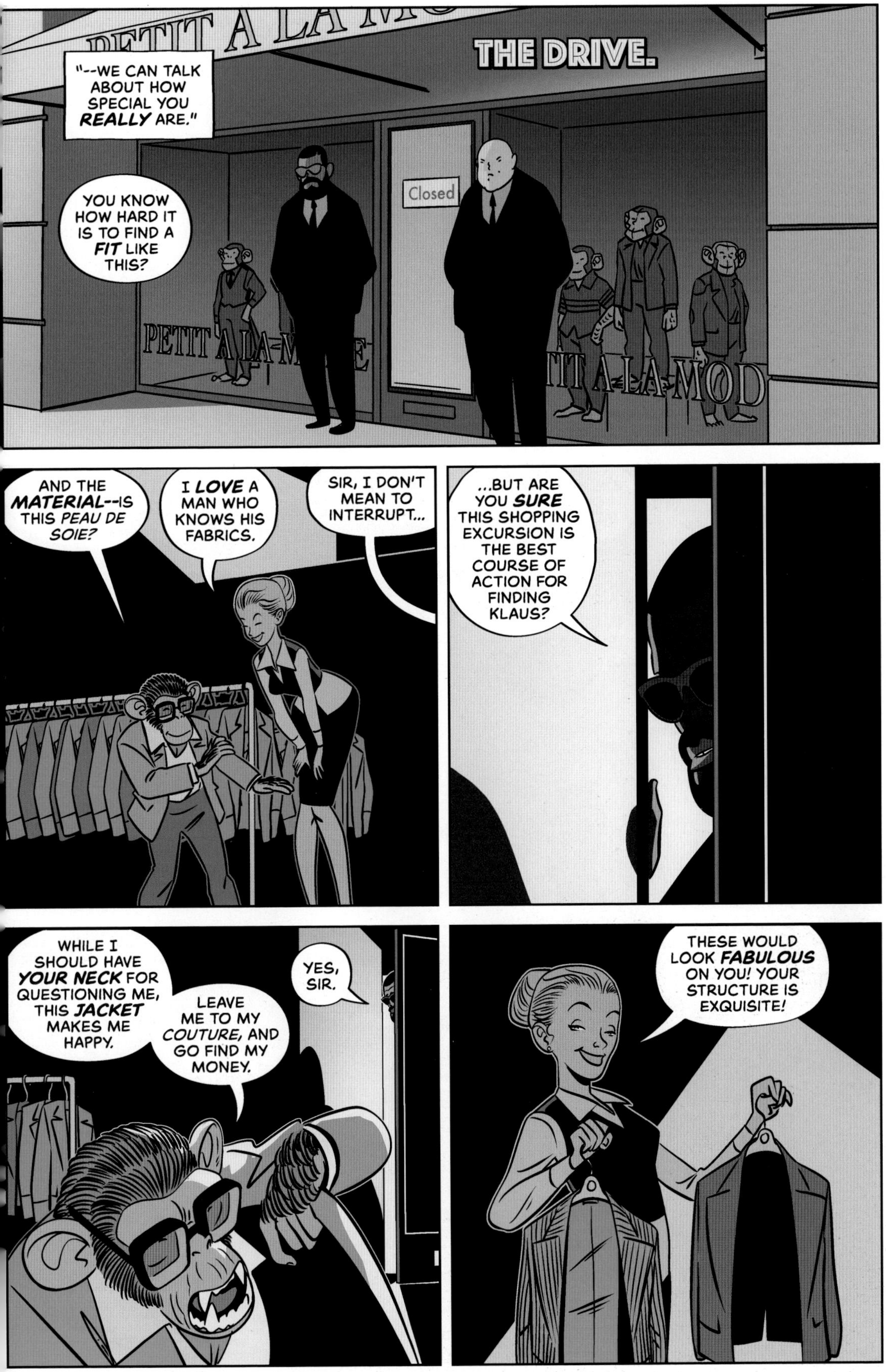
PETIT A LA MO
THE DRIVE.
"--WE CAN TALK ABOUT HOW SPECIAL YOU *REALLY* ARE."
Closed
YOU KNOW HOW HARD IT IS TO FIND A *FIT* LIKE THIS?
PETIT A LA M E
TIT A LA MOD
AND THE *MATERIAL*--IS THIS *PEAU DE SOIE?*
I *LOVE* A MAN WHO KNOWS HIS FABRICS.
SIR, I DON'T MEAN TO INTERRUPT...
...BUT ARE YOU *SURE* THIS SHOPPING EXCURSION IS THE BEST COURSE OF ACTION FOR FINDING KLAUS?
WHILE I SHOULD HAVE *YOUR NECK* FOR QUESTIONING ME, THIS *JACKET* MAKES ME HAPPY.
LEAVE ME TO MY *COUTURE,* AND GO FIND MY MONEY.
YES, SIR.
THESE WOULD LOOK *FABULOUS* ON YOU! YOUR STRUCTURE IS EXQUISITE!

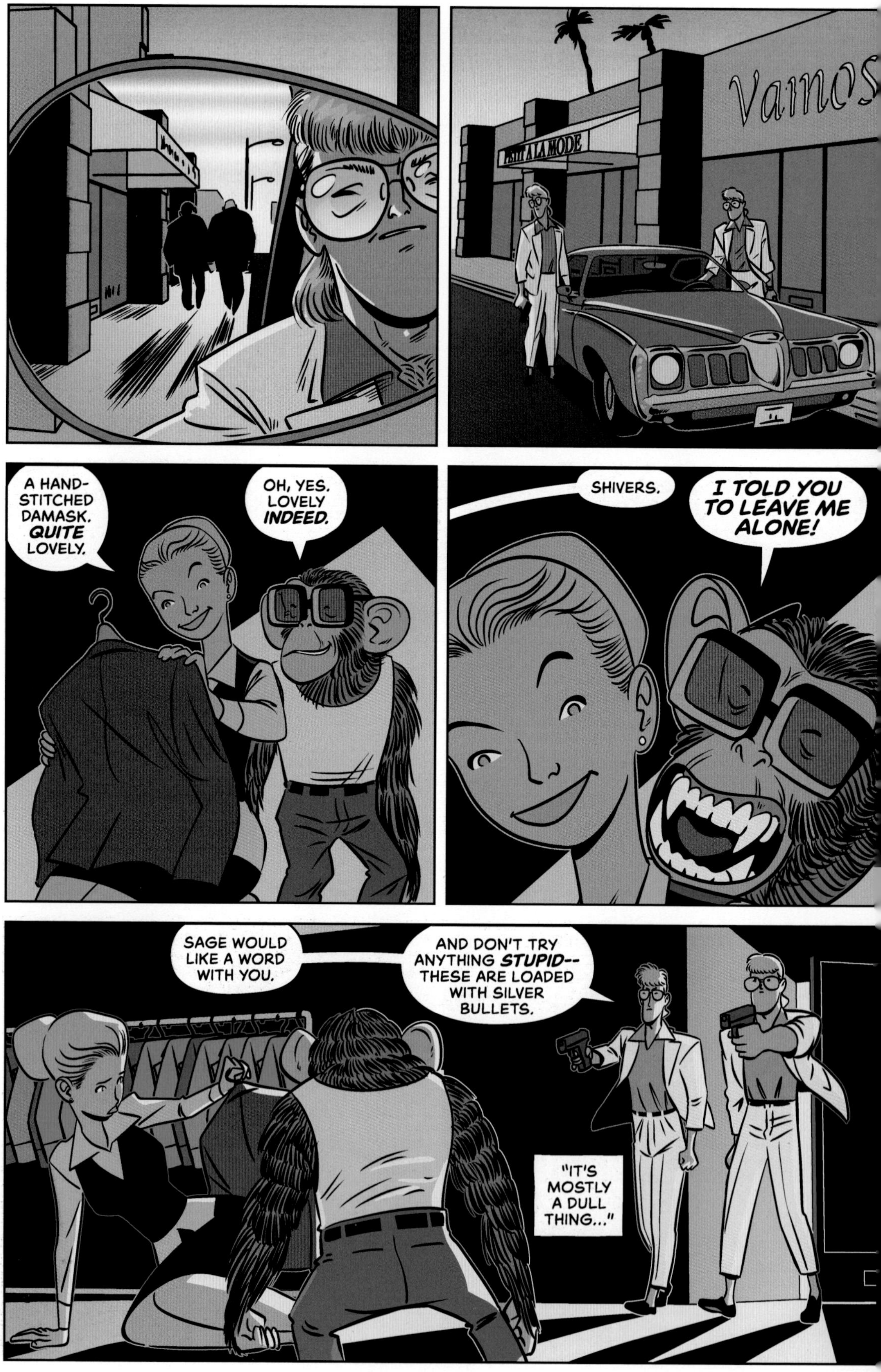

Vamos
PETIT A LA MODE
A HAND-STITCHED DAMASK. QUITE LOVELY.
OH, YES. LOVELY INDEED.
SHIVERS.
I TOLD YOU TO LEAVE ME ALONE!
SAGE WOULD LIKE A WORD WITH YOU.
AND DON'T TRY ANYTHING STUPID-- THESE ARE LOADED WITH SILVER BULLETS.
"IT'S MOSTLY A DULL THING..."

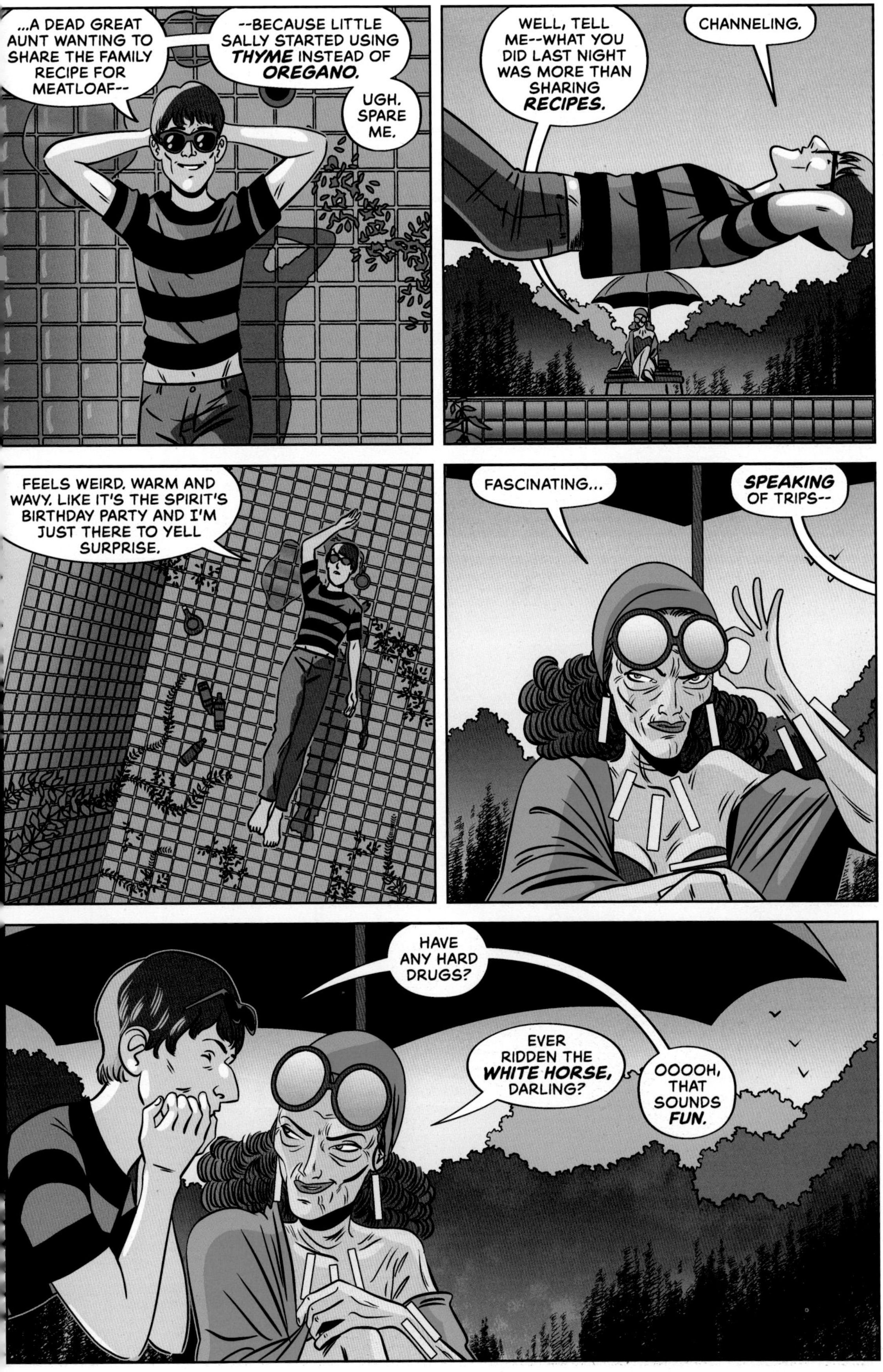
...A DEAD GREAT AUNT WANTING TO SHARE THE FAMILY RECIPE FOR MEATLOAF--
--BECAUSE LITTLE SALLY STARTED USING THYME INSTEAD OF OREGANO.
UGH. SPARE ME.
WELL, TELL ME--WHAT YOU DID LAST NIGHT WAS MORE THAN SHARING RECIPES.
CHANNELING.
FEELS WEIRD. WARM AND WAVY. LIKE IT'S THE SPIRIT'S BIRTHDAY PARTY AND I'M JUST THERE TO YELL SURPRISE.
FASCINATING...
SPEAKING OF TRIPS--
HAVE ANY HARD DRUGS?
EVER RIDDEN THE WHITE HORSE, DARLING?
OOOOH, THAT SOUNDS FUN.

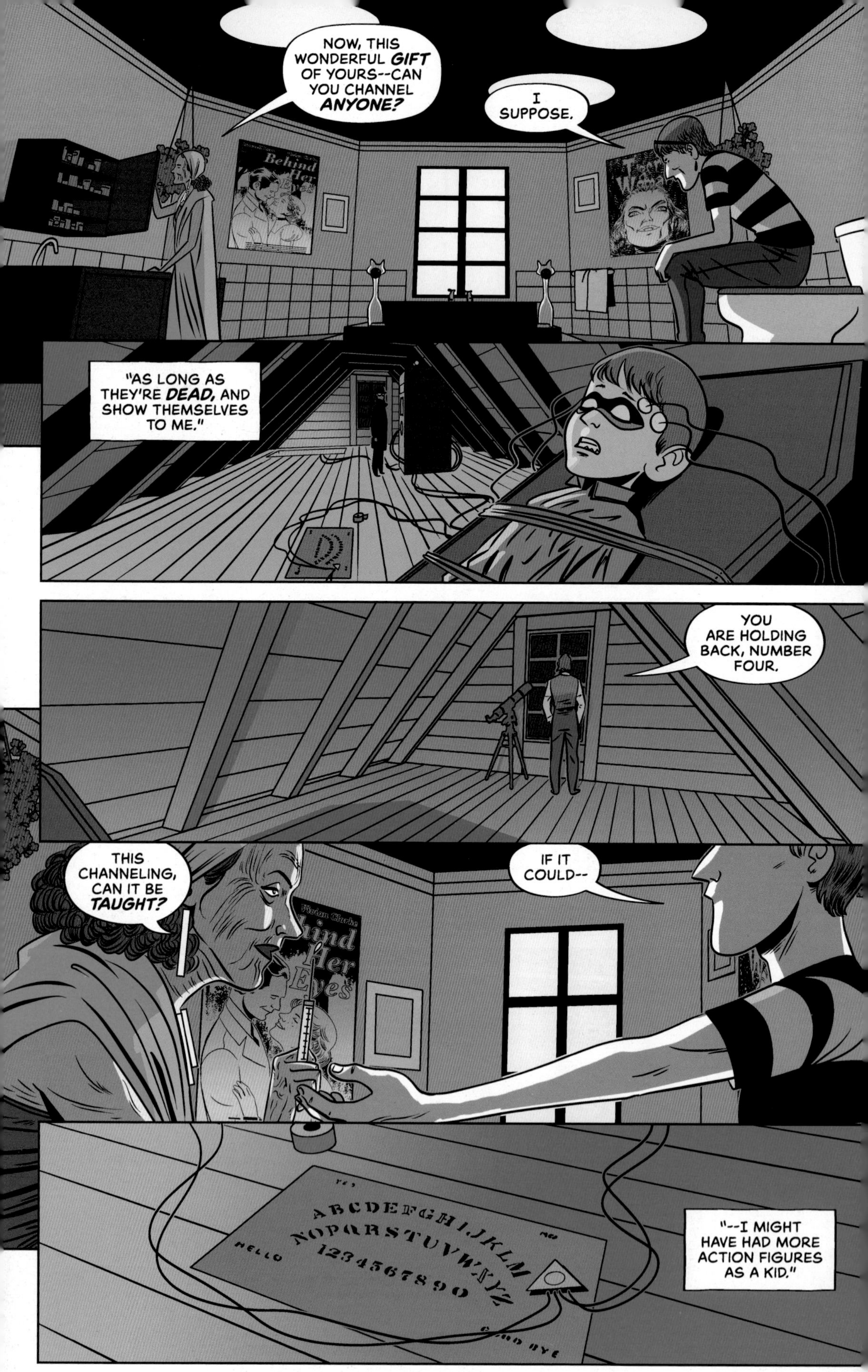
NOW, THIS WONDERFUL *GIFT* OF YOURS--CAN YOU CHANNEL ***ANYONE?***
I SUPPOSE.
"AS LONG AS THEY'RE ***DEAD,*** AND SHOW THEMSELVES TO ME."
YOU ARE HOLDING BACK, NUMBER FOUR.
THIS CHANNELING, CAN IT BE ***TAUGHT?***
IF IT COULD--
"--I MIGHT HAVE HAD MORE ACTION FIGURES AS A KID."

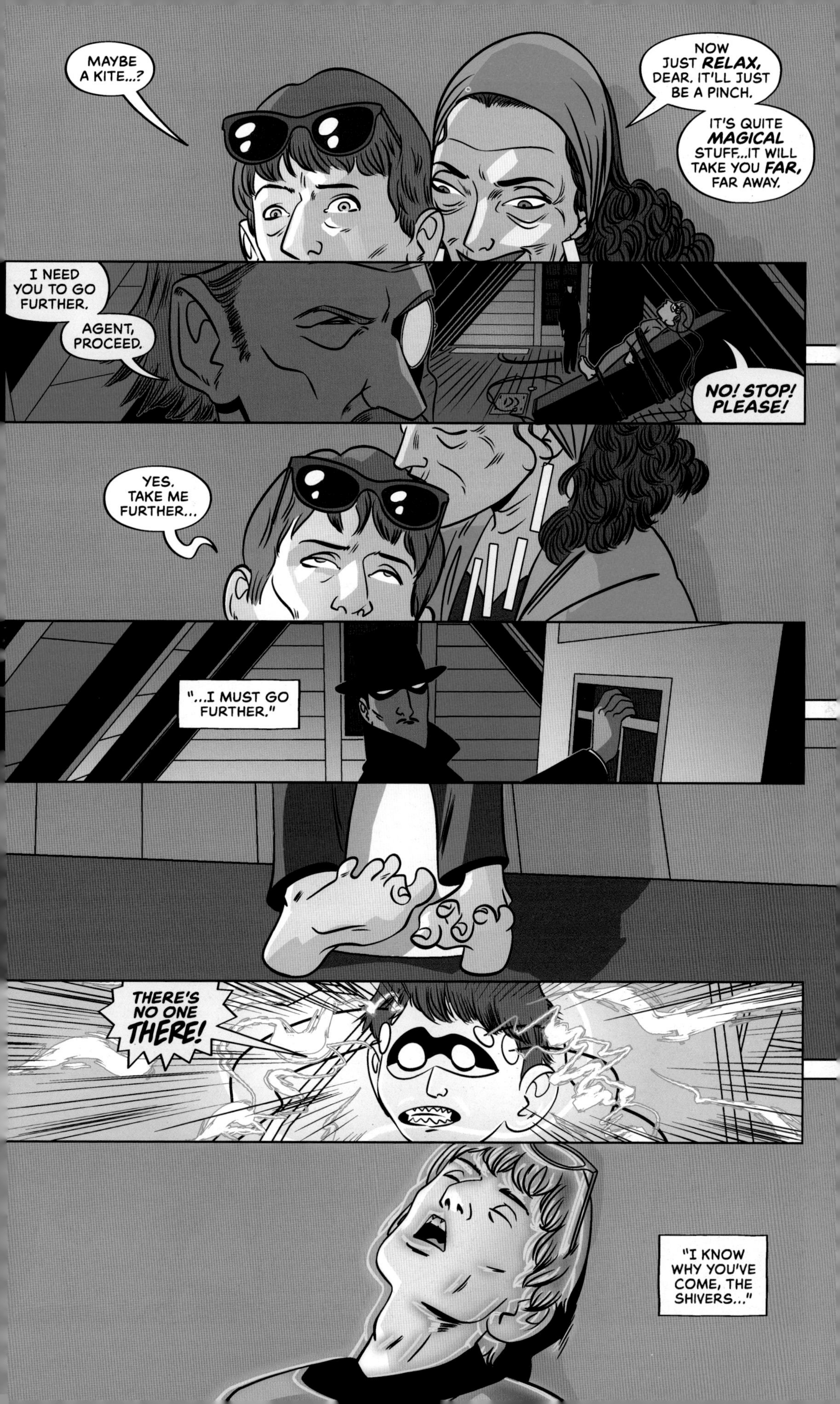
MAYBE A KITE...?
NOW JUST RELAX, DEAR. IT'LL JUST BE A PINCH.
IT'S QUITE MAGICAL STUFF...IT WILL TAKE YOU FAR, FAR AWAY.
I NEED YOU TO GO FURTHER.
AGENT, PROCEED.
NO! STOP! PLEASE!
YES. TAKE ME FURTHER...
"...I MUST GO FURTHER."
THERE'S NO ONE THERE!
"I KNOW WHY YOU'VE COME, THE SHIVERS..."

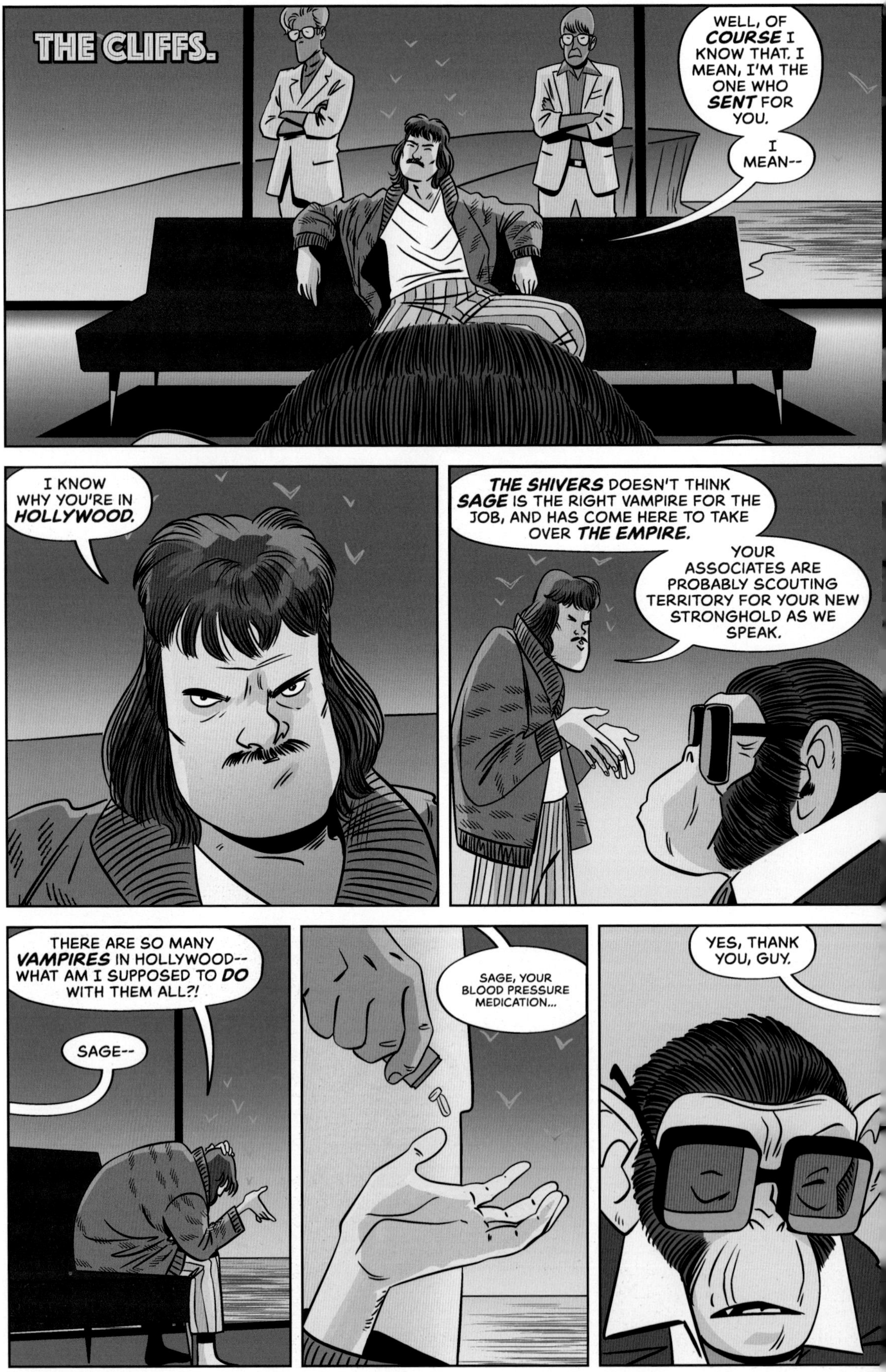

THE CLIFFS.
WELL, OF COURSE I KNOW THAT. I MEAN, I'M THE ONE WHO SENT FOR YOU.
I MEAN--
I KNOW WHY YOU'RE IN HOLLYWOOD.
THE SHIVERS DOESN'T THINK SAGE IS THE RIGHT VAMPIRE FOR THE JOB, AND HAS COME HERE TO TAKE OVER THE EMPIRE.
YOUR ASSOCIATES ARE PROBABLY SCOUTING TERRITORY FOR YOUR NEW STRONGHOLD AS WE SPEAK.
THERE ARE SO MANY VAMPIRES IN HOLLYWOOD--WHAT AM I SUPPOSED TO DO WITH THEM ALL?!
SAGE--
SAGE, YOUR BLOOD PRESSURE MEDICATION...
YES, THANK YOU, GUY.

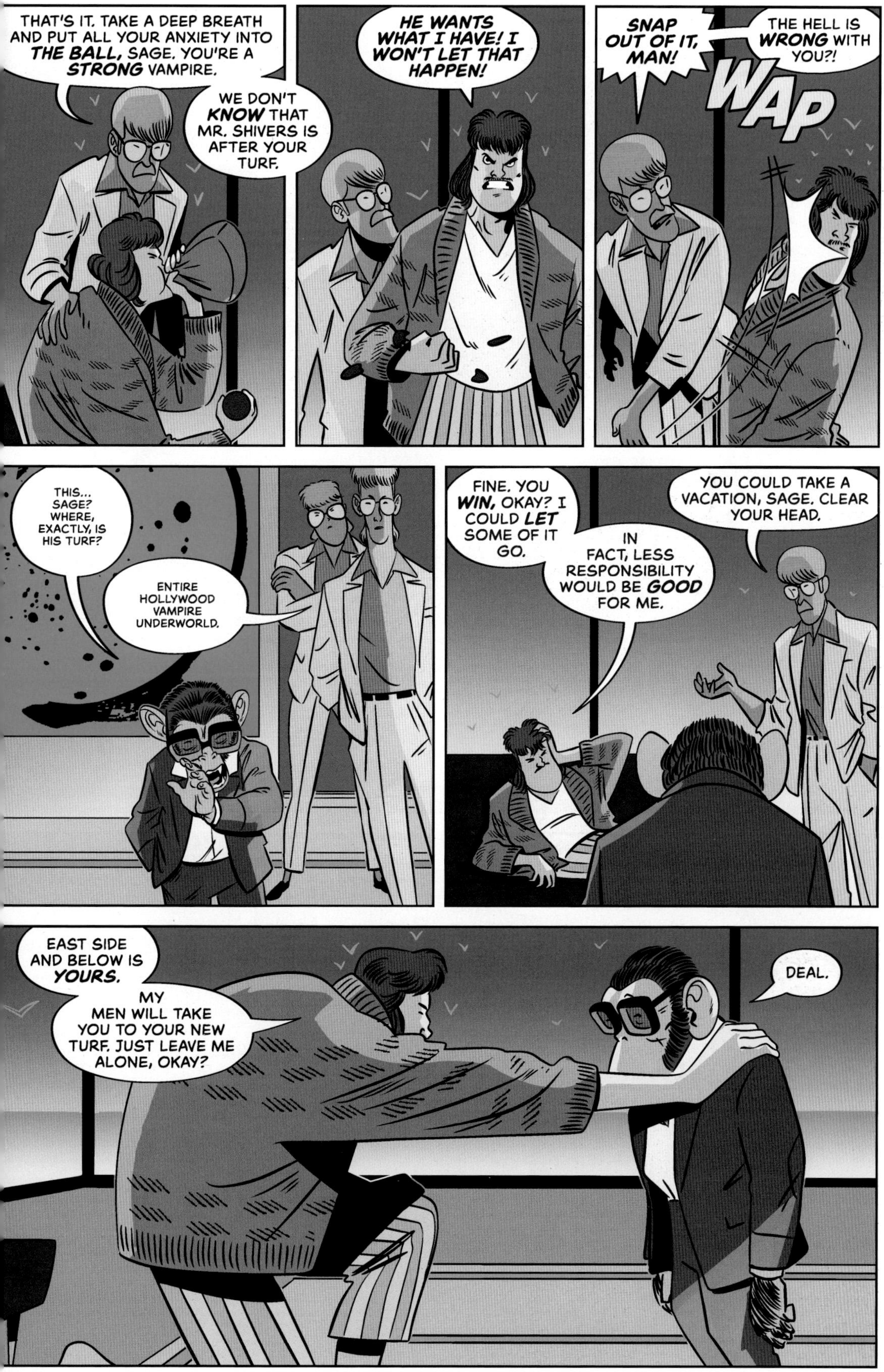
THAT'S IT. TAKE A DEEP BREATH AND PUT ALL YOUR ANXIETY INTO THE BALL, SAGE. YOU'RE A STRONG VAMPIRE.
WE DON'T KNOW THAT MR. SHIVERS IS AFTER YOUR TURF.
HE WANTS WHAT I HAVE! I WON'T LET THAT HAPPEN!
SNAP OUT OF IT, MAN!
THE HELL IS WRONG WITH YOU?!
WAP
THIS... SAGE? WHERE, EXACTLY, IS HIS TURF?
ENTIRE HOLLYWOOD VAMPIRE UNDERWORLD.
FINE. YOU WIN, OKAY? I COULD LET SOME OF IT GO.
IN FACT, LESS RESPONSIBILITY WOULD BE GOOD FOR ME.
YOU COULD TAKE A VACATION, SAGE. CLEAR YOUR HEAD.
EAST SIDE AND BELOW IS YOURS.
MY MEN WILL TAKE YOU TO YOUR NEW TURF. JUST LEAVE ME ALONE, OKAY?
DEAL.

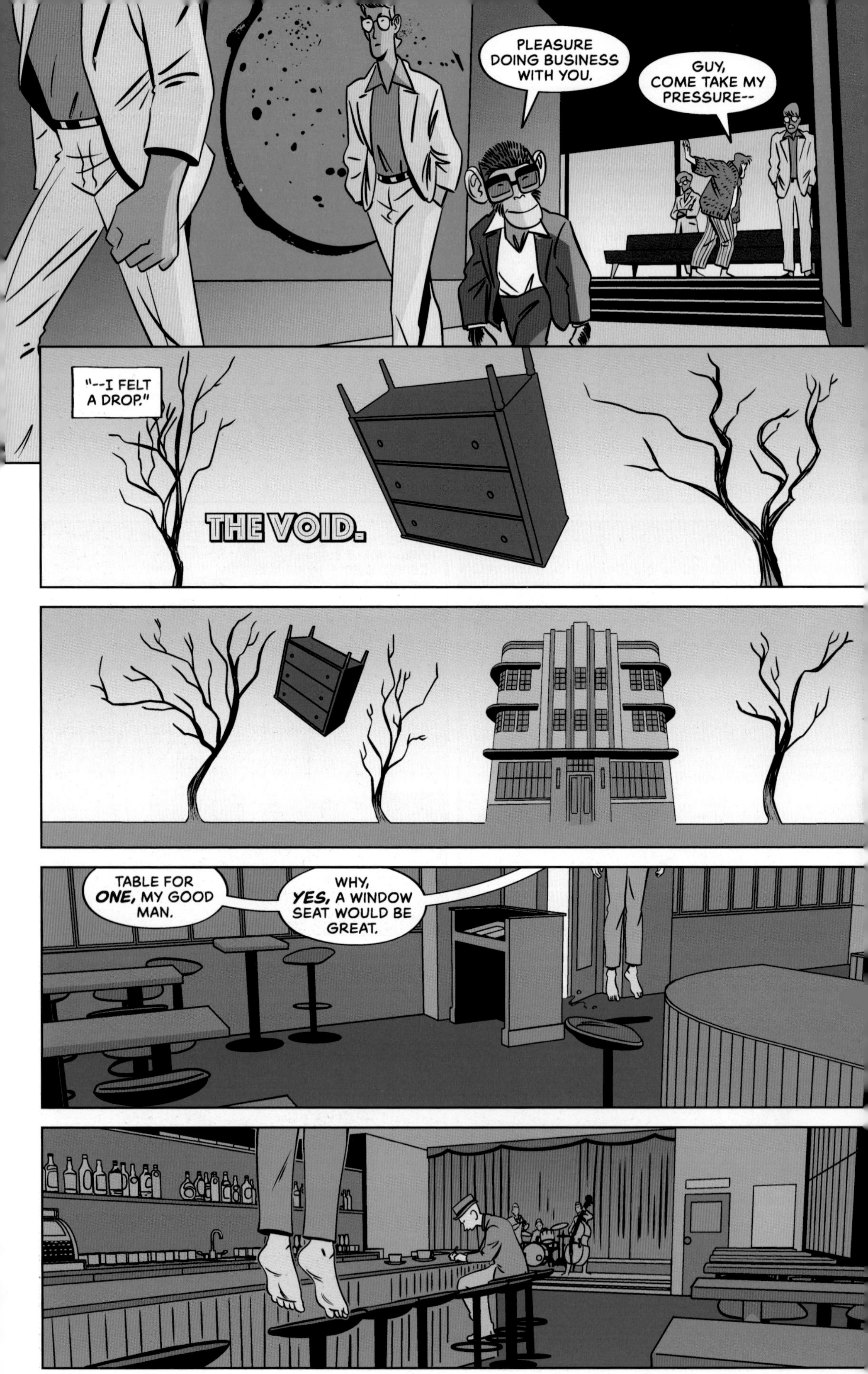
PLEASURE DOING BUSINESS WITH YOU.
GUY, COME TAKE MY PRESSURE--
"--I FELT A DROP."
THE VOID.
TABLE FOR *ONE*, MY GOOD MAN.
WHY, *YES*, A WINDOW SEAT WOULD BE GREAT.

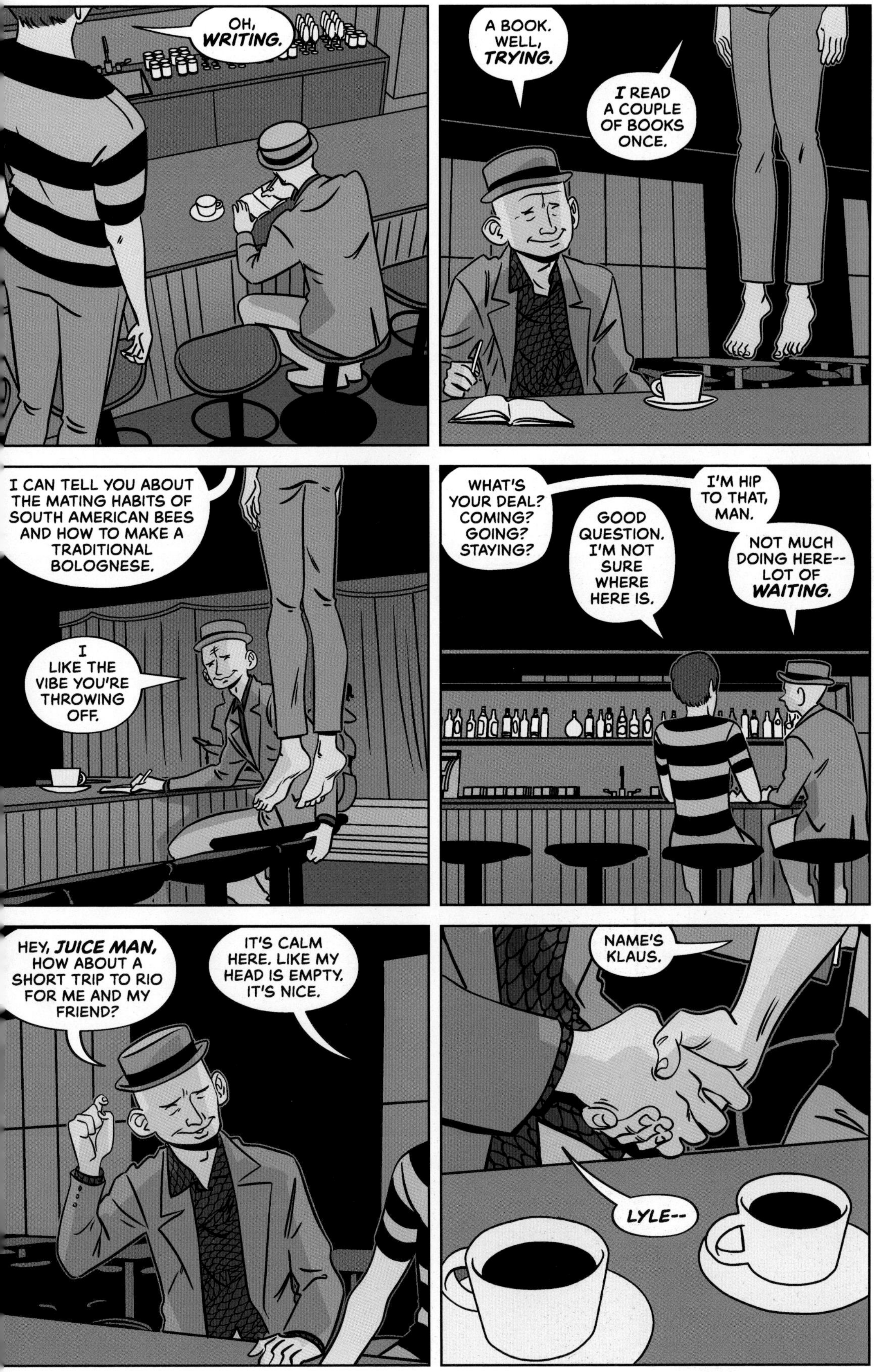
OH, WRITING.
A BOOK. WELL, TRYING.
I READ A COUPLE OF BOOKS ONCE.
I CAN TELL YOU ABOUT THE MATING HABITS OF SOUTH AMERICAN BEES AND HOW TO MAKE A TRADITIONAL BOLOGNESE.
I LIKE THE VIBE YOU'RE THROWING OFF.
WHAT'S YOUR DEAL? COMING? GOING? STAYING?
GOOD QUESTION. I'M NOT SURE WHERE HERE IS.
I'M HIP TO THAT, MAN.
NOT MUCH DOING HERE-- LOT OF WAITING.
HEY, JUICE MAN, HOW ABOUT A SHORT TRIP TO RIO FOR ME AND MY FRIEND?
IT'S CALM HERE. LIKE MY HEAD IS EMPTY. IT'S NICE.
NAME'S KLAUS.
LYLE--

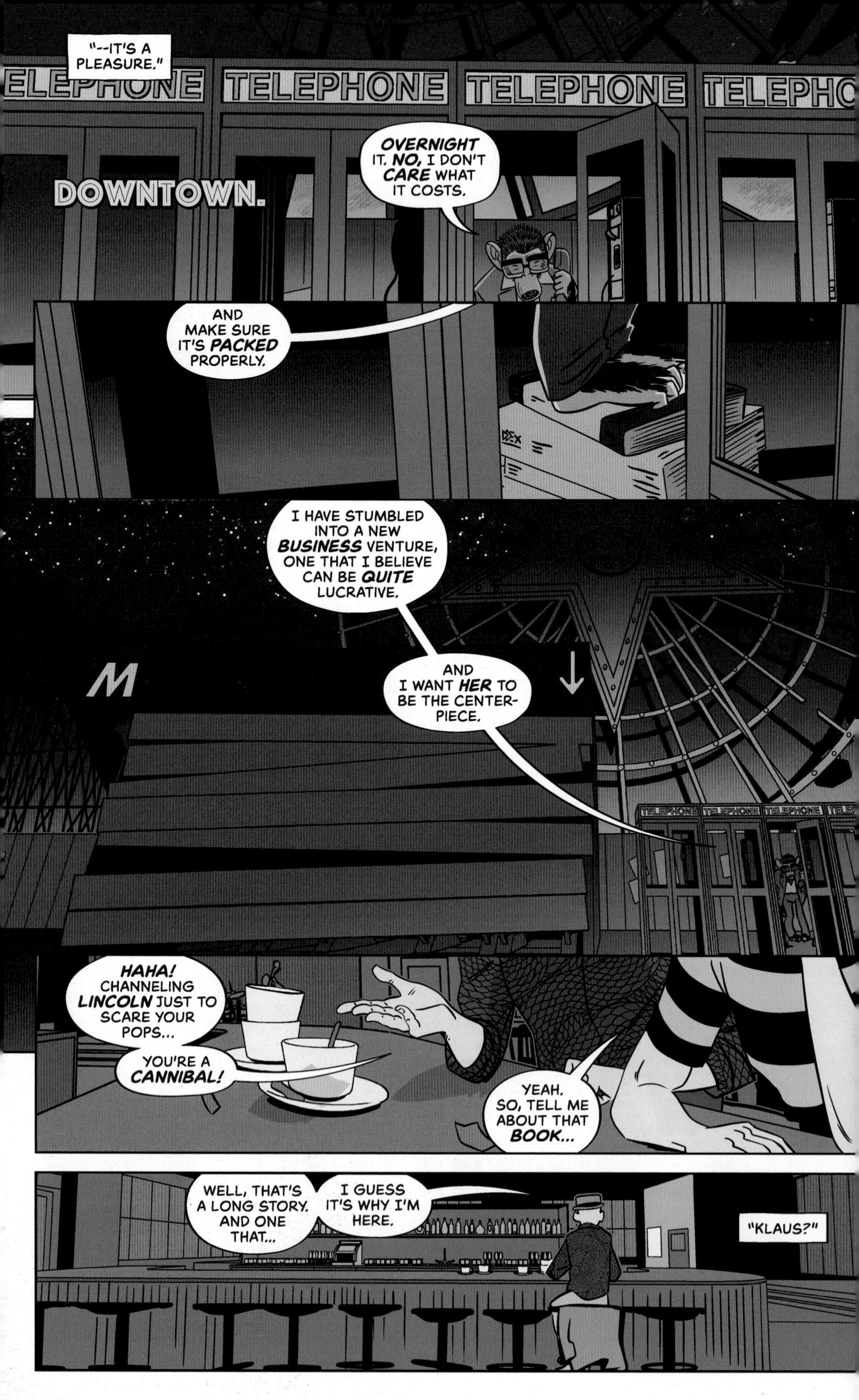
"--IT'S A PLEASURE."
TELEPHONE
TELEPHONE
DOWNTOWN.
OVERNIGHT IT. NO, I DON'T CARE WHAT IT COSTS.
AND MAKE SURE IT'S PACKED PROPERLY.
I HAVE STUMBLED INTO A NEW BUSINESS VENTURE, ONE THAT I BELIEVE CAN BE QUITE LUCRATIVE.
AND I WANT HER TO BE THE CENTER-PIECE.
HAHA! CHANNELING LINCOLN JUST TO SCARE YOUR POPS...
YOU'RE A CANNIBAL!
YEAH. SO, TELL ME ABOUT THAT BOOK...
WELL, THAT'S A LONG STORY. AND ONE THAT...
I GUESS IT'S WHY I'M HERE.
"KLAUS?"

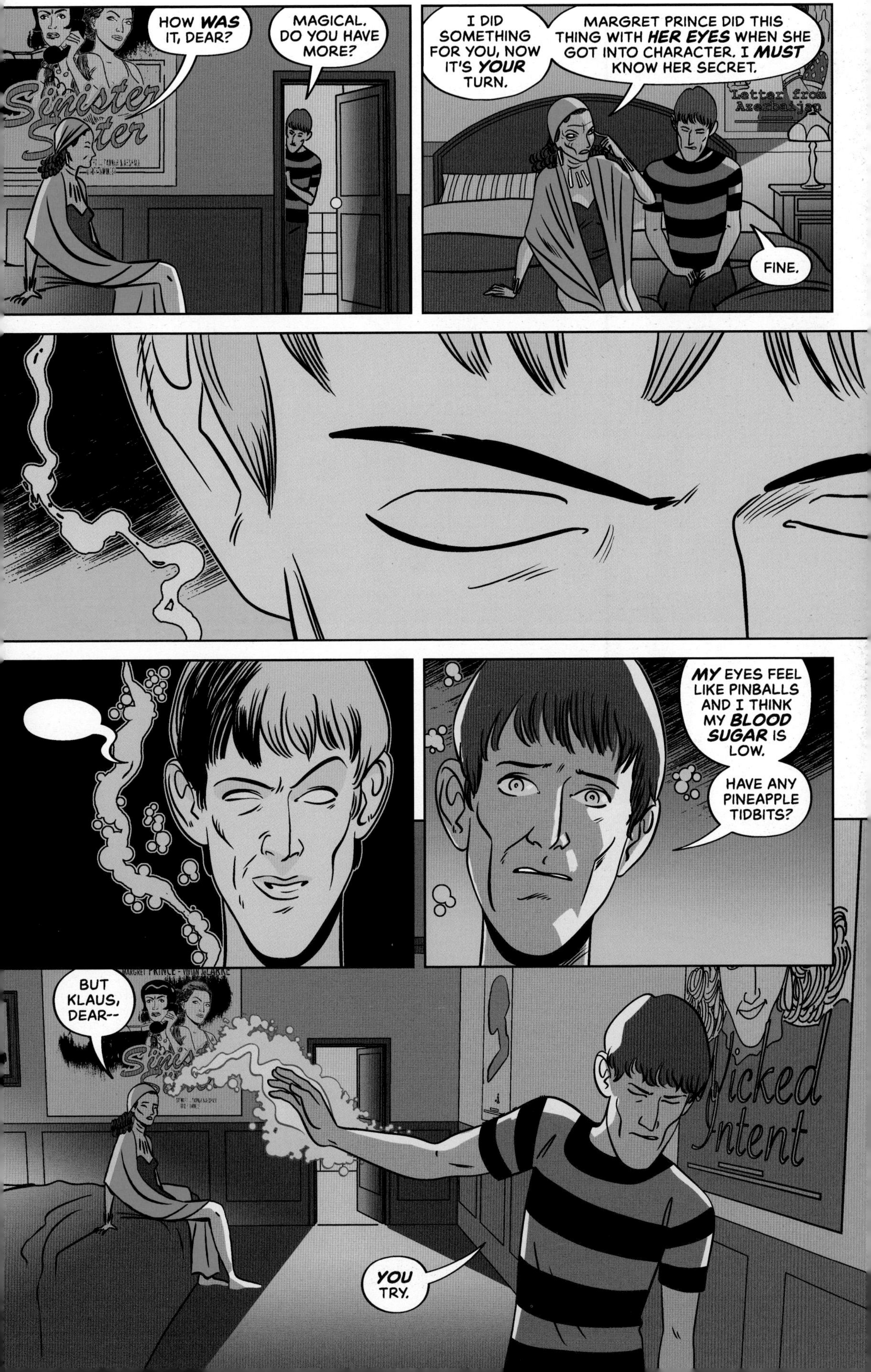
Sinister Sister
HOW WAS IT, DEAR?
MAGICAL. DO YOU HAVE MORE?
I DID SOMETHING FOR YOU, NOW IT'S YOUR TURN.
MARGRET PRINCE DID THIS THING WITH HER EYES WHEN SHE GOT INTO CHARACTER. I MUST KNOW HER SECRET.
Letter from Azerbaijan
FINE.
MY EYES FEEL LIKE PINBALLS AND I THINK MY BLOOD SUGAR IS LOW.
HAVE ANY PINEAPPLE TIDBITS?
BUT KLAUS, DEAR--
Wicked Intent
YOU TRY.

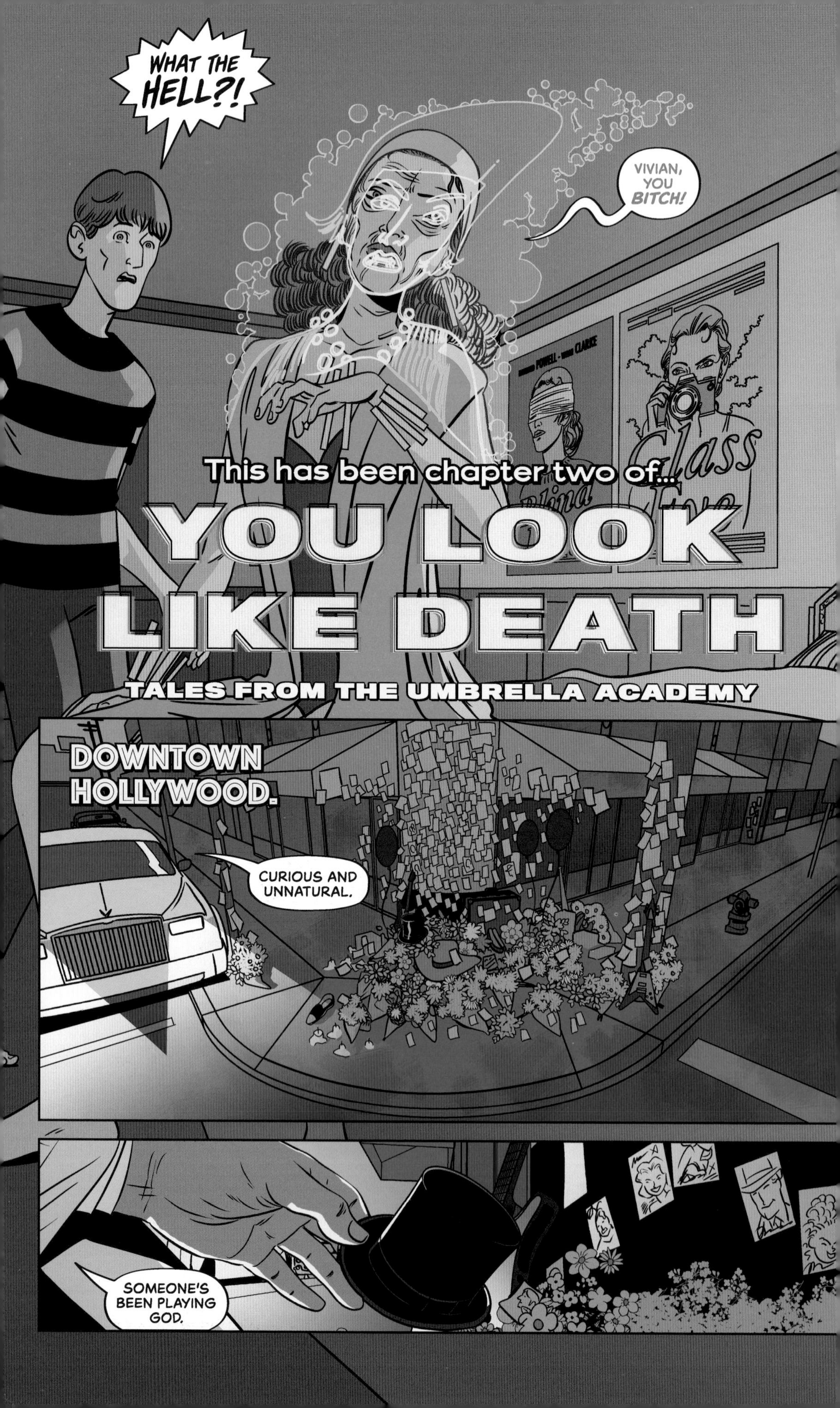
WHAT THE HELL?!
VIVIAN, YOU BITCH!
This has been chapter two of...
YOU LOOK LIKE DEATH
TALES FROM THE UMBRELLA ACADEMY
DOWNTOWN HOLLYWOOD.
CURIOUS AND UNNATURAL.
SOMEONE'S BEEN PLAYING GOD.

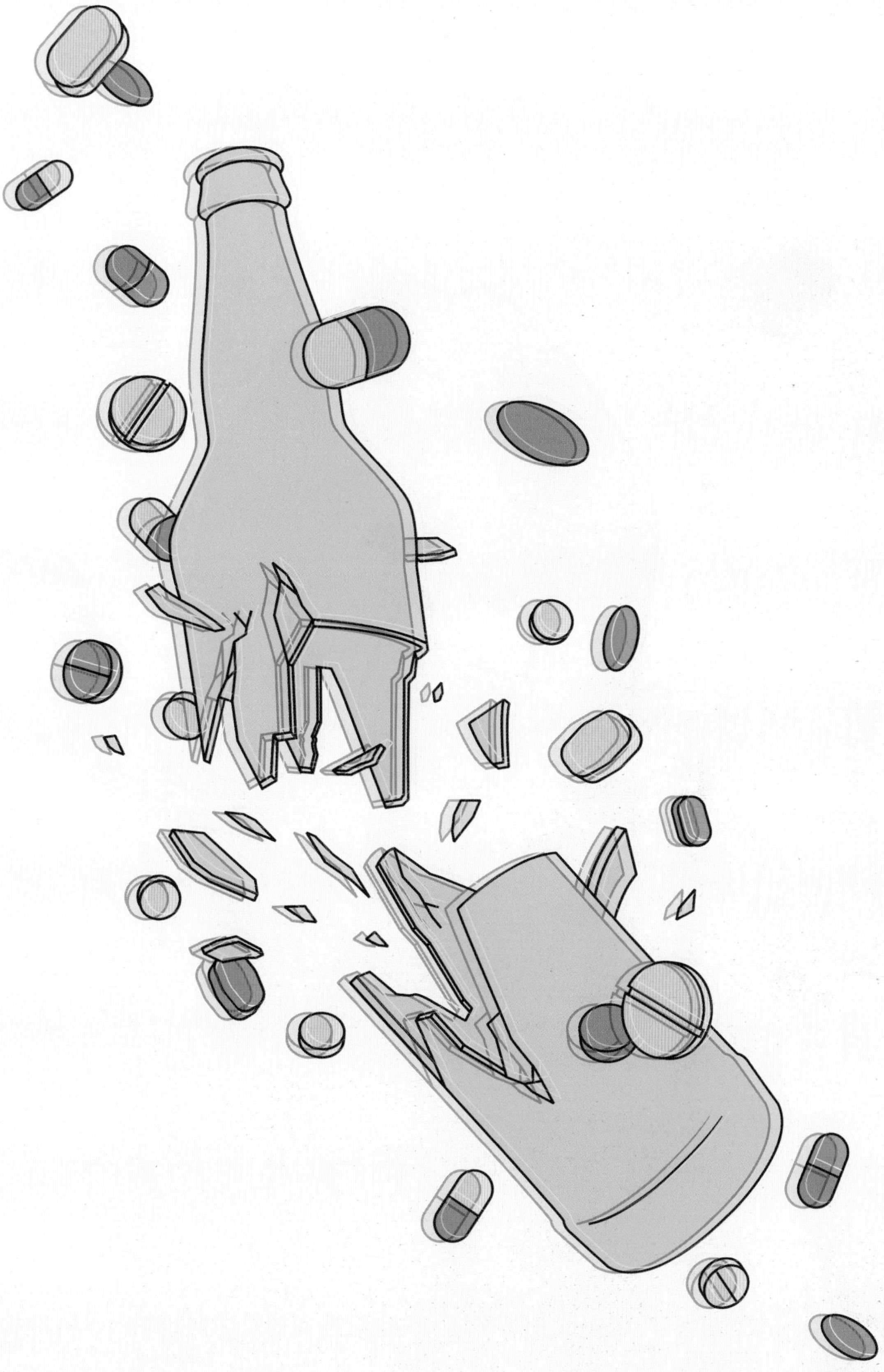

CHAPTER THREE

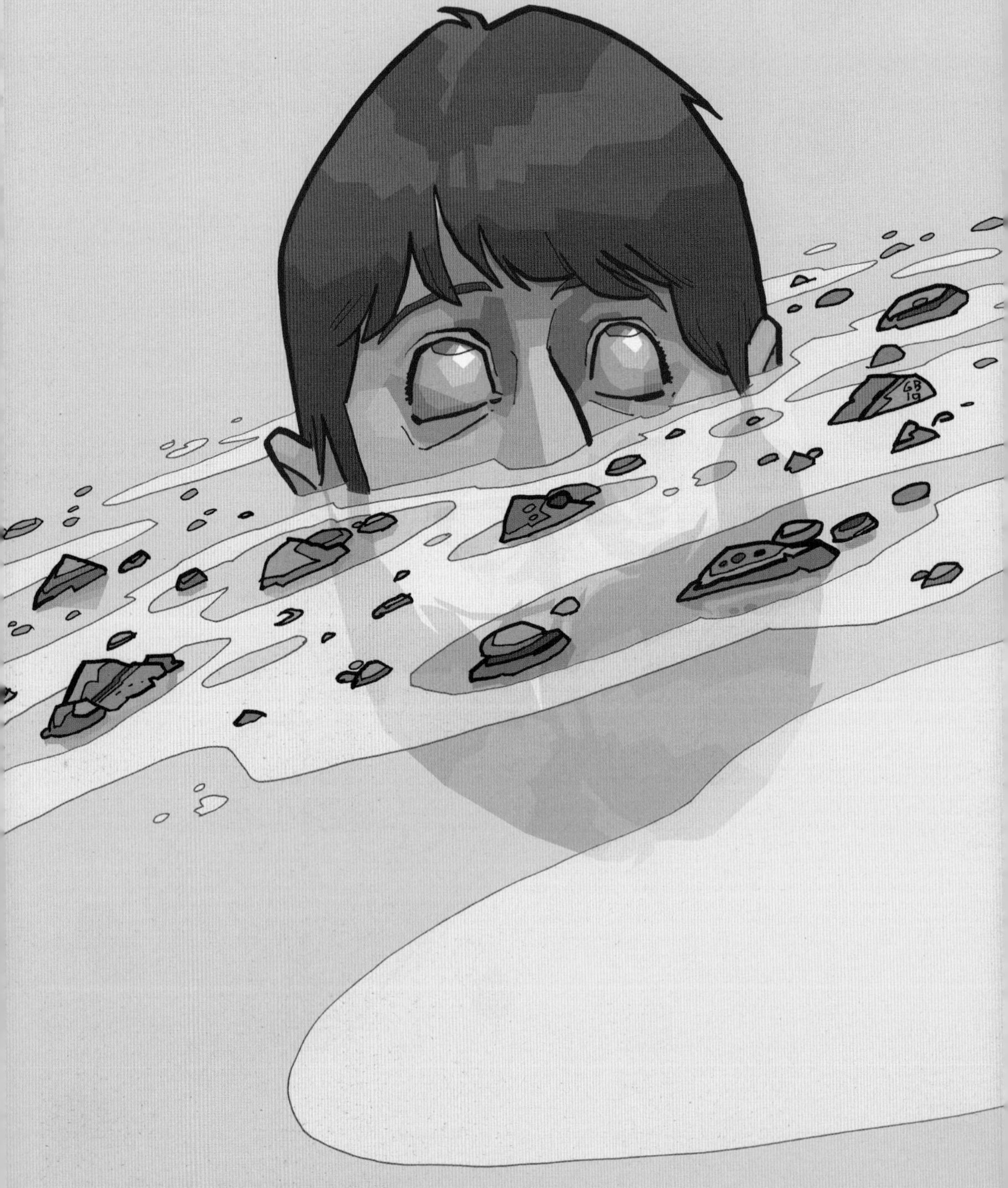

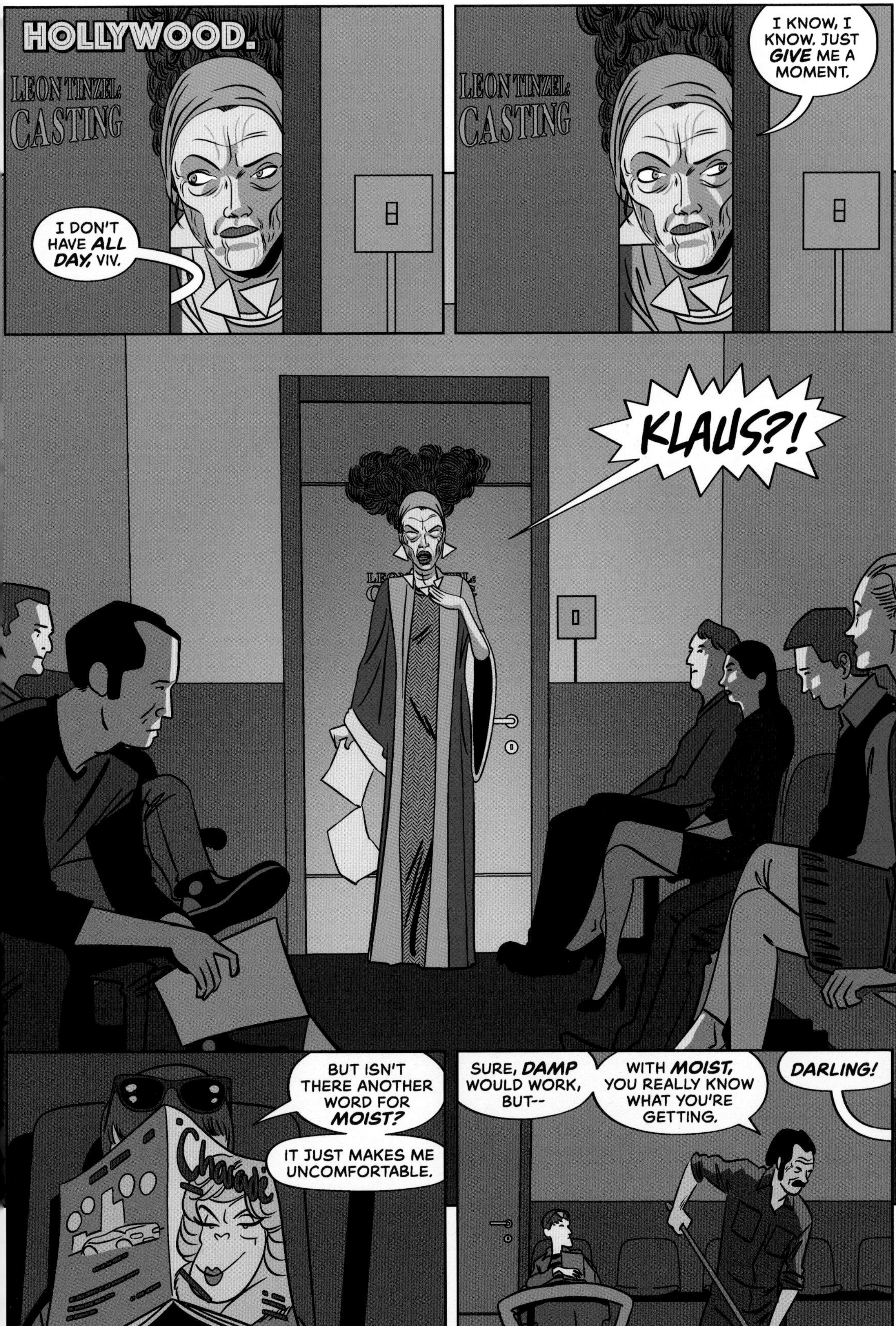
HOLLYWOOD.
LEON TINZEL: CASTING
I DON'T HAVE ALL DAY, VIV.
LEON TINZEL: CASTING
I KNOW, I KNOW. JUST GIVE ME A MOMENT.
KLAUS?!
BUT ISN'T THERE ANOTHER WORD FOR MOIST?
IT JUST MAKES ME UNCOMFORTABLE.
Charade
SURE, DAMP WOULD WORK, BUT--
WITH MOIST, YOU REALLY KNOW WHAT YOU'RE GETTING.
DARLING!

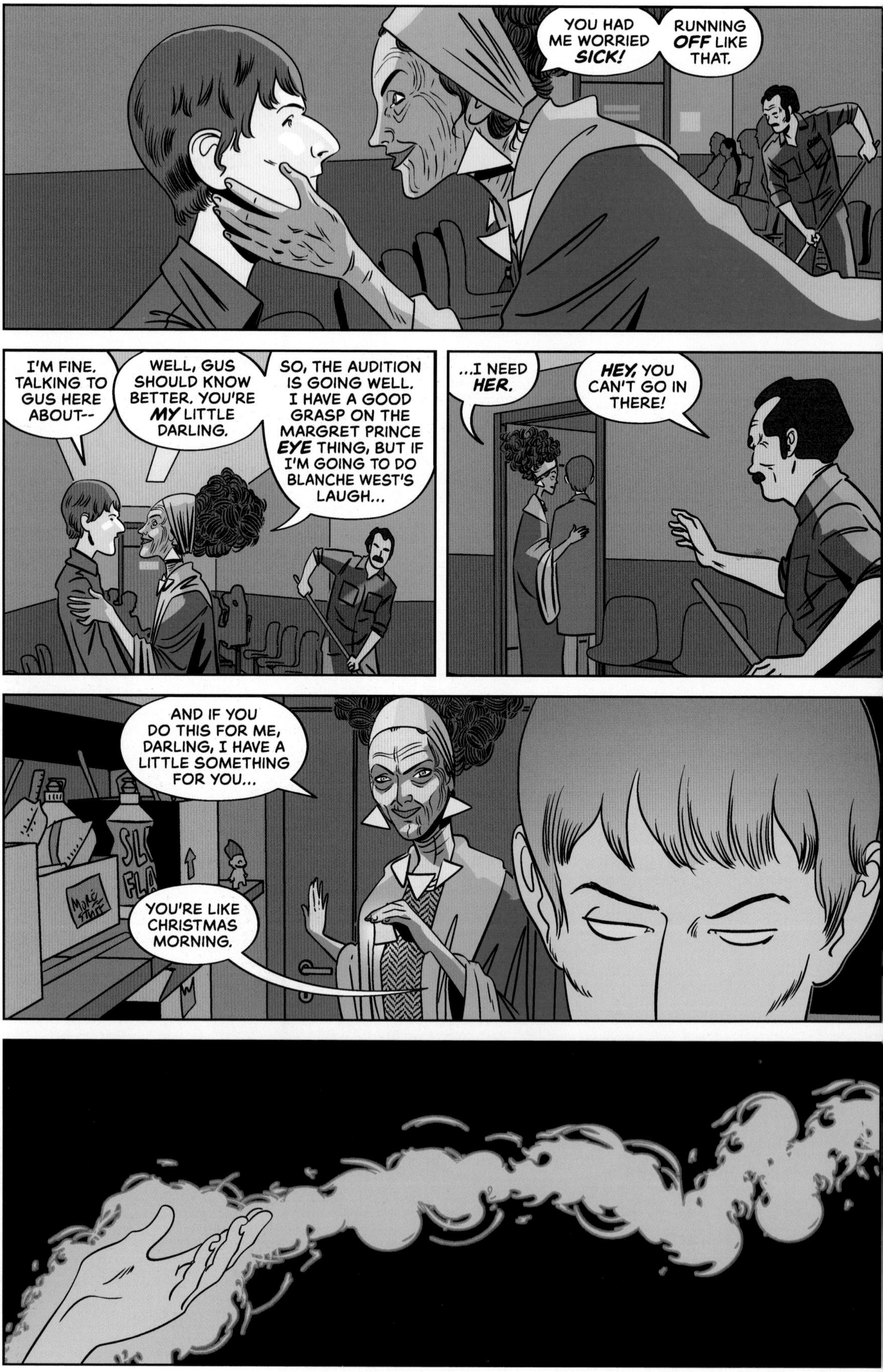

YOU HAD ME WORRIED SICK!
RUNNING OFF LIKE THAT.
I'M FINE, TALKING TO GUS HERE ABOUT--
WELL, GUS SHOULD KNOW BETTER. YOU'RE MY LITTLE DARLING.
SO, THE AUDITION IS GOING WELL. I HAVE A GOOD GRASP ON THE MARGRET PRINCE EYE THING, BUT IF I'M GOING TO DO BLANCHE WEST'S LAUGH...
...I NEED HER.
HEY, YOU CAN'T GO IN THERE!
AND IF YOU DO THIS FOR ME, DARLING, I HAVE A LITTLE SOMETHING FOR YOU...
YOU'RE LIKE CHRISTMAS MORNING.
MORE STUFF

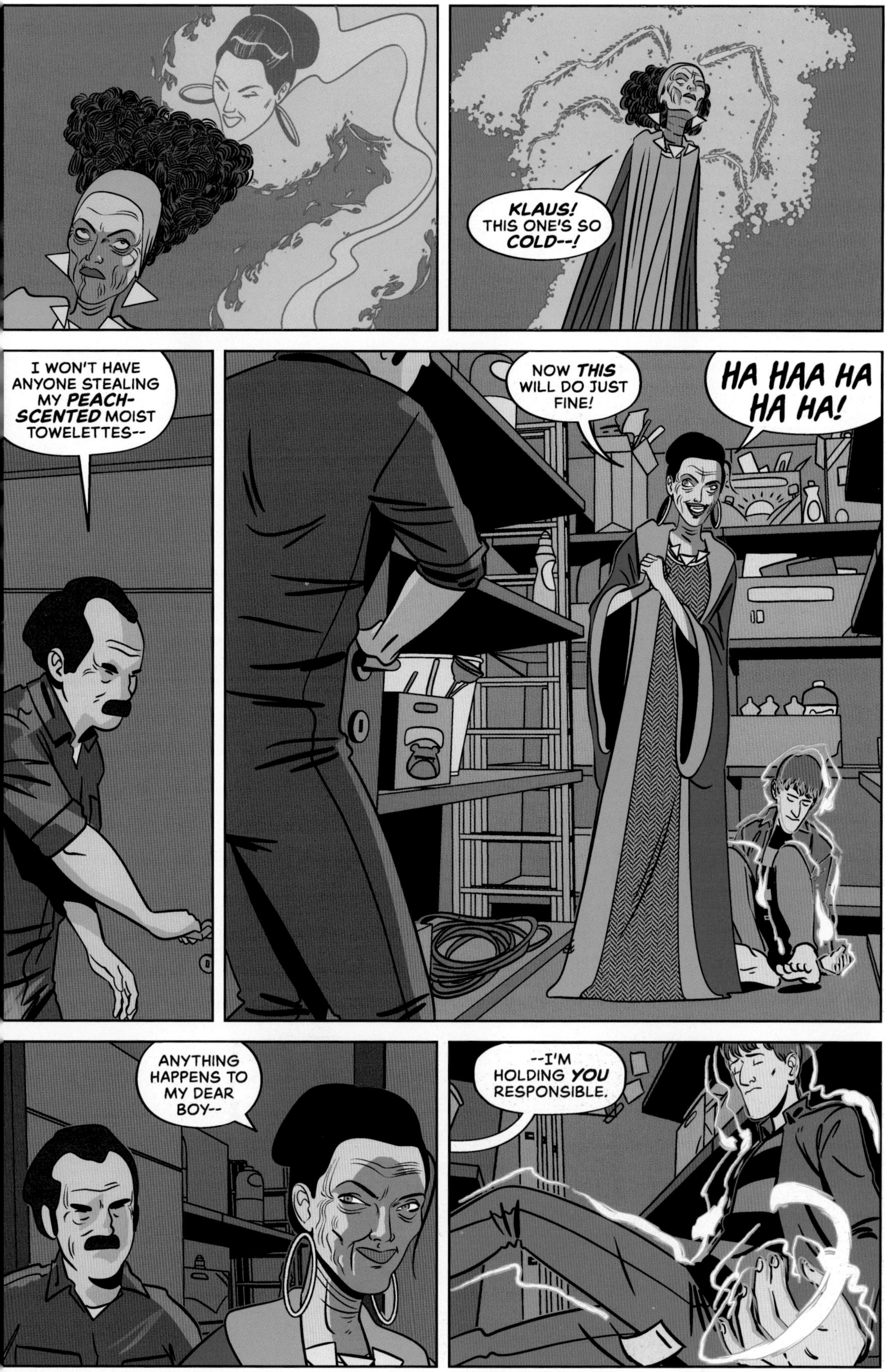

KLAUS! THIS ONE'S SO COLD--!
I WON'T HAVE ANYONE STEALING MY PEACH-SCENTED MOIST TOWELETTES--
NOW THIS WILL DO JUST FINE!
HA HAA HA HA HA!
ANYTHING HAPPENS TO MY DEAR BOY--
--I'M HOLDING YOU RESPONSIBLE.

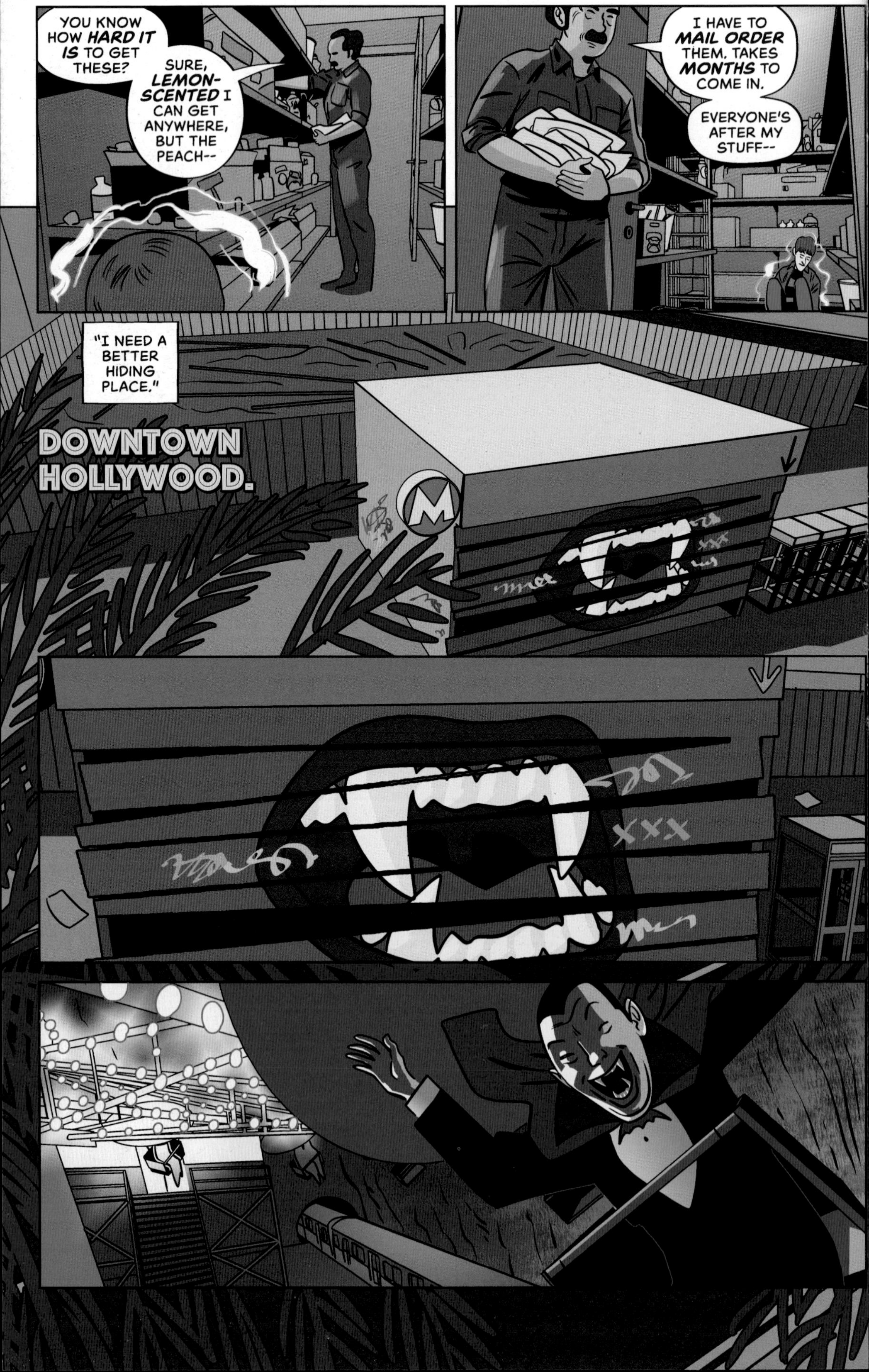
YOU KNOW HOW HARD IT IS TO GET THESE?
SURE, LEMON-SCENTED I CAN GET ANYWHERE, BUT THE PEACH--
I HAVE TO MAIL ORDER THEM. TAKES MONTHS TO COME IN.
EVERYONE'S AFTER MY STUFF--
"I NEED A BETTER HIDING PLACE."
DOWNTOWN HOLLYWOOD.
XXX

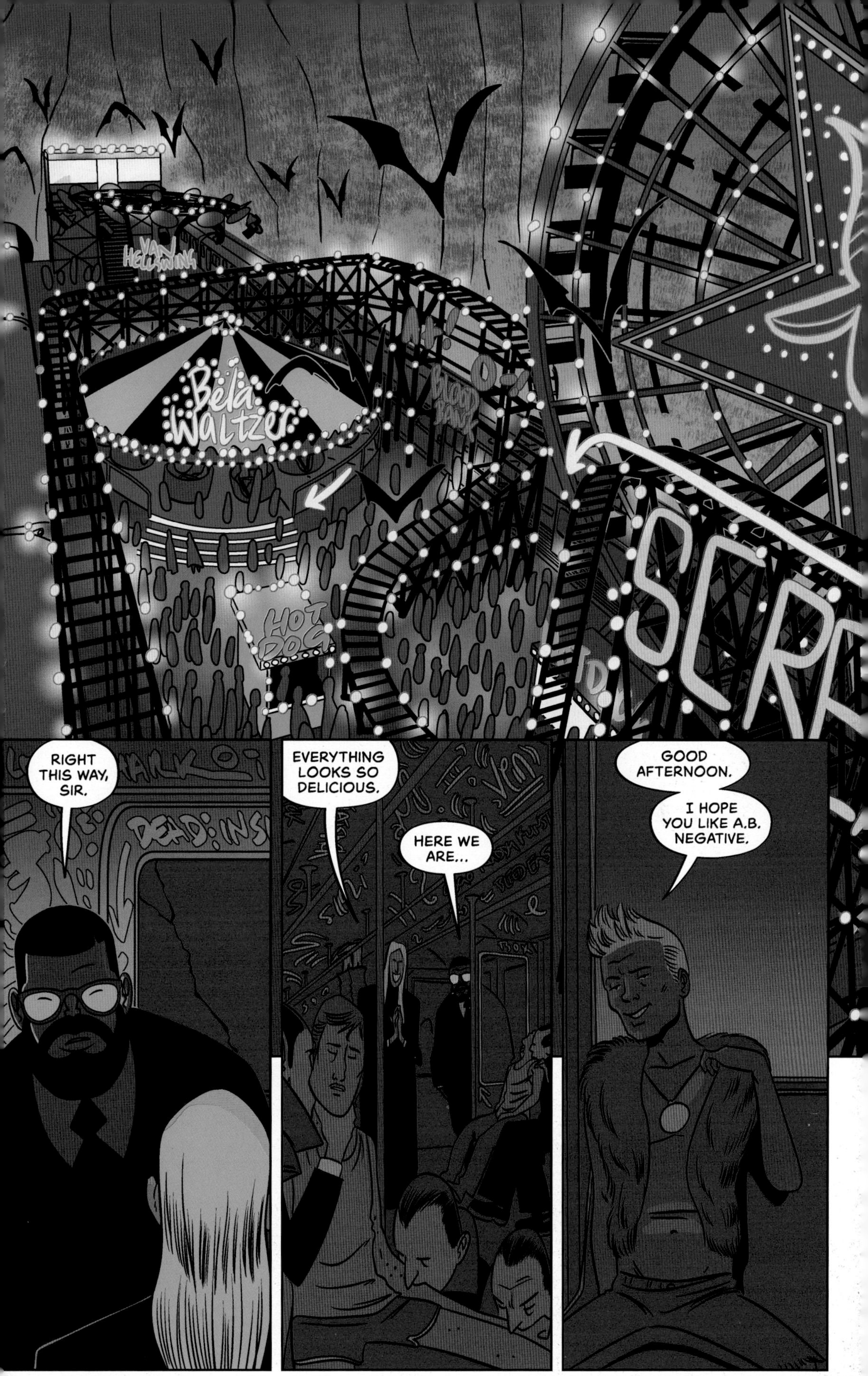

VAN HELLSWING
Bela Waltzer
BLOOD BANK
HOT DOG
SCR
RIGHT THIS WAY, SIR.
EVERYTHING LOOKS SO DELICIOUS.
HERE WE ARE...
GOOD AFTERNOON.
I HOPE YOU LIKE A.B. NEGATIVE.

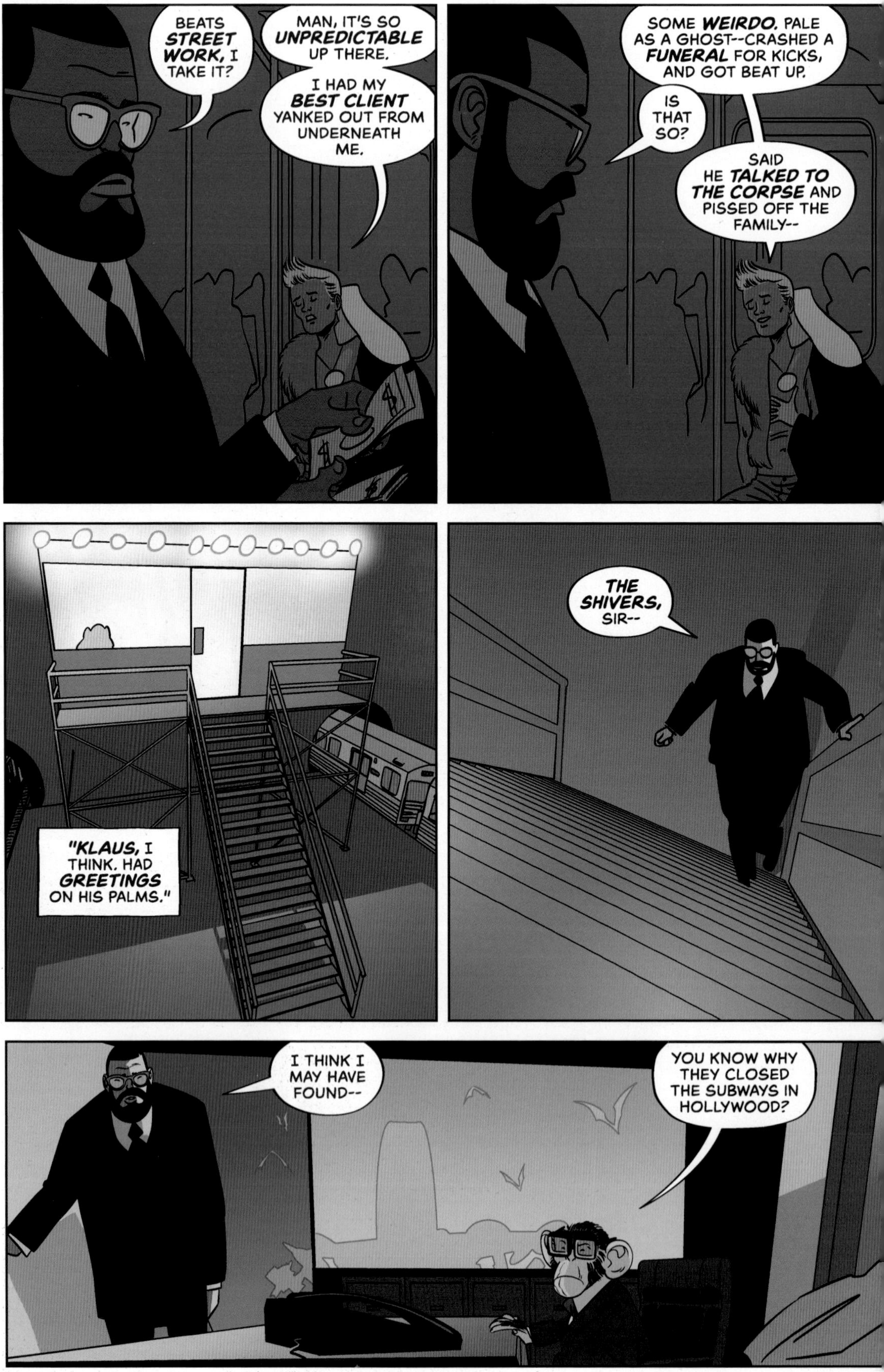
BEATS STREET WORK, I TAKE IT?
MAN, IT'S SO UNPREDICTABLE UP THERE.
I HAD MY BEST CLIENT YANKED OUT FROM UNDERNEATH ME.
SOME WEIRDO. PALE AS A GHOST--CRASHED A FUNERAL FOR KICKS, AND GOT BEAT UP.
IS THAT SO?
SAID HE TALKED TO THE CORPSE AND PISSED OFF THE FAMILY--
"KLAUS, I THINK. HAD GREETINGS ON HIS PALMS."
THE SHIVERS, SIR--
I THINK I MAY HAVE FOUND--
YOU KNOW WHY THEY CLOSED THE SUBWAYS IN HOLLYWOOD?

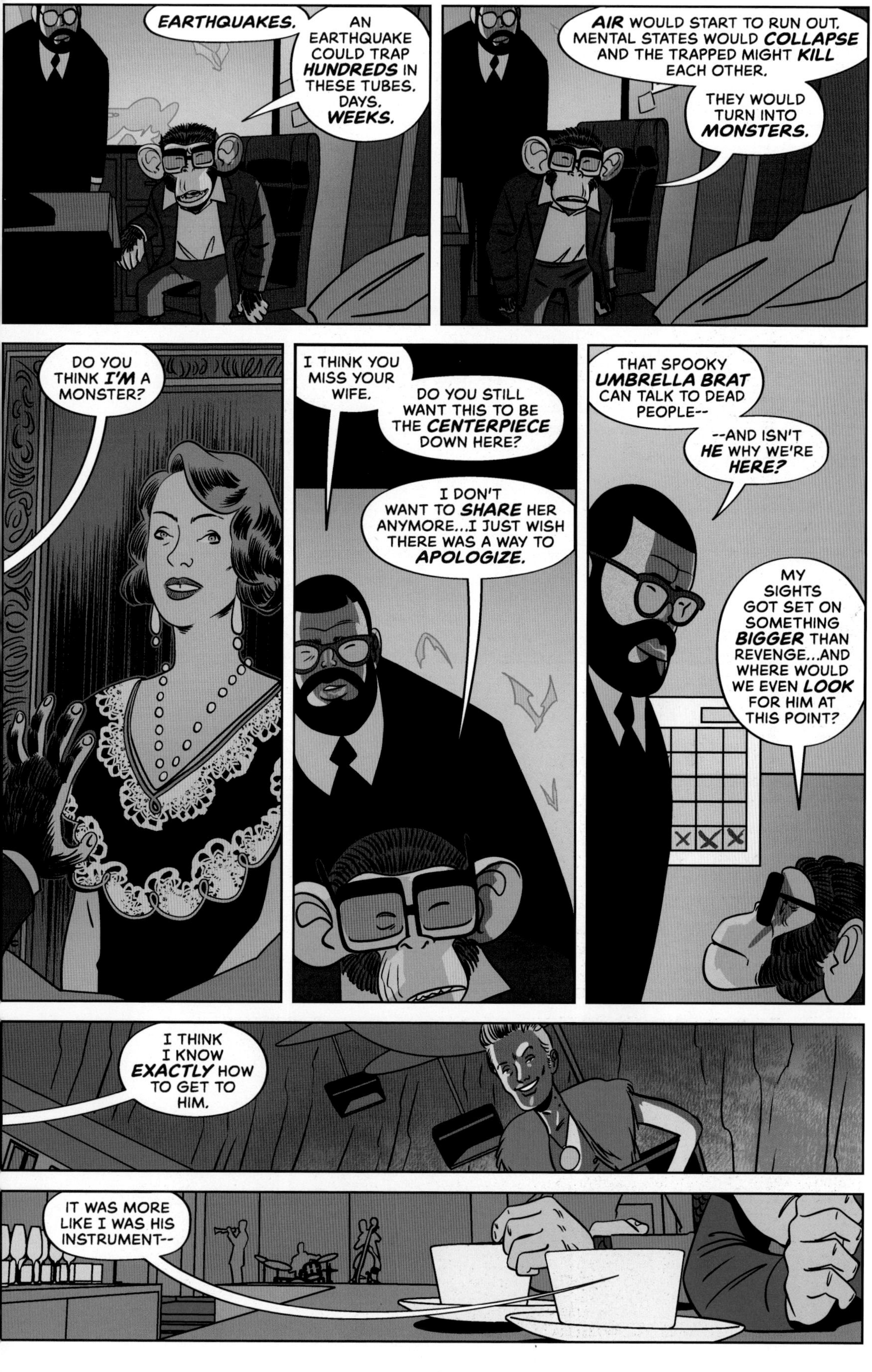
EARTHQUAKES.
AN EARTHQUAKE COULD TRAP HUNDREDS IN THESE TUBES. DAYS. WEEKS.
AIR WOULD START TO RUN OUT. MENTAL STATES WOULD COLLAPSE AND THE TRAPPED MIGHT KILL EACH OTHER.
THEY WOULD TURN INTO MONSTERS.
DO YOU THINK I'M A MONSTER?
I THINK YOU MISS YOUR WIFE.
DO YOU STILL WANT THIS TO BE THE CENTERPIECE DOWN HERE?
I DON'T WANT TO SHARE HER ANYMORE...I JUST WISH THERE WAS A WAY TO APOLOGIZE.
THAT SPOOKY UMBRELLA BRAT CAN TALK TO DEAD PEOPLE--
--AND ISN'T HE WHY WE'RE HERE?
MY SIGHTS GOT SET ON SOMETHING BIGGER THAN REVENGE...AND WHERE WOULD WE EVEN LOOK FOR HIM AT THIS POINT?
I THINK I KNOW EXACTLY HOW TO GET TO HIM.
IT WAS MORE LIKE I WAS HIS INSTRUMENT--

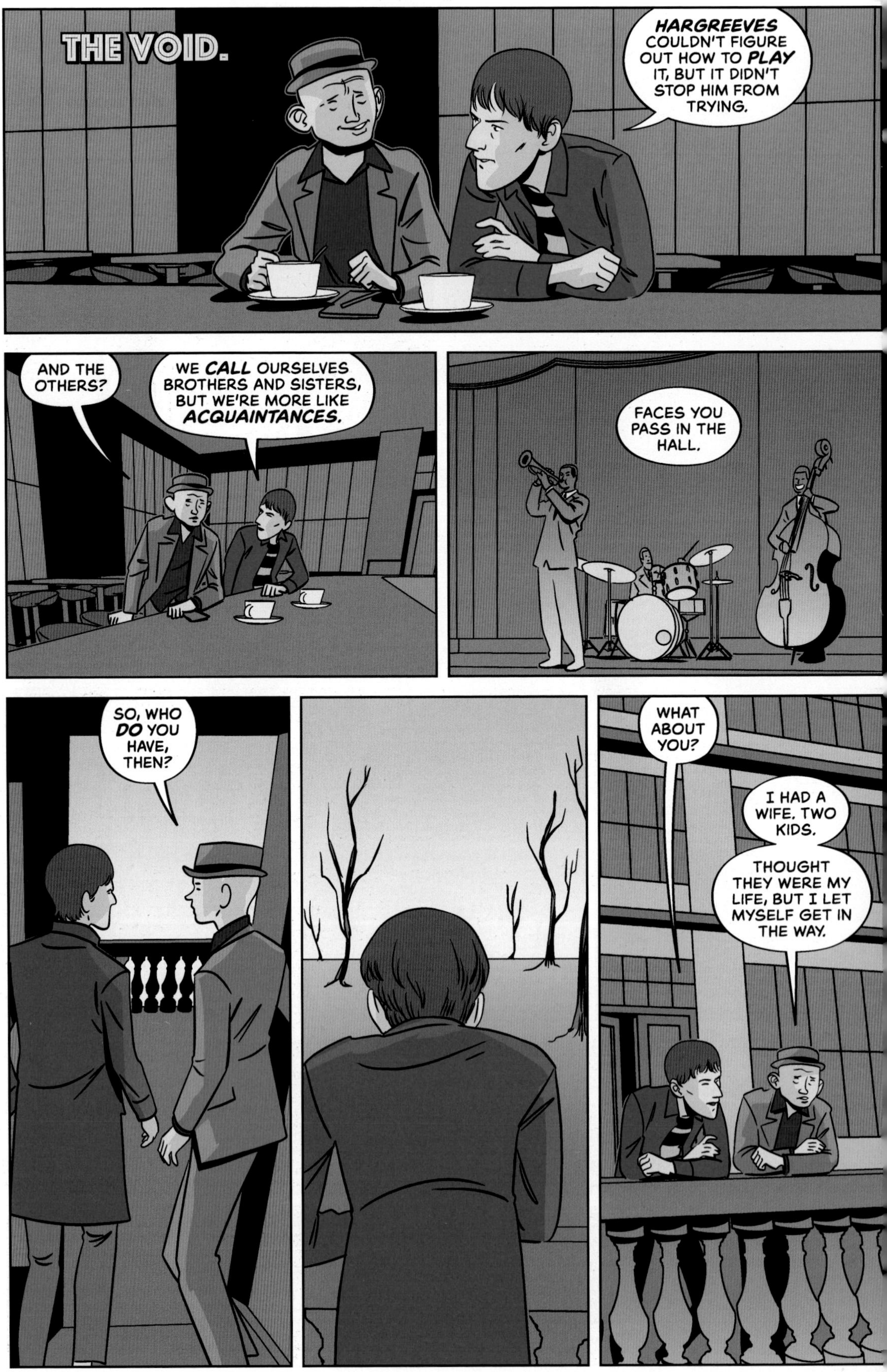
THE VOID.
HARGREEVES COULDN'T FIGURE OUT HOW TO PLAY IT, BUT IT DIDN'T STOP HIM FROM TRYING.
AND THE OTHERS?
WE CALL OURSELVES BROTHERS AND SISTERS, BUT WE'RE MORE LIKE ACQUAINTANCES.
FACES YOU PASS IN THE HALL.
SO, WHO DO YOU HAVE, THEN?
WHAT ABOUT YOU?
I HAD A WIFE. TWO KIDS.
THOUGHT THEY WERE MY LIFE, BUT I LET MYSELF GET IN THE WAY.

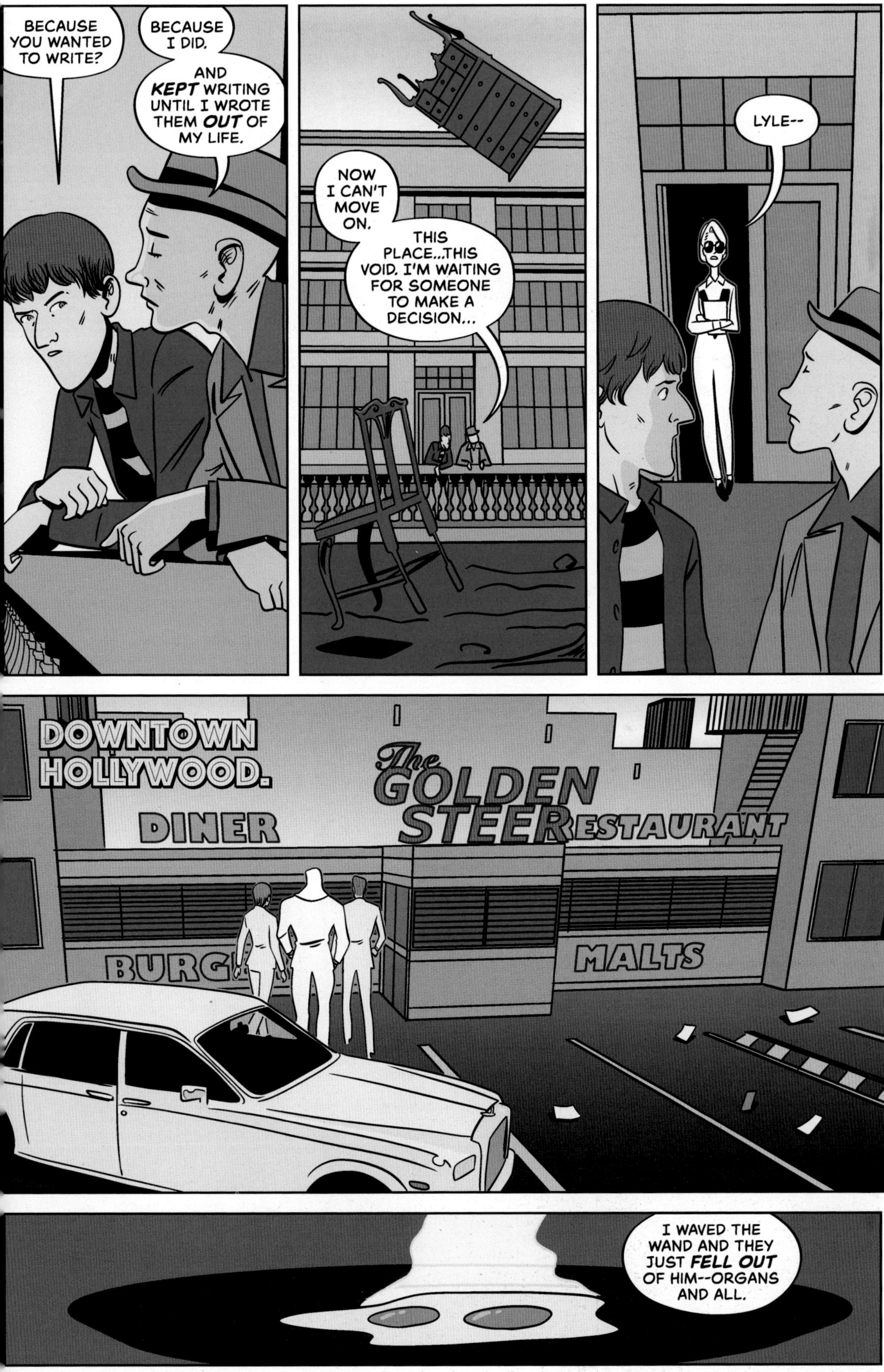

BECAUSE YOU WANTED TO WRITE?
BECAUSE I DID.
AND **KEPT** WRITING UNTIL I WROTE THEM **OUT** OF MY LIFE.
NOW I CAN'T MOVE ON.
THIS PLACE...THIS VOID. I'M WAITING FOR SOMEONE TO MAKE A DECISION...
LYLE--
DOWNTOWN HOLLYWOOD.
The GOLDEN STEER RESTAURANT
DINER
BURG
MALTS
I WAVED THE WAND AND THEY JUST **FELL OUT** OF HIM--ORGANS AND ALL.

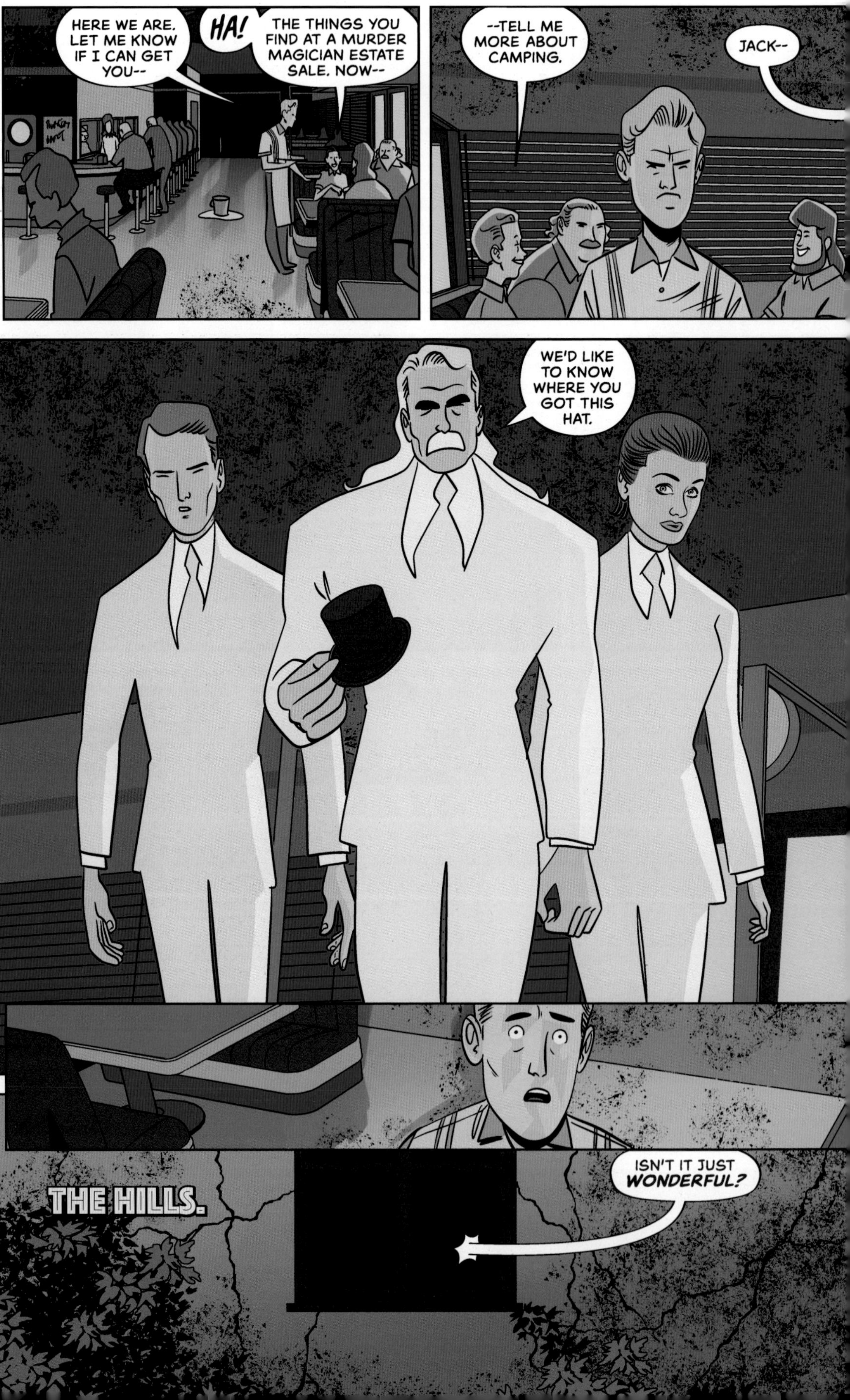
HERE WE ARE. LET ME KNOW IF I CAN GET YOU--
HA!
THE THINGS YOU FIND AT A MURDER MAGICIAN ESTATE SALE. NOW--
--TELL ME MORE ABOUT CAMPING.
JACK--
WE'D LIKE TO KNOW WHERE YOU GOT THIS HAT.
THE HILLS.
ISN'T IT JUST *WONDERFUL?*

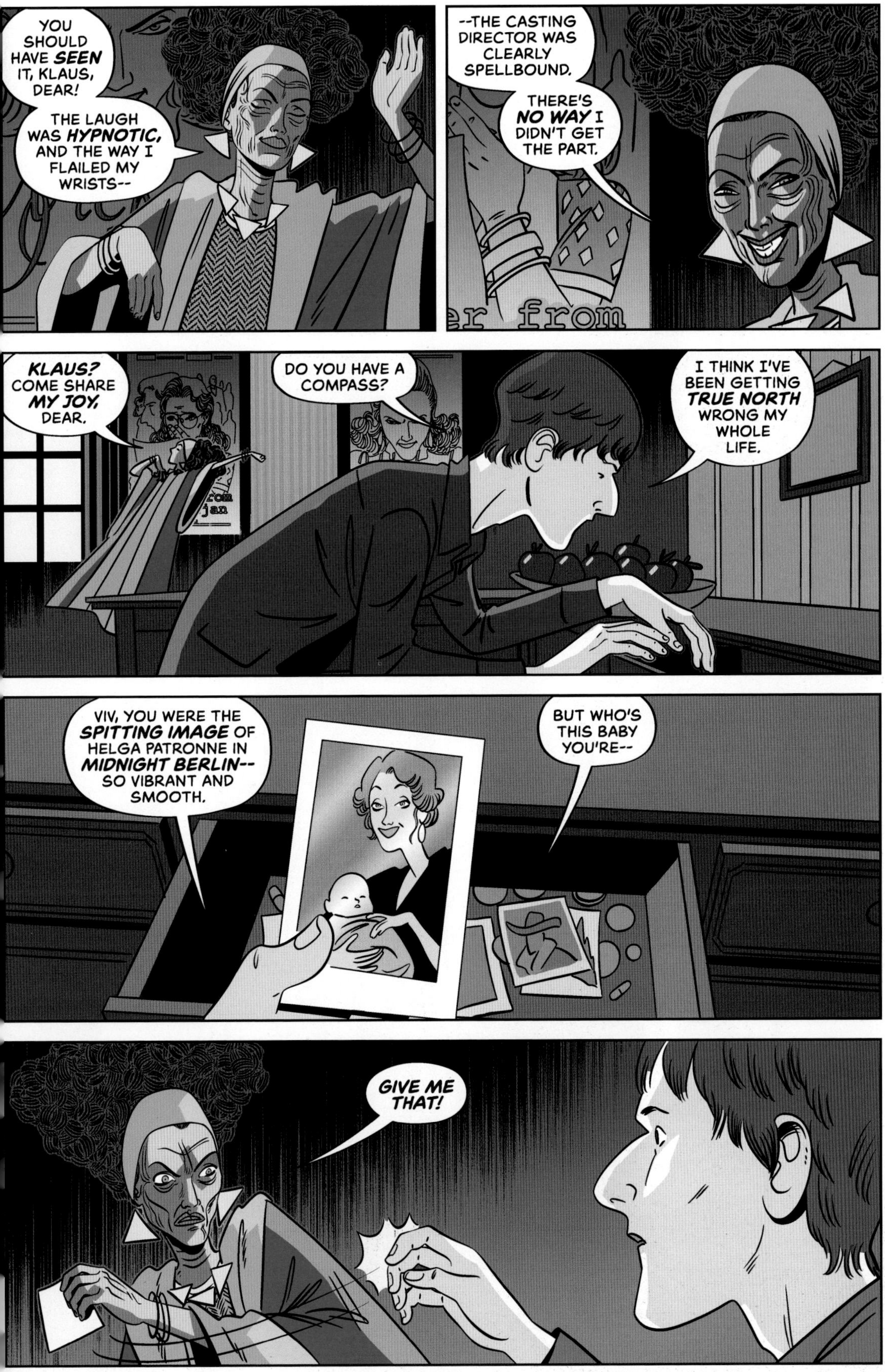
YOU SHOULD HAVE SEEN IT, KLAUS, DEAR!
THE LAUGH WAS HYPNOTIC, AND THE WAY I FLAILED MY WRISTS--
--THE CASTING DIRECTOR WAS CLEARLY SPELLBOUND.
THERE'S NO WAY I DIDN'T GET THE PART.
er from
KLAUS? COME SHARE MY JOY, DEAR.
DO YOU HAVE A COMPASS?
I THINK I'VE BEEN GETTING TRUE NORTH WRONG MY WHOLE LIFE.
VIV, YOU WERE THE SPITTING IMAGE OF HELGA PATRONNE IN MIDNIGHT BERLIN-- SO VIBRANT AND SMOOTH.
BUT WHO'S THIS BABY YOU'RE--
GIVE ME THAT!

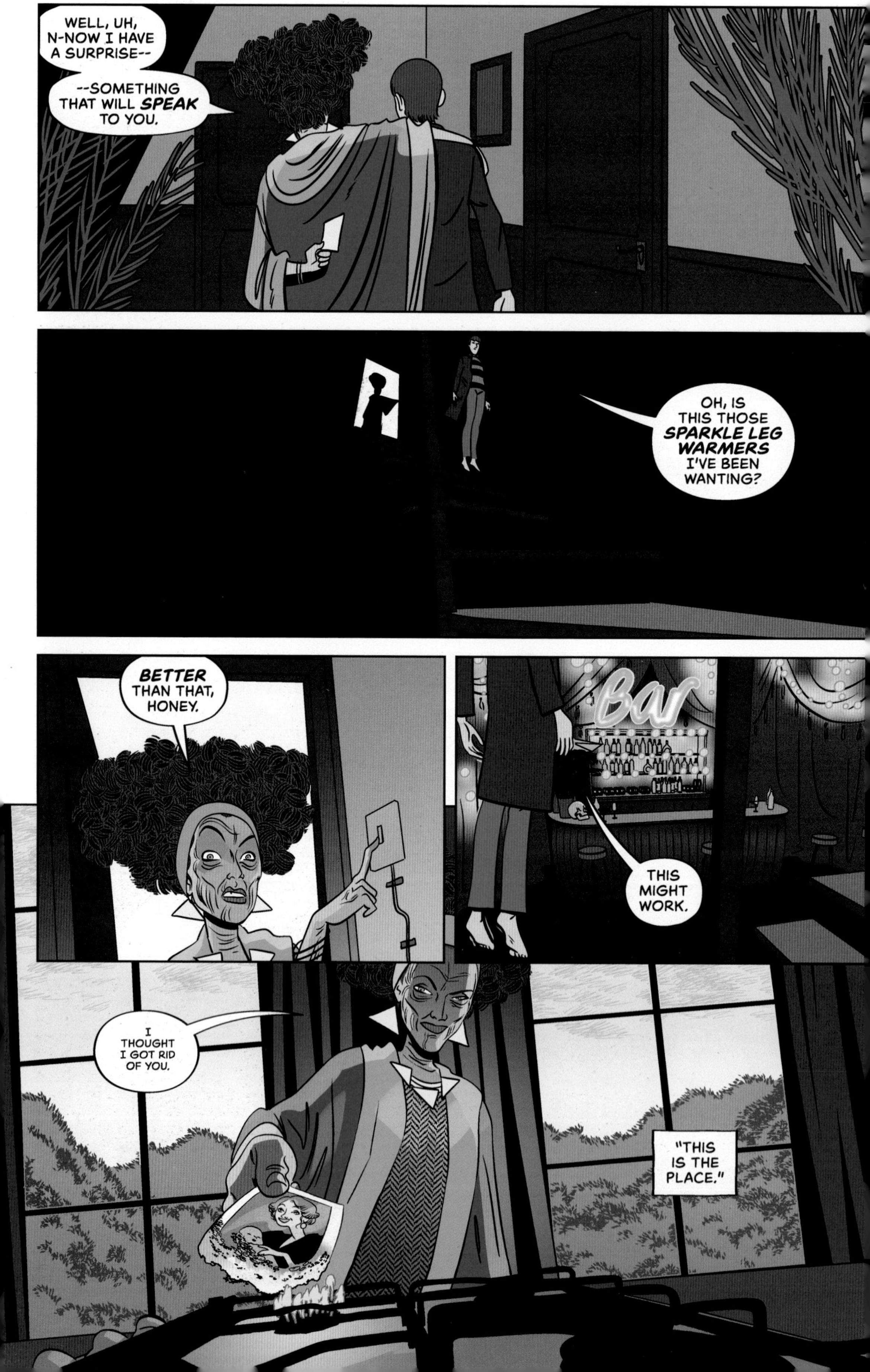
WELL, UH, N-NOW I HAVE A SURPRISE--
--SOMETHING THAT WILL SPEAK TO YOU.
OH, IS THIS THOSE SPARKLE LEG WARMERS I'VE BEEN WANTING?
BETTER THAN THAT, HONEY.
Bar
THIS MIGHT WORK.
I THOUGHT I GOT RID OF YOU.
"THIS IS THE PLACE."

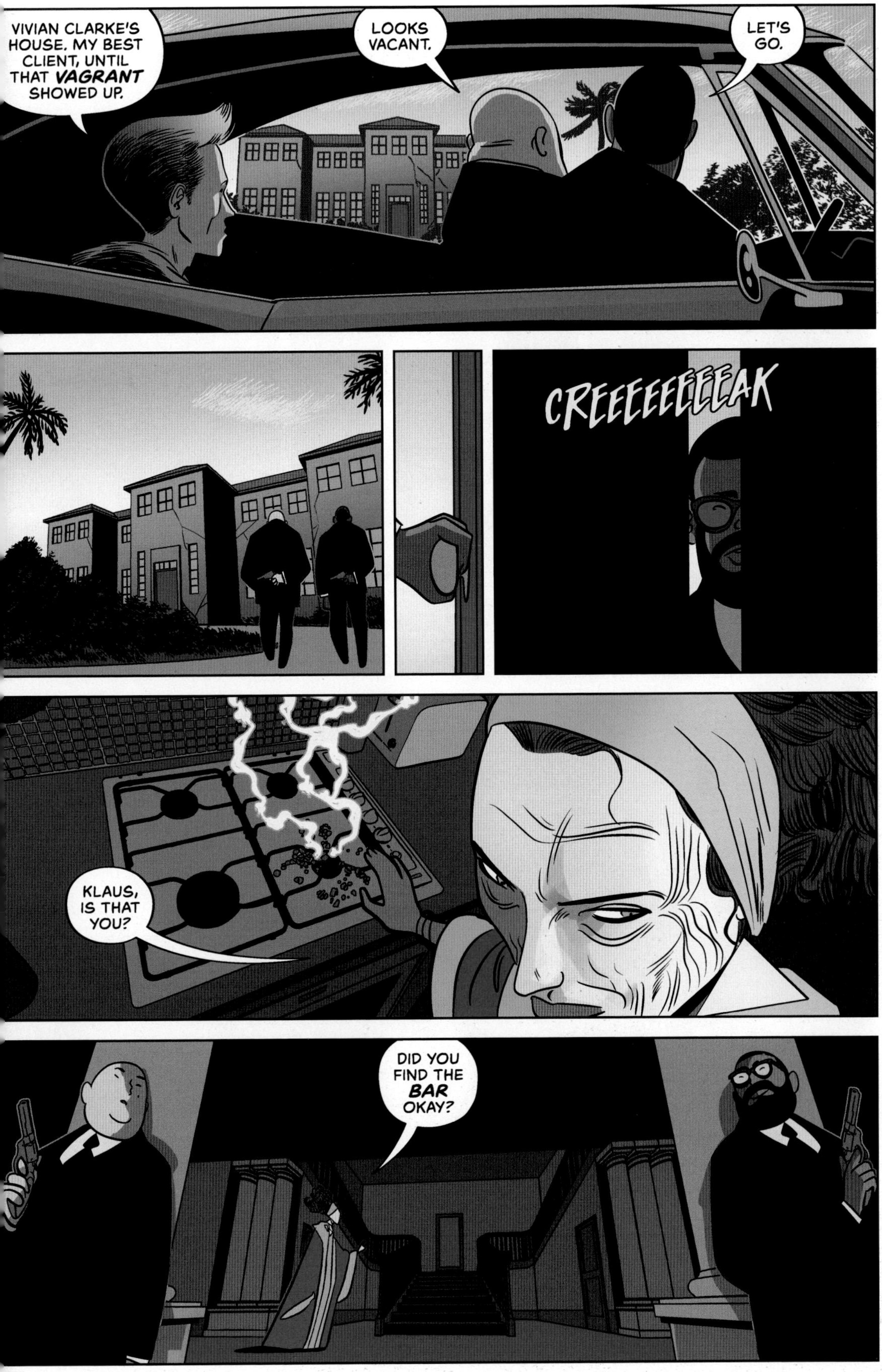
VIVIAN CLARKE'S HOUSE. MY BEST CLIENT, UNTIL THAT ***VAGRANT*** SHOWED UP.
LOOKS VACANT.
LET'S GO.
CREEEEEEEEAK
KLAUS, IS THAT YOU?
DID YOU FIND THE ***BAR*** OKAY?

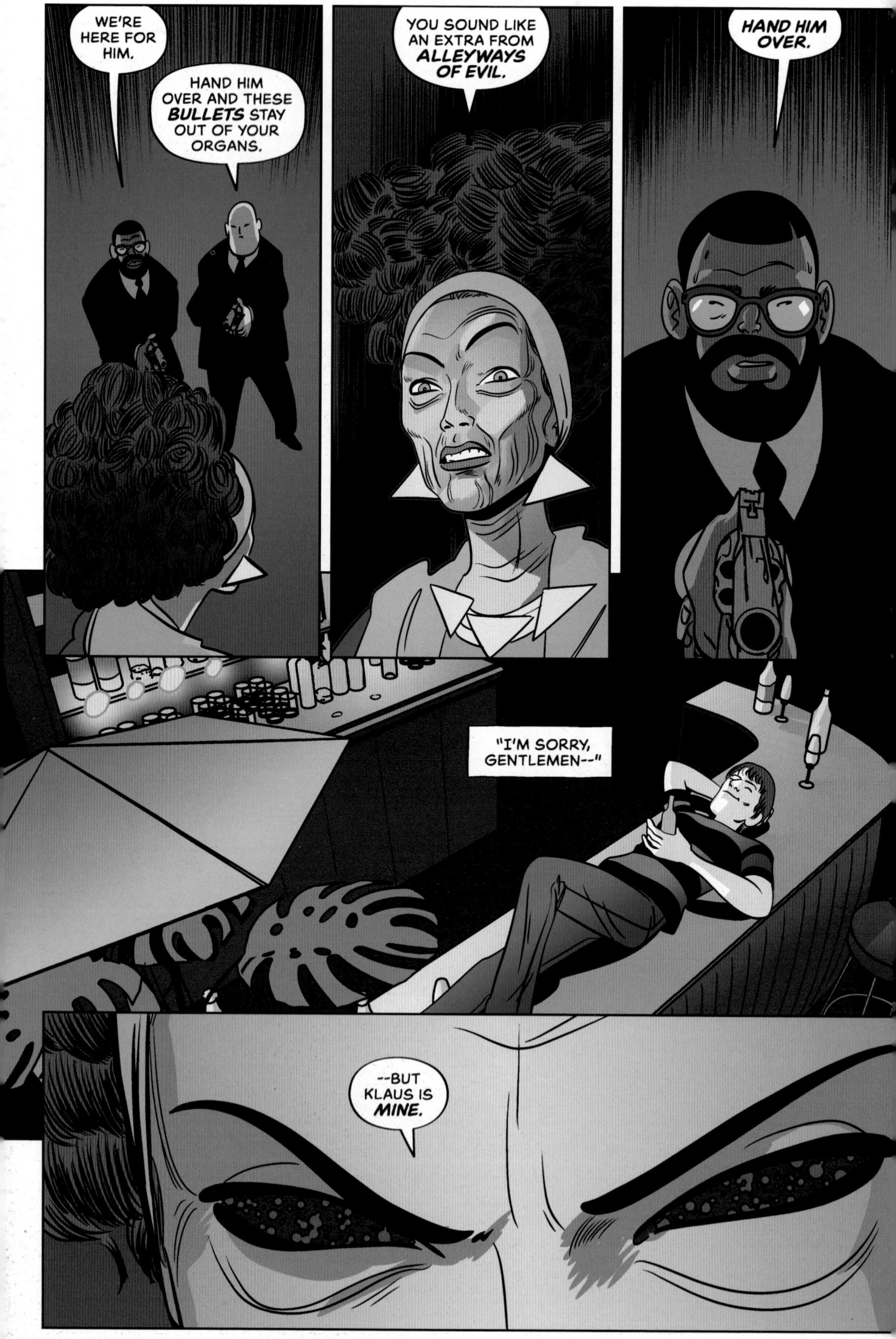
WE'RE HERE FOR HIM.
HAND HIM OVER AND THESE **BULLETS** STAY OUT OF YOUR ORGANS.
YOU SOUND LIKE AN EXTRA FROM ***ALLEYWAYS OF EVIL.***
HAND HIM OVER.
"I'M SORRY, GENTLEMEN--"
--BUT KLAUS IS ***MINE.***

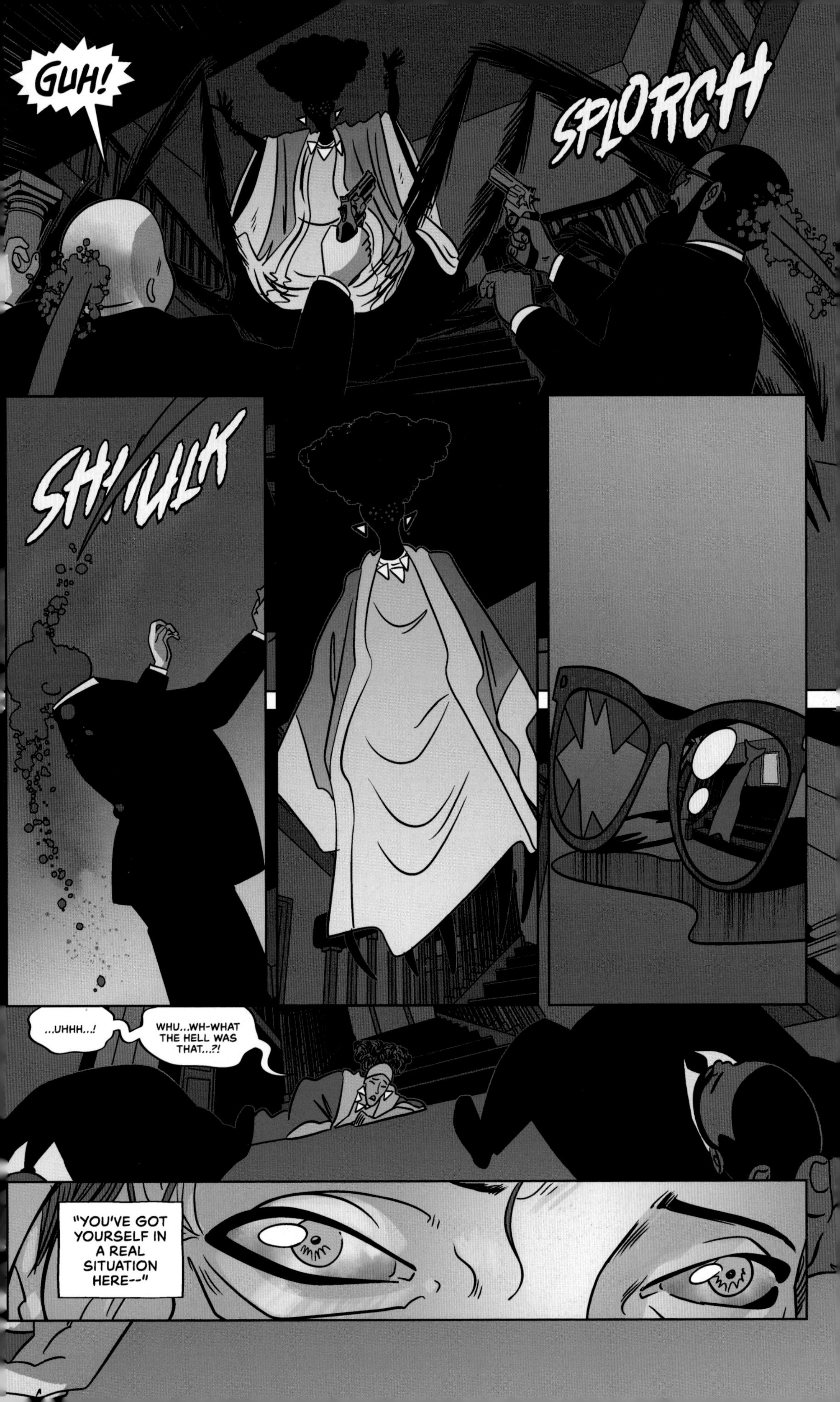
GUH!
SPLORCH
SHLULK
...UHHH...!
WHU...WH-WHAT THE HELL WAS THAT...?!
"YOU'VE GOT YOURSELF IN A REAL SITUATION HERE--"

I'VE BEEN GOING OVER YOUR RECORDS AND--

--IS THERE ANYTHING *ELSE* YOU CAN GIVE ME TO GO ON?

HEAVEN

ANY TIMES YOU SWERVED--

YOU ARE HERE

--AND SAVED A *SQUIRREL?* OR LET SOMEONE HAVE THE LAST PIECE OF CAKE?

ANY TIMES WHERE YOU PUT *YOUR KIDS* TO BED--

HELL

CHOOSE YOUR PATH TO ETERNITY

HELL

CHOOSE YOUR PATH TO ETERNITY

--AND STEPPED *AWAY* FROM THE NOVEL?

HEAVEN

HELL

CHOOSE YOUR PATH TO ETERNITY

I SEE.

IT'S NOT THAT YOU WERE A TERRIBLE PERSON, IT'S THAT I CAN'T FIND MUCH GOOD.

AND WITH YOUR HEARING COMING UP...I JUST DON'T KNOW HOW TO PRESENT YOUR CASE.

I'M SORRY.

HELL

CHOOSE YOUR PATH TO ETERNITY

RRIIINGG

74

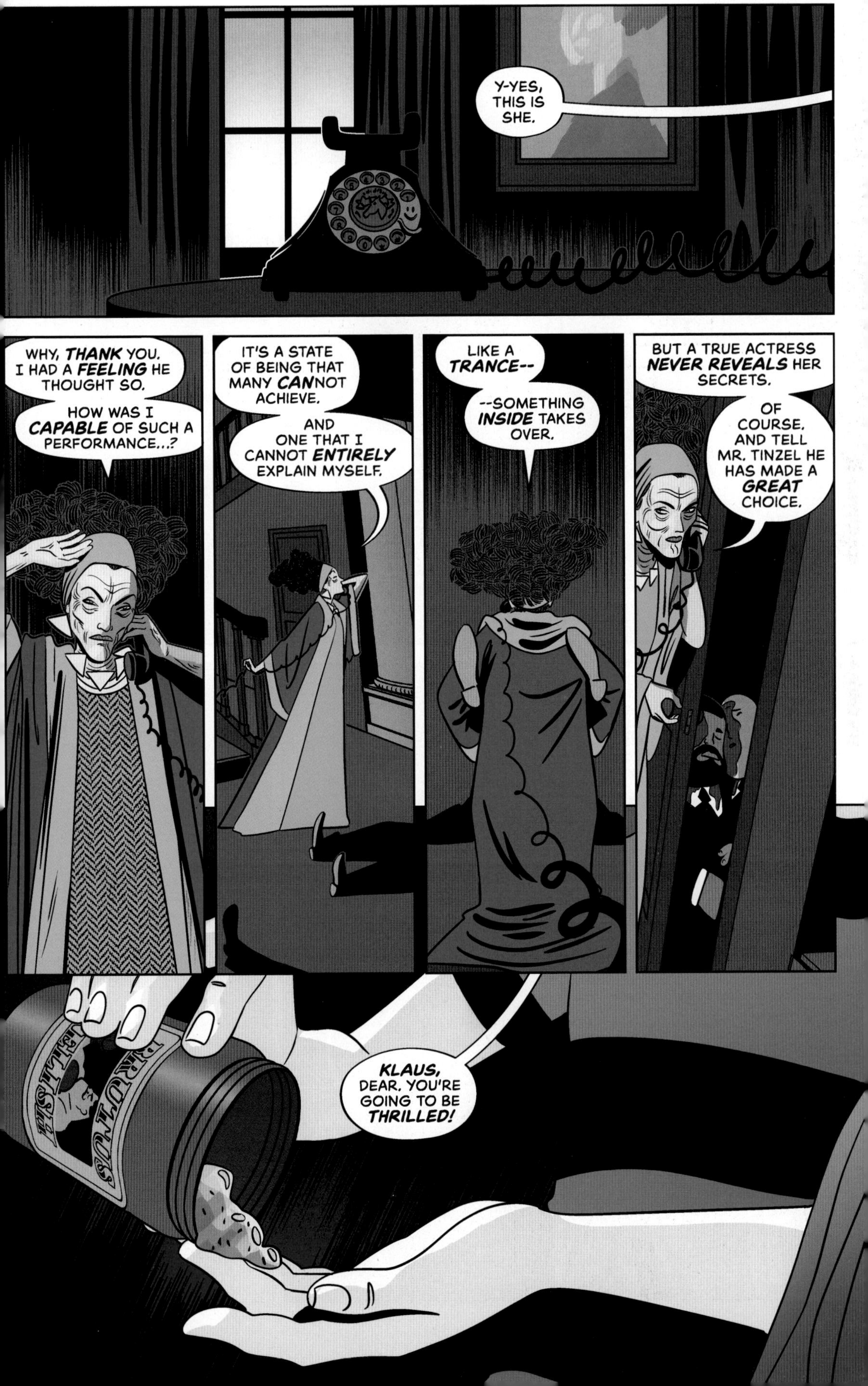
Y-YES, THIS IS SHE.
WHY, THANK YOU. I HAD A FEELING HE THOUGHT SO.
HOW WAS I CAPABLE OF SUCH A PERFORMANCE...?
IT'S A STATE OF BEING THAT MANY CANNOT ACHIEVE.
AND ONE THAT I CANNOT ENTIRELY EXPLAIN MYSELF.
LIKE A TRANCE--
--SOMETHING INSIDE TAKES OVER.
BUT A TRUE ACTRESS NEVER REVEALS HER SECRETS.
OF COURSE. AND TELL MR. TINZEL HE HAS MADE A GREAT CHOICE.
BRUTUS
KLAUS, DEAR. YOU'RE GOING TO BE THRILLED!

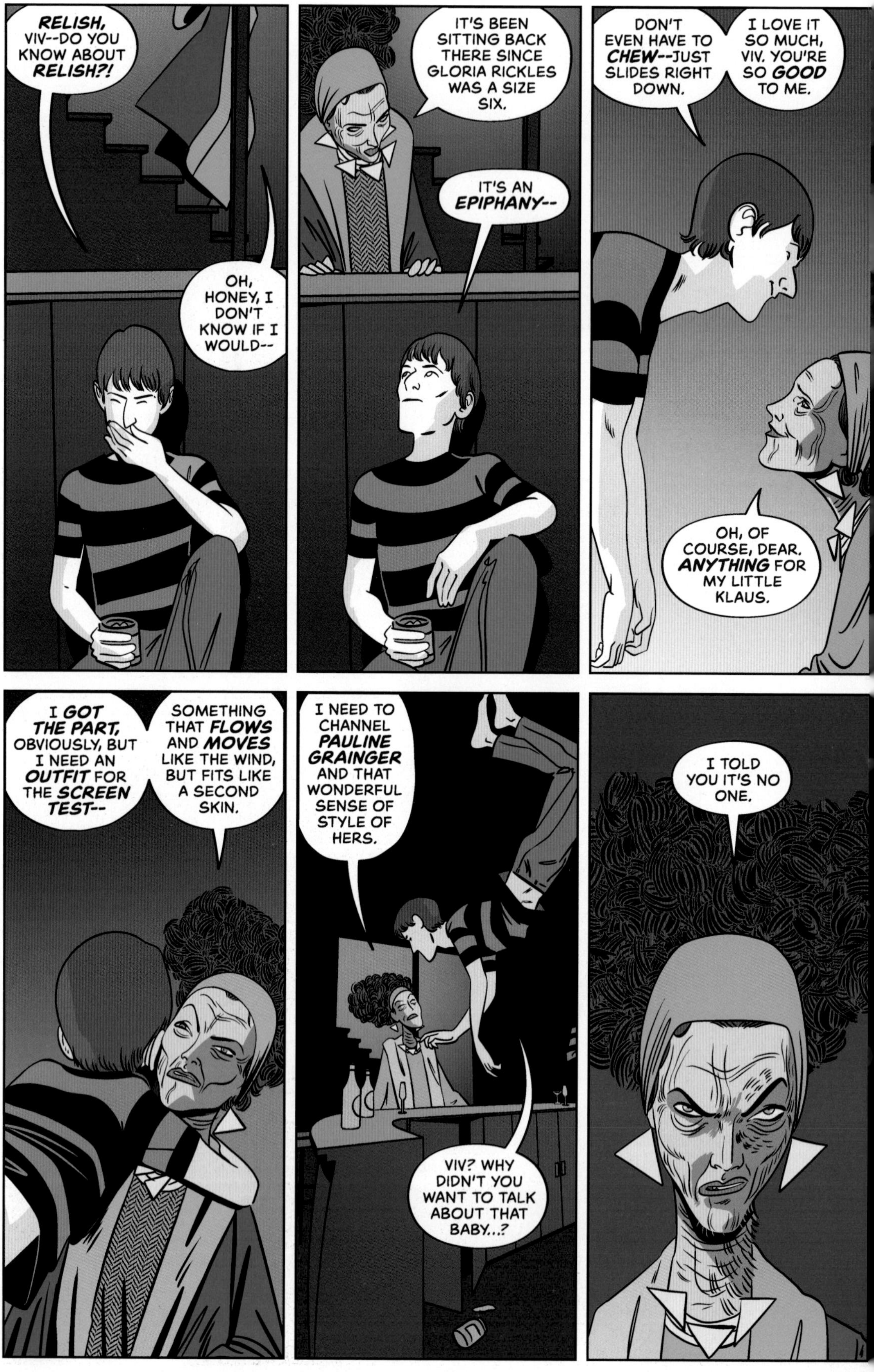
RELISH, VIV--DO YOU KNOW ABOUT RELISH?!
OH, HONEY, I DON'T KNOW IF I WOULD--
IT'S BEEN SITTING BACK THERE SINCE GLORIA RICKLES WAS A SIZE SIX.
IT'S AN EPIPHANY--
DON'T EVEN HAVE TO CHEW--JUST SLIDES RIGHT DOWN.
I LOVE IT SO MUCH, VIV. YOU'RE SO GOOD TO ME.
OH, OF COURSE, DEAR. ANYTHING FOR MY LITTLE KLAUS.
I GOT THE PART, OBVIOUSLY, BUT I NEED AN OUTFIT FOR THE SCREEN TEST--
SOMETHING THAT FLOWS AND MOVES LIKE THE WIND, BUT FITS LIKE A SECOND SKIN.
I NEED TO CHANNEL PAULINE GRAINGER AND THAT WONDERFUL SENSE OF STYLE OF HERS.
VIV? WHY DIDN'T YOU WANT TO TALK ABOUT THAT BABY...?
I TOLD YOU IT'S NO ONE.

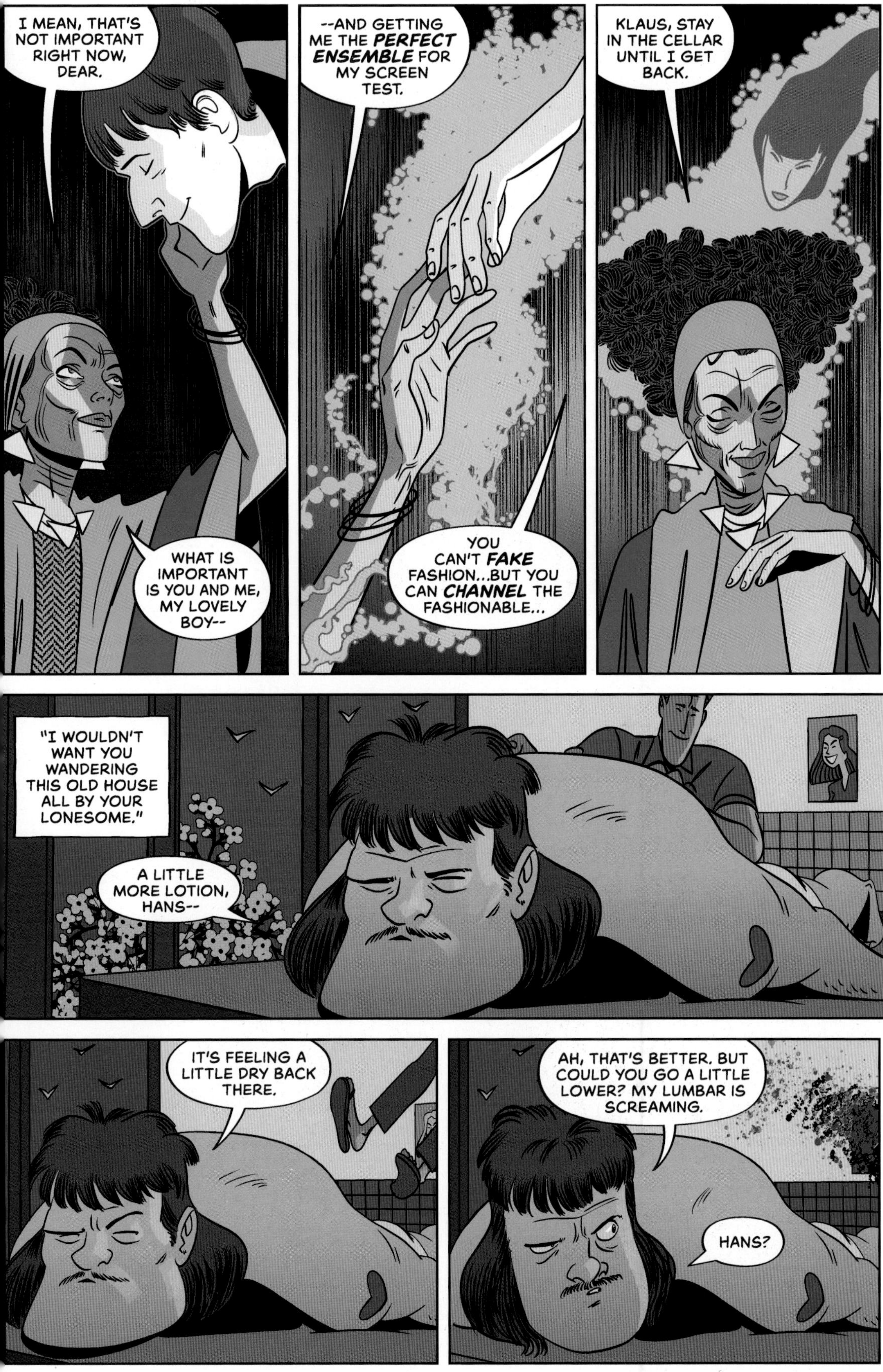
I MEAN, THAT'S NOT IMPORTANT RIGHT NOW, DEAR.
WHAT IS IMPORTANT IS YOU AND ME, MY LOVELY BOY--
--AND GETTING ME THE PERFECT ENSEMBLE FOR MY SCREEN TEST.
YOU CAN'T FAKE FASHION...BUT YOU CAN CHANNEL THE FASHIONABLE...
KLAUS, STAY IN THE CELLAR UNTIL I GET BACK.
"I WOULDN'T WANT YOU WANDERING THIS OLD HOUSE ALL BY YOUR LONESOME."
A LITTLE MORE LOTION, HANS--
IT'S FEELING A LITTLE DRY BACK THERE.
AH, THAT'S BETTER. BUT COULD YOU GO A LITTLE LOWER? MY LUMBAR IS SCREAMING.
HANS?

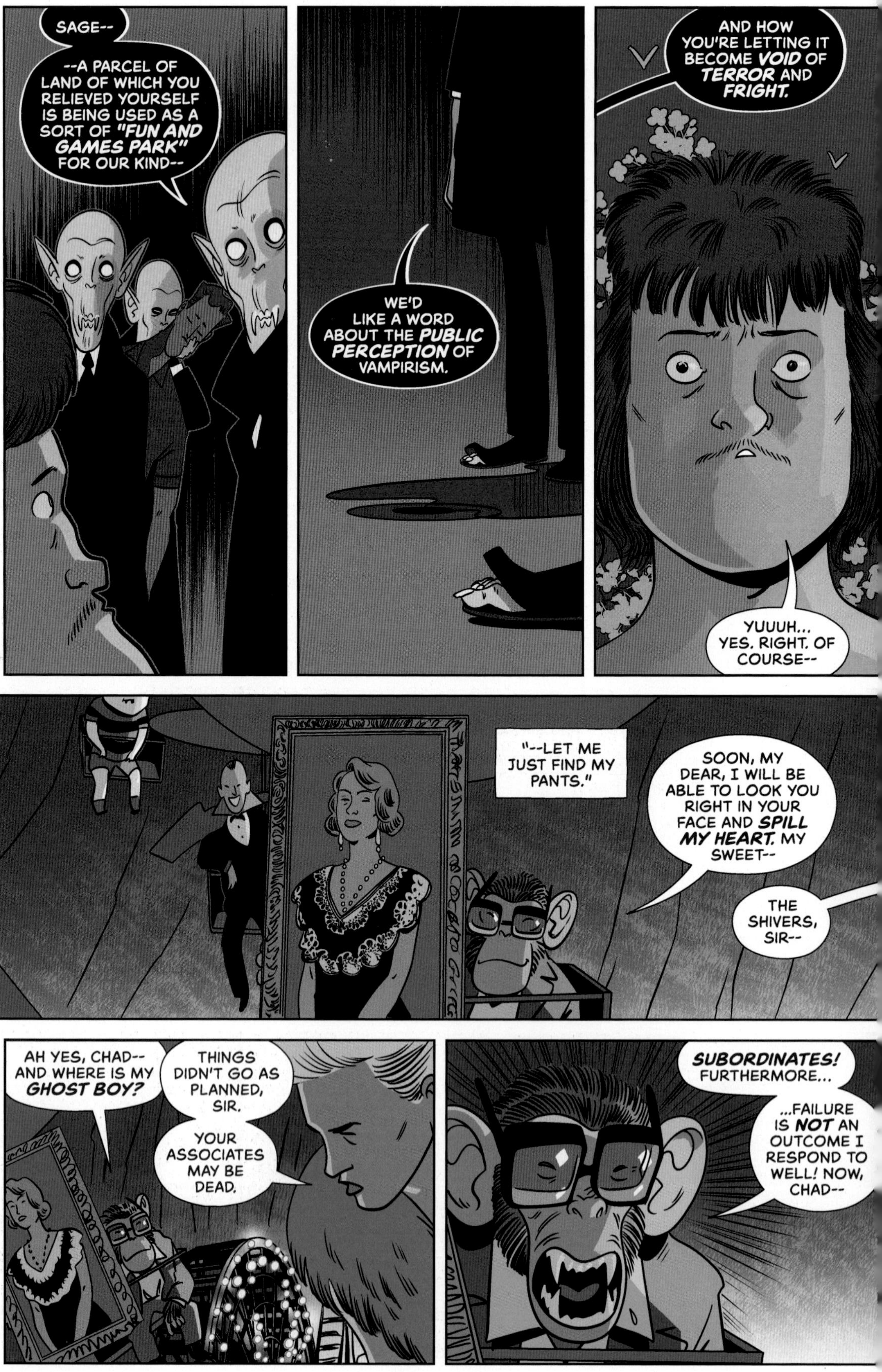

SAGE--
--A PARCEL OF LAND OF WHICH YOU RELIEVED YOURSELF IS BEING USED AS A SORT OF "FUN AND GAMES PARK" FOR OUR KIND--
WE'D LIKE A WORD ABOUT THE PUBLIC PERCEPTION OF VAMPIRISM.
AND HOW YOU'RE LETTING IT BECOME VOID OF TERROR AND FRIGHT.
YUUUH... YES. RIGHT. OF COURSE--
"--LET ME JUST FIND MY PANTS."
SOON, MY DEAR, I WILL BE ABLE TO LOOK YOU RIGHT IN YOUR FACE AND SPILL MY HEART. MY SWEET--
THE SHIVERS, SIR--
AH YES, CHAD-- AND WHERE IS MY GHOST BOY?
THINGS DIDN'T GO AS PLANNED, SIR.
YOUR ASSOCIATES MAY BE DEAD.
SUBORDINATES! FURTHERMORE...
...FAILURE IS NOT AN OUTCOME I RESPOND TO WELL! NOW, CHAD--

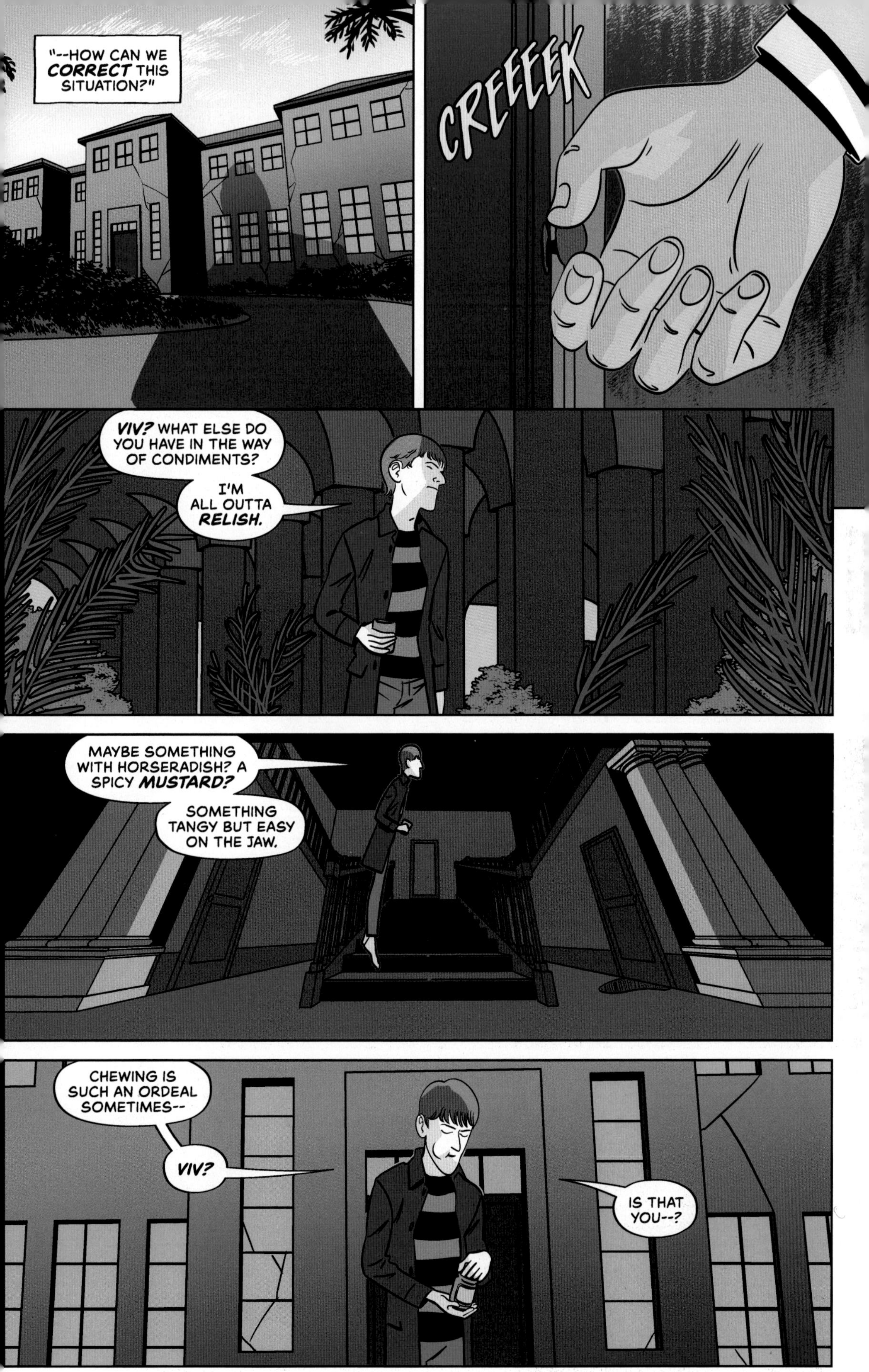
"--HOW CAN WE CORRECT THIS SITUATION?"
CREEEEK
VIV? WHAT ELSE DO YOU HAVE IN THE WAY OF CONDIMENTS?
I'M ALL OUTTA RELISH.
MAYBE SOMETHING WITH HORSERADISH? A SPICY MUSTARD?
SOMETHING TANGY BUT EASY ON THE JAW.
CHEWING IS SUCH AN ORDEAL SOMETIMES--
VIV?
IS THAT YOU--?

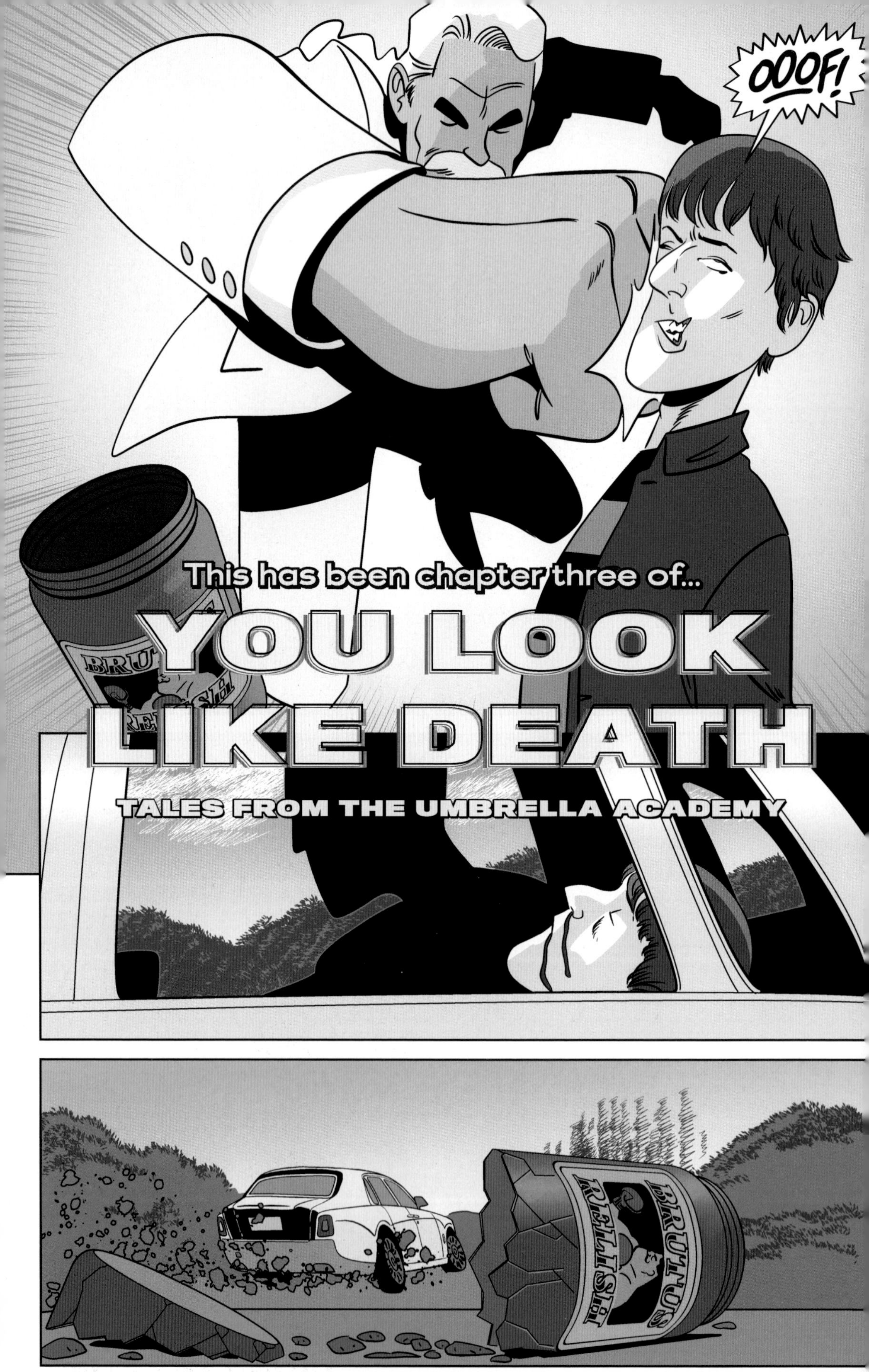

OOOF!
This has been chapter three of...
YOU LOOK LIKE DEATH
TALES FROM THE UMBRELLA ACADEMY
BRUTUS RELISH

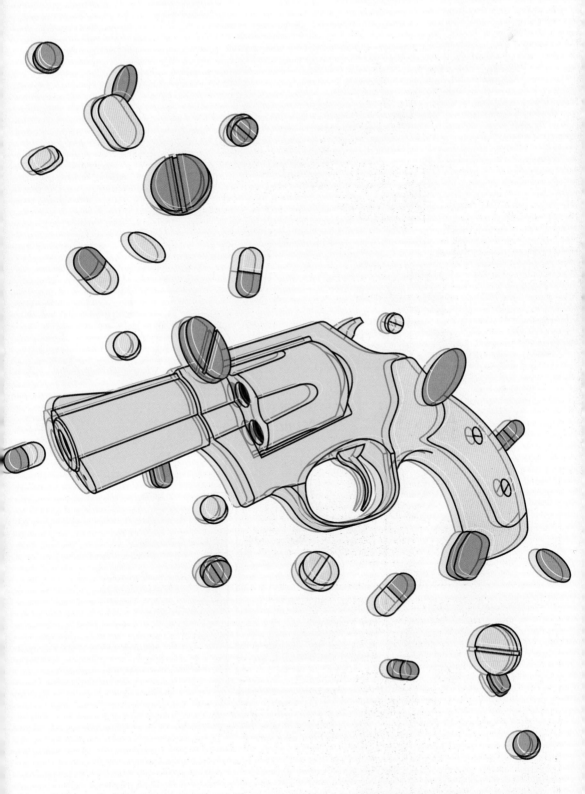

CHAPTER FOUR

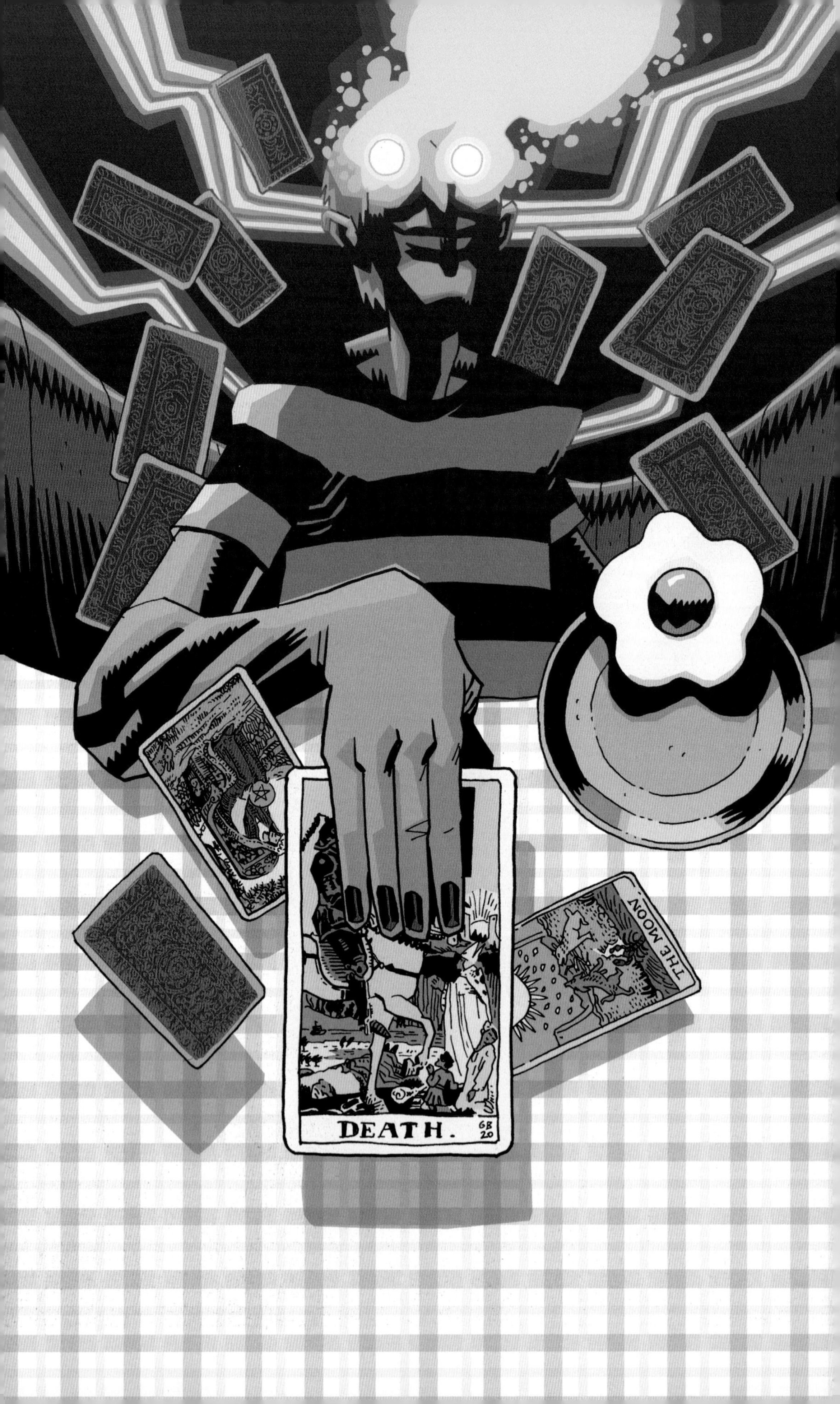
DEATH.
GB 20
THE MOON

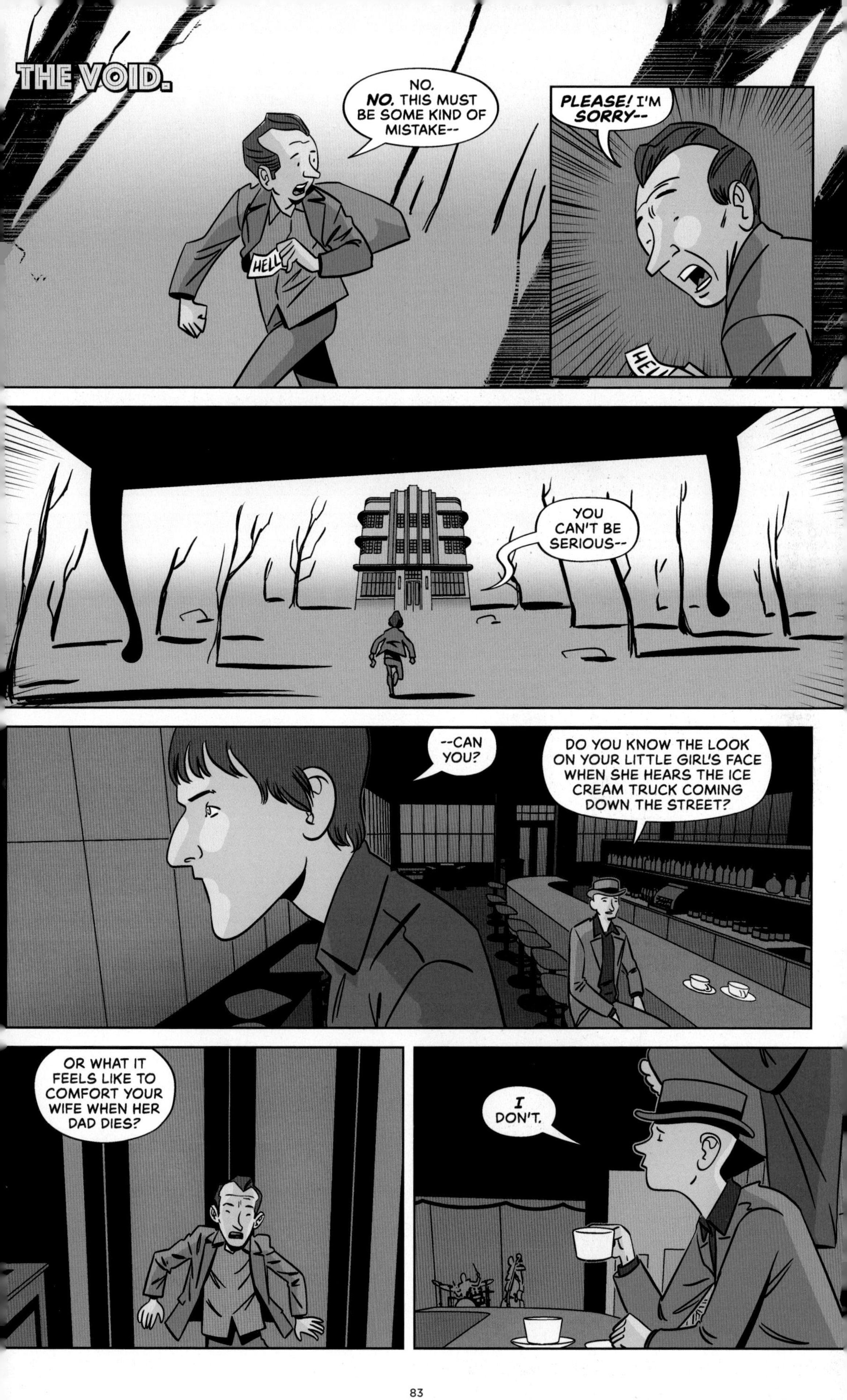
THE VOID.
NO, *NO.* THIS MUST BE SOME KIND OF MISTAKE--
HELL
PLEASE! I'M *SORRY--*
YOU CAN'T BE SERIOUS--
--CAN YOU?
DO YOU KNOW THE LOOK ON YOUR LITTLE GIRL'S FACE WHEN SHE HEARS THE ICE CREAM TRUCK COMING DOWN THE STREET?
OR WHAT IT FEELS LIKE TO COMFORT YOUR WIFE WHEN HER DAD DIES?
I DON'T.

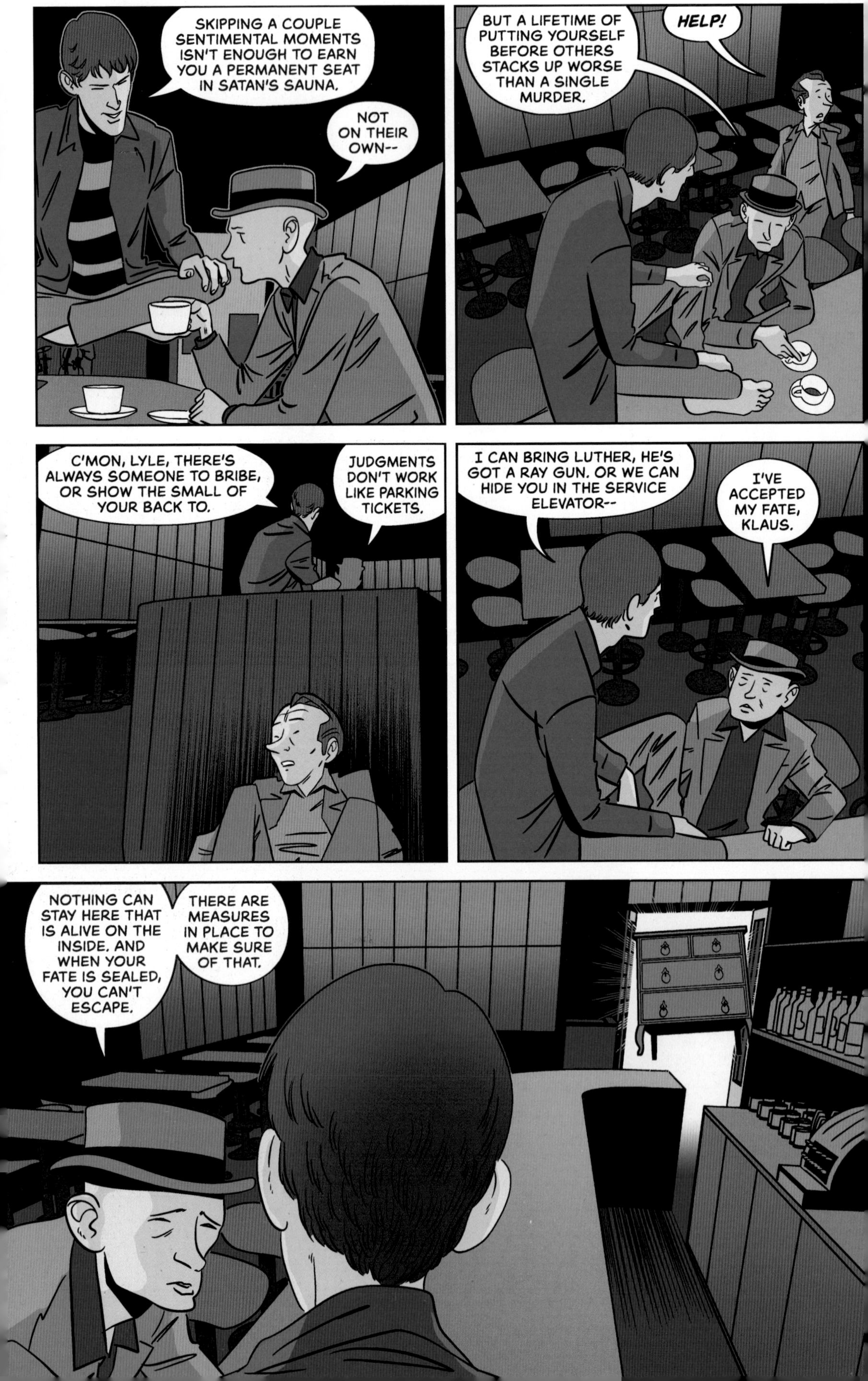
SKIPPING A COUPLE SENTIMENTAL MOMENTS ISN'T ENOUGH TO EARN YOU A PERMANENT SEAT IN SATAN'S SAUNA.
NOT ON THEIR OWN--
BUT A LIFETIME OF PUTTING YOURSELF BEFORE OTHERS STACKS UP WORSE THAN A SINGLE MURDER.
HELP!
C'MON, LYLE, THERE'S ALWAYS SOMEONE TO BRIBE, OR SHOW THE SMALL OF YOUR BACK TO.
JUDGMENTS DON'T WORK LIKE PARKING TICKETS.
I CAN BRING LUTHER, HE'S GOT A RAY GUN. OR WE CAN HIDE YOU IN THE SERVICE ELEVATOR--
I'VE ACCEPTED MY FATE, KLAUS.
NOTHING CAN STAY HERE THAT IS ALIVE ON THE INSIDE. AND WHEN YOUR FATE IS SEALED, YOU CAN'T ESCAPE.
THERE ARE MEASURES IN PLACE TO MAKE SURE OF THAT.

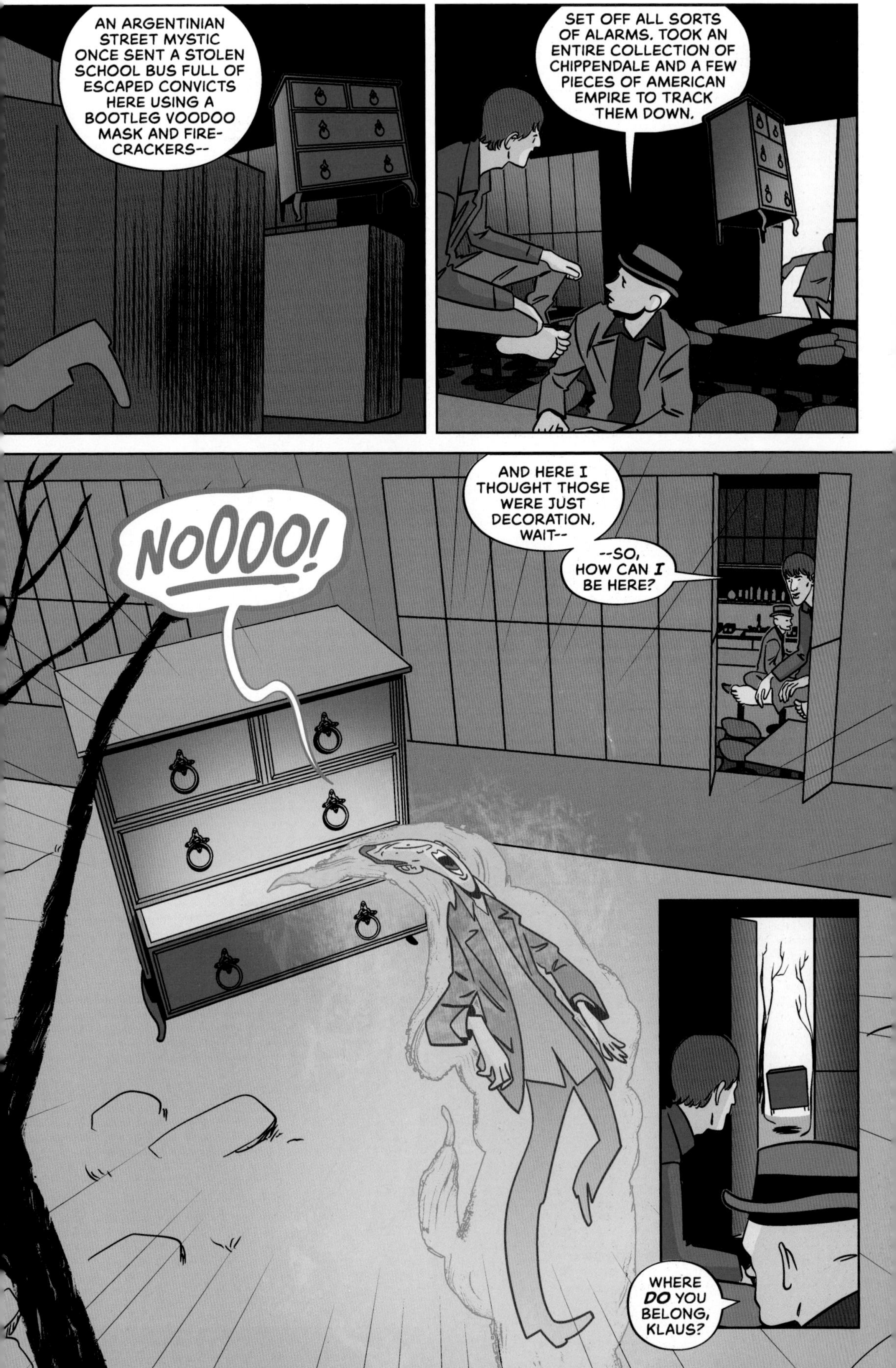
AN ARGENTINIAN STREET MYSTIC ONCE SENT A STOLEN SCHOOL BUS FULL OF ESCAPED CONVICTS HERE USING A BOOTLEG VOODOO MASK AND FIRE-CRACKERS--
SET OFF ALL SORTS OF ALARMS. TOOK AN ENTIRE COLLECTION OF CHIPPENDALE AND A FEW PIECES OF AMERICAN EMPIRE TO TRACK THEM DOWN.
NOOOO!
AND HERE I THOUGHT THOSE WERE JUST DECORATION. WAIT--
--SO, HOW CAN I BE HERE?
WHERE DO YOU BELONG, KLAUS?

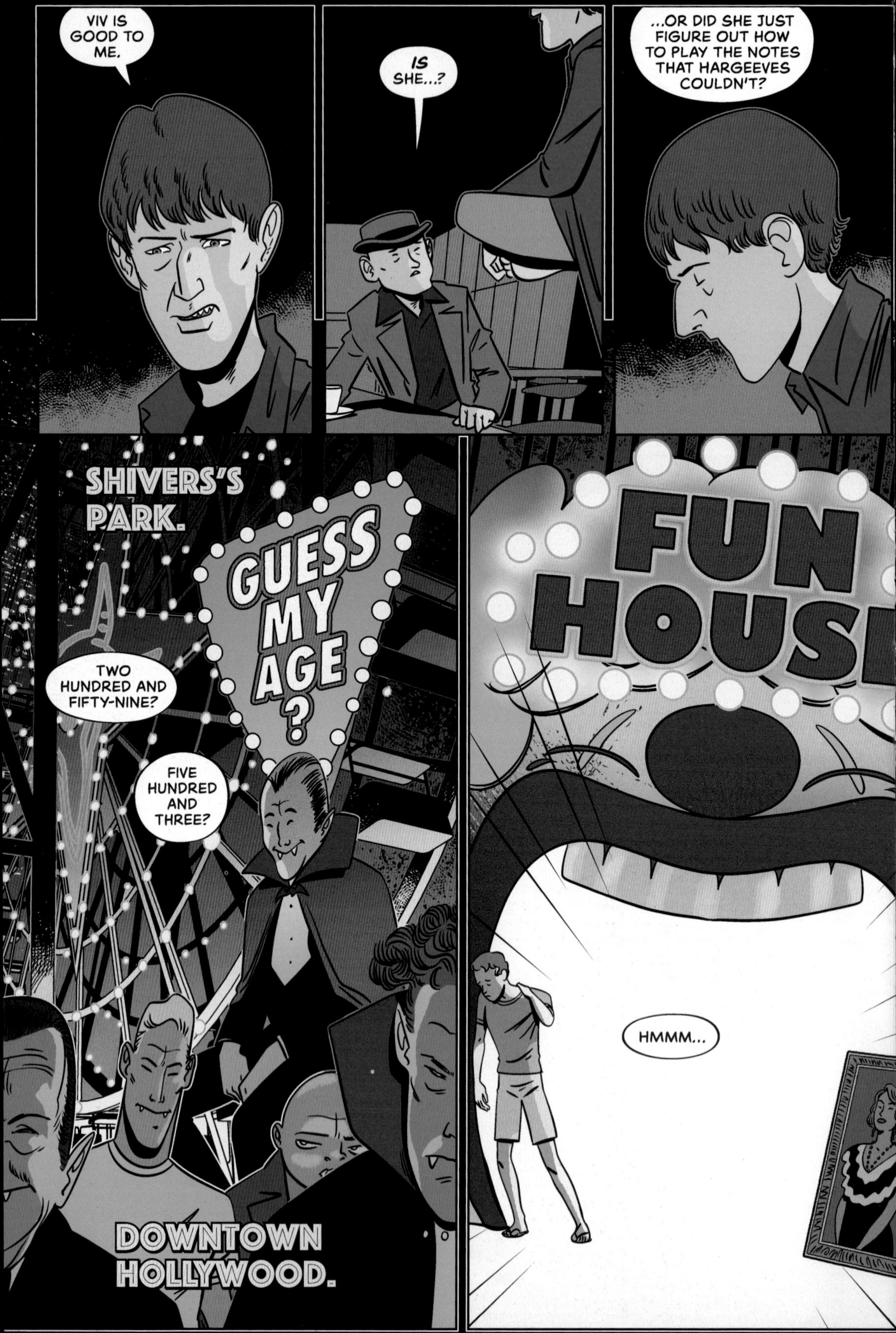
VIV IS GOOD TO ME.
IS SHE...?
...OR DID SHE JUST FIGURE OUT HOW TO PLAY THE NOTES THAT HARGEEVES COULDN'T?
SHIVERS'S PARK.
GUESS MY AGE ?
TWO HUNDRED AND FIFTY-NINE?
FIVE HUNDRED AND THREE?
DOWNTOWN HOLLYWOOD.
FUN HOUS
HMMM...

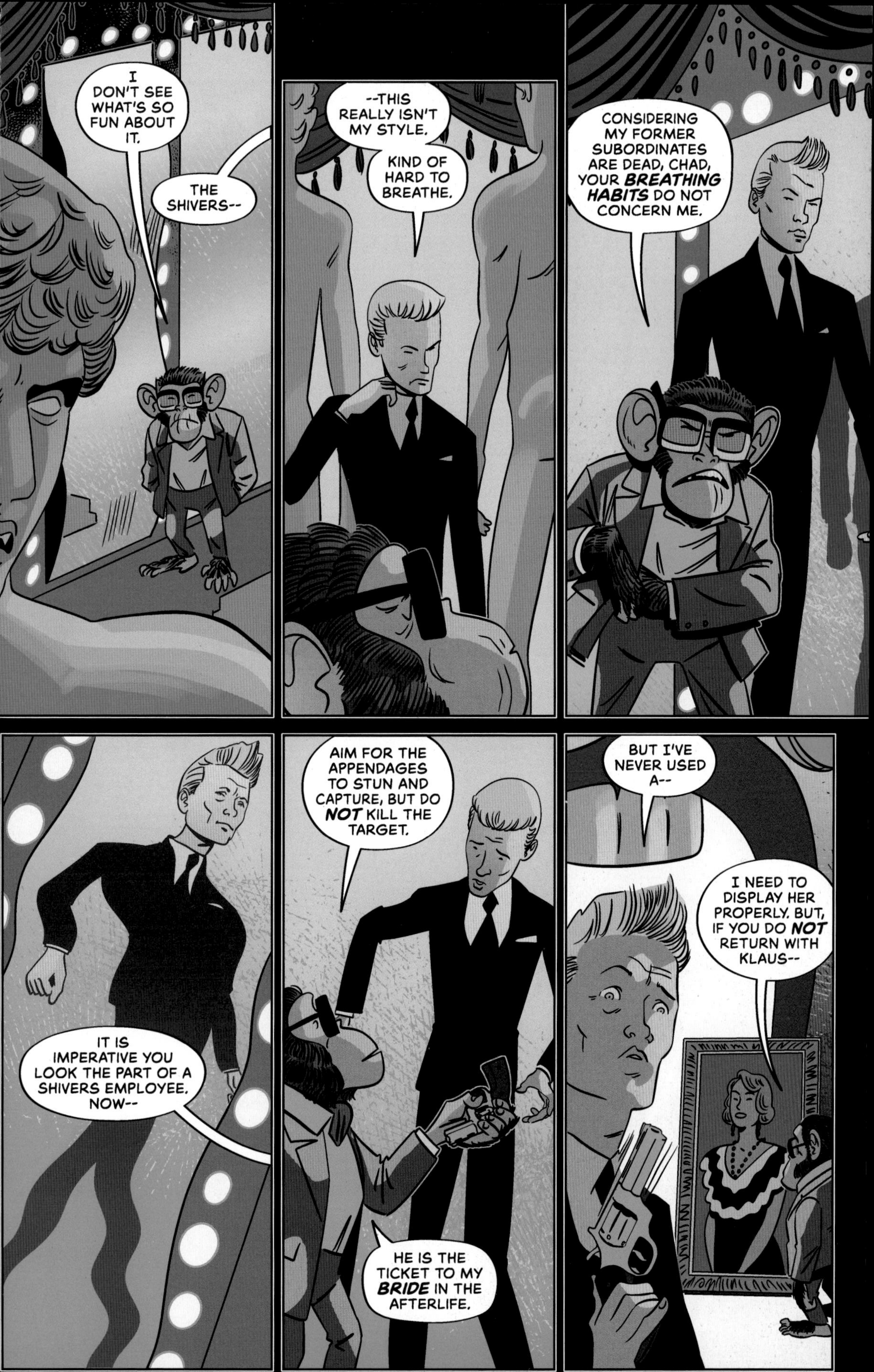
I DON'T SEE WHAT'S SO FUN ABOUT IT.
THE SHIVERS--
--THIS REALLY ISN'T MY STYLE.
KIND OF HARD TO BREATHE.
CONSIDERING MY FORMER SUBORDINATES ARE DEAD, CHAD, YOUR BREATHING HABITS DO NOT CONCERN ME.
IT IS IMPERATIVE YOU LOOK THE PART OF A SHIVERS EMPLOYEE. NOW--
AIM FOR THE APPENDAGES TO STUN AND CAPTURE, BUT DO NOT KILL THE TARGET.
HE IS THE TICKET TO MY BRIDE IN THE AFTERLIFE.
BUT I'VE NEVER USED A--
I NEED TO DISPLAY HER PROPERLY. BUT, IF YOU DO NOT RETURN WITH KLAUS--

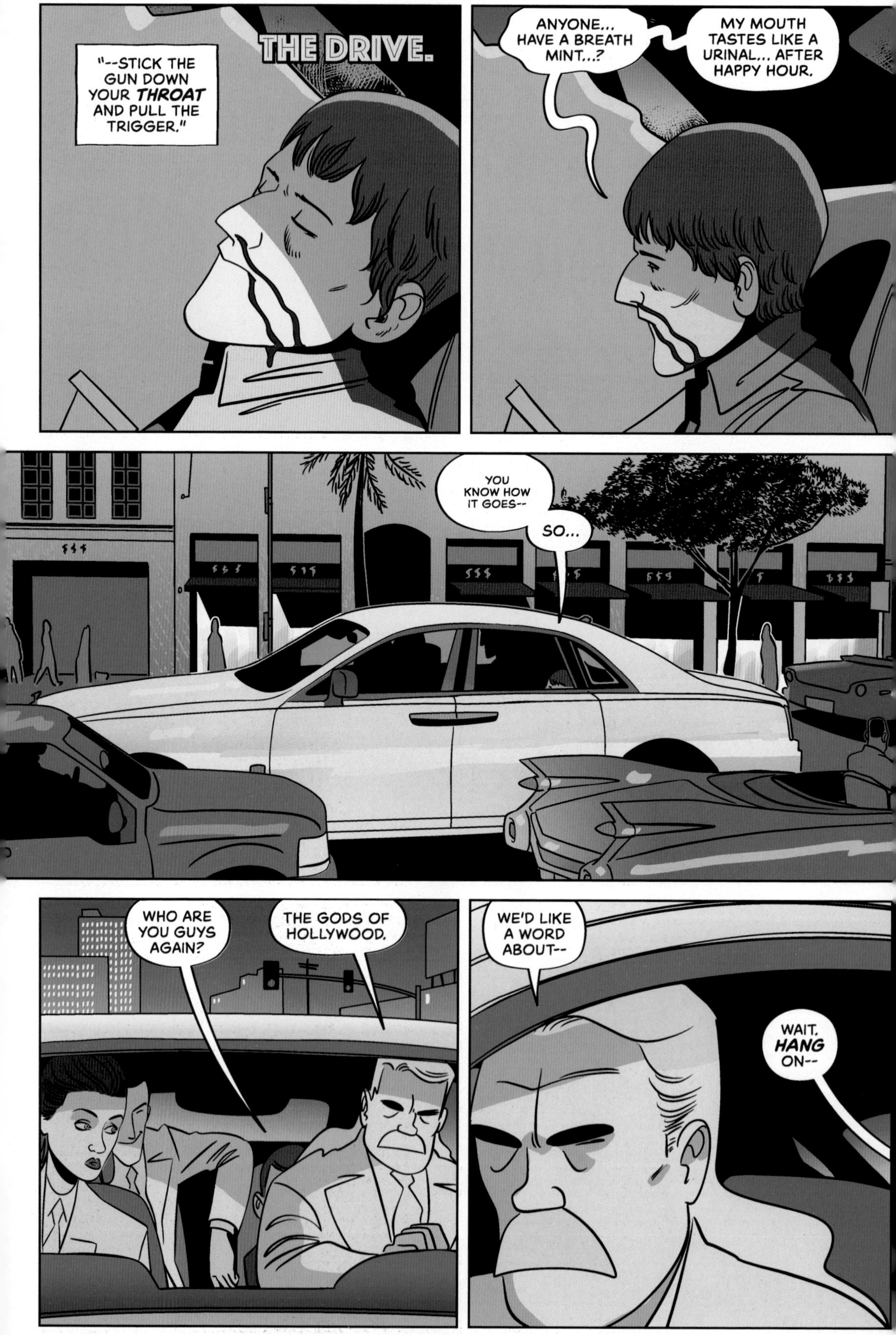
"--STICK THE GUN DOWN YOUR THROAT AND PULL THE TRIGGER."
THE DRIVE.
ANYONE... HAVE A BREATH MINT...?
MY MOUTH TASTES LIKE A URINAL... AFTER HAPPY HOUR.
YOU KNOW HOW IT GOES--
SO...
WHO ARE YOU GUYS AGAIN?
THE GODS OF HOLLYWOOD.
WE'D LIKE A WORD ABOUT--
WAIT. HANG ON--

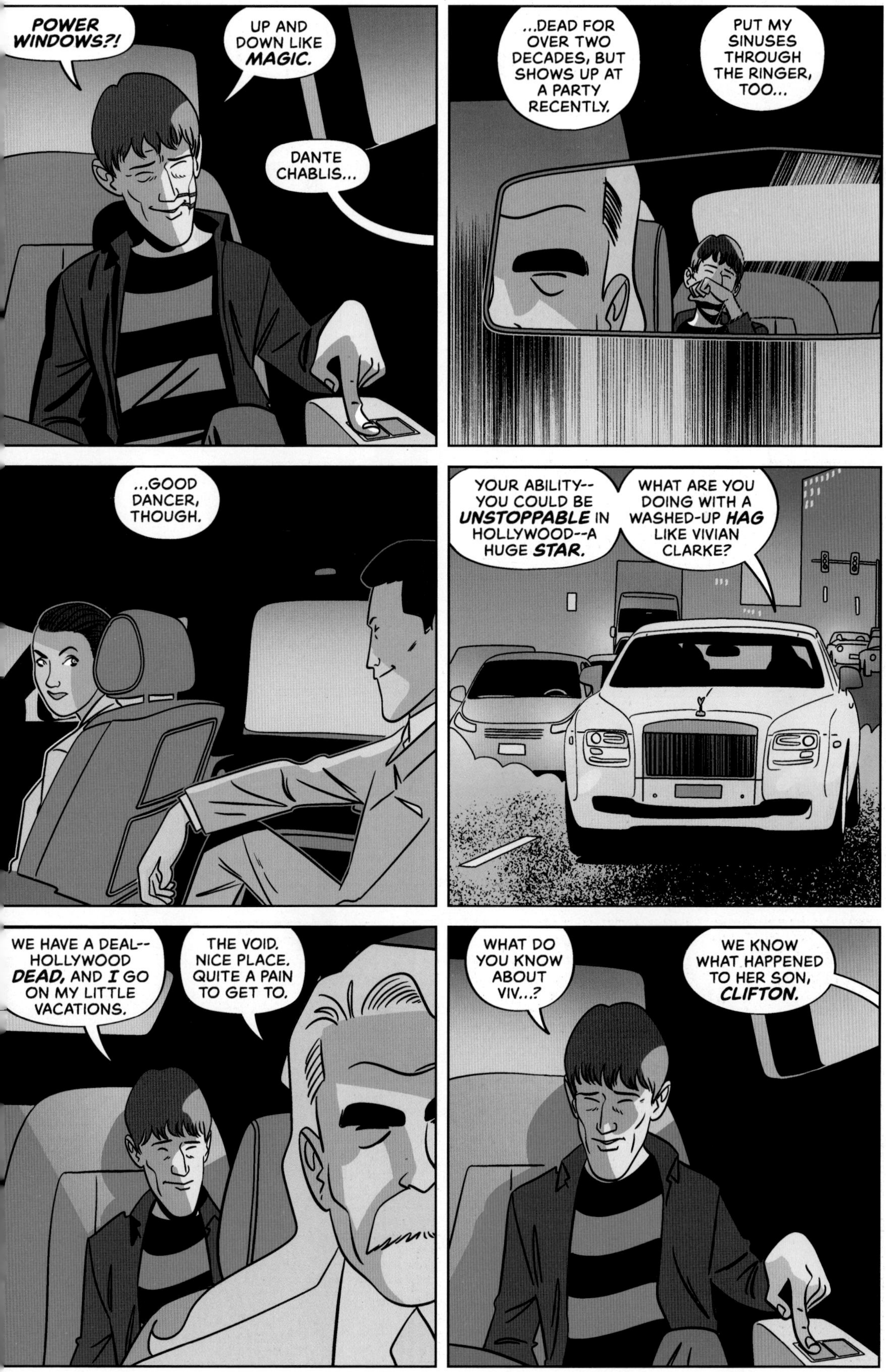
POWER WINDOWS?!
UP AND DOWN LIKE MAGIC.
DANTE CHABLIS...
...DEAD FOR OVER TWO DECADES, BUT SHOWS UP AT A PARTY RECENTLY.
PUT MY SINUSES THROUGH THE RINGER, TOO...
...GOOD DANCER, THOUGH.
YOUR ABILITY-- YOU COULD BE UNSTOPPABLE IN HOLLYWOOD--A HUGE STAR.
WHAT ARE YOU DOING WITH A WASHED-UP HAG LIKE VIVIAN CLARKE?
WE HAVE A DEAL-- HOLLYWOOD DEAD, AND I GO ON MY LITTLE VACATIONS.
THE VOID. NICE PLACE. QUITE A PAIN TO GET TO.
WHAT DO YOU KNOW ABOUT VIV...?
WE KNOW WHAT HAPPENED TO HER SON, CLIFTON.

SO, **GODS**, HUH? LIKE A PERFORMING MIRACLES THING?

WE'VE BEEN KNOWN TO.

KLAUS--

WE'D LIKE YOU TO WORK FOR US.

HENRY FONTANE   LAURA LOX

THE GHOST IN MR. WHITE

THE GHOST IN MR. WHITE

AND WHAT'S IN IT FOR ME?

SNAP

KLAUS HARGREEVES

THE GHOST IN M

THE HILLS.

OH, KLAUS, IT WAS JUST **WONDERFUL**.

I WISH YOU COULD HAVE BEEN--

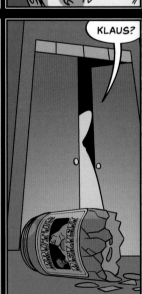

KLAUS?

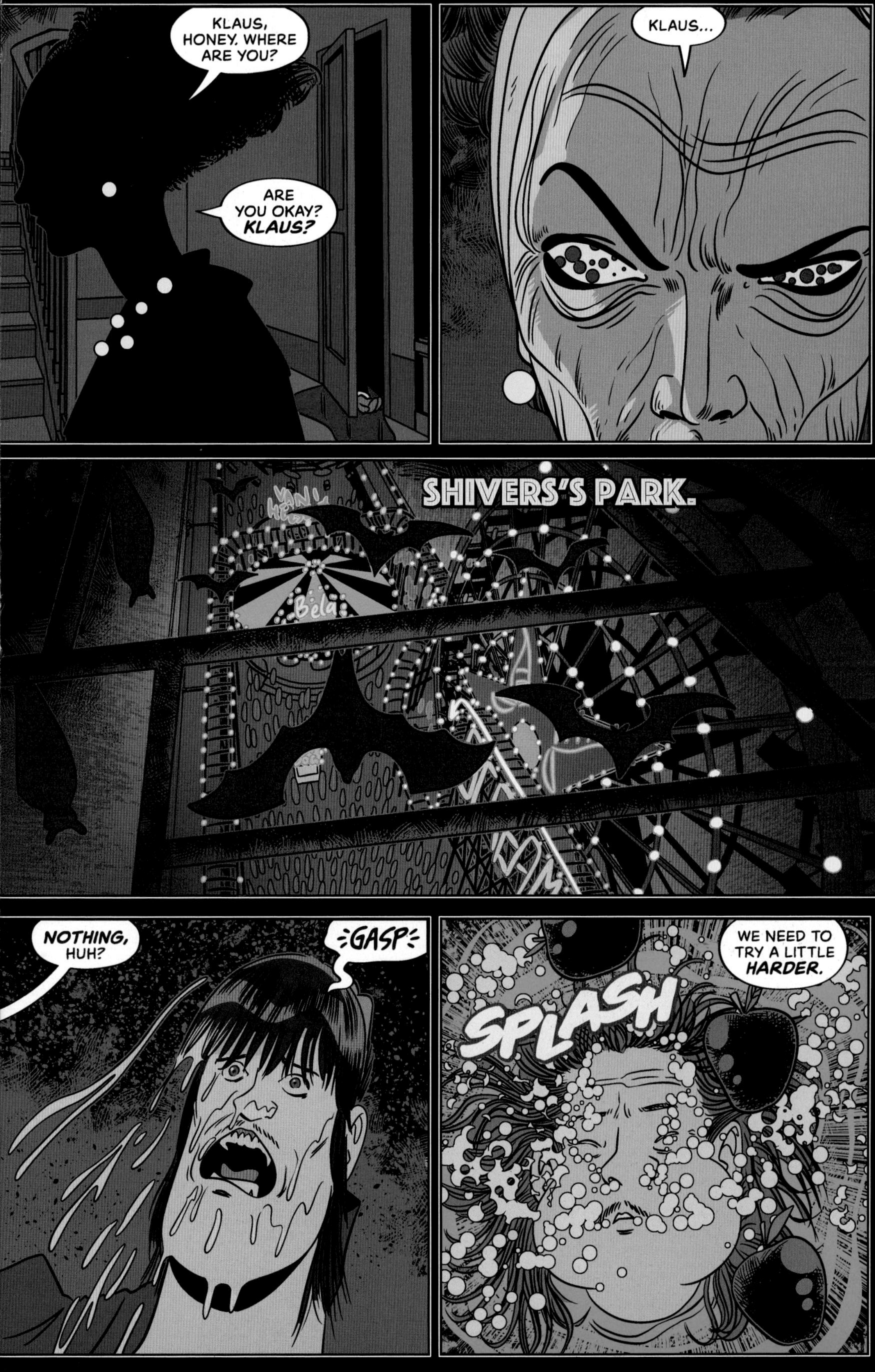
KLAUS, HONEY. WHERE ARE YOU?
ARE YOU OKAY? KLAUS?
KLAUS...
SHIVERS'S PARK.
NOTHING, HUH?
GASP
SPLASH
WE NEED TO TRY A LITTLE HARDER.

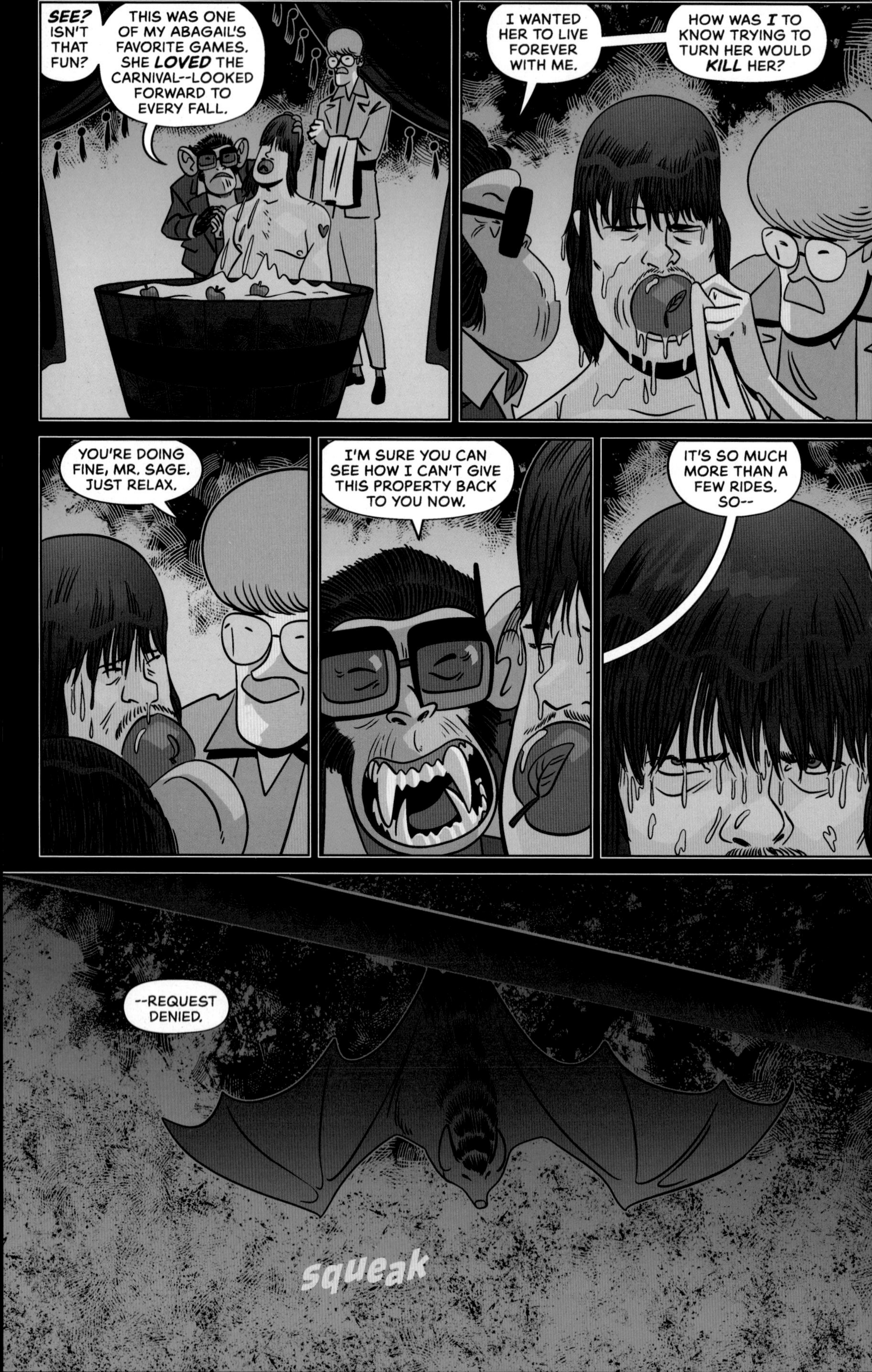
SEE? ISN'T THAT FUN?
THIS WAS ONE OF MY ABAGAIL'S FAVORITE GAMES. SHE LOVED THE CARNIVAL--LOOKED FORWARD TO EVERY FALL.
I WANTED HER TO LIVE FOREVER WITH ME.
HOW WAS I TO KNOW TRYING TO TURN HER WOULD KILL HER?
YOU'RE DOING FINE, MR. SAGE. JUST RELAX.
I'M SURE YOU CAN SEE HOW I CAN'T GIVE THIS PROPERTY BACK TO YOU NOW.
IT'S SO MUCH MORE THAN A FEW RIDES. SO--
--REQUEST DENIED.
squeak

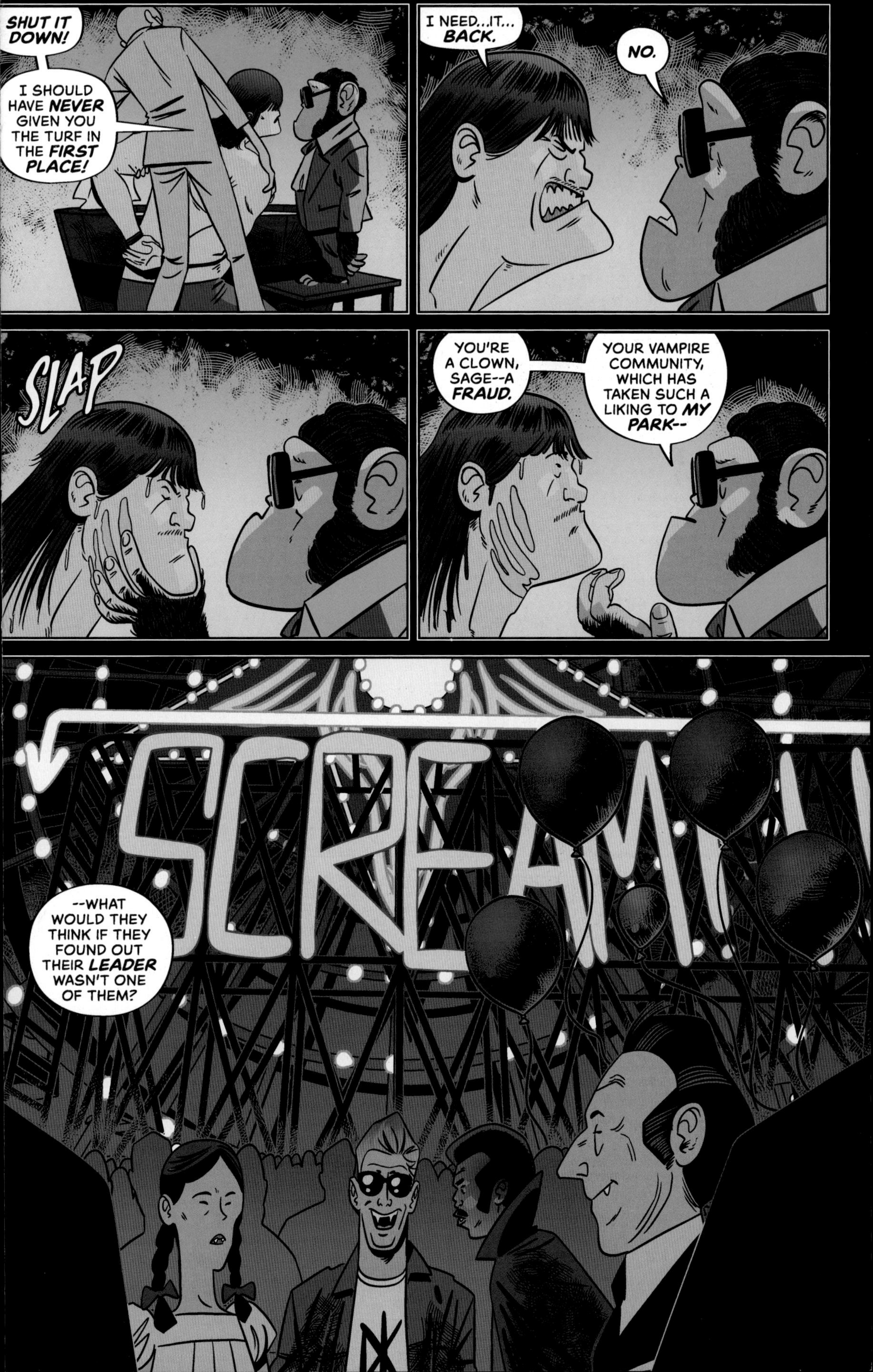
SHUT IT DOWN!
I SHOULD HAVE NEVER GIVEN YOU THE TURF IN THE FIRST PLACE!
I NEED...IT... BACK.
NO.
SLAP
YOU'RE A CLOWN, SAGE--A FRAUD.
YOUR VAMPIRE COMMUNITY, WHICH HAS TAKEN SUCH A LIKING TO MY PARK--
SCREAM
--WHAT WOULD THEY THINK IF THEY FOUND OUT THEIR LEADER WASN'T ONE OF THEM?

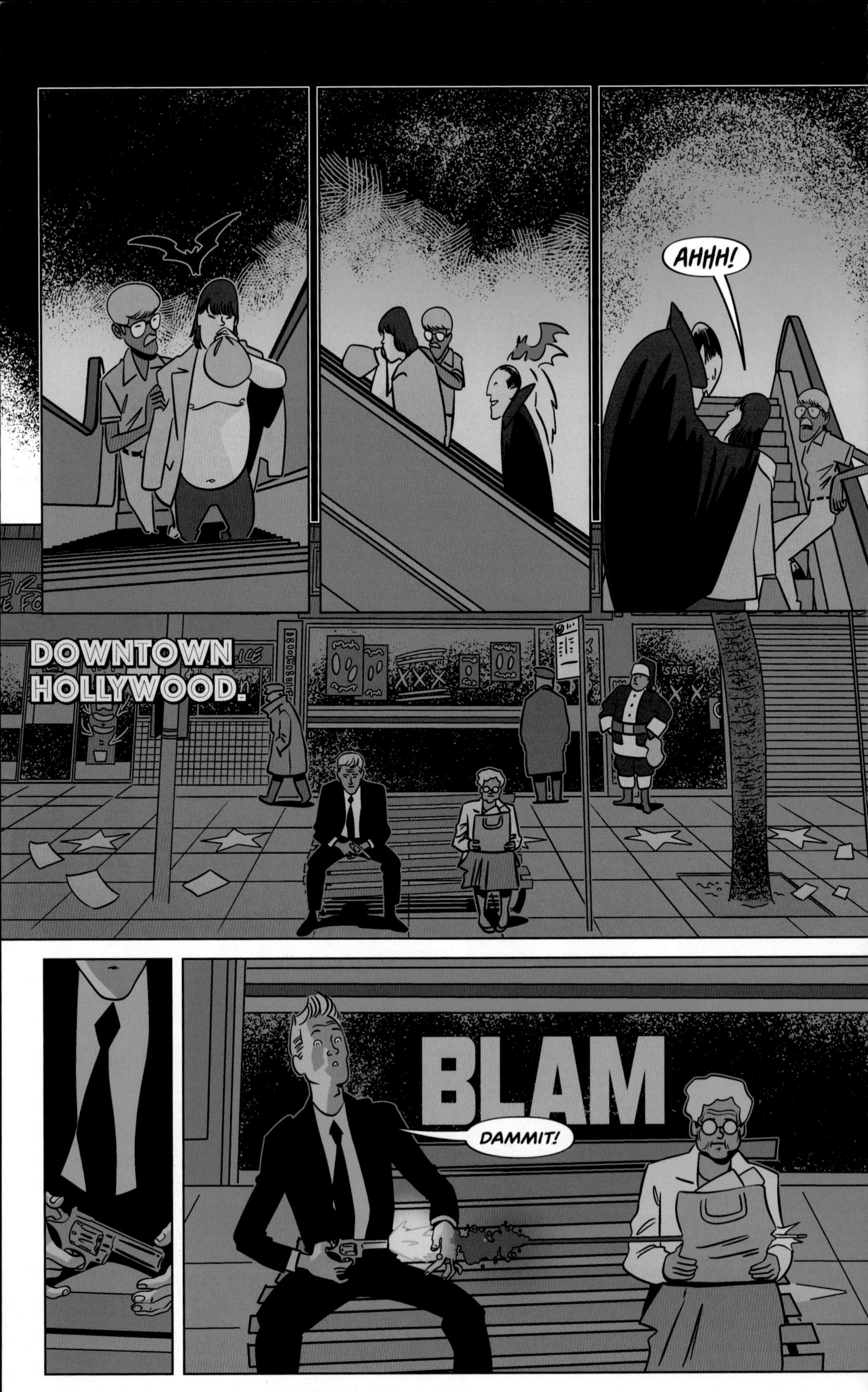
AHHH!
DOWNTOWN HOLLYWOOD.
BLAM
DAMMIT!

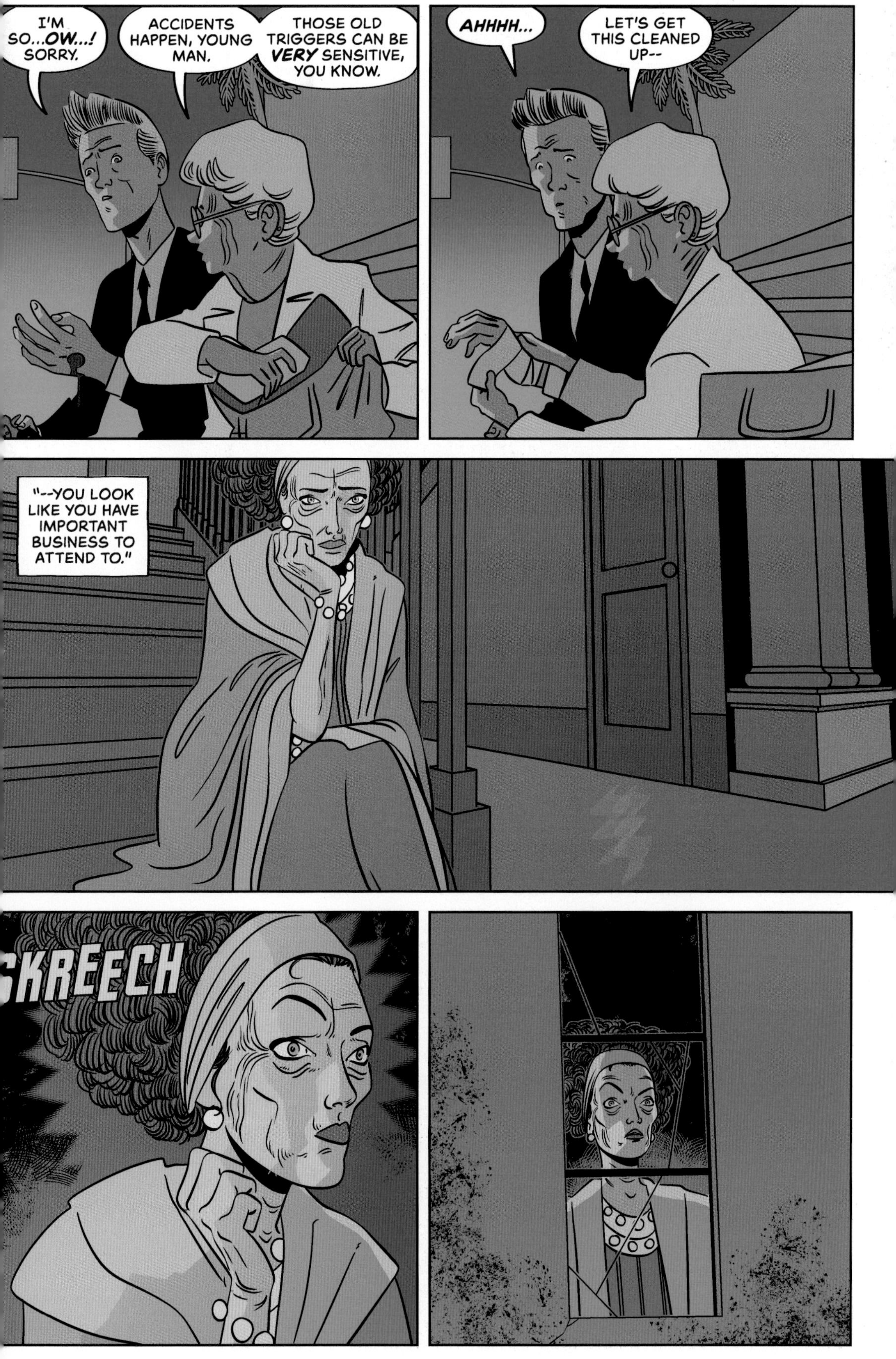
I'M SO...OW...! SORRY.
ACCIDENTS HAPPEN, YOUNG MAN.
THOSE OLD TRIGGERS CAN BE VERY SENSITIVE, YOU KNOW.
AHHHH...
LET'S GET THIS CLEANED UP--
"--YOU LOOK LIKE YOU HAVE IMPORTANT BUSINESS TO ATTEND TO."
SKREECH

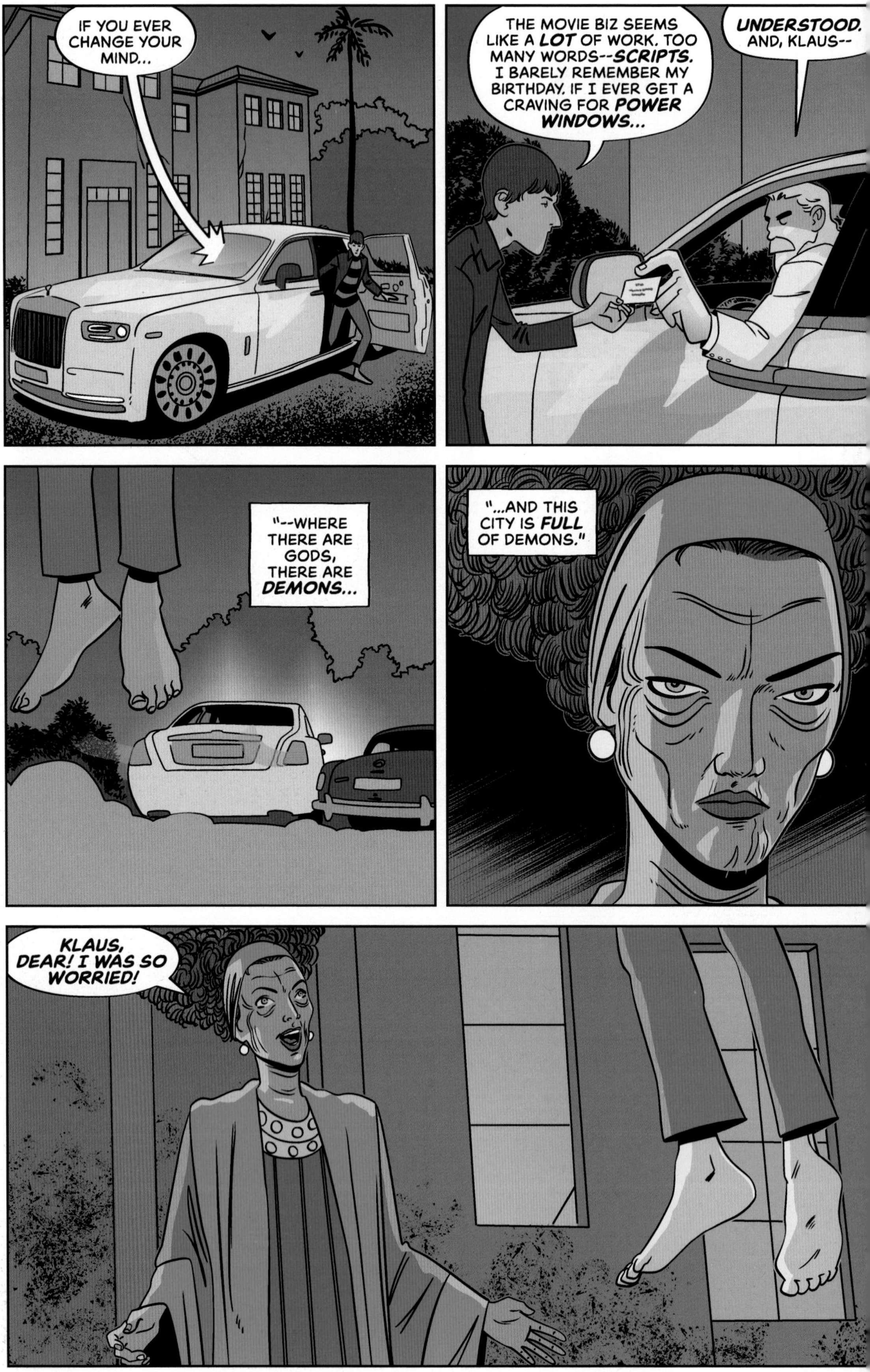
IF YOU EVER CHANGE YOUR MIND...
THE MOVIE BIZ SEEMS LIKE A **LOT** OF WORK. TOO MANY WORDS--**SCRIPTS.** I BARELY REMEMBER MY BIRTHDAY. IF I EVER GET A CRAVING FOR **POWER WINDOWS...**
UNDERSTOOD. AND, KLAUS--
"--WHERE THERE ARE GODS, THERE ARE **DEMONS...**
"...AND THIS CITY IS **FULL** OF DEMONS."
KLAUS, DEAR! I WAS SO WORRIED!

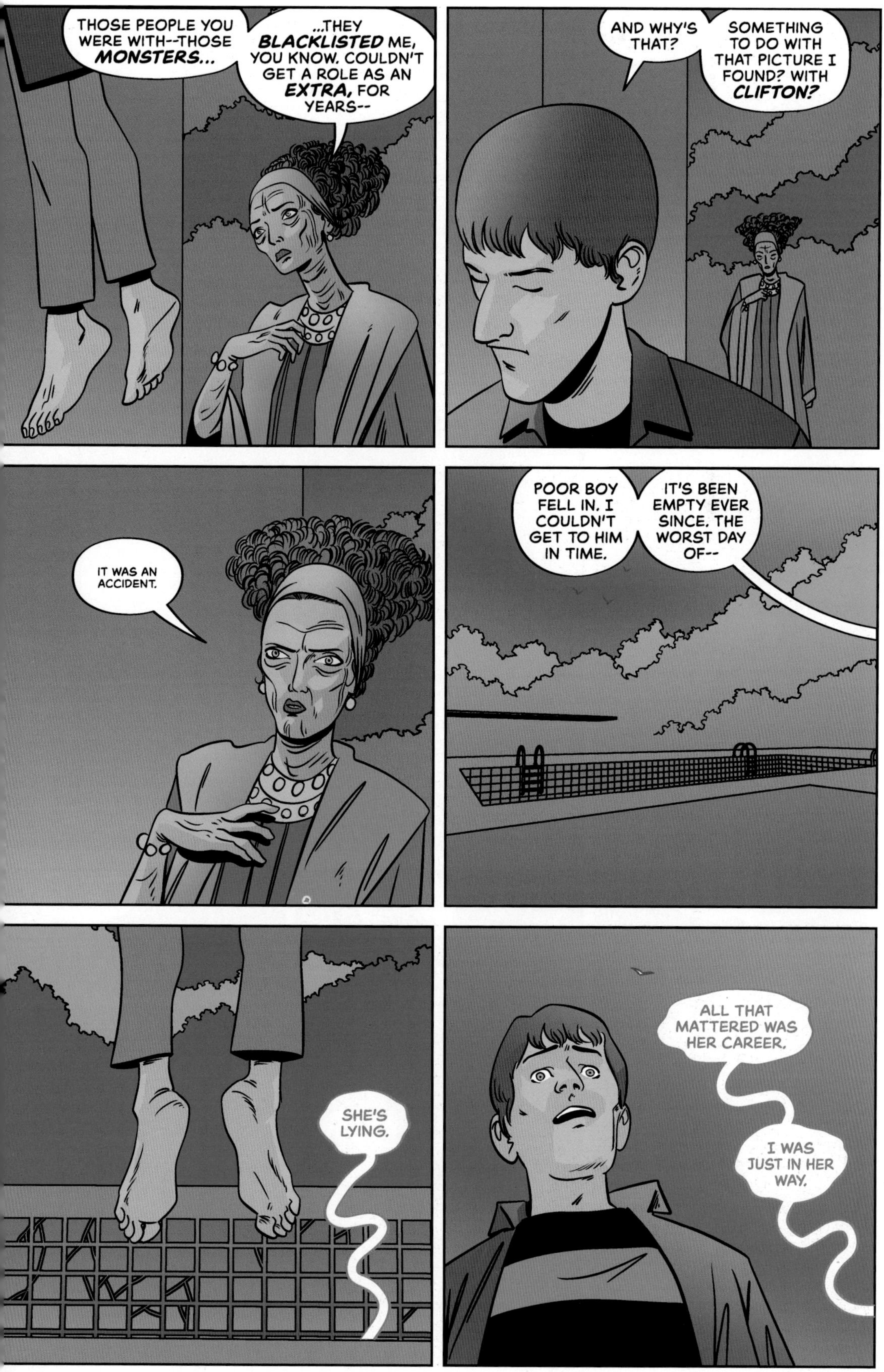
THOSE PEOPLE YOU WERE WITH--THOSE **MONSTERS...**
...THEY **BLACKLISTED** ME, YOU KNOW. COULDN'T GET A ROLE AS AN **EXTRA,** FOR YEARS--
AND WHY'S THAT?
SOMETHING TO DO WITH THAT PICTURE I FOUND? WITH **CLIFTON?**
IT WAS AN ACCIDENT.
POOR BOY FELL IN. I COULDN'T GET TO HIM IN TIME.
IT'S BEEN EMPTY EVER SINCE. THE WORST DAY OF--
SHE'S LYING.
ALL THAT MATTERED WAS HER CAREER.
I WAS JUST IN HER WAY.

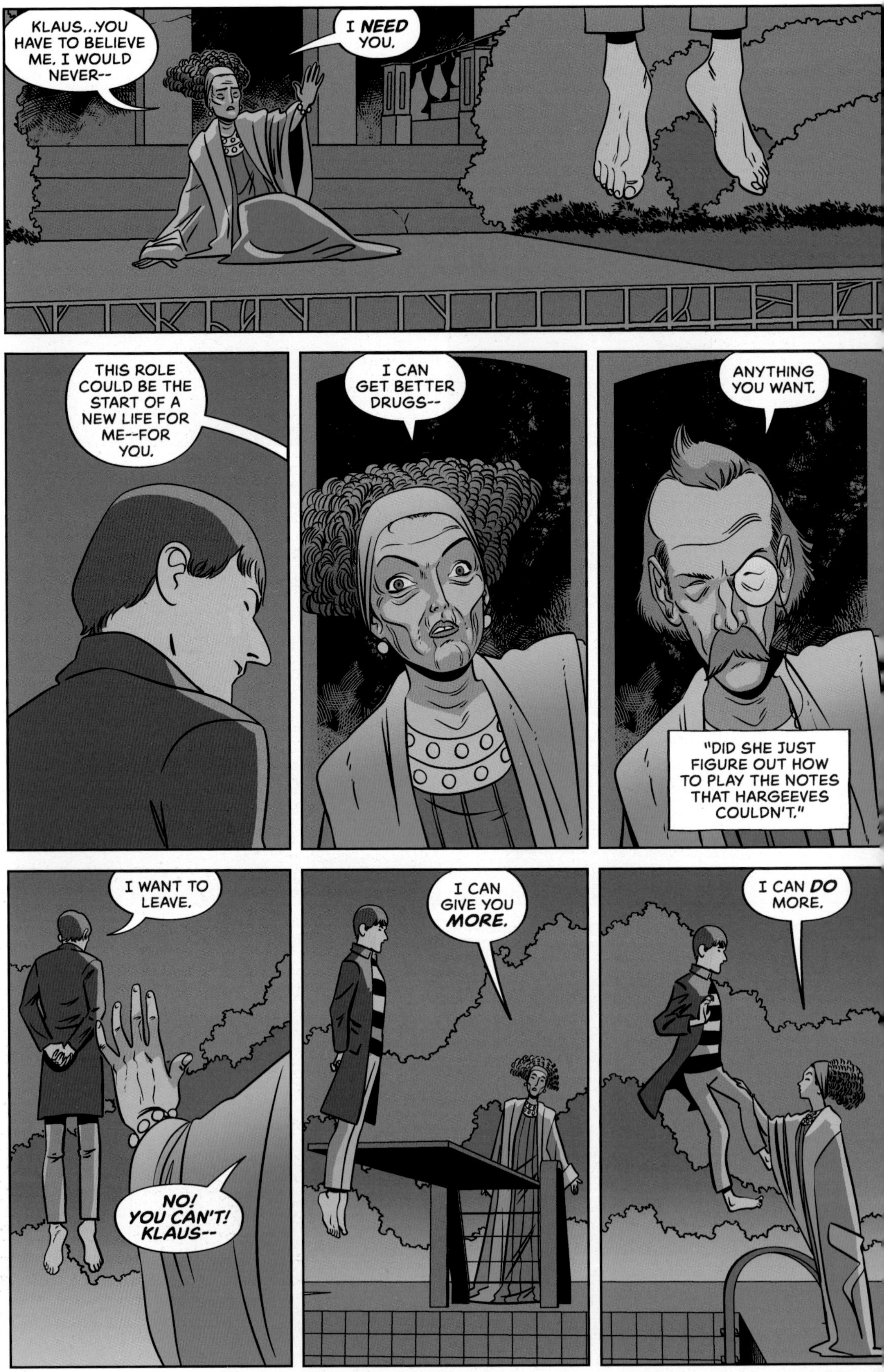
KLAUS...YOU HAVE TO BELIEVE ME. I WOULD NEVER--
I NEED YOU.
THIS ROLE COULD BE THE START OF A NEW LIFE FOR ME--FOR YOU.
I CAN GET BETTER DRUGS--
ANYTHING YOU WANT.
"DID SHE JUST FIGURE OUT HOW TO PLAY THE NOTES THAT HARGEEVES COULDN'T."
I WANT TO LEAVE.
NO! YOU CAN'T! KLAUS--
I CAN GIVE YOU MORE.
I CAN DO MORE.

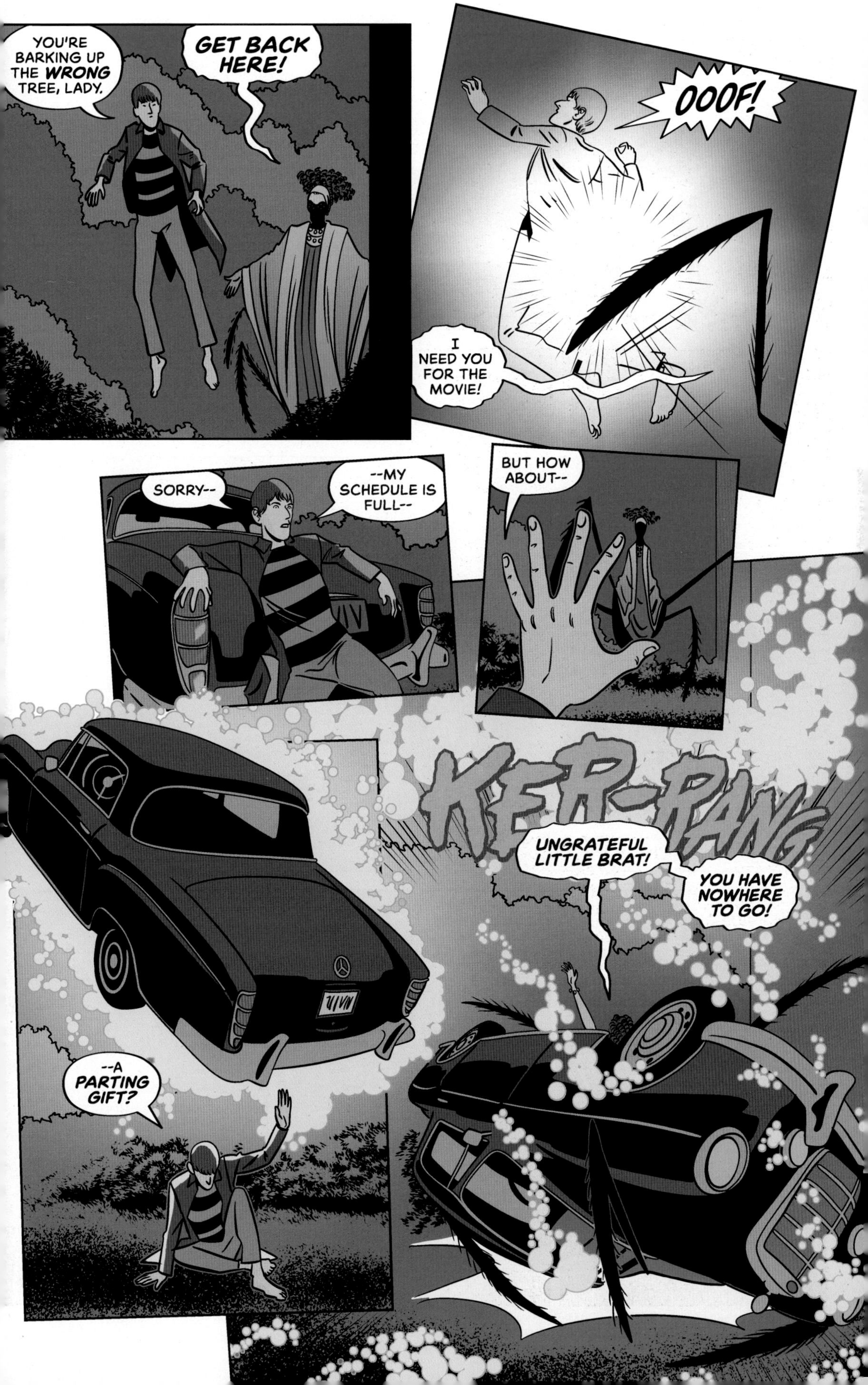

YOU'RE BARKING UP THE WRONG TREE, LADY.
GET BACK HERE!
OOOF!
I NEED YOU FOR THE MOVIE!
SORRY--
--MY SCHEDULE IS FULL--
BUT HOW ABOUT--
KER-RANG
UNGRATEFUL LITTLE BRAT!
YOU HAVE NOWHERE TO GO!
--A PARTING GIFT?

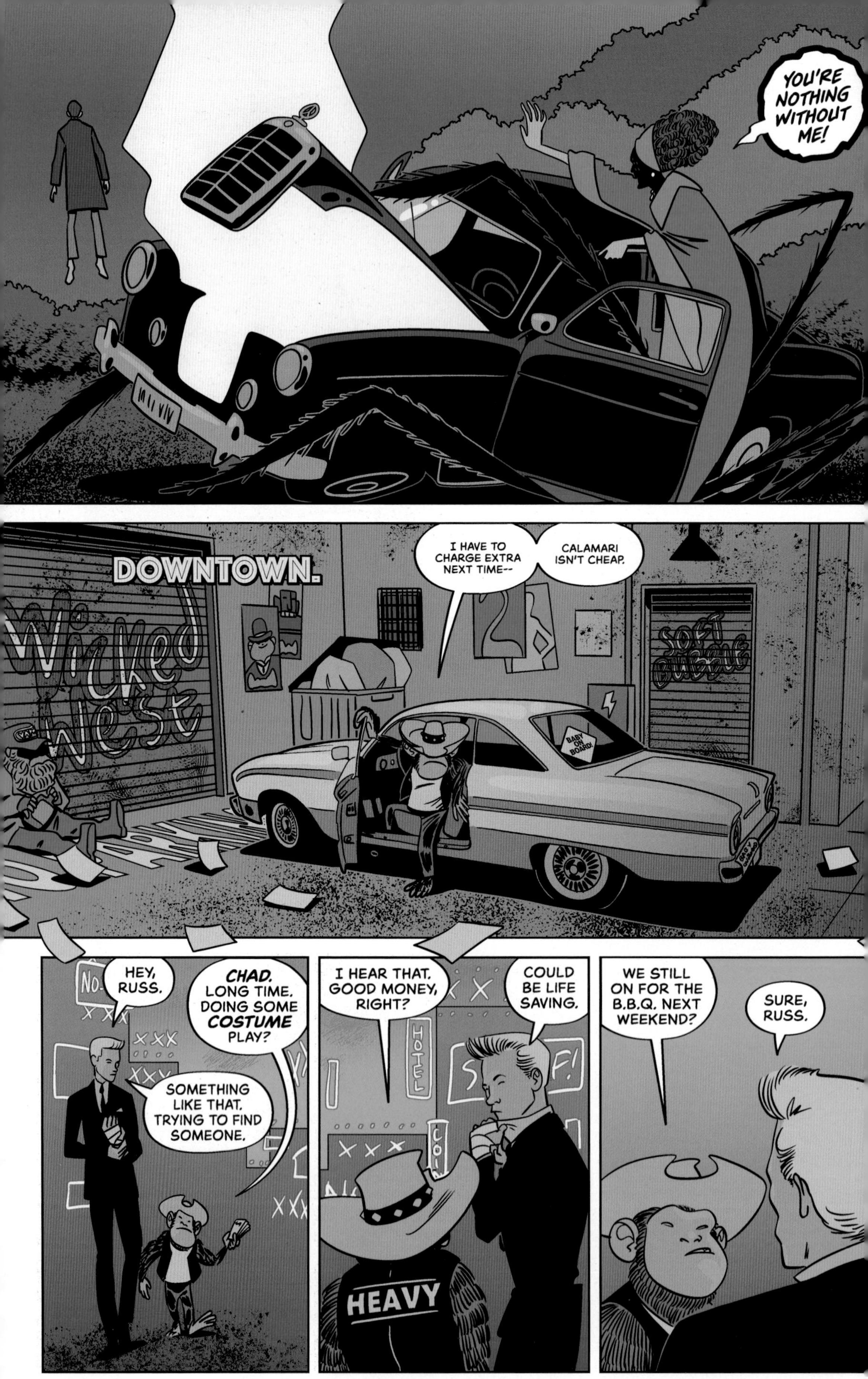
YOU'RE NOTHING WITHOUT ME!
DOWNTOWN.
I HAVE TO CHARGE EXTRA NEXT TIME--
CALAMARI ISN'T CHEAP.
Wicked West
BABY ON BOARD!
HEY, RUSS.
CHAD. LONG TIME. DOING SOME COSTUME PLAY?
SOMETHING LIKE THAT. TRYING TO FIND SOMEONE.
I HEAR THAT. GOOD MONEY, RIGHT?
COULD BE LIFE SAVING.
HOTEL
HEAVY
WE STILL ON FOR THE B.B.Q. NEXT WEEKEND?
SURE, RUSS.

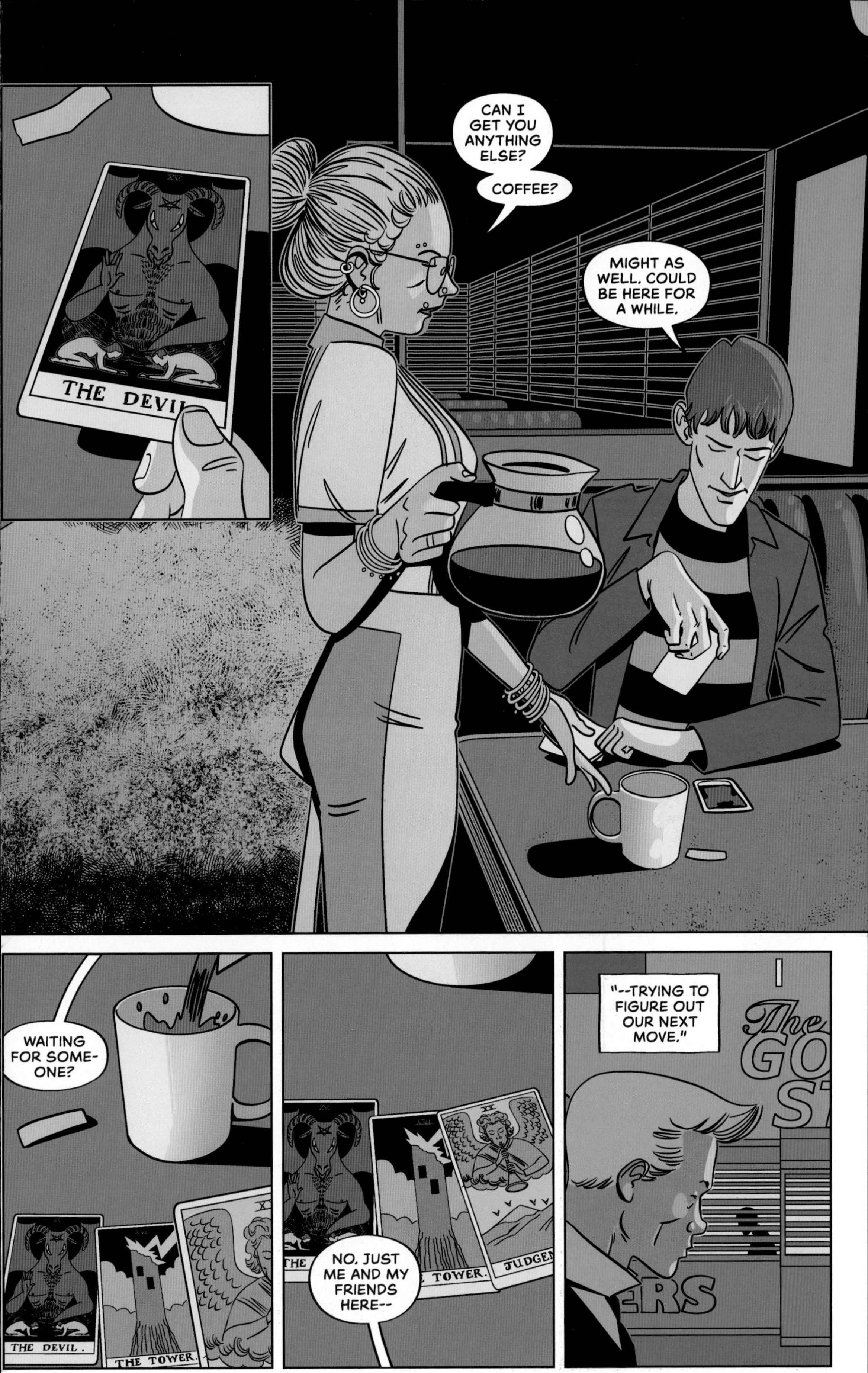
THE DEVIL
CAN I GET YOU ANYTHING ELSE?
COFFEE?
MIGHT AS WELL. COULD BE HERE FOR A WHILE.
WAITING FOR SOME-ONE?
THE DEVIL.
THE TOWER.
NO. JUST ME AND MY FRIENDS HERE--
THE TOWER.
"--TRYING TO FIGURE OUT OUR NEXT MOVE."

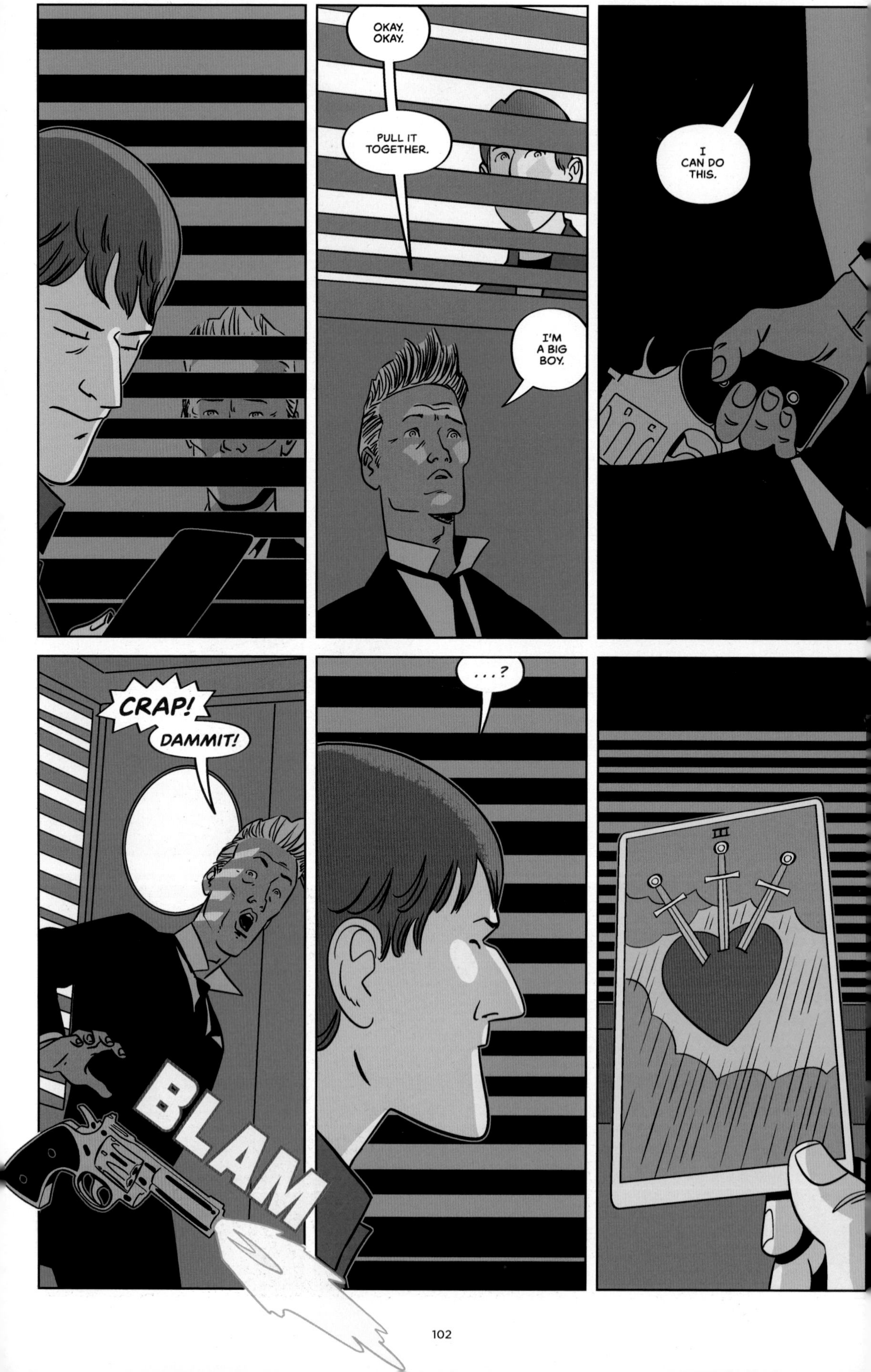
OKAY. OKAY.
PULL IT TOGETHER.
I'M A BIG BOY.
I CAN DO THIS.
CRAP!
DAMMIT!
BLAM
...?
III

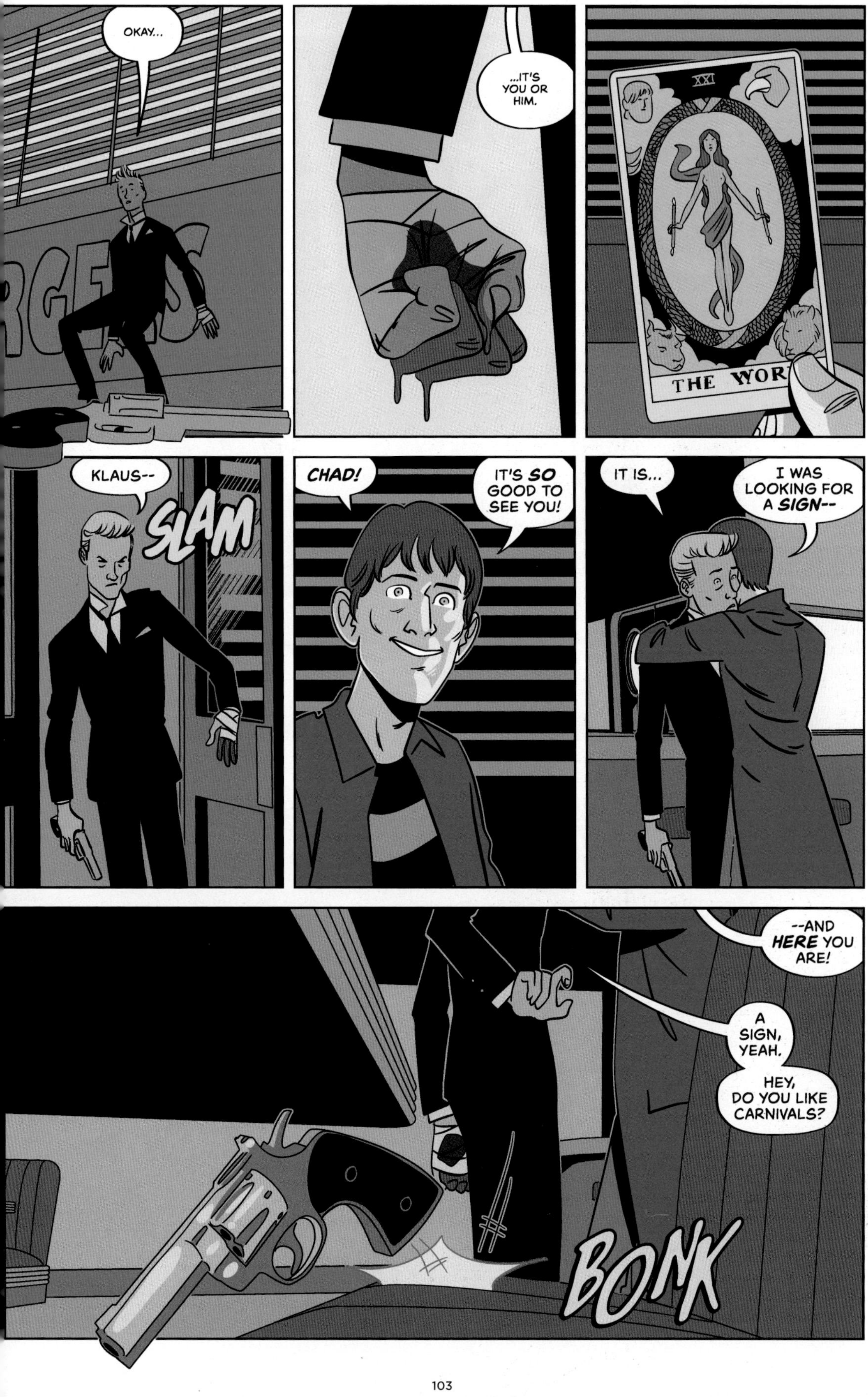
OKAY...
...IT'S YOU OR HIM.
XXI
THE WOR
KLAUS--
SLAM
CHAD!
IT'S SO GOOD TO SEE YOU!
IT IS...
I WAS LOOKING FOR A SIGN--
--AND HERE YOU ARE!
A SIGN, YEAH.
HEY, DO YOU LIKE CARNIVALS?
BONK

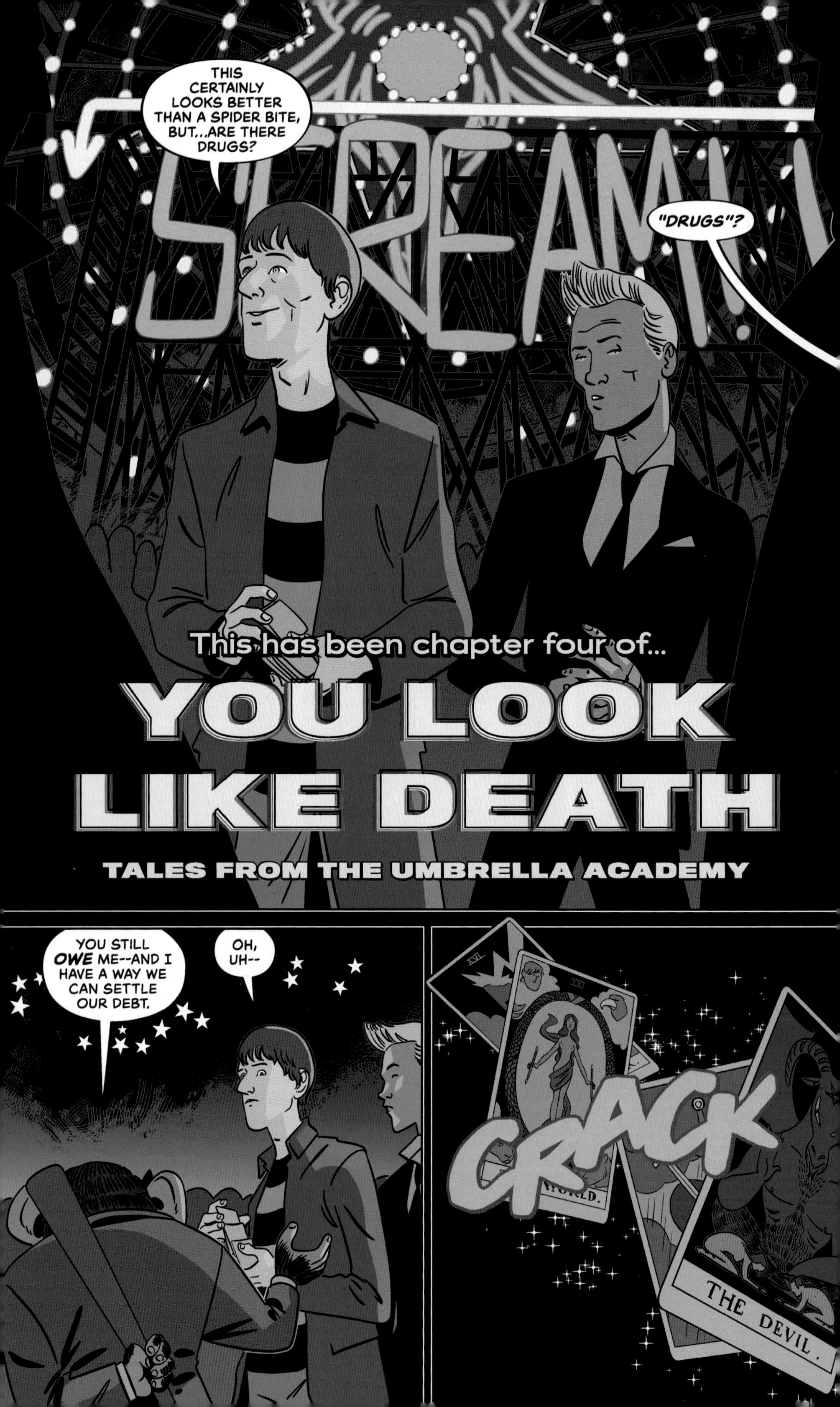
THIS CERTAINLY LOOKS BETTER THAN A SPIDER BITE, BUT...ARE THERE DRUGS?
"DRUGS"?
This has been chapter four of...
YOU LOOK LIKE DEATH
TALES FROM THE UMBRELLA ACADEMY
YOU STILL *OWE* ME--AND I HAVE A WAY WE CAN SETTLE OUR DEBT.
OH, UH--
CRACK
THE DEVIL.

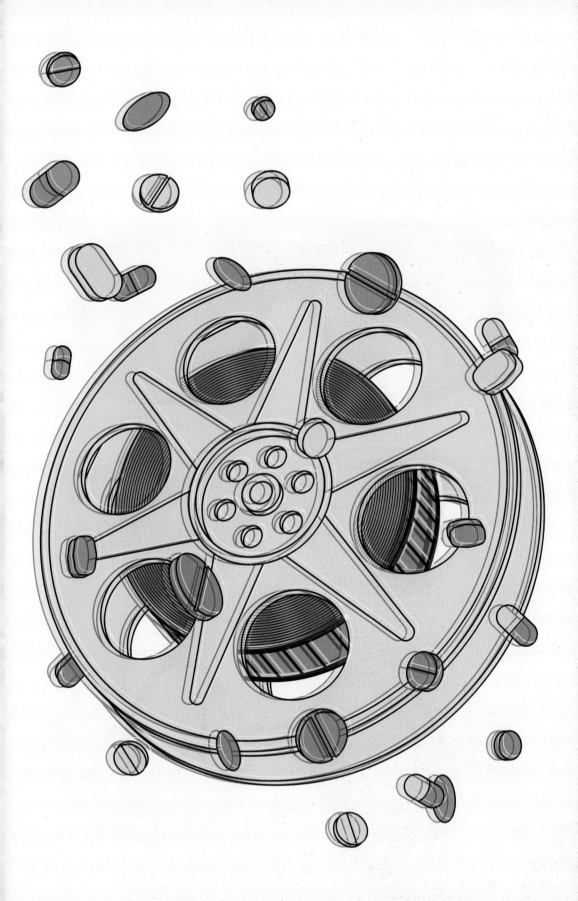

CHAPTER FIVE

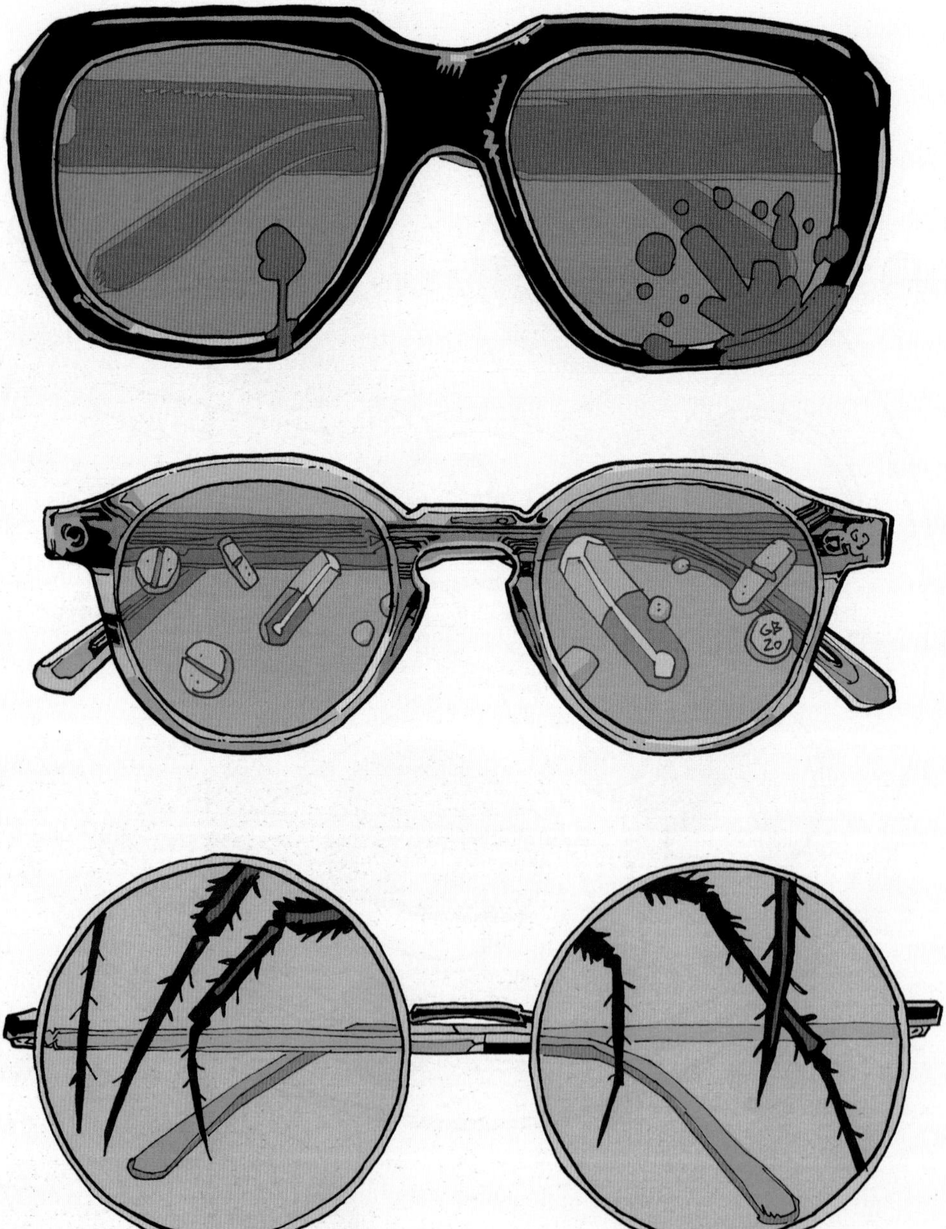

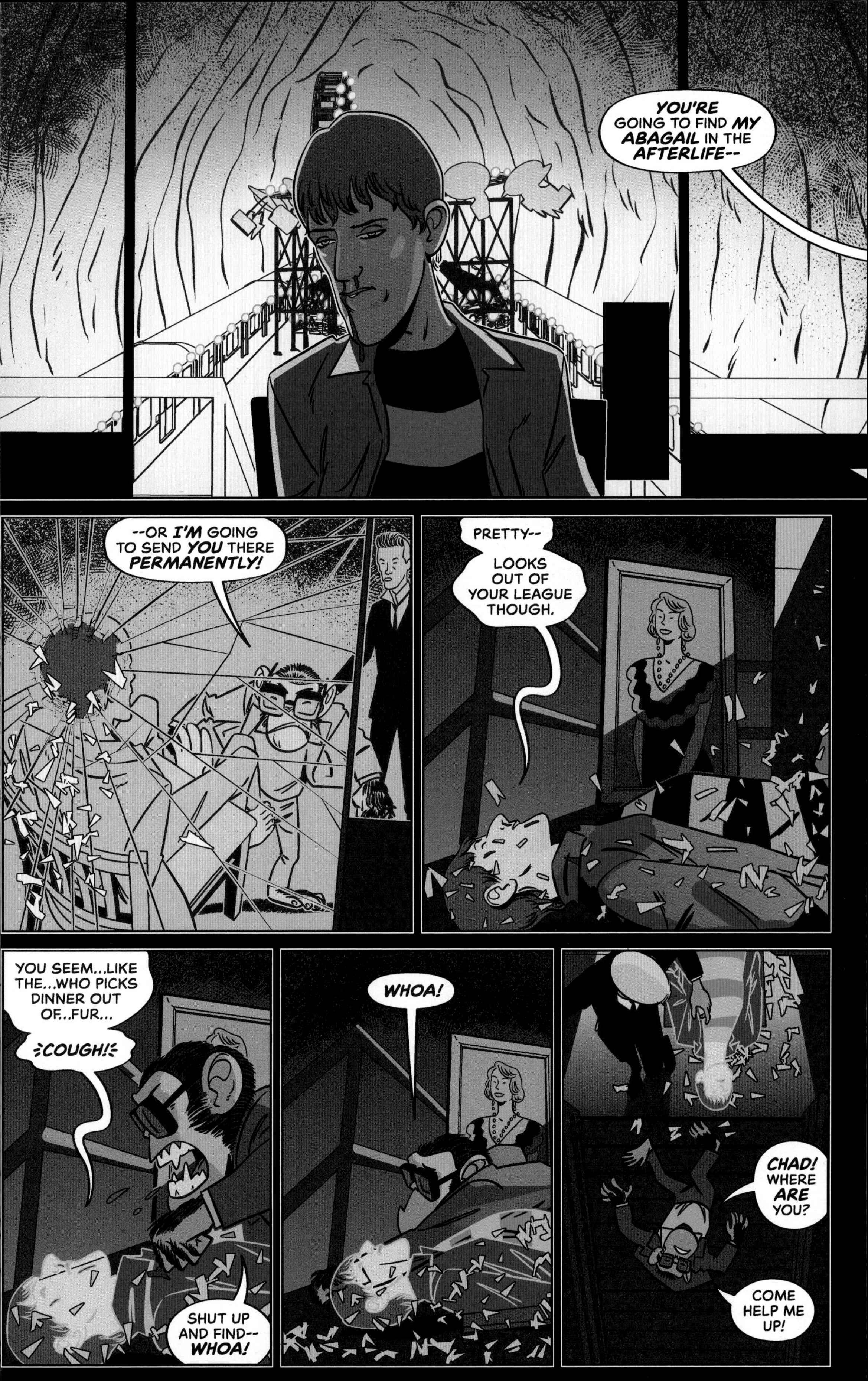

YOU'RE GOING TO FIND MY ABAGAIL IN THE AFTERLIFE--
--OR I'M GOING TO SEND YOU THERE PERMANENTLY!
PRETTY--
LOOKS OUT OF YOUR LEAGUE THOUGH.
YOU SEEM...LIKE THE...WHO PICKS DINNER OUT OF...FUR...
COUGH!
SHUT UP AND FIND-- WHOA!
WHOA!
CHAD! WHERE ARE YOU?
COME HELP ME UP!

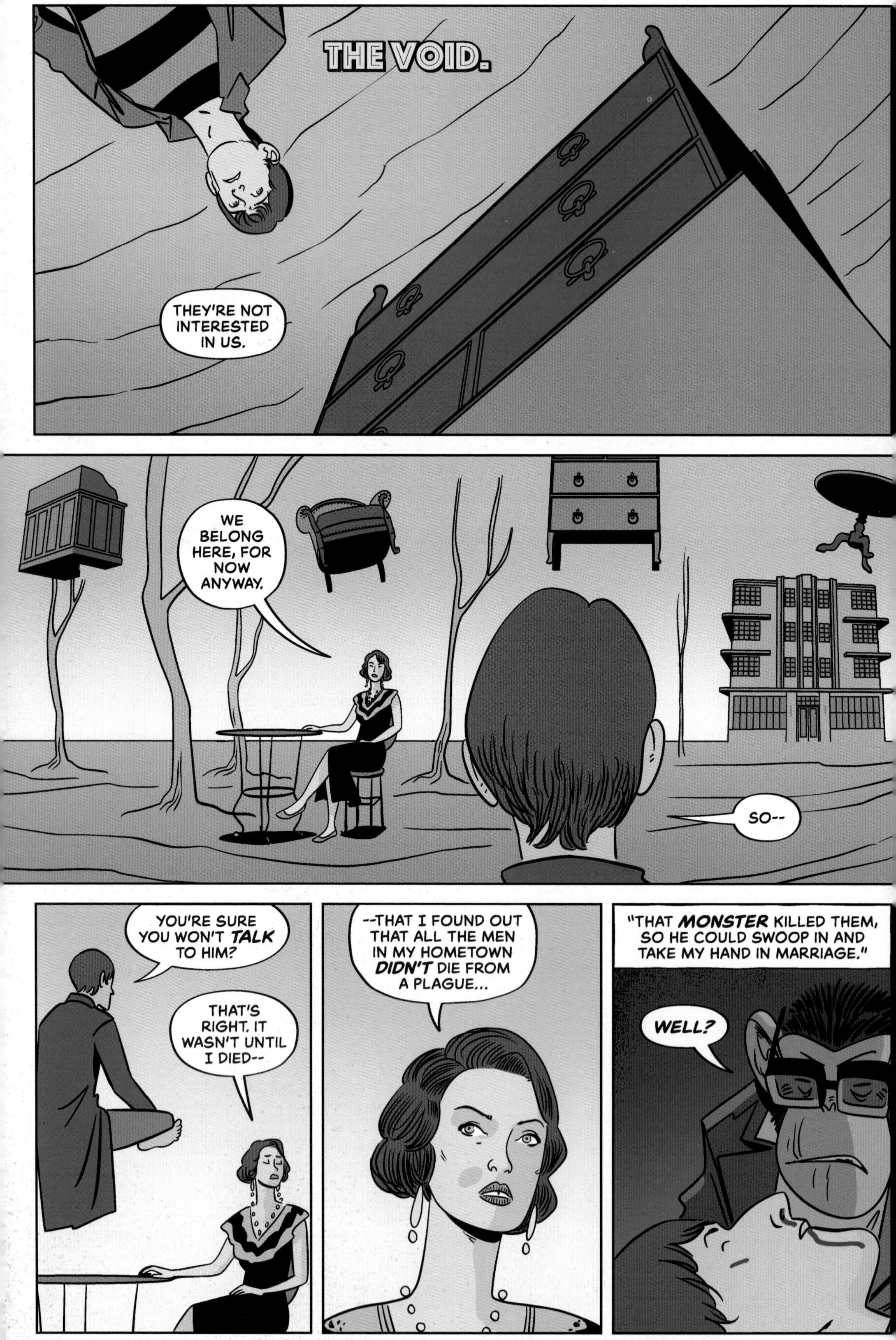
THE VOID.
THEY'RE NOT INTERESTED IN US.
WE BELONG HERE, FOR NOW ANYWAY.
SO--
YOU'RE SURE YOU WON'T TALK TO HIM?
THAT'S RIGHT. IT WASN'T UNTIL I DIED--
--THAT I FOUND OUT THAT ALL THE MEN IN MY HOMETOWN DIDN'T DIE FROM A PLAGUE...
"THAT MONSTER KILLED THEM, SO HE COULD SWOOP IN AND TAKE MY HAND IN MARRIAGE."
WELL?

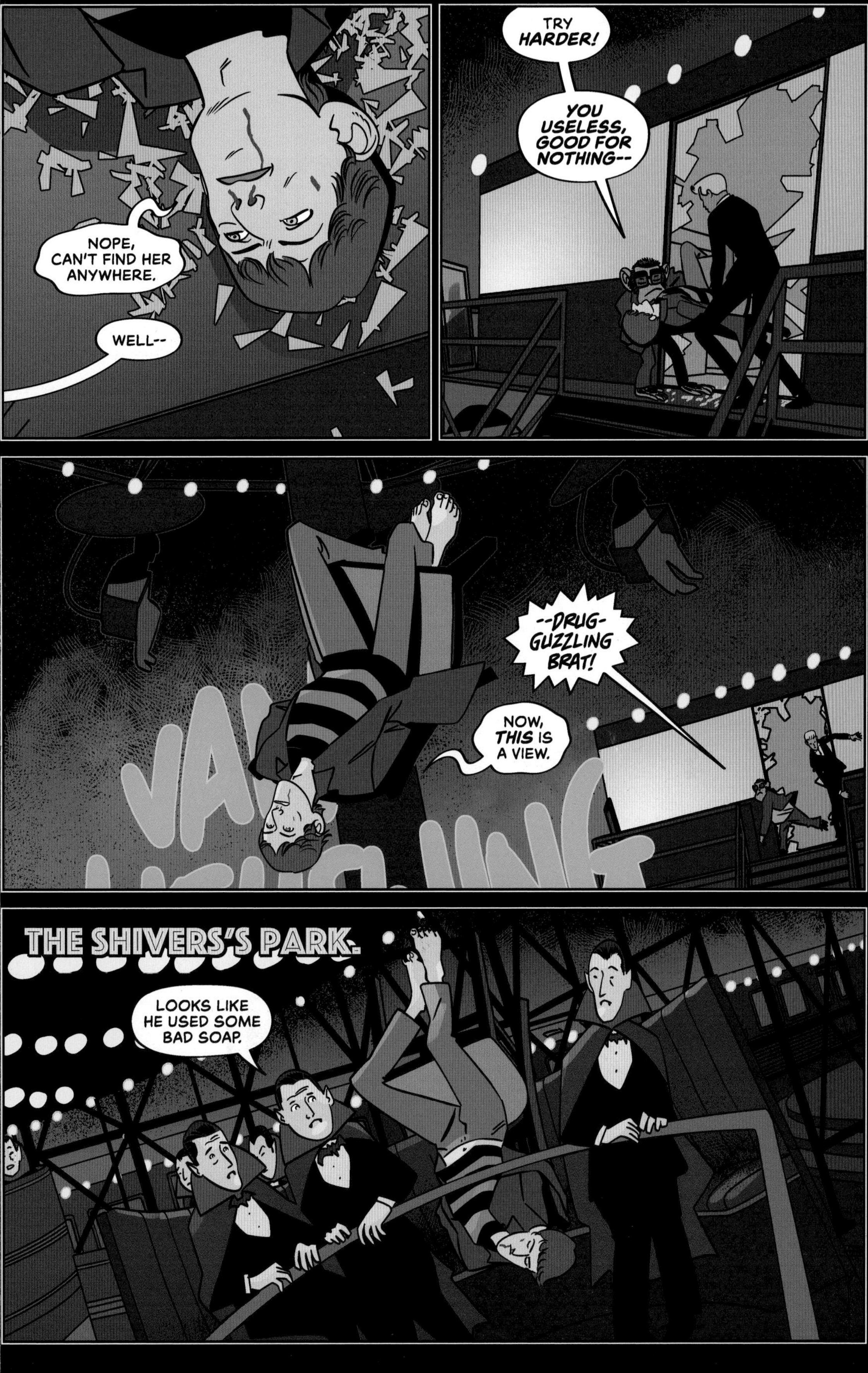
NOPE, CAN'T FIND HER ANYWHERE.
WELL--
TRY HARDER!
YOU USELESS, GOOD FOR NOTHING--
--DRUG-GUZZLING BRAT!
NOW, THIS IS A VIEW.
THE SHIVERS'S PARK.
LOOKS LIKE HE USED SOME BAD SOAP.

THE VOID.
MORE COFFEE?
NO--
The end
I THINK I'M DONE HERE.
THE END
AGENTS--
poof
THE UMBRELLA ACADEMY.
FETCH ME NUMBER FOUR.
HIS MOTHER IS BEING DIFFICULT AGAIN.

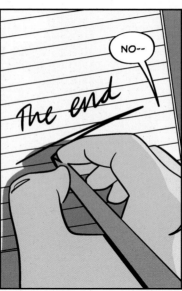

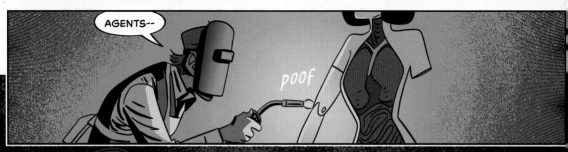

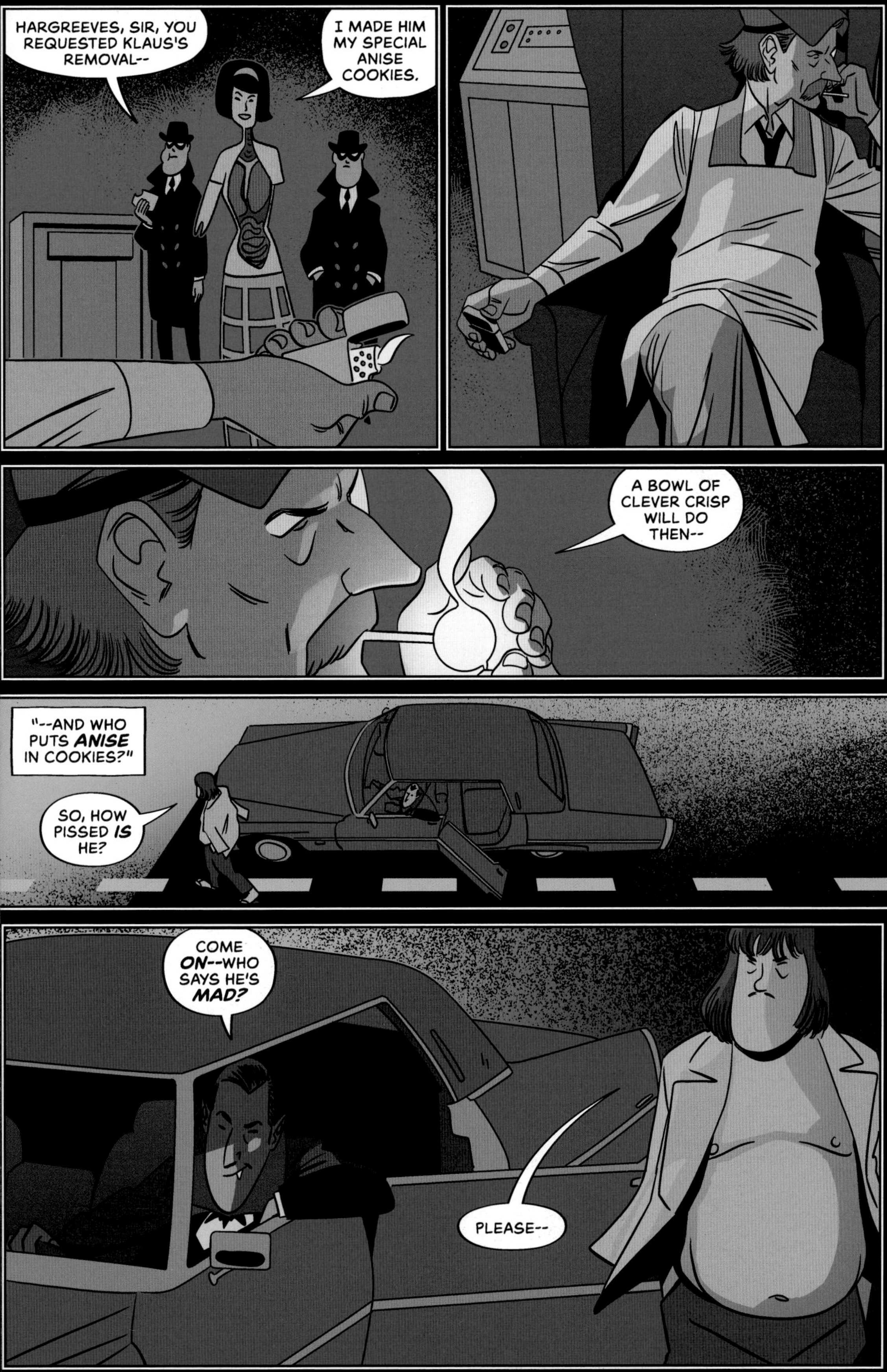
HARGREEVES, SIR, YOU REQUESTED KLAUS'S REMOVAL--
I MADE HIM MY SPECIAL ANISE COOKIES.
A BOWL OF CLEVER CRISP WILL DO THEN--
"--AND WHO PUTS ANISE IN COOKIES?"
SO, HOW PISSED IS HE?
COME ON--WHO SAYS HE'S MAD?
PLEASE--

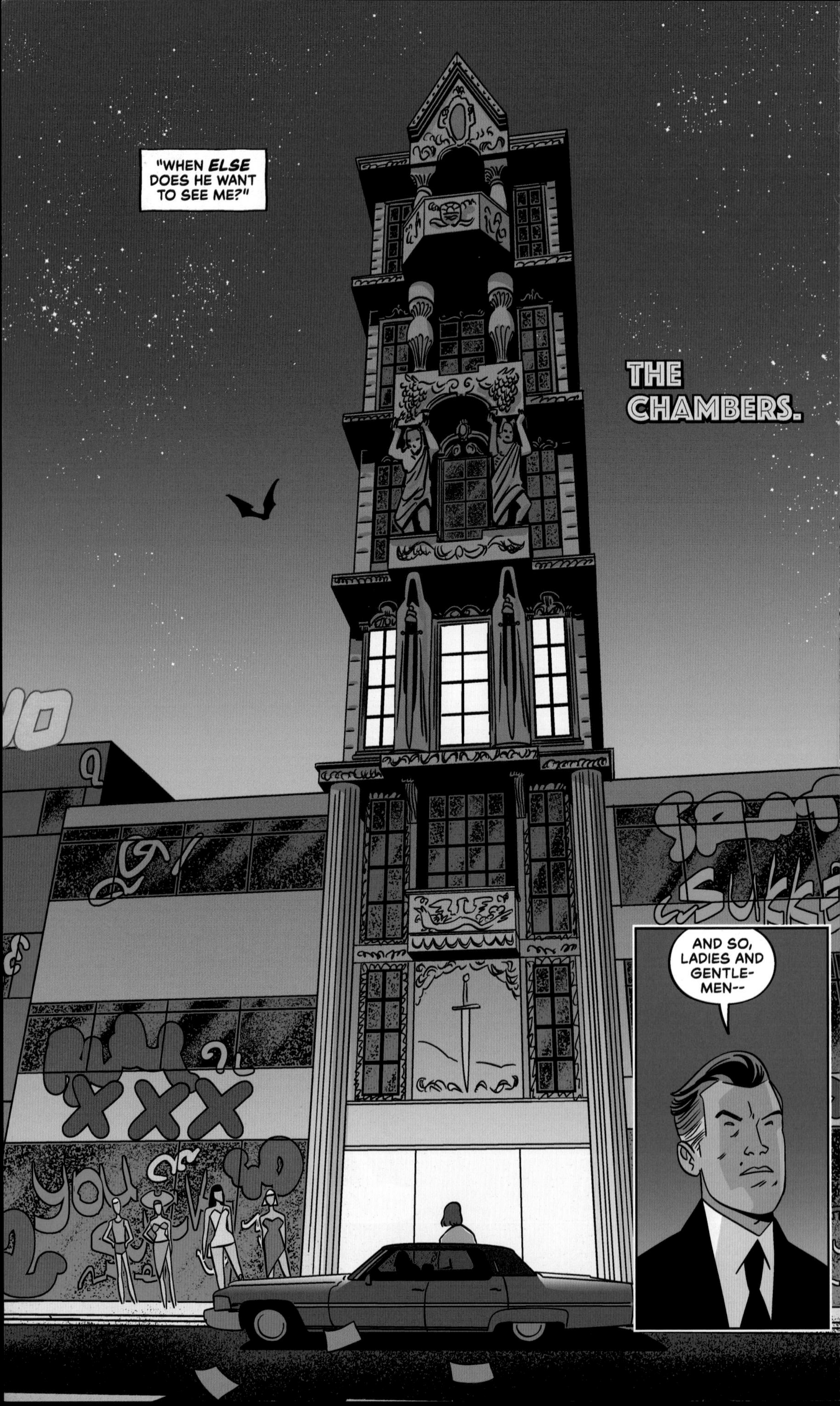
"WHEN ELSE DOES HE WANT TO SEE ME?"
THE CHAMBERS.
AND SO, LADIES AND GENTLE-MEN--

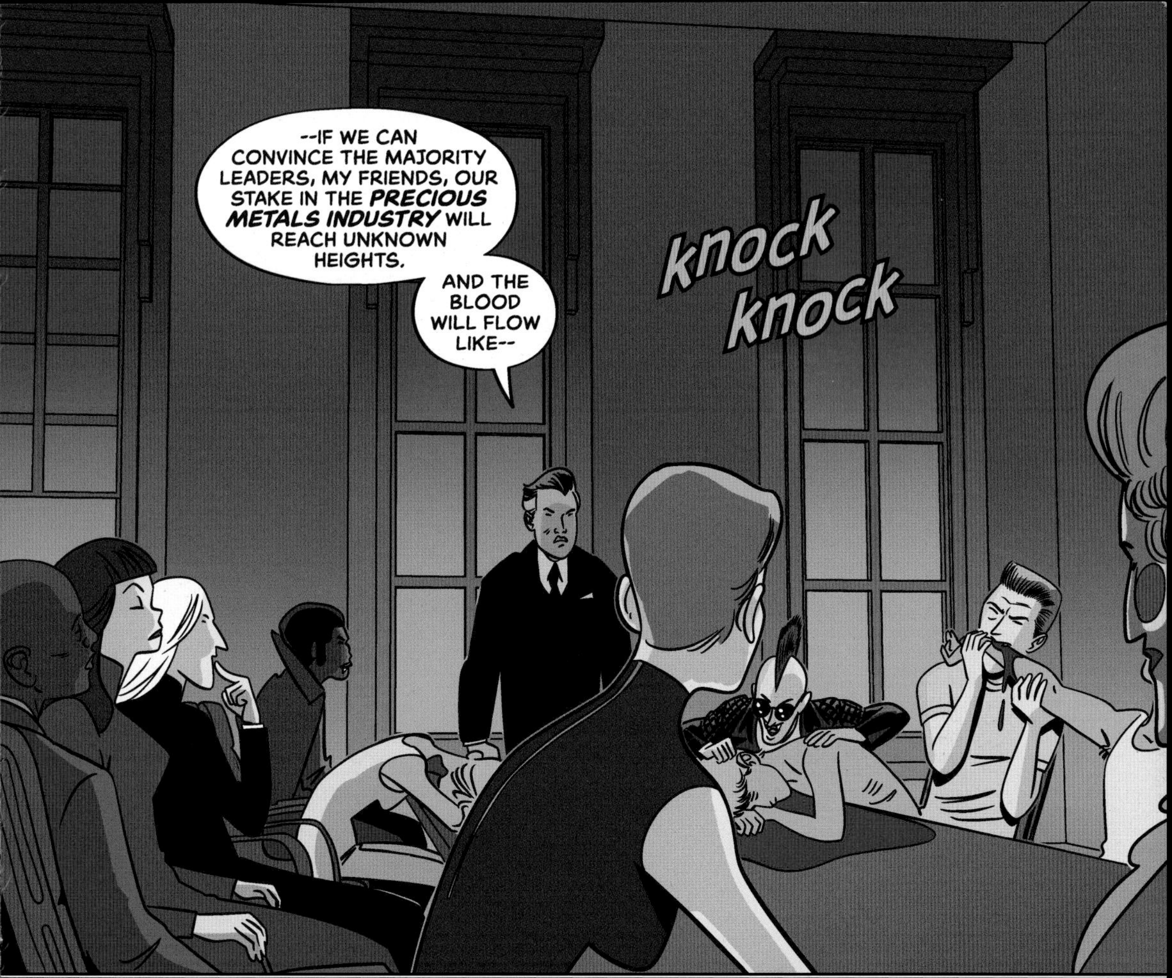
--IF WE CAN CONVINCE THE MAJORITY LEADERS, MY FRIENDS, OUR STAKE IN THE **PRECIOUS METALS INDUSTRY** WILL REACH UNKNOWN HEIGHTS.
AND THE BLOOD WILL FLOW LIKE--
knock knock

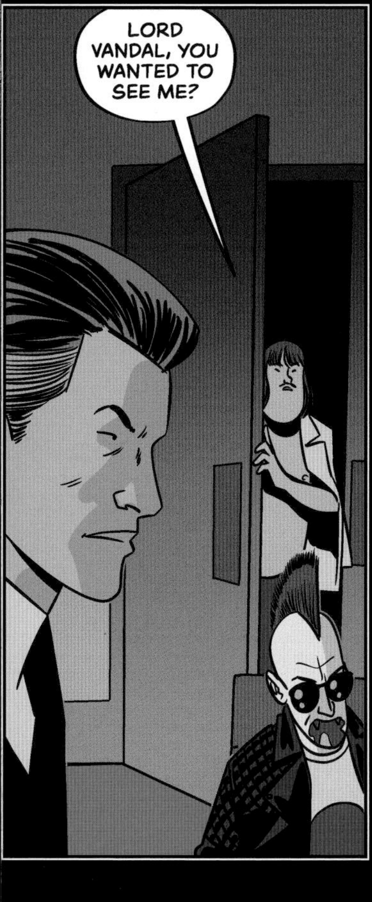
LORD VANDAL, YOU WANTED TO SEE ME?

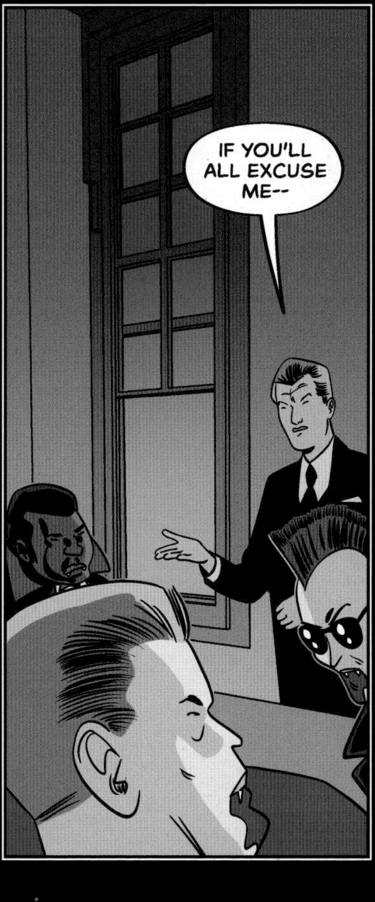
IF YOU'LL ALL EXCUSE ME--

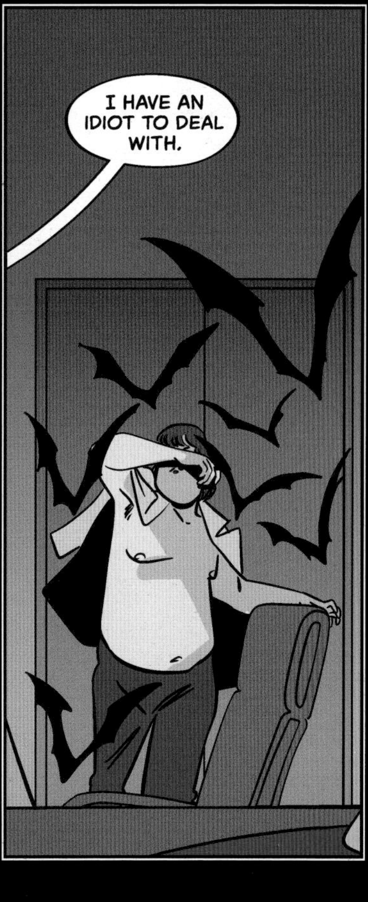
I HAVE AN IDIOT TO DEAL WITH.

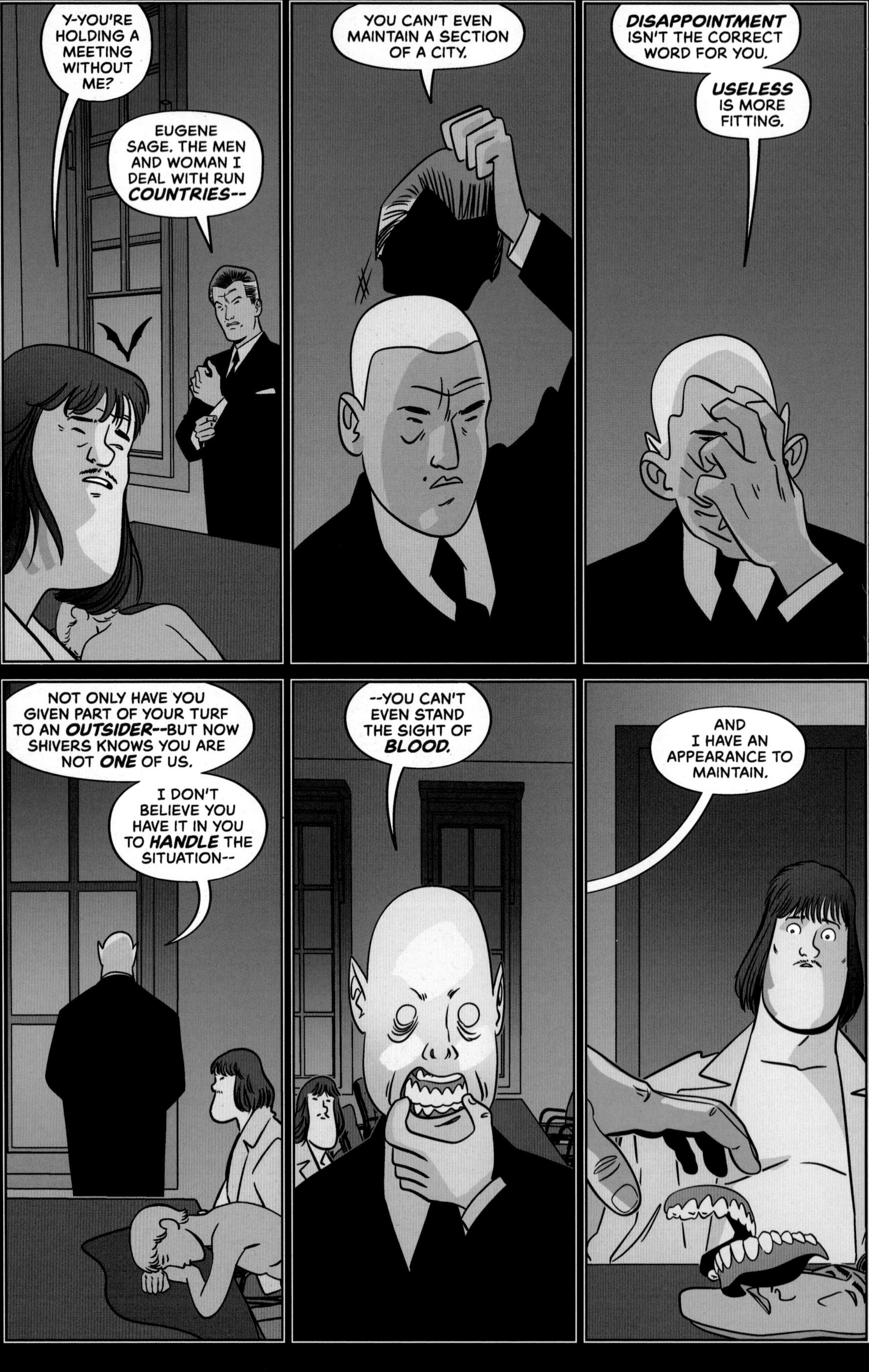
Y-YOU'RE HOLDING A MEETING WITHOUT ME?
EUGENE SAGE. THE MEN AND WOMAN I DEAL WITH RUN COUNTRIES--
YOU CAN'T EVEN MAINTAIN A SECTION OF A CITY.
DISAPPOINTMENT ISN'T THE CORRECT WORD FOR YOU.
USELESS IS MORE FITTING.
NOT ONLY HAVE YOU GIVEN PART OF YOUR TURF TO AN OUTSIDER--BUT NOW SHIVERS KNOWS YOU ARE NOT ONE OF US.
I DON'T BELIEVE YOU HAVE IT IN YOU TO HANDLE THE SITUATION--
--YOU CAN'T EVEN STAND THE SIGHT OF BLOOD.
AND I HAVE AN APPEARANCE TO MAINTAIN.

"I WILL GIVE YOU A CHANCE TO **CORRECT** THIS, BUT IN THE MEANTIME--

"I CAN NO LONGER BE ASSOCIATED WITH OR **PROTECT** YOU. YOU WILL BE **CUT OFF.**

"YOU HAVE FAILED ME AND THIS FAMILY."

HOW DID IT GO?

AH, HE'LL COME AROUND.

YOU KNOW YOUR DAD.

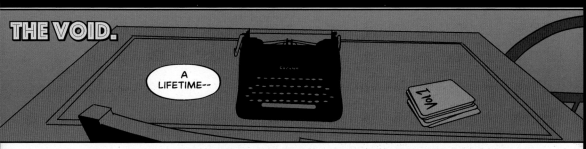

THE VOID.

A LIFETIME--

--AND THIS IS WHAT I HAVE TO SHOW FOR IT.

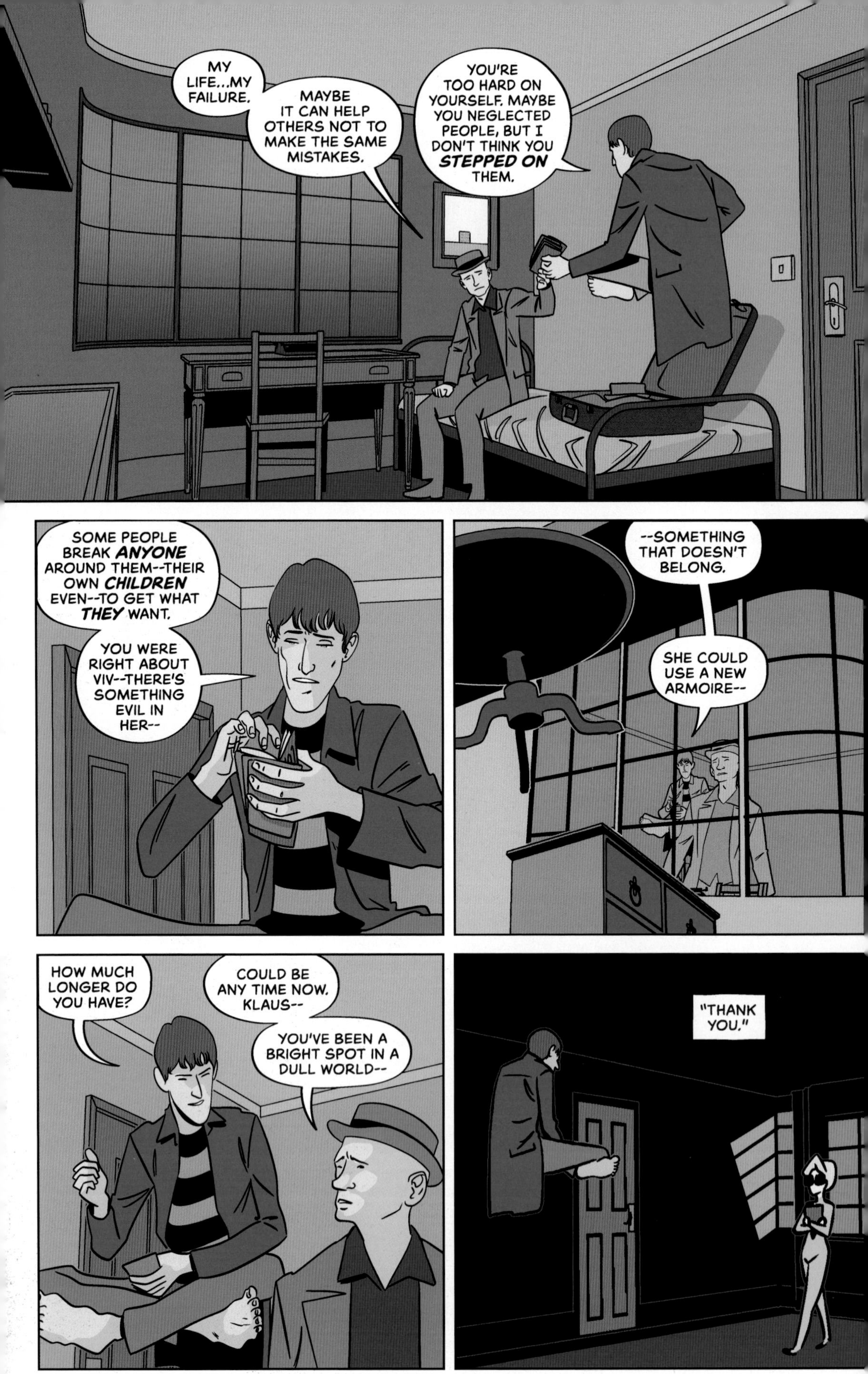
MY LIFE...MY FAILURE.
MAYBE IT CAN HELP OTHERS NOT TO MAKE THE SAME MISTAKES.
YOU'RE TOO HARD ON YOURSELF. MAYBE YOU NEGLECTED PEOPLE, BUT I DON'T THINK YOU *STEPPED ON* THEM.
SOME PEOPLE BREAK *ANYONE* AROUND THEM--THEIR OWN *CHILDREN* EVEN--TO GET WHAT *THEY* WANT.
YOU WERE RIGHT ABOUT VIV--THERE'S SOMETHING EVIL IN HER--
--SOMETHING THAT DOESN'T BELONG.
SHE COULD USE A NEW ARMOIRE--
HOW MUCH LONGER DO YOU HAVE?
COULD BE ANY TIME NOW. KLAUS--
YOU'VE BEEN A BRIGHT SPOT IN A DULL WORLD--
"THANK YOU."

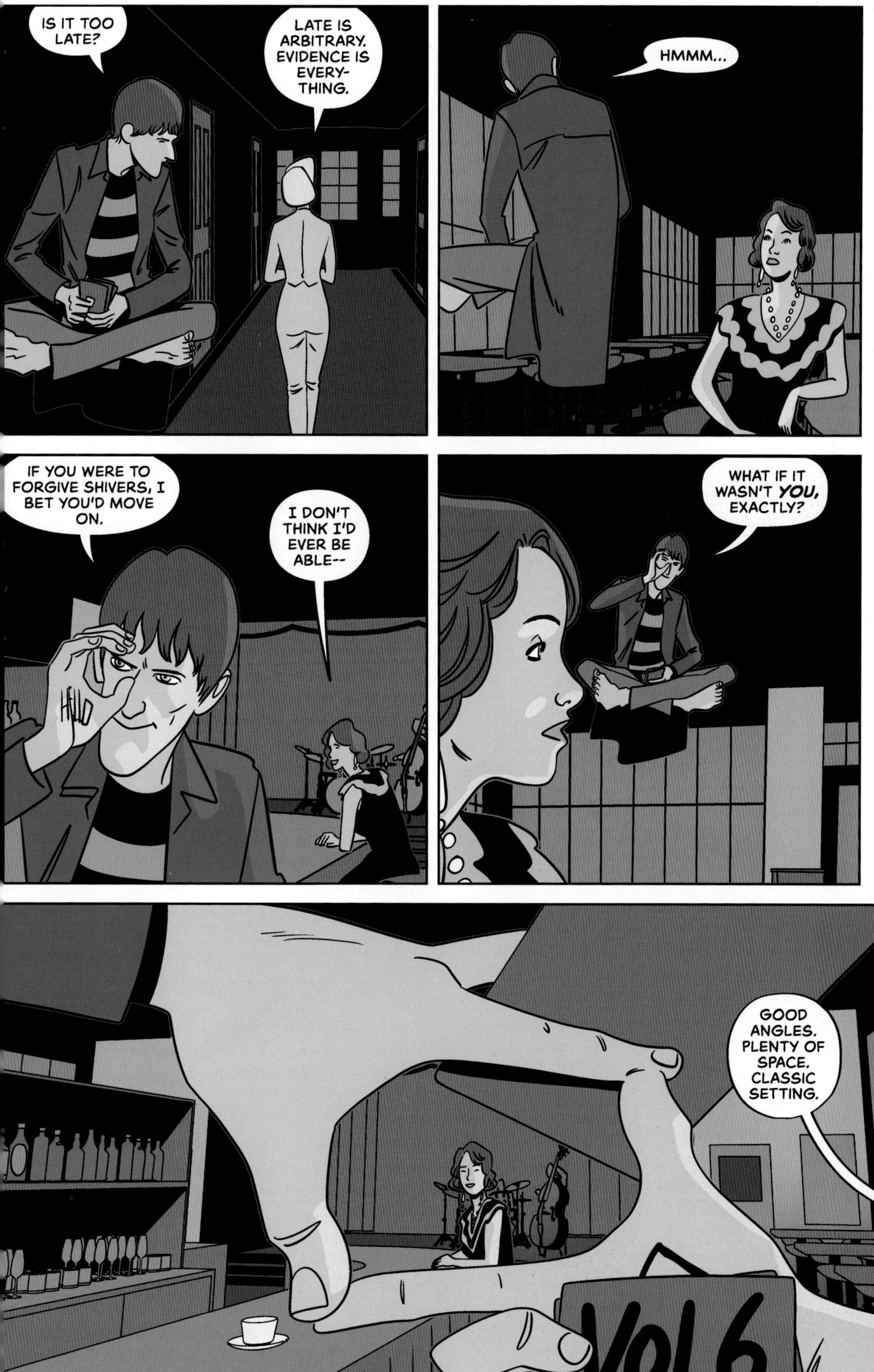
IS IT TOO LATE?
LATE IS ARBITRARY. EVIDENCE IS EVERY-THING.
HMMM...
IF YOU WERE TO FORGIVE SHIVERS, I BET YOU'D MOVE ON.
I DON'T THINK I'D EVER BE ABLE--
HELLO
WHAT IF IT WASN'T *YOU,* EXACTLY?
GOOD ANGLES. PLENTY OF SPACE. CLASSIC SETTING.
VOL 6

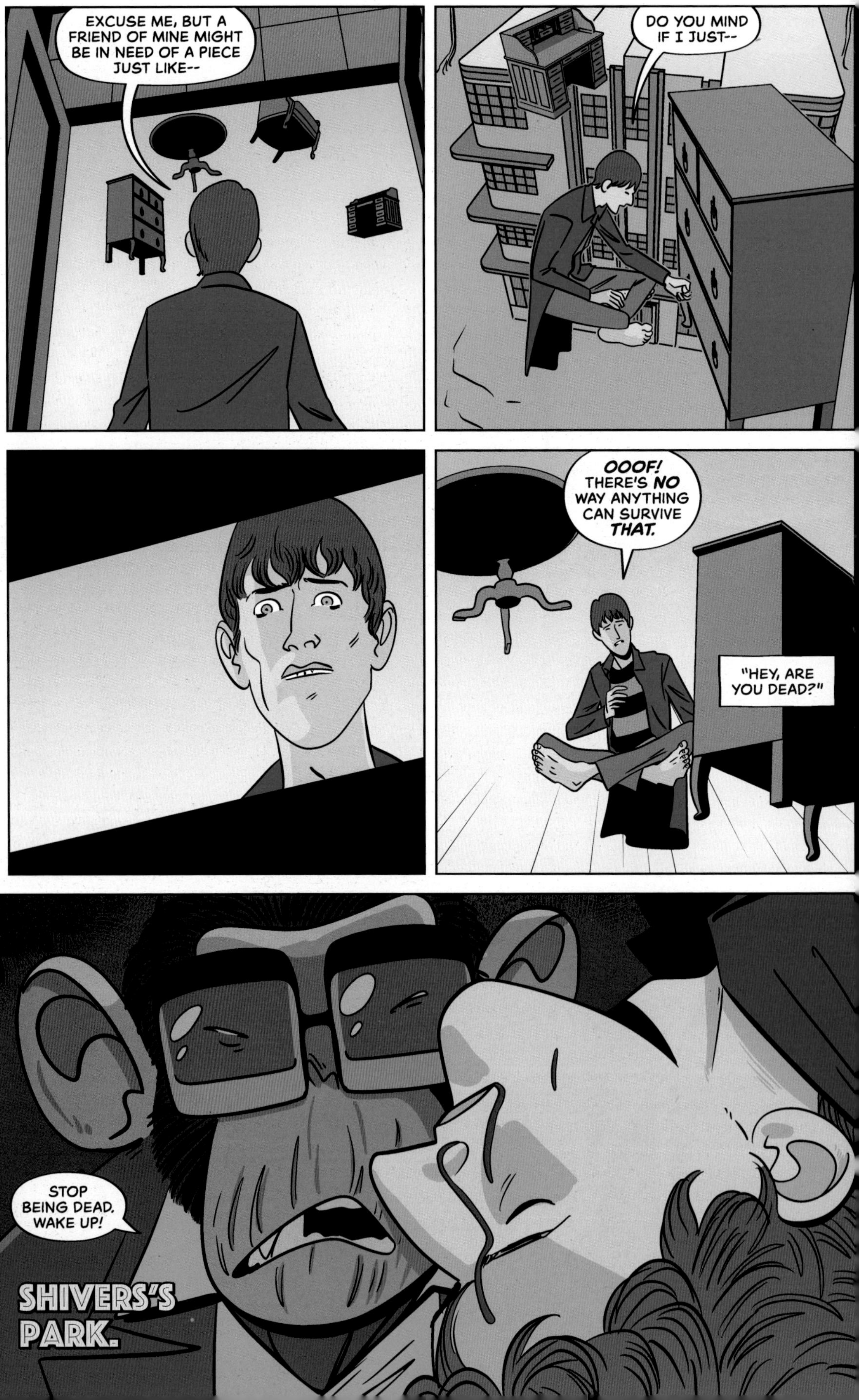

EXCUSE ME, BUT A FRIEND OF MINE MIGHT BE IN NEED OF A PIECE JUST LIKE--
DO YOU MIND IF I JUST--
OOOF! THERE'S NO WAY ANYTHING CAN SURVIVE THAT.
"HEY, ARE YOU DEAD?"
STOP BEING DEAD. WAKE UP!
SHIVERS'S PARK.

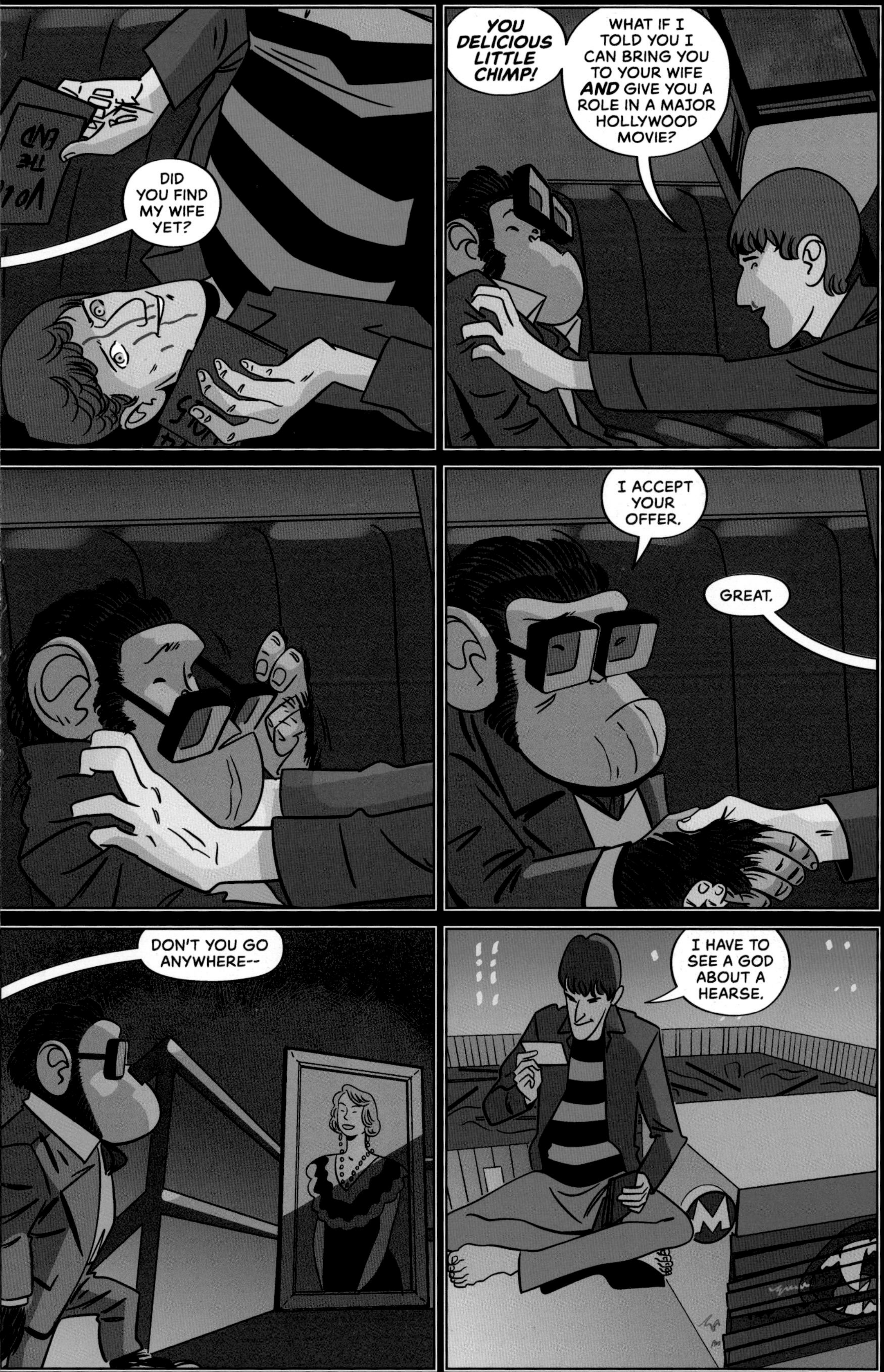
DID YOU FIND MY WIFE YET?
YOU DELICIOUS LITTLE CHIMP!
WHAT IF I TOLD YOU I CAN BRING YOU TO YOUR WIFE AND GIVE YOU A ROLE IN A MAJOR HOLLYWOOD MOVIE?
I ACCEPT YOUR OFFER.
GREAT.
DON'T YOU GO ANYWHERE--
I HAVE TO SEE A GOD ABOUT A HEARSE.

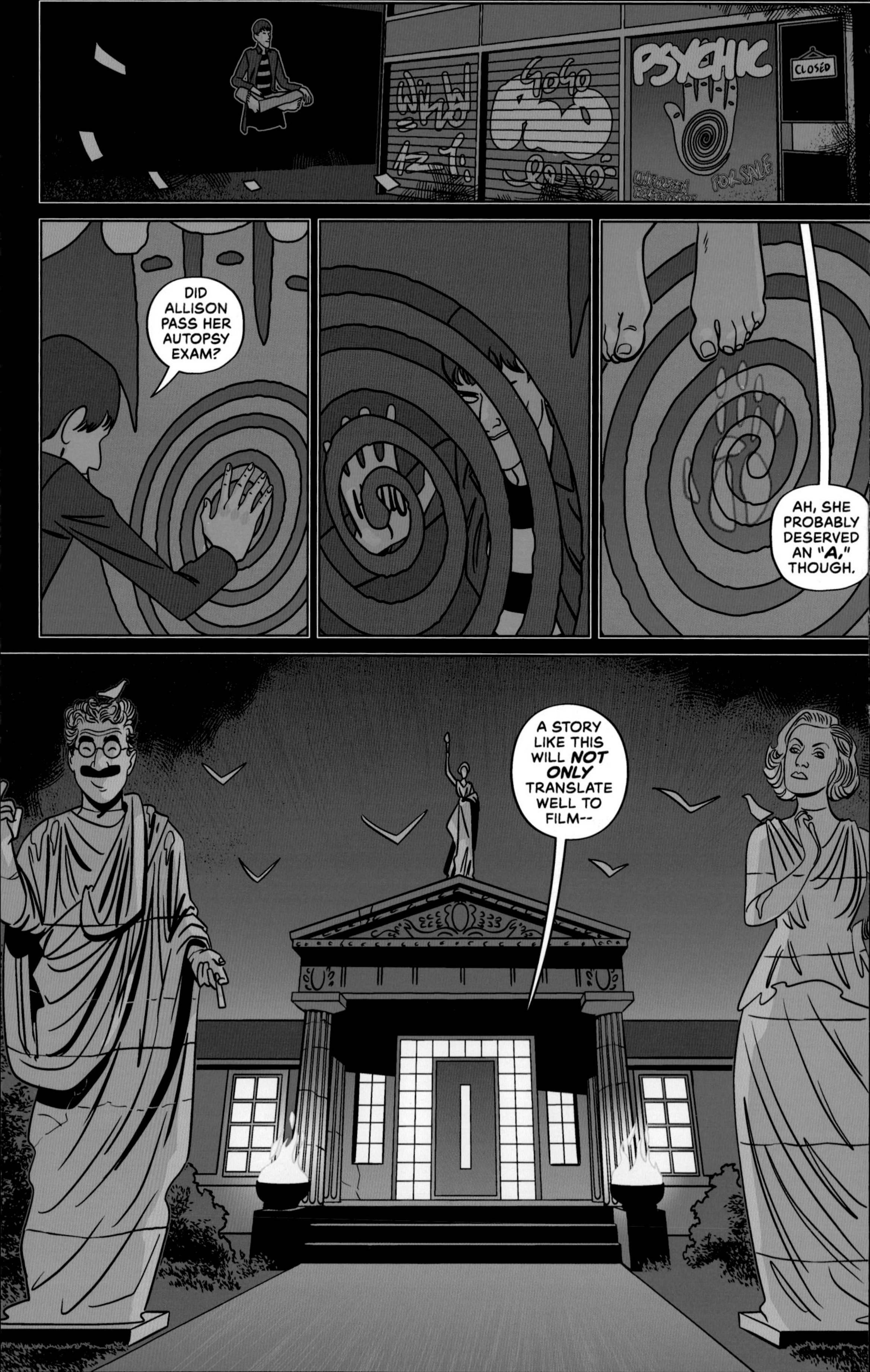
PSYCHIC
CLOSED
FOR SALE
DID ALLISON PASS HER AUTOPSY EXAM?
AH, SHE PROBABLY DESERVED AN "A," THOUGH.
A STORY LIKE THIS WILL NOT ONLY TRANSLATE WELL TO FILM--

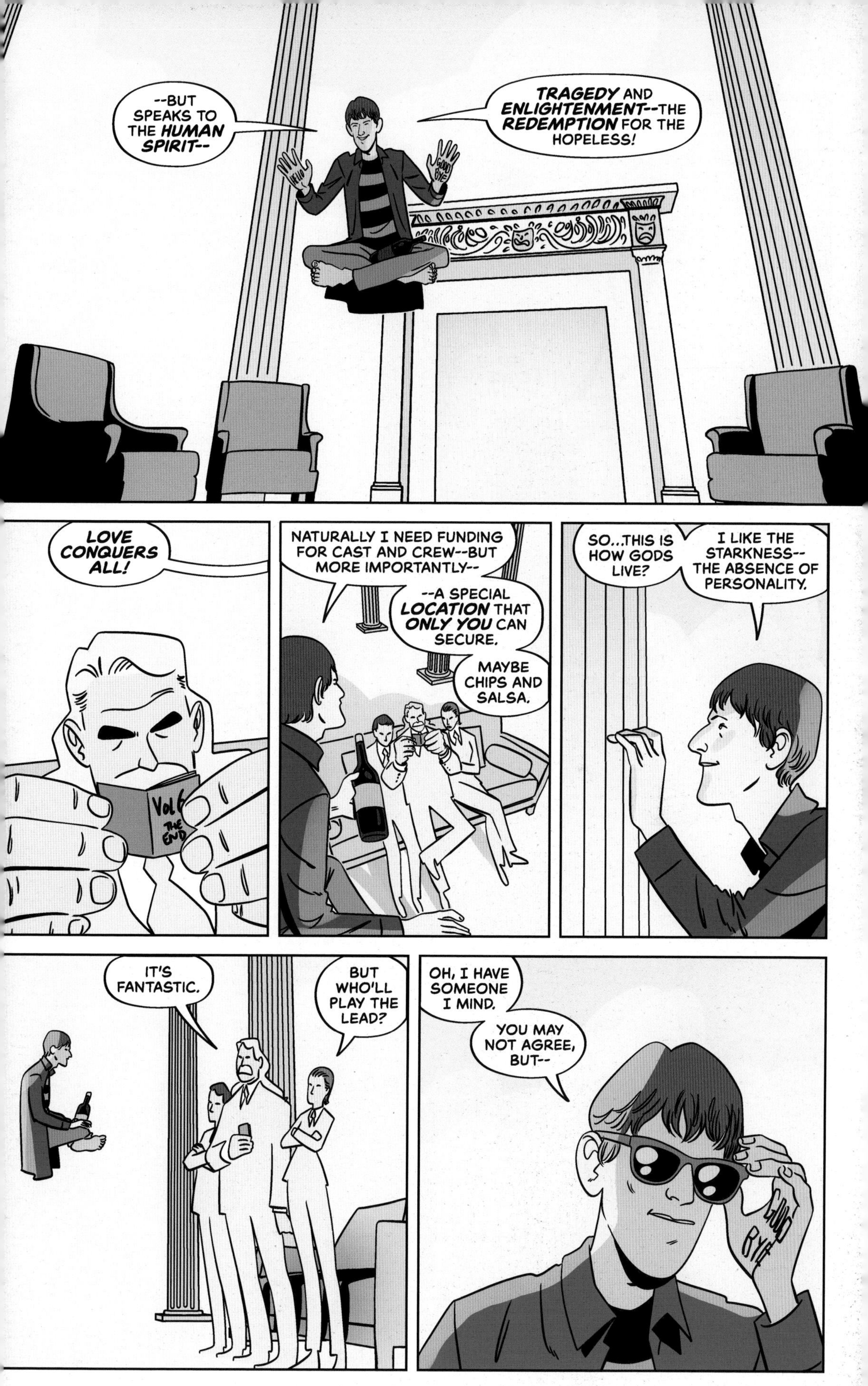

--BUT SPEAKS TO THE HUMAN SPIRIT--
TRAGEDY AND ENLIGHTENMENT--THE REDEMPTION FOR THE HOPELESS!
HELLO
GOOD BYE
LOVE CONQUERS ALL!
Vol 6 THE END
NATURALLY I NEED FUNDING FOR CAST AND CREW--BUT MORE IMPORTANTLY--
--A SPECIAL LOCATION THAT ONLY YOU CAN SECURE.
MAYBE CHIPS AND SALSA.
SO...THIS IS HOW GODS LIVE?
I LIKE THE STARKNESS--THE ABSENCE OF PERSONALITY.
IT'S FANTASTIC.
BUT WHO'LL PLAY THE LEAD?
OH, I HAVE SOMEONE I MIND.
YOU MAY NOT AGREE, BUT--
GOOD BYE

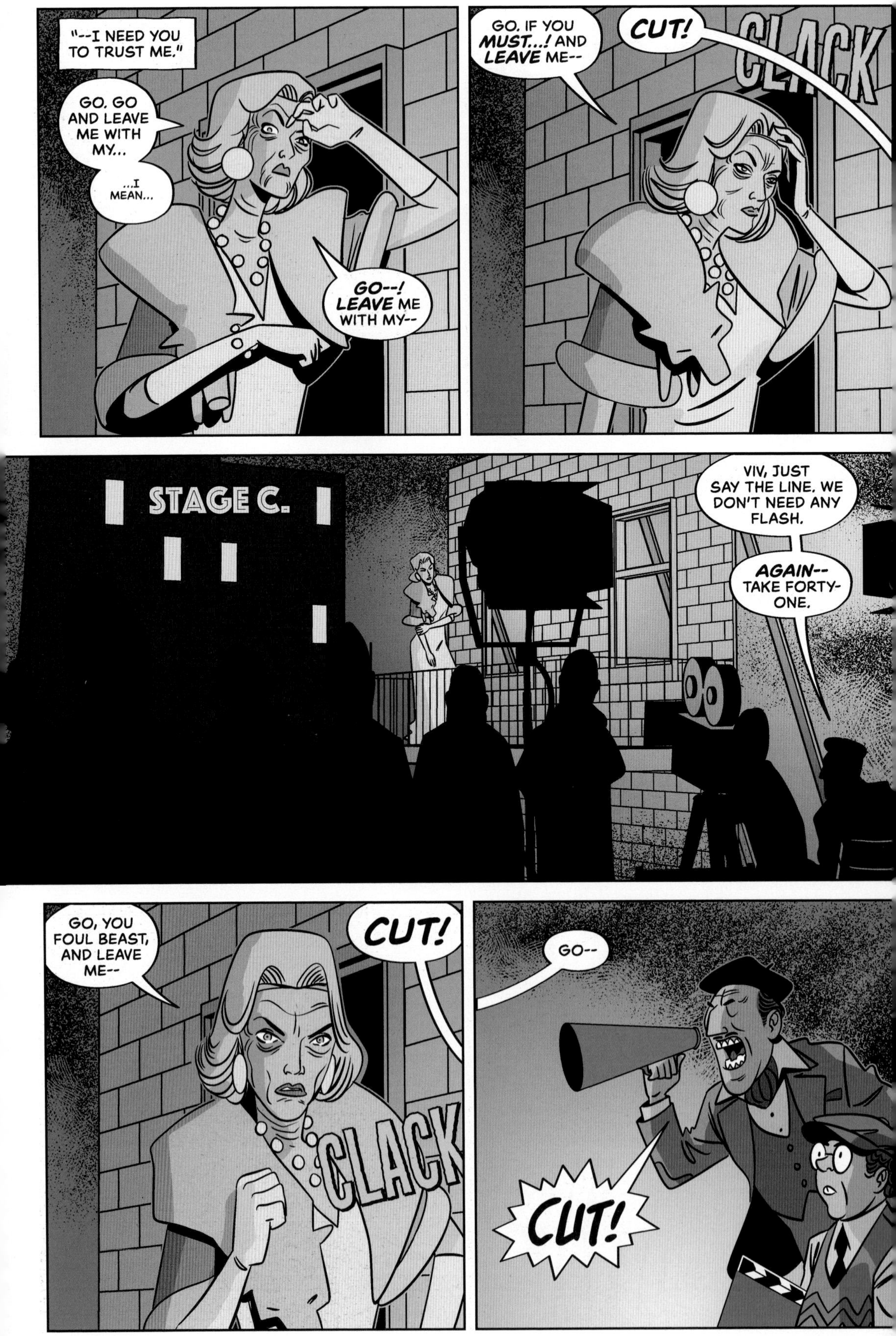
"--I NEED YOU TO TRUST ME."
GO, GO AND LEAVE ME WITH MY...
...I MEAN...
GO--! LEAVE ME WITH MY--
GO, IF YOU MUST...! AND LEAVE ME--
CUT!
CLACK
STAGE C.
VIV, JUST SAY THE LINE. WE DON'T NEED ANY FLASH.
AGAIN-- TAKE FORTY-ONE.
GO, YOU FOUL BEAST, AND LEAVE ME--
CUT!
CLACK
GO--
CUT!

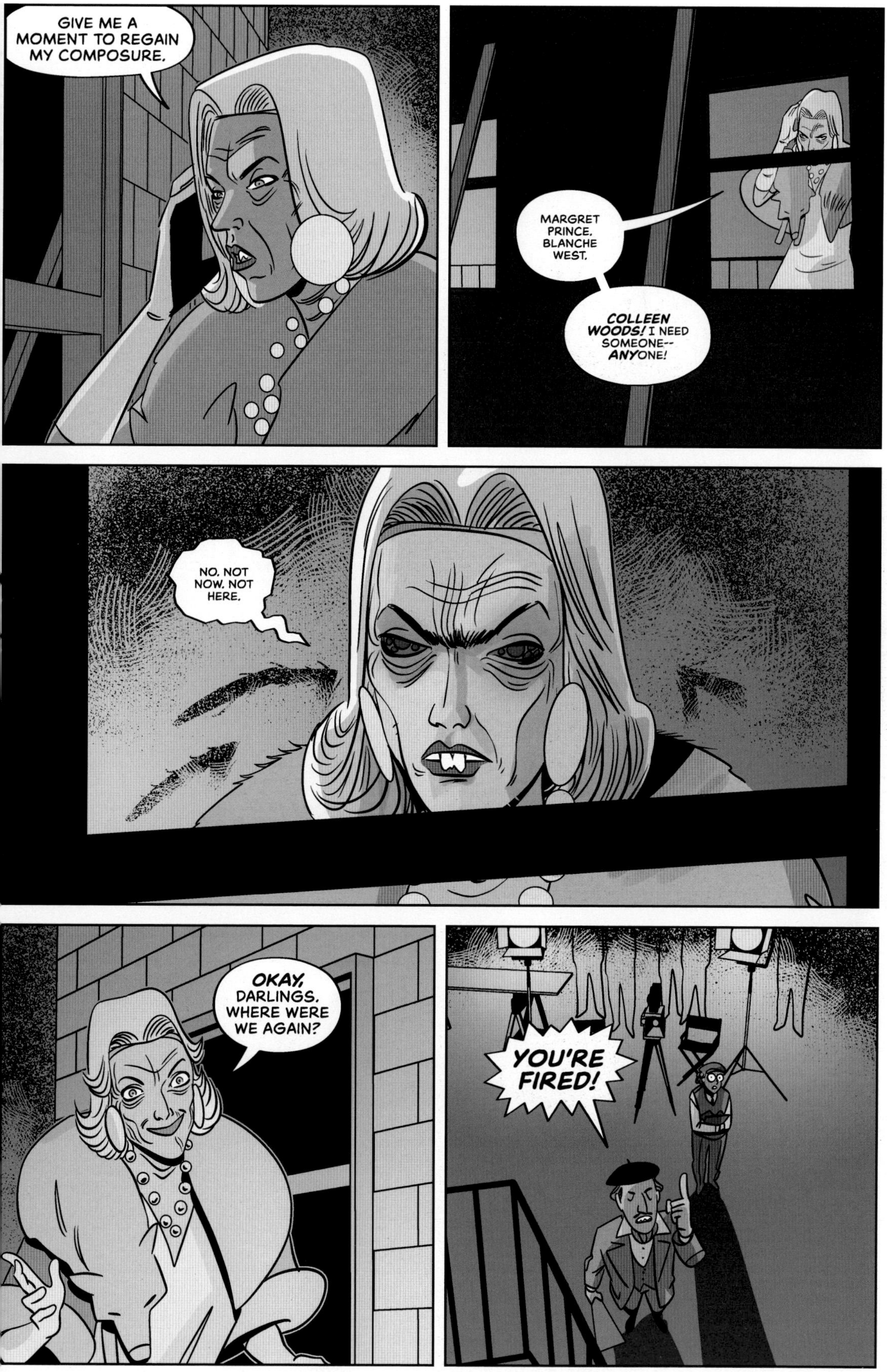
GIVE ME A MOMENT TO REGAIN MY COMPOSURE.
MARGRET PRINCE. BLANCHE WEST.
COLLEEN WOODS! I NEED SOMEONE-- ANYONE!
NO. NOT NOW. NOT HERE.
OKAY, DARLINGS. WHERE WERE WE AGAIN?
YOU'RE FIRED!

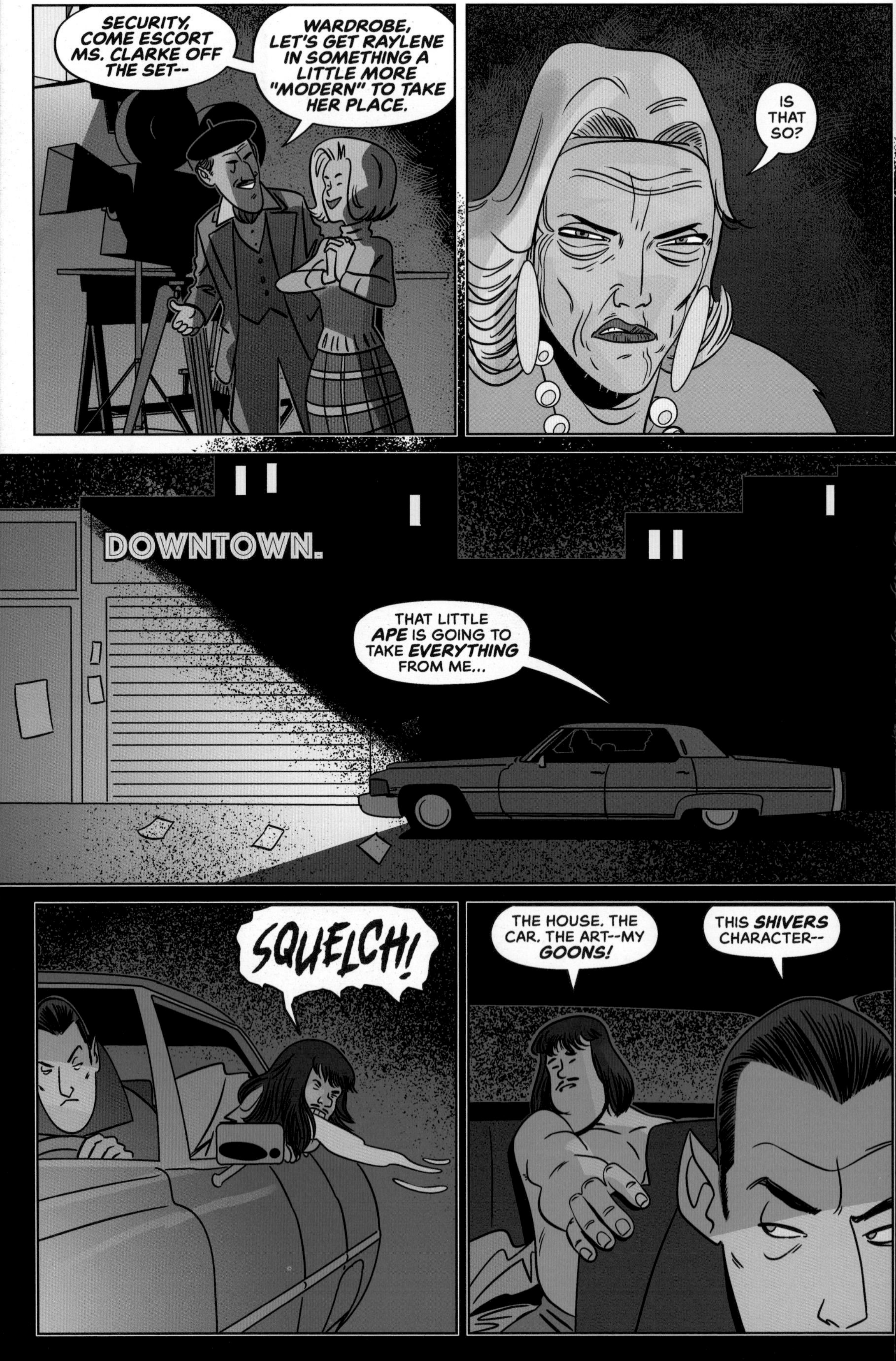
SECURITY, COME ESCORT MS. CLARKE OFF THE SET--
WARDROBE, LET'S GET RAYLENE IN SOMETHING A LITTLE MORE "MODERN" TO TAKE HER PLACE.
IS THAT SO?
DOWNTOWN.
THAT LITTLE APE IS GOING TO TAKE EVERYTHING FROM ME...
SQUELCH!
THE HOUSE. THE CAR. THE ART--MY GOONS!
THIS SHIVERS CHARACTER--

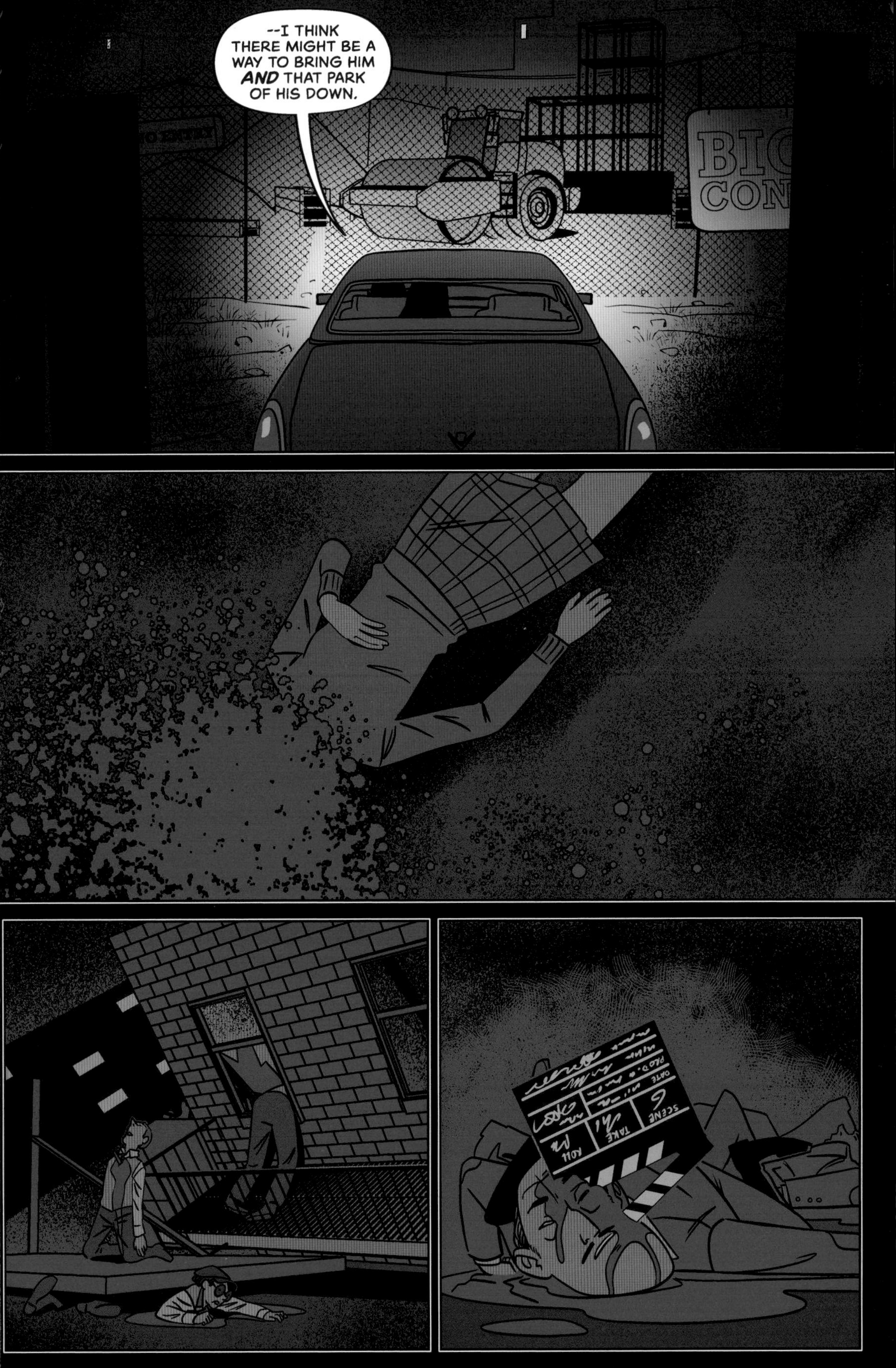
--I THINK THERE MIGHT BE A WAY TO BRING HIM *AND* THAT PARK OF HIS DOWN.

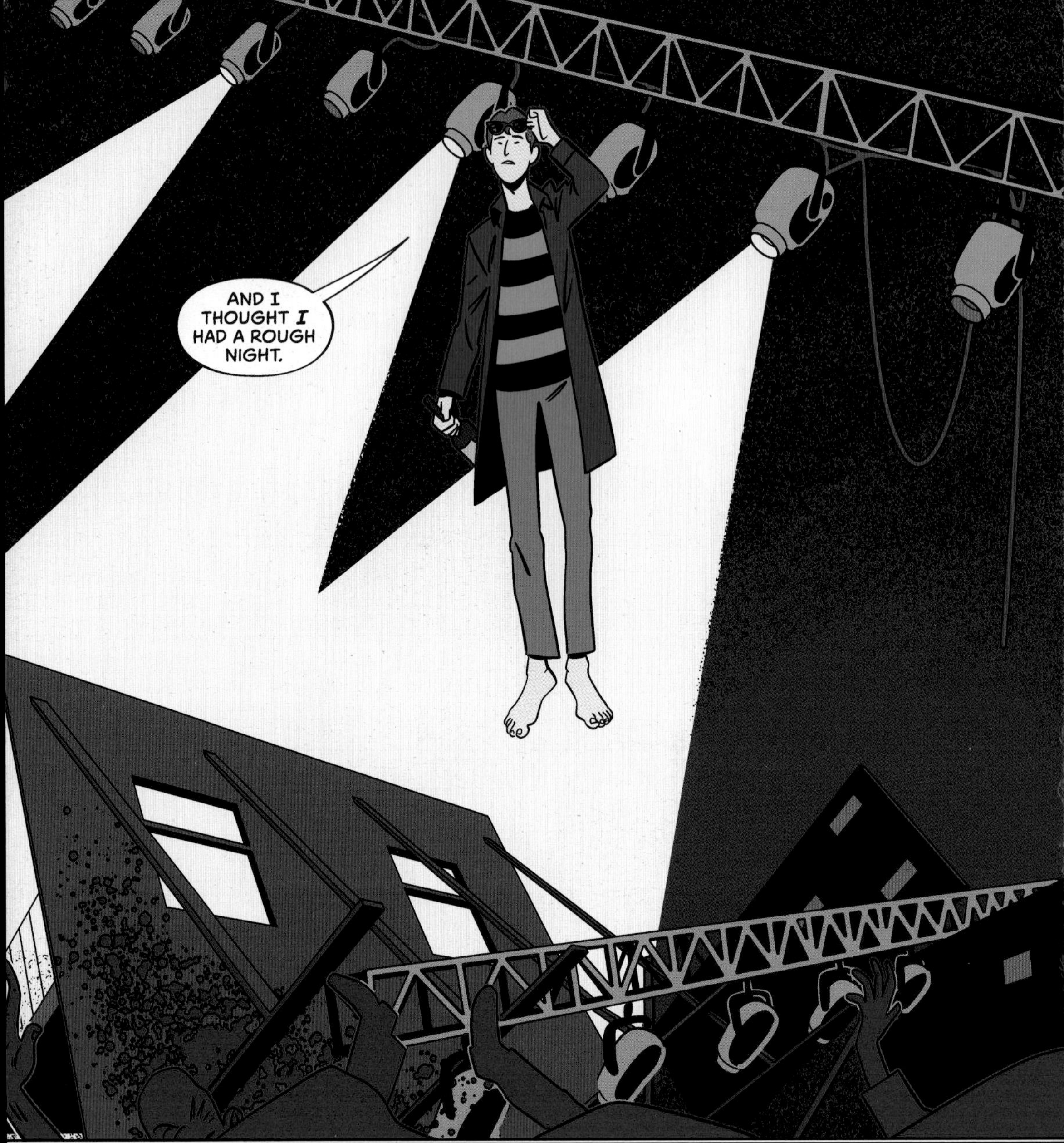
AND I THOUGHT I HAD A ROUGH NIGHT.

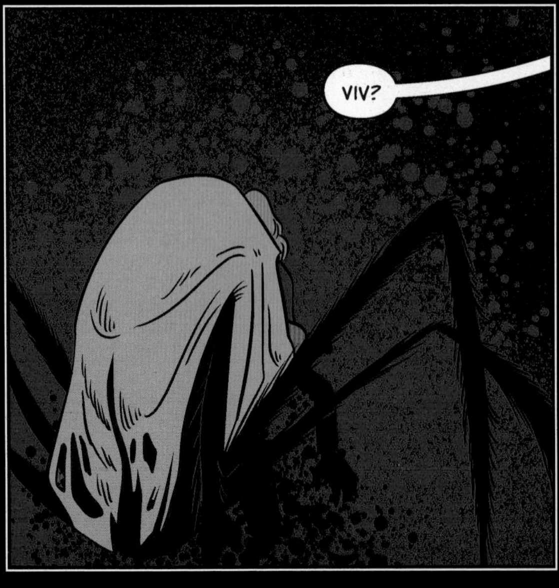
VIV?

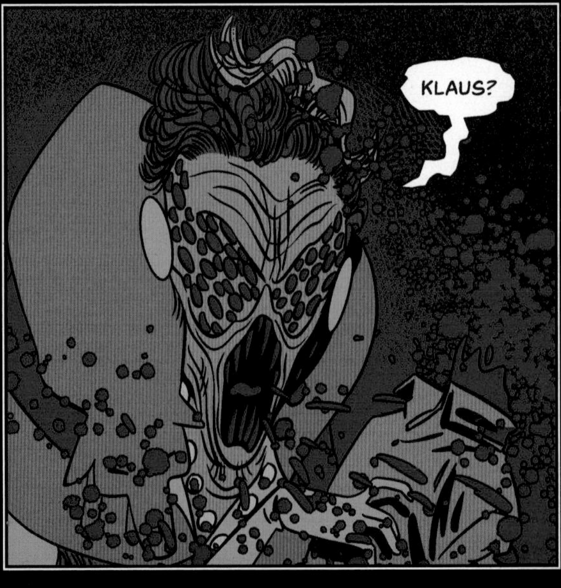
KLAUS?

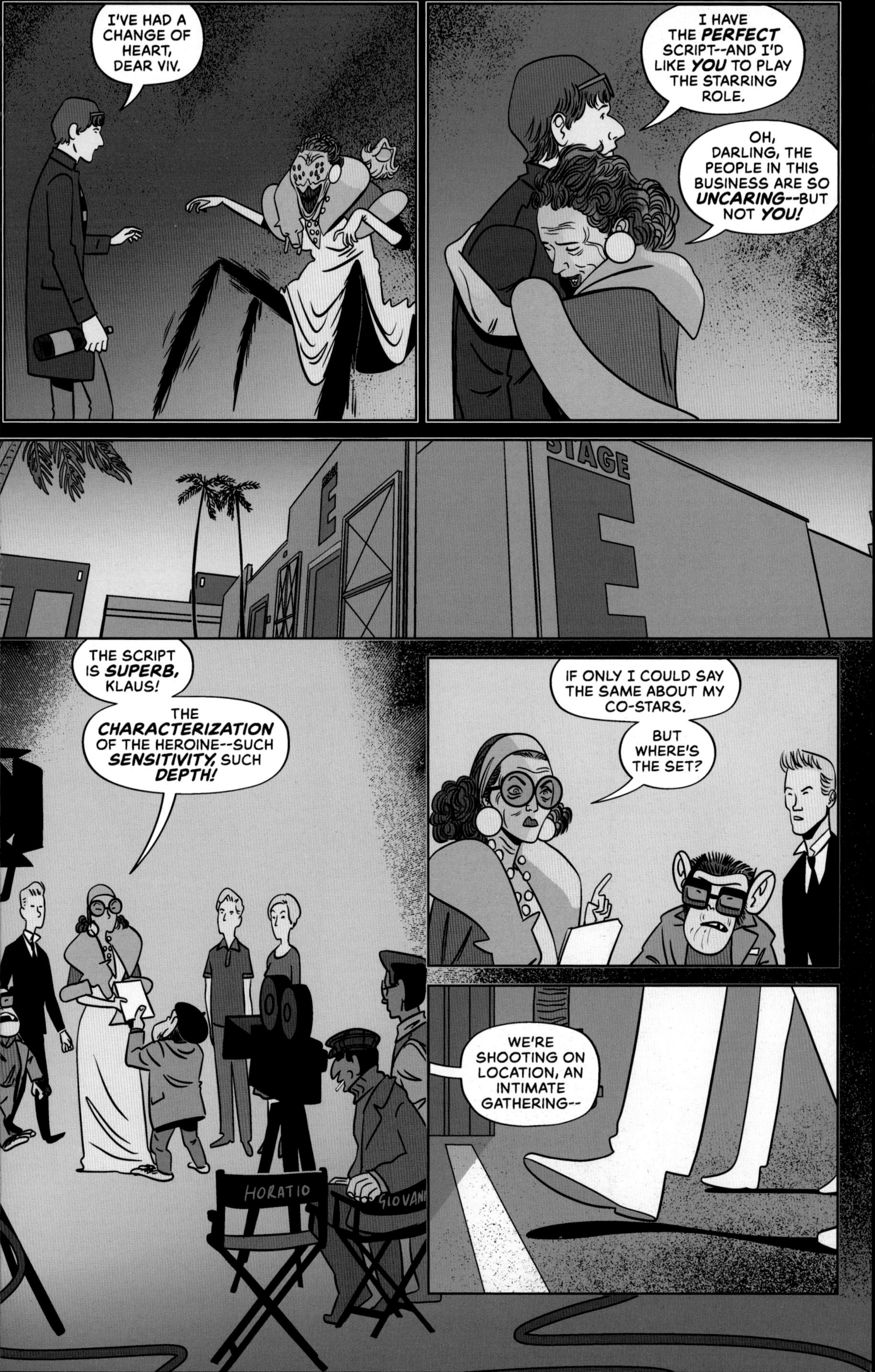

I'VE HAD A CHANGE OF HEART, DEAR VIV.
I HAVE THE PERFECT SCRIPT--AND I'D LIKE YOU TO PLAY THE STARRING ROLE.
OH, DARLING, THE PEOPLE IN THIS BUSINESS ARE SO UNCARING--BUT NOT YOU!
STAGE
E
THE SCRIPT IS SUPERB, KLAUS!
THE CHARACTERIZATION OF THE HEROINE--SUCH SENSITIVITY, SUCH DEPTH!
HORATIO
IF ONLY I COULD SAY THE SAME ABOUT MY CO-STARS.
BUT WHERE'S THE SET?
WE'RE SHOOTING ON LOCATION, AN INTIMATE GATHERING--

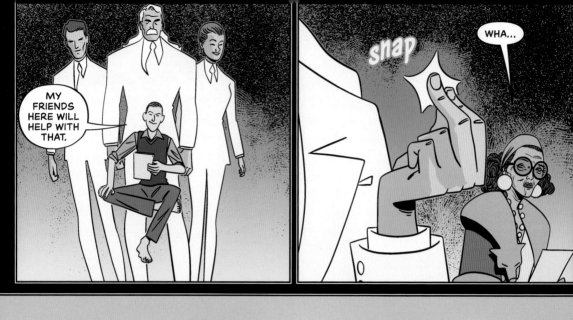

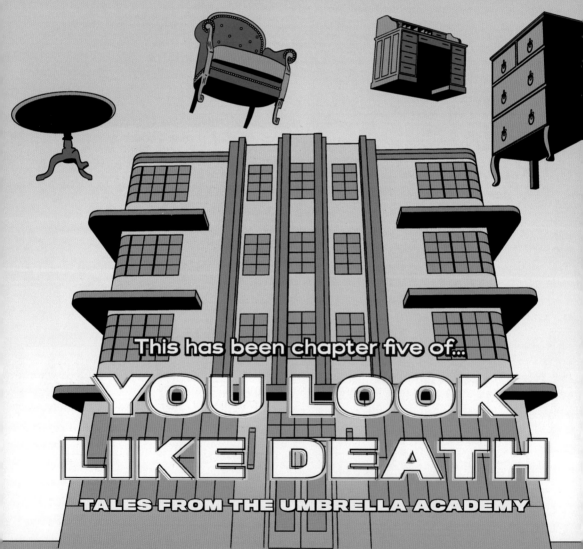

MY FRIENDS HERE WILL HELP WITH THAT.
snap
WHA...
This has been chapter five of...
YOU LOOK LIKE DEATH
TALES FROM THE UMBRELLA ACADEMY

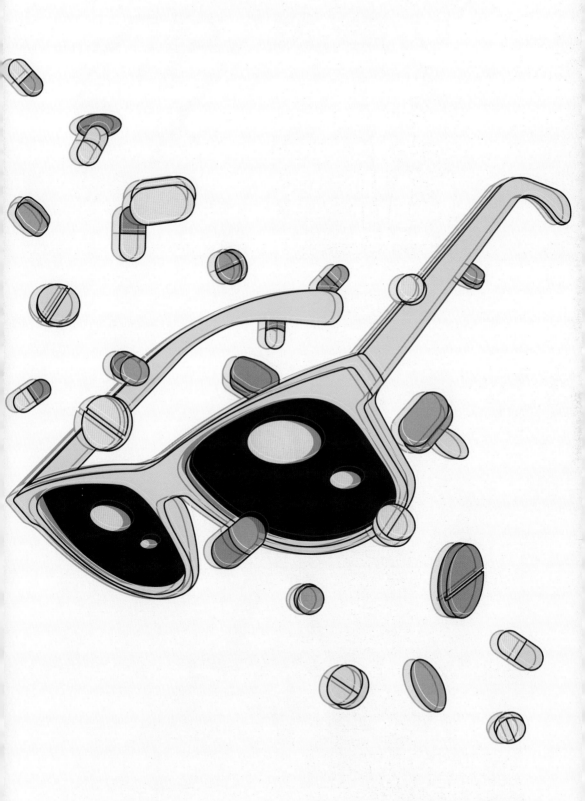

CHAPTER SIX

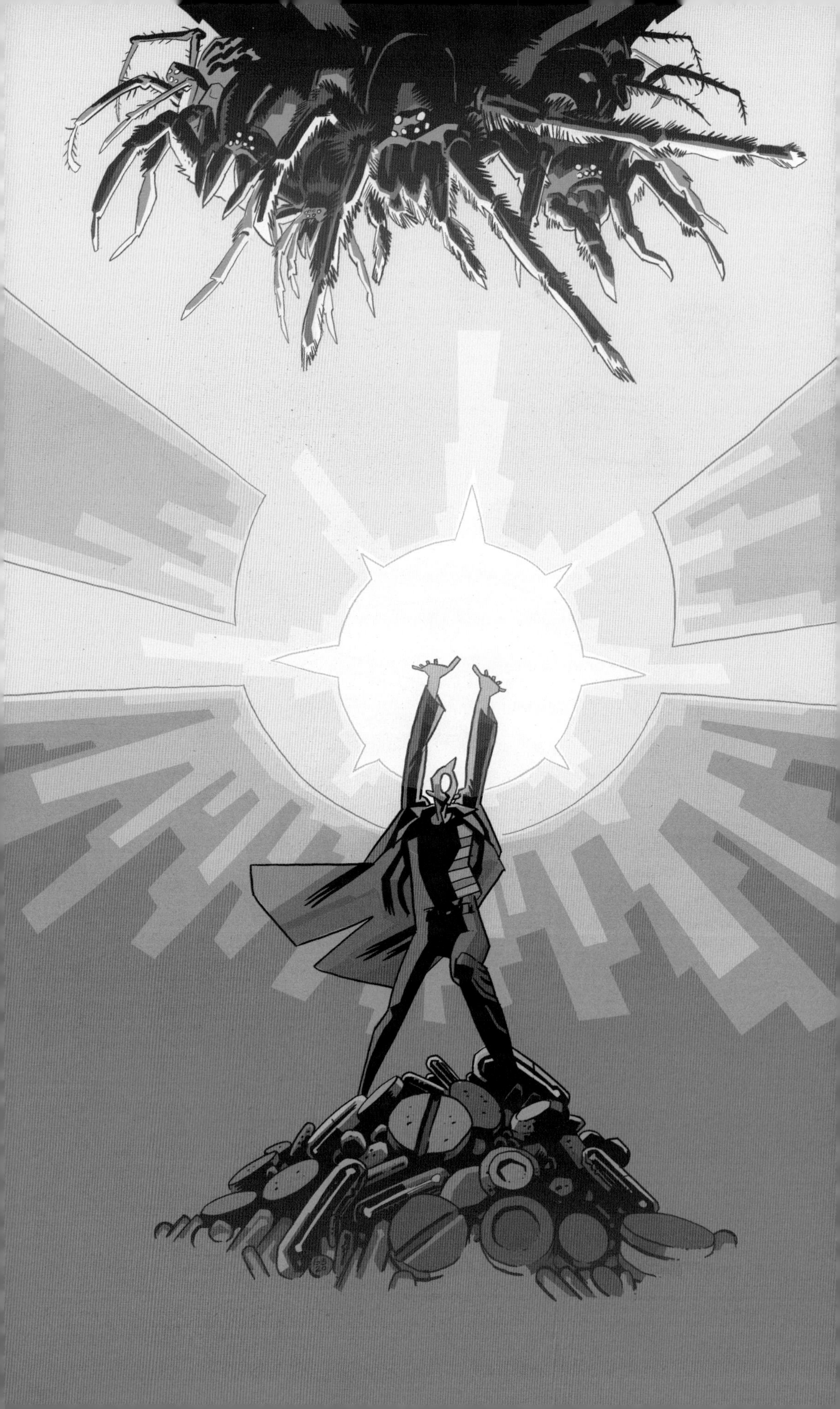

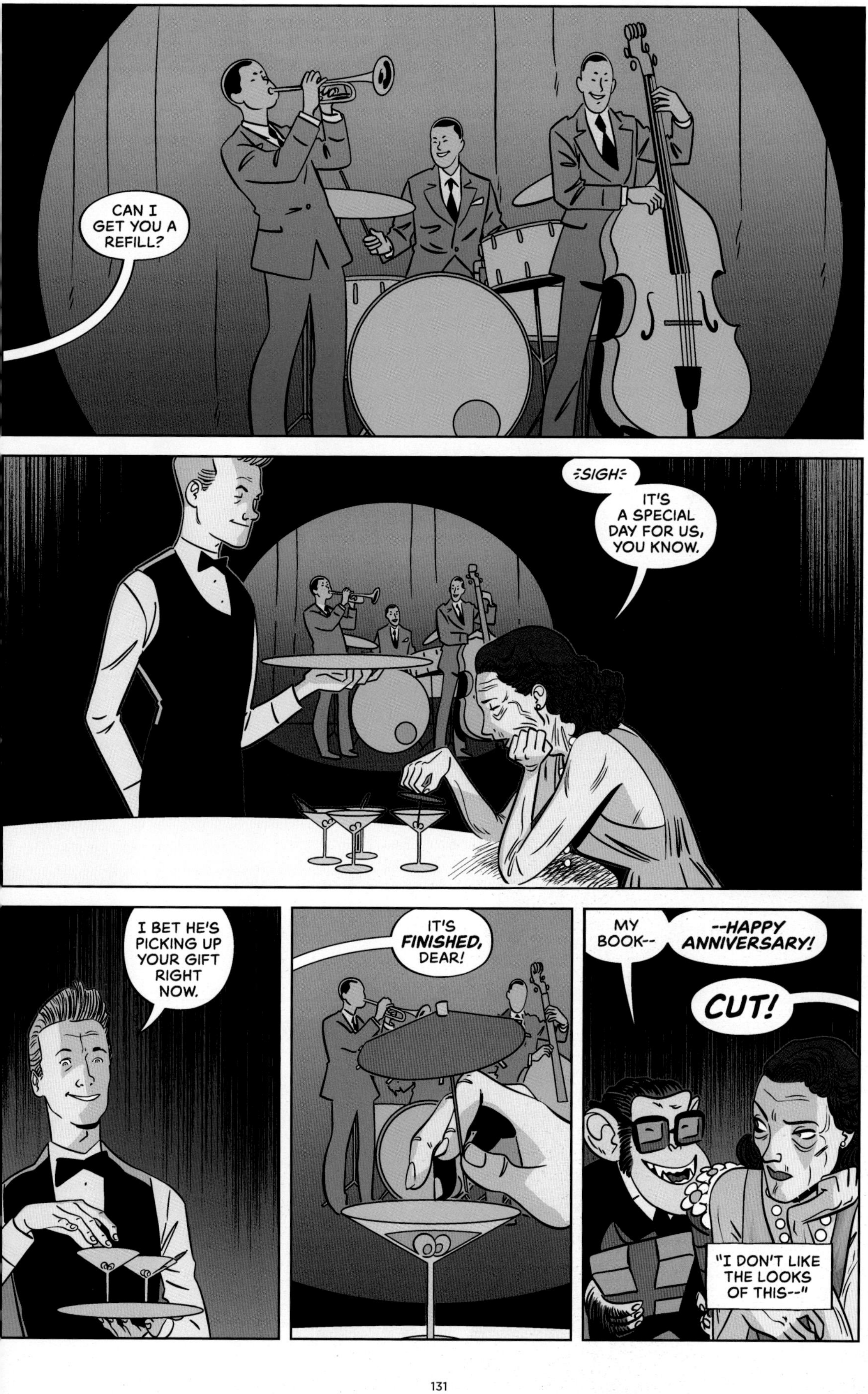

CAN I GET YOU A REFILL?
=SIGH=
IT'S A SPECIAL DAY FOR US, YOU KNOW.
I BET HE'S PICKING UP YOUR GIFT RIGHT NOW.
IT'S *FINISHED,* DEAR!
MY BOOK--
--HAPPY ANNIVERSARY!
CUT!
"I DON'T LIKE THE LOOKS OF THIS--"

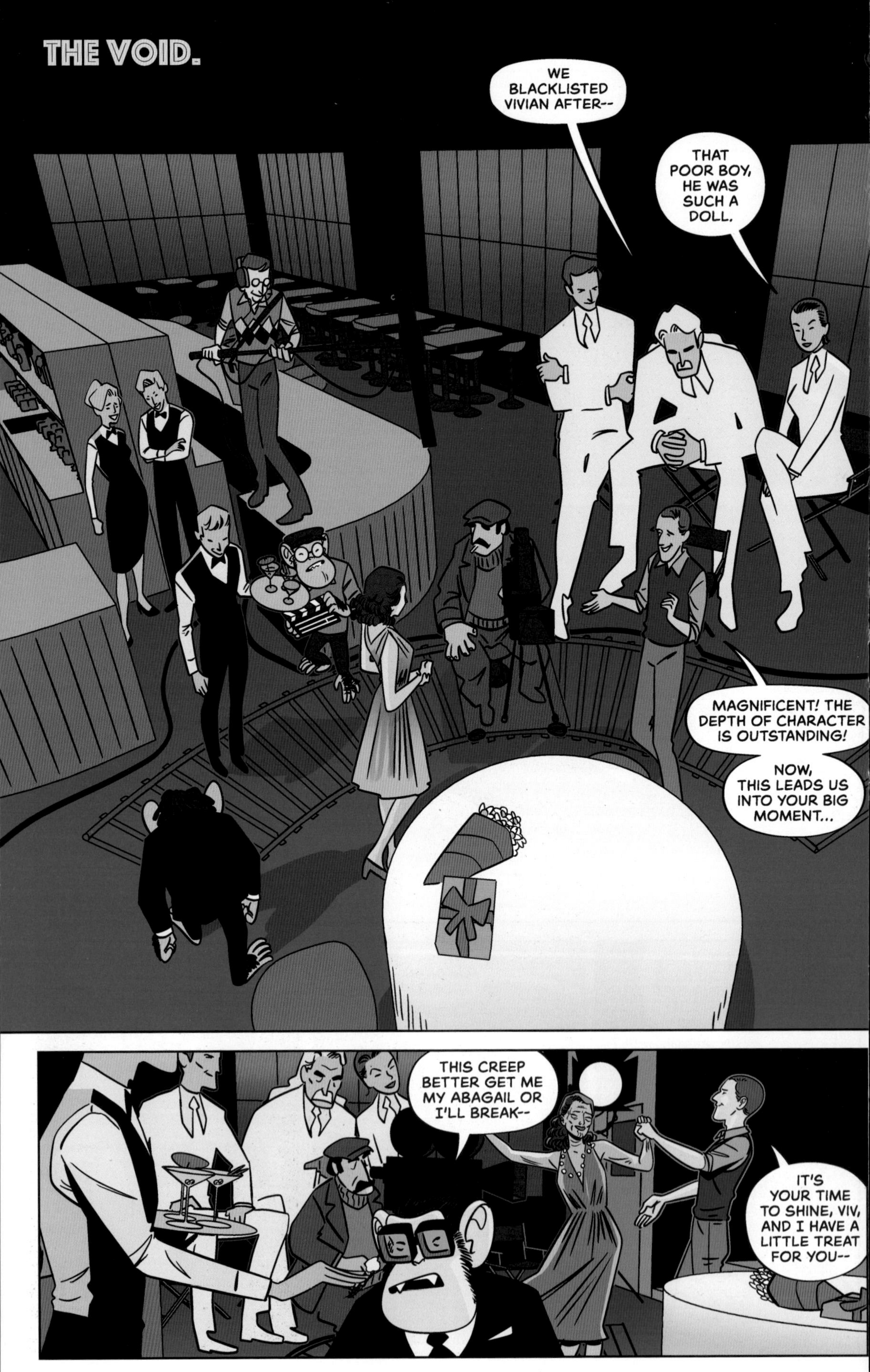
THE VOID.
WE BLACKLISTED VIVIAN AFTER--
THAT POOR BOY, HE WAS SUCH A DOLL.
MAGNIFICENT! THE DEPTH OF CHARACTER IS OUTSTANDING!
NOW, THIS LEADS US INTO YOUR BIG MOMENT...
THIS CREEP BETTER GET ME MY ABAGAIL OR I'LL BREAK--
IT'S YOUR TIME TO SHINE, VIV, AND I HAVE A LITTLE TREAT FOR YOU--

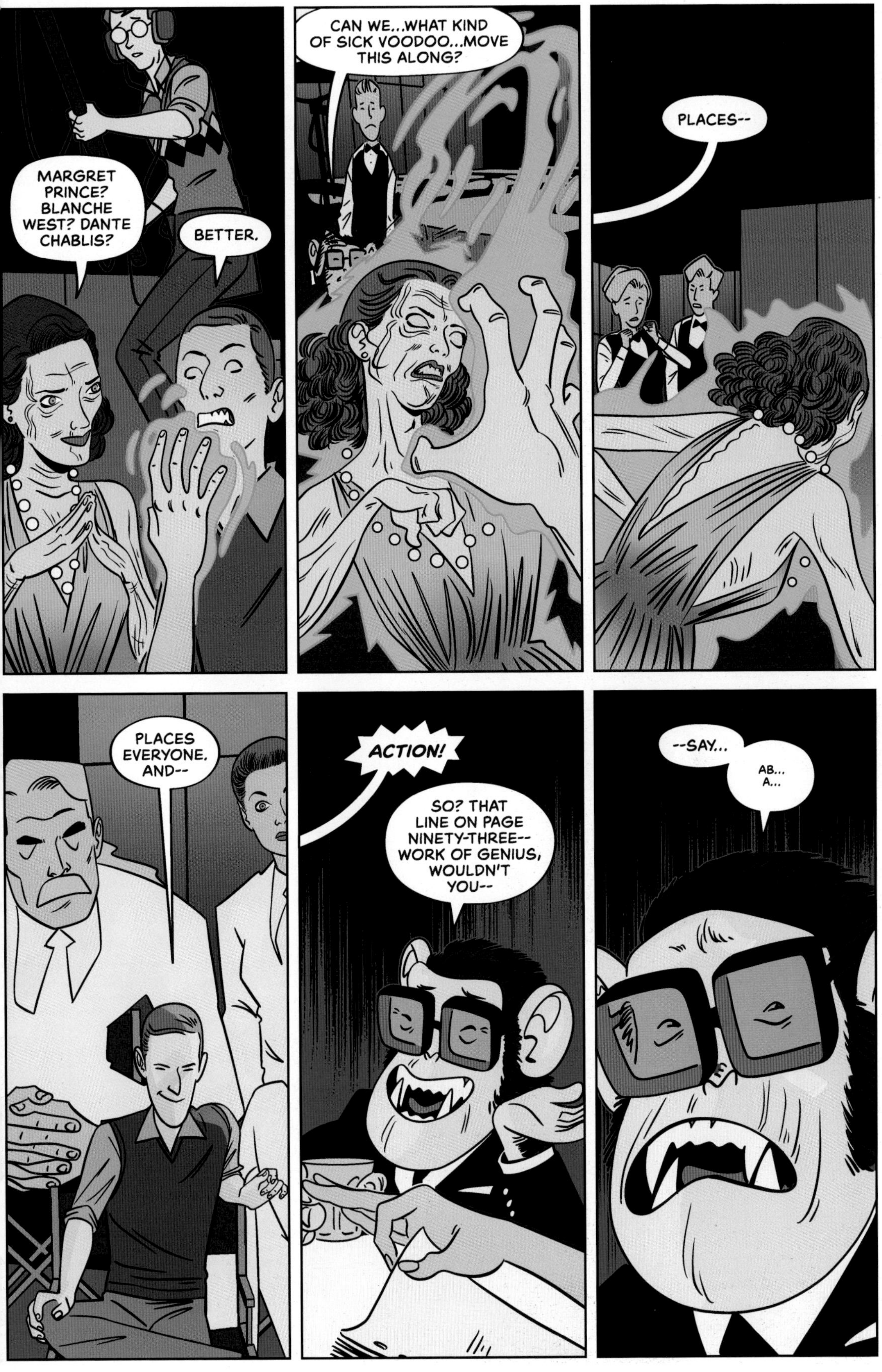
MARGRET PRINCE? BLANCHE WEST? DANTE CHABLIS?
BETTER.
CAN WE...WHAT KIND OF SICK VOODOO...MOVE THIS ALONG?
PLACES--
PLACES EVERYONE, AND--
ACTION!
SO? THAT LINE ON PAGE NINETY-THREE-- WORK OF GENIUS, WOULDN'T YOU--
--SAY...
AB... A...

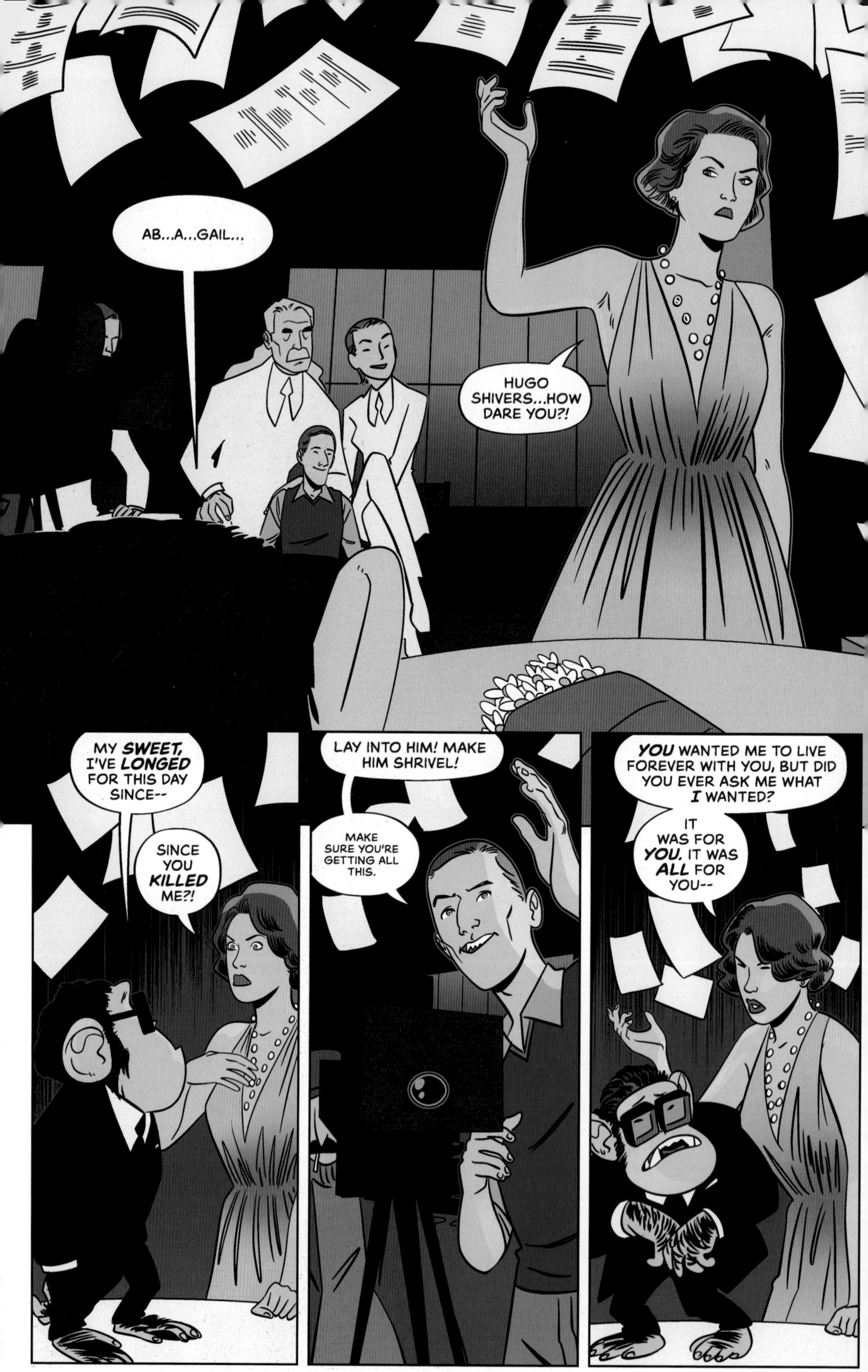
AB...A...GAIL...
HUGO SHIVERS...HOW DARE YOU?!
MY **SWEET**, I'VE **LONGED** FOR THIS DAY SINCE--
SINCE YOU **KILLED** ME?!
LAY INTO HIM! MAKE HIM SHRIVEL!
MAKE SURE YOU'RE GETTING ALL THIS.
YOU WANTED ME TO LIVE FOREVER WITH YOU, BUT DID YOU EVER ASK ME WHAT **I** WANTED?
IT WAS FOR **YOU**. IT WAS **ALL** FOR YOU--

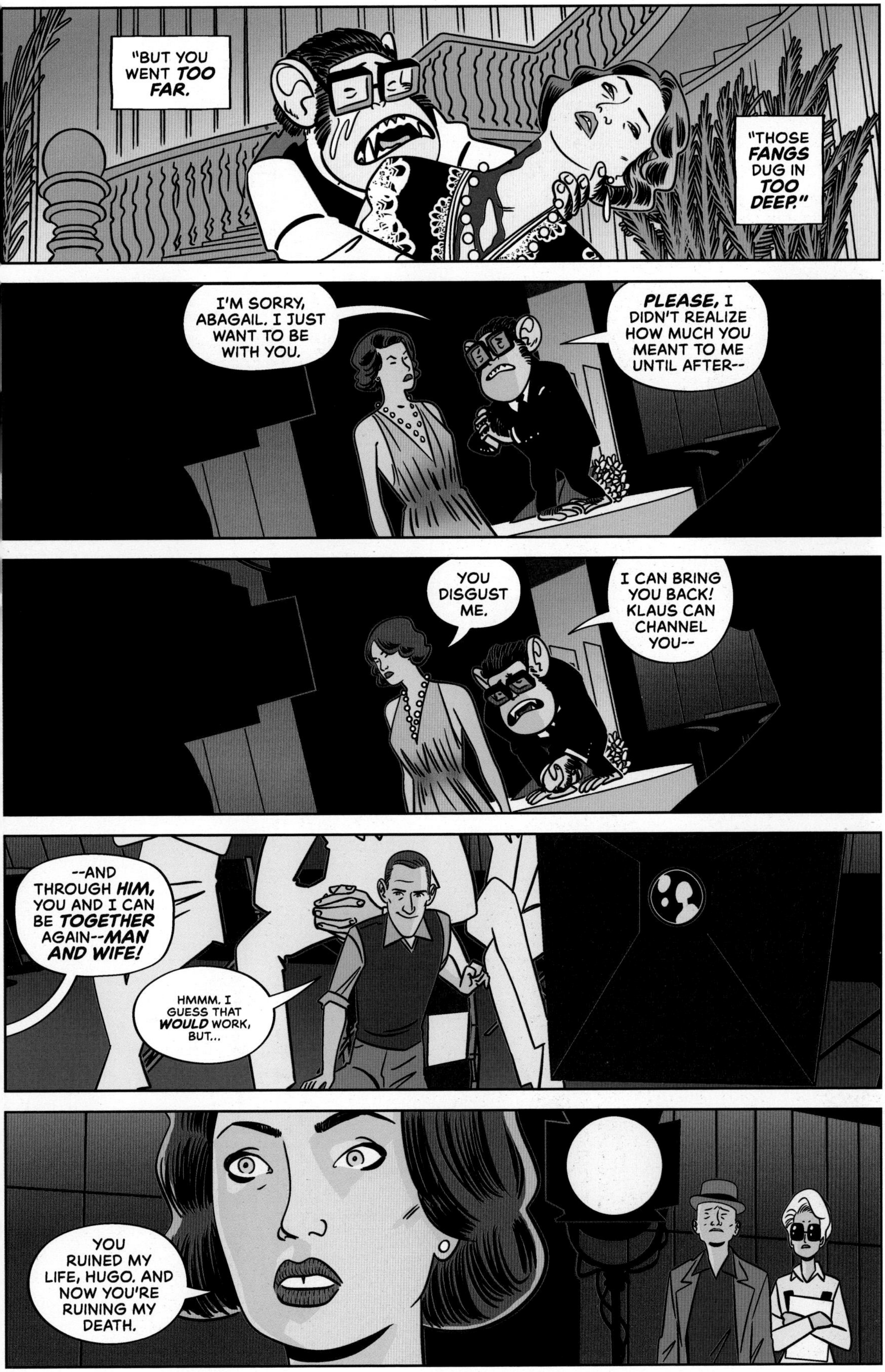
"BUT YOU WENT TOO FAR.
"THOSE FANGS DUG IN TOO DEEP."
I'M SORRY, ABAGAIL. I JUST WANT TO BE WITH YOU.
PLEASE, I DIDN'T REALIZE HOW MUCH YOU MEANT TO ME UNTIL AFTER--
YOU DISGUST ME.
I CAN BRING YOU BACK! KLAUS CAN CHANNEL YOU--
--AND THROUGH HIM, YOU AND I CAN BE TOGETHER AGAIN--MAN AND WIFE!
HMMM. I GUESS THAT WOULD WORK, BUT...
YOU RUINED MY LIFE, HUGO. AND NOW YOU'RE RUINING MY DEATH.

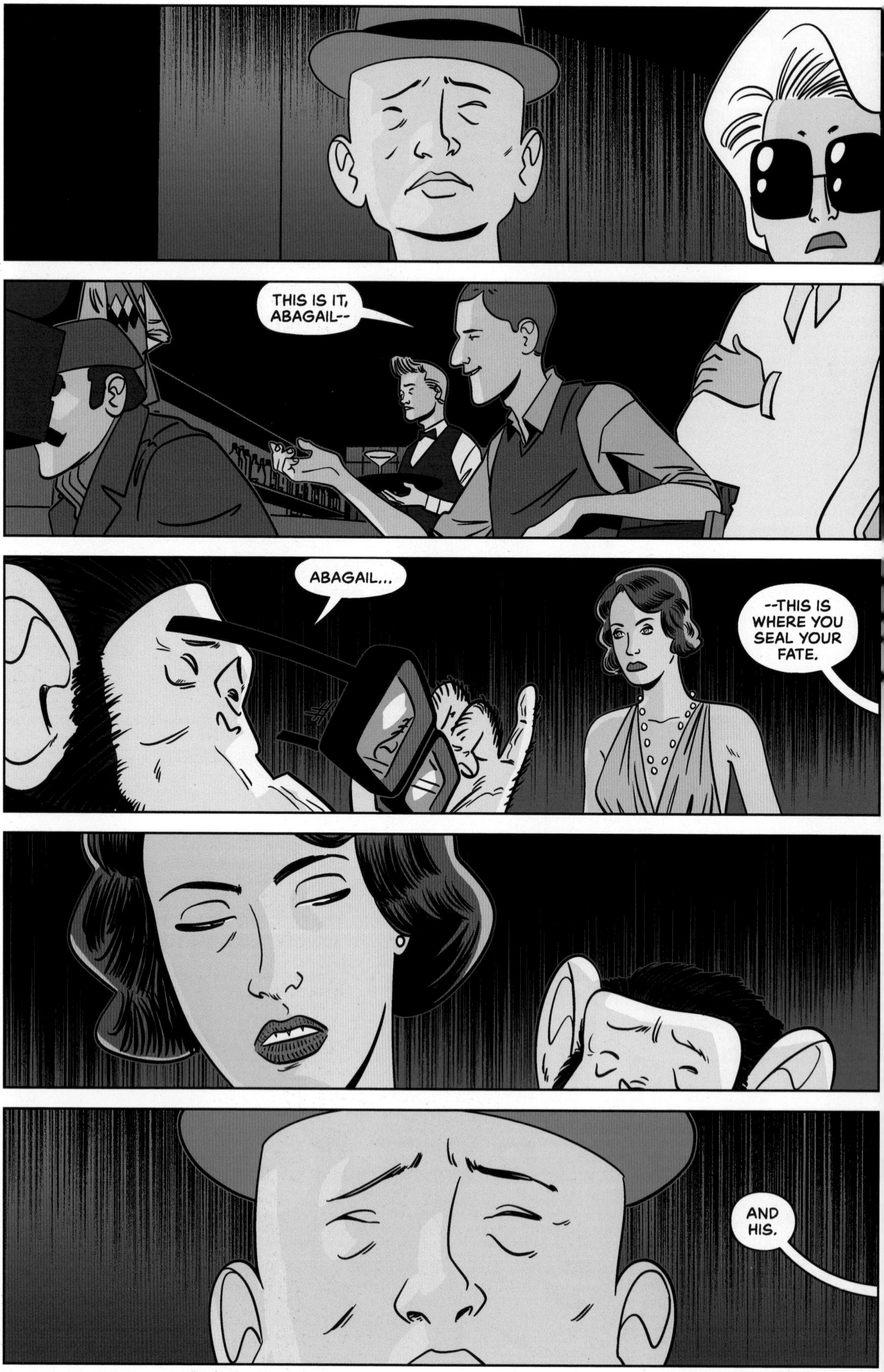
THIS IS IT, ABAGAIL--
ABAGAIL...
--THIS IS WHERE YOU SEAL YOUR FATE.
AND HIS.

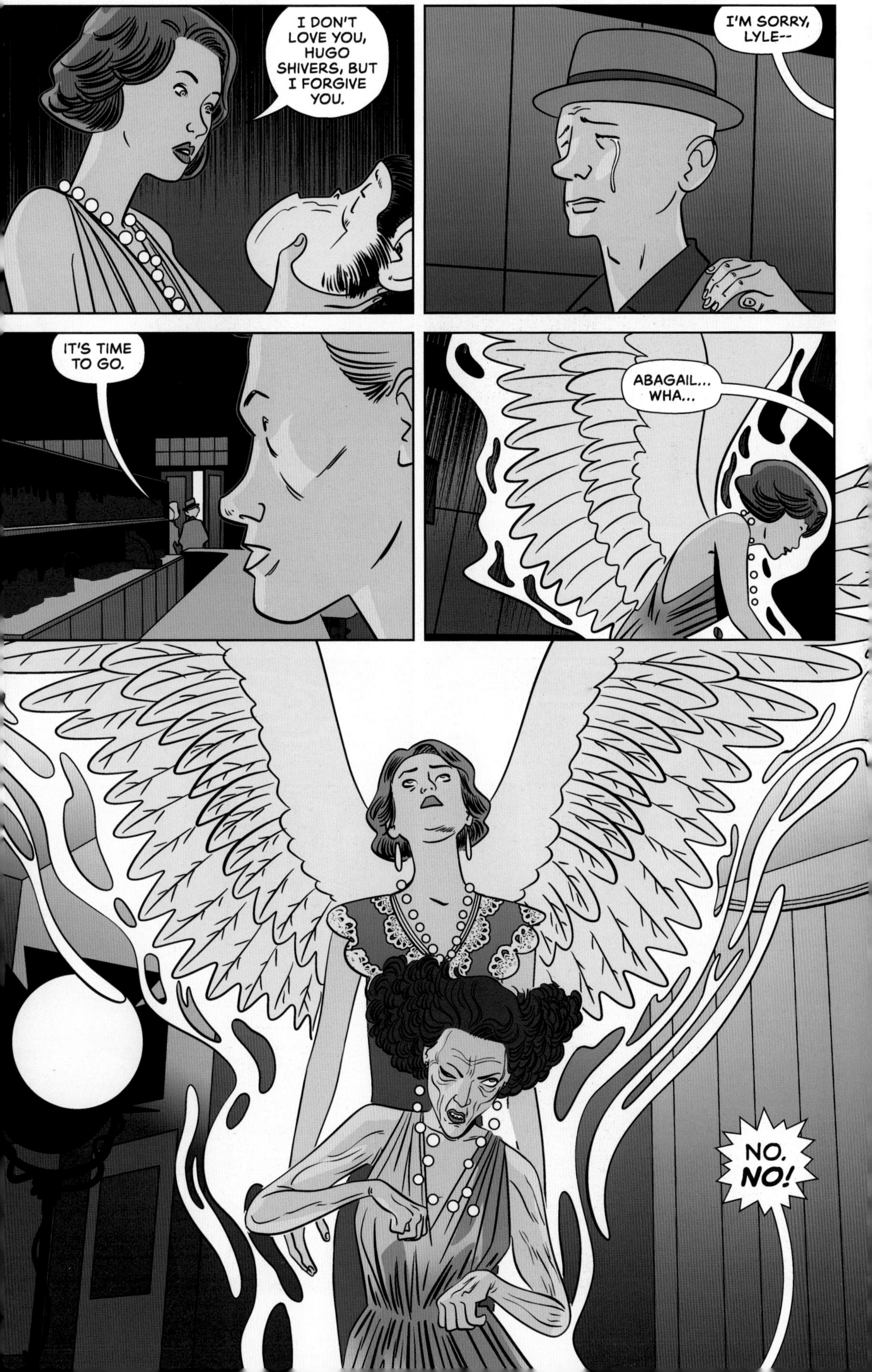
I DON'T LOVE YOU, HUGO SHIVERS, BUT I FORGIVE YOU.
I'M SORRY, LYLE--
IT'S TIME TO GO.
ABAGAIL... WHA...
NO. NO!

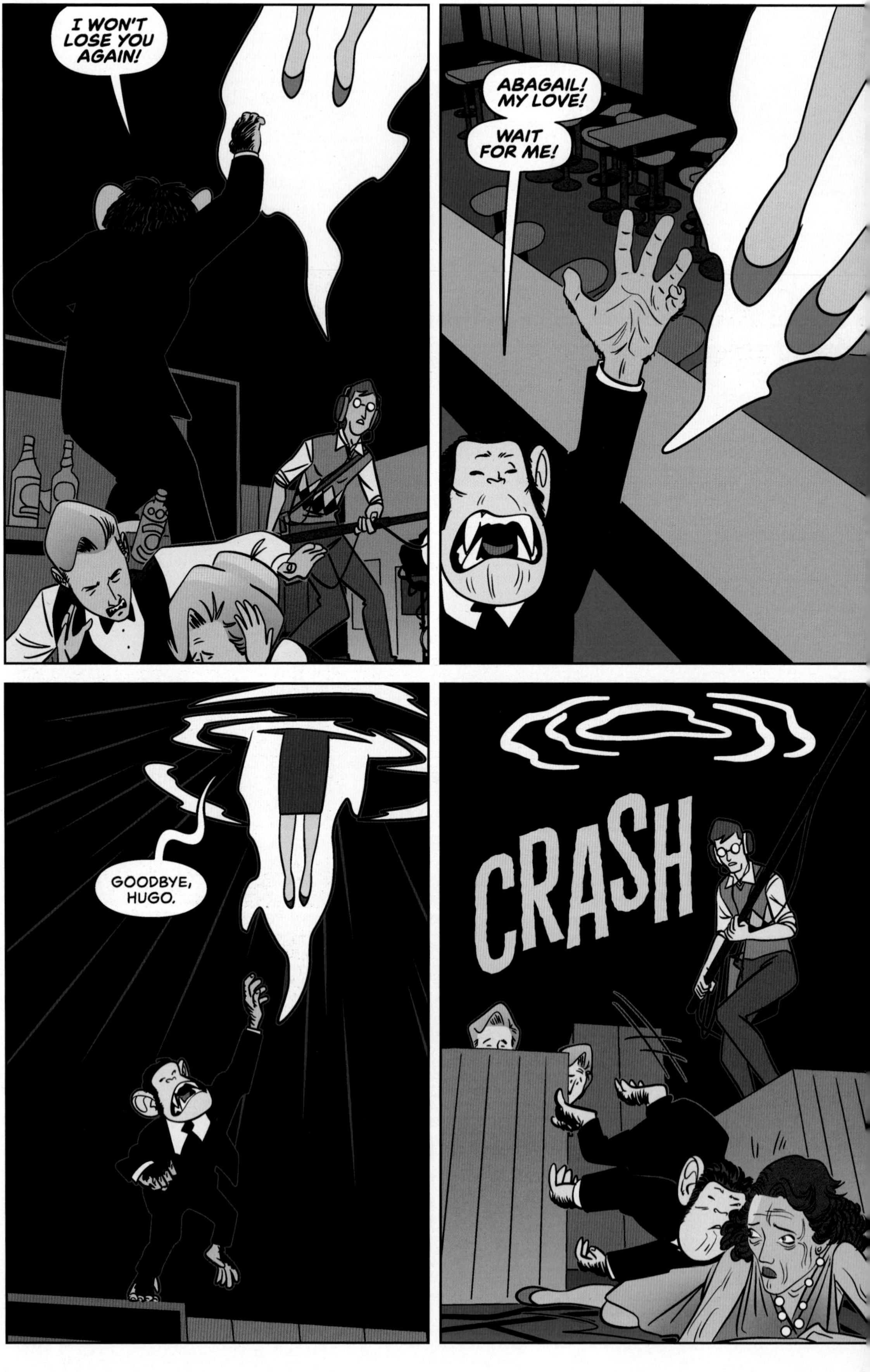
I WON'T LOSE YOU AGAIN!
ABAGAIL! MY LOVE!
WAIT FOR ME!
GOODBYE, HUGO.
CRASH

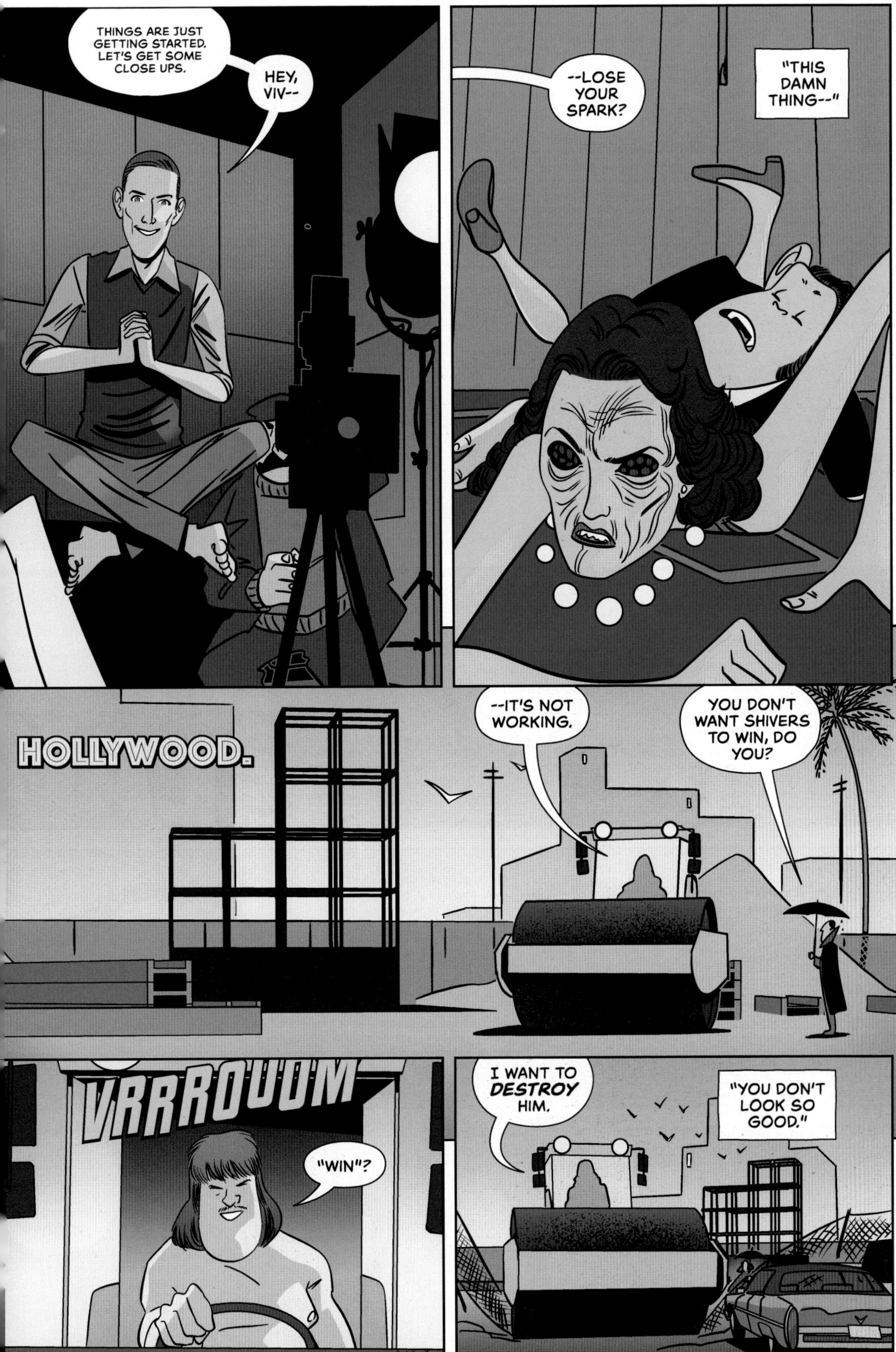
THINGS ARE JUST GETTING STARTED. LET'S GET SOME CLOSE UPS.
HEY, VIV--
--LOSE YOUR SPARK?
"THIS DAMN THING--"
HOLLYWOOD.
--IT'S NOT WORKING.
YOU DON'T WANT SHIVERS TO WIN, DO YOU?
VRRROUUM
"WIN"?
I WANT TO *DESTROY* HIM.
"YOU DON'T LOOK SO GOOD."

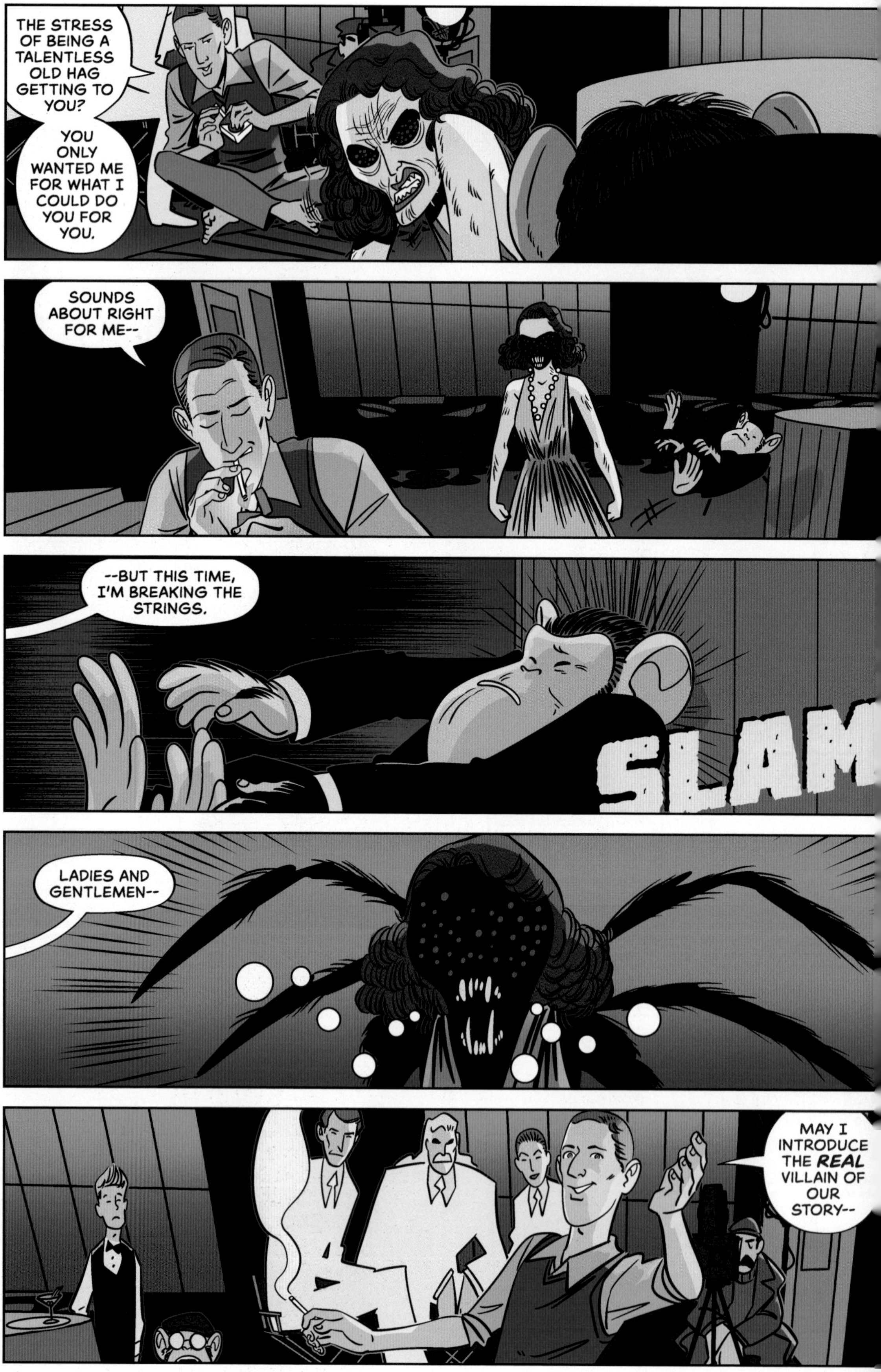
THE STRESS OF BEING A TALENTLESS OLD HAG GETTING TO YOU?
YOU ONLY WANTED ME FOR WHAT I COULD DO YOU FOR YOU.
SOUNDS ABOUT RIGHT FOR ME--
--BUT THIS TIME, I'M BREAKING THE STRINGS.
SLAM
LADIES AND GENTLEMEN--
MAY I INTRODUCE THE ***REAL*** VILLAIN OF OUR STORY--

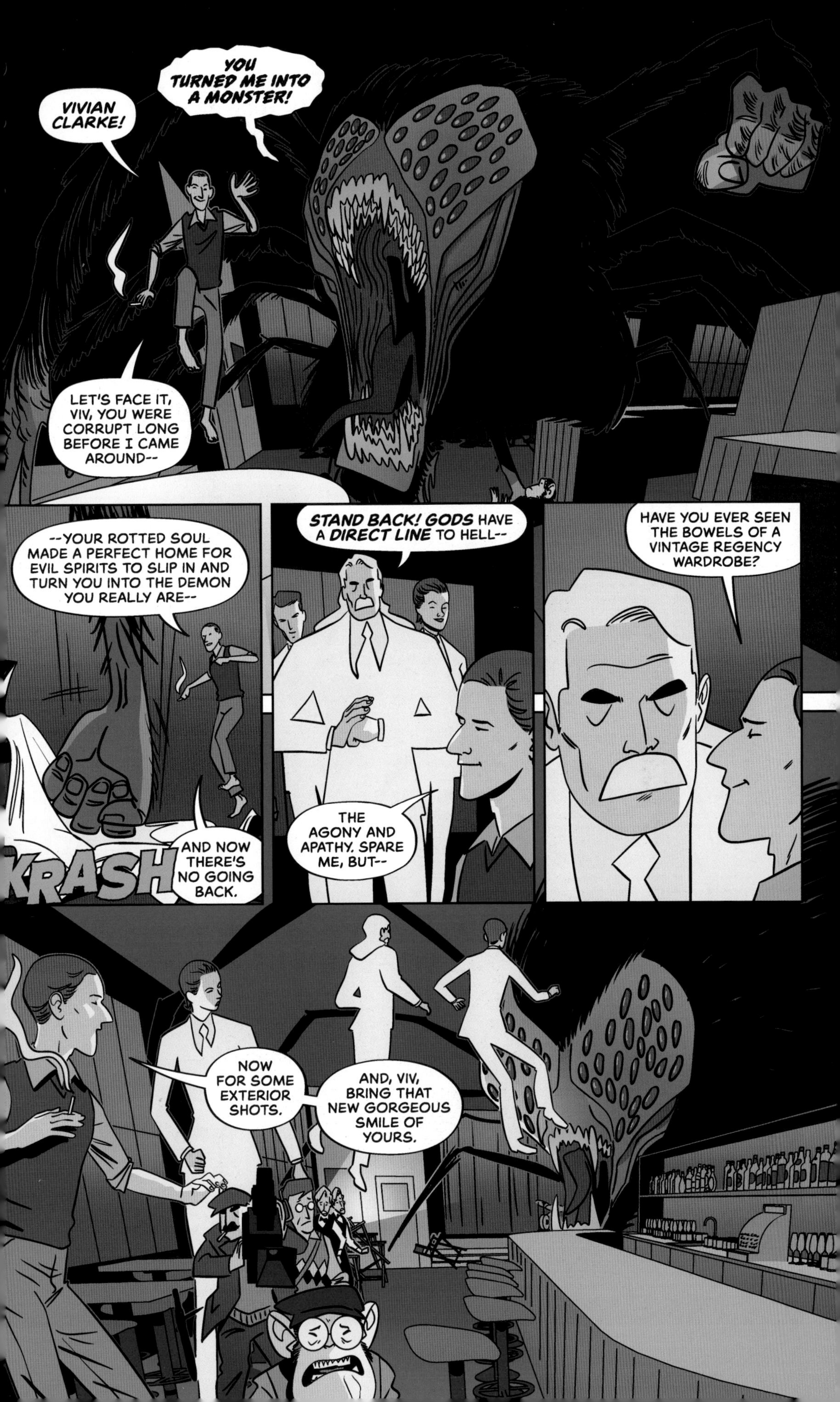

VIVIAN CLARKE!
YOU TURNED ME INTO A MONSTER!
LET'S FACE IT, VIV, YOU WERE CORRUPT LONG BEFORE I CAME AROUND--
--YOUR ROTTED SOUL MADE A PERFECT HOME FOR EVIL SPIRITS TO SLIP IN AND TURN YOU INTO THE DEMON YOU REALLY ARE--
KRASH
AND NOW THERE'S NO GOING BACK.
STAND BACK! GODS HAVE A DIRECT LINE TO HELL--
THE AGONY AND APATHY. SPARE ME, BUT--
HAVE YOU EVER SEEN THE BOWELS OF A VINTAGE REGENCY WARDROBE?
NOW FOR SOME EXTERIOR SHOTS.
AND, VIV, BRING THAT NEW GORGEOUS SMILE OF YOURS.

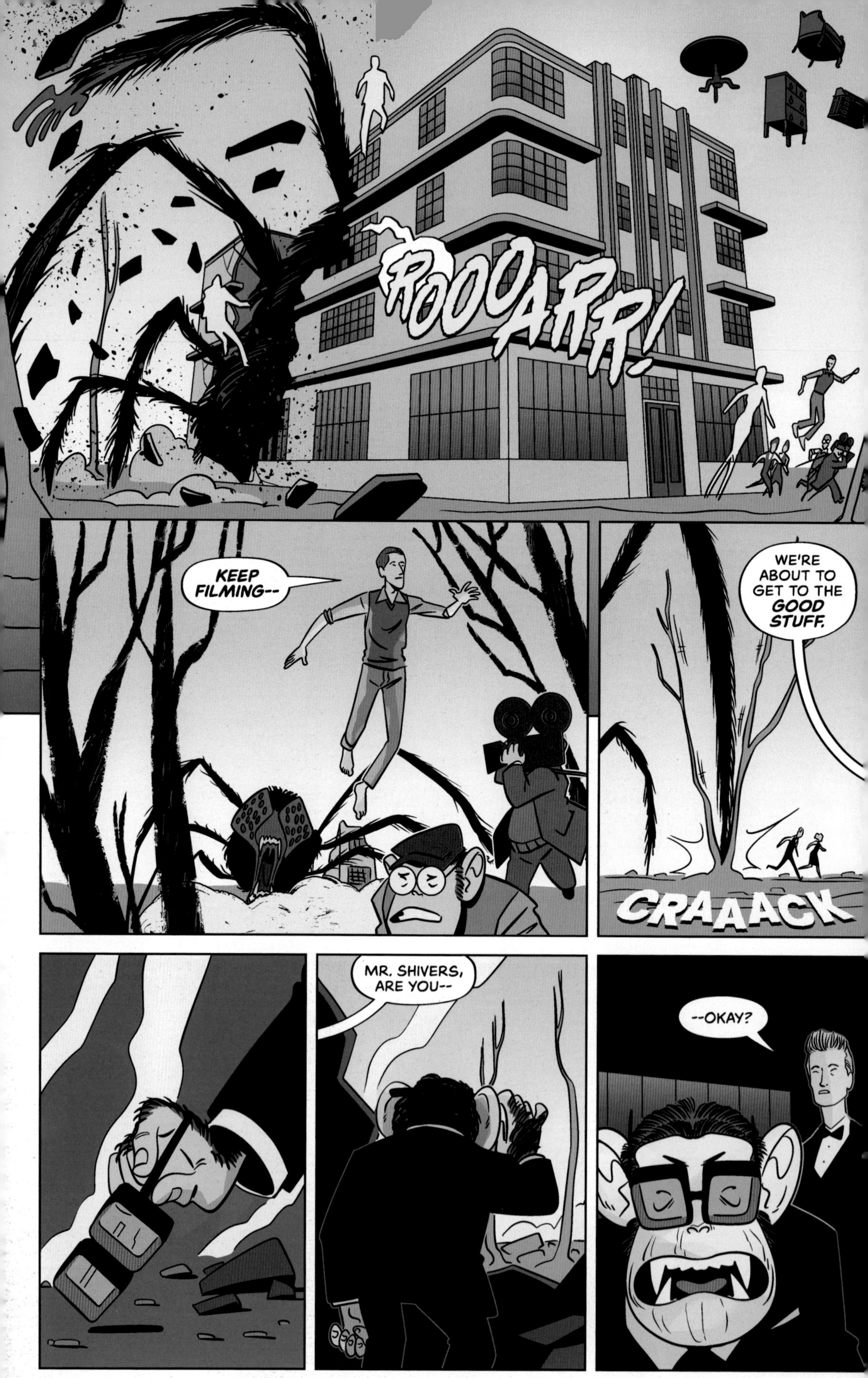
ROOOARRR!
KEEP FILMING--
WE'RE ABOUT TO GET TO THE GOOD STUFF.
CRAAACK
MR. SHIVERS, ARE YOU--
--OKAY?

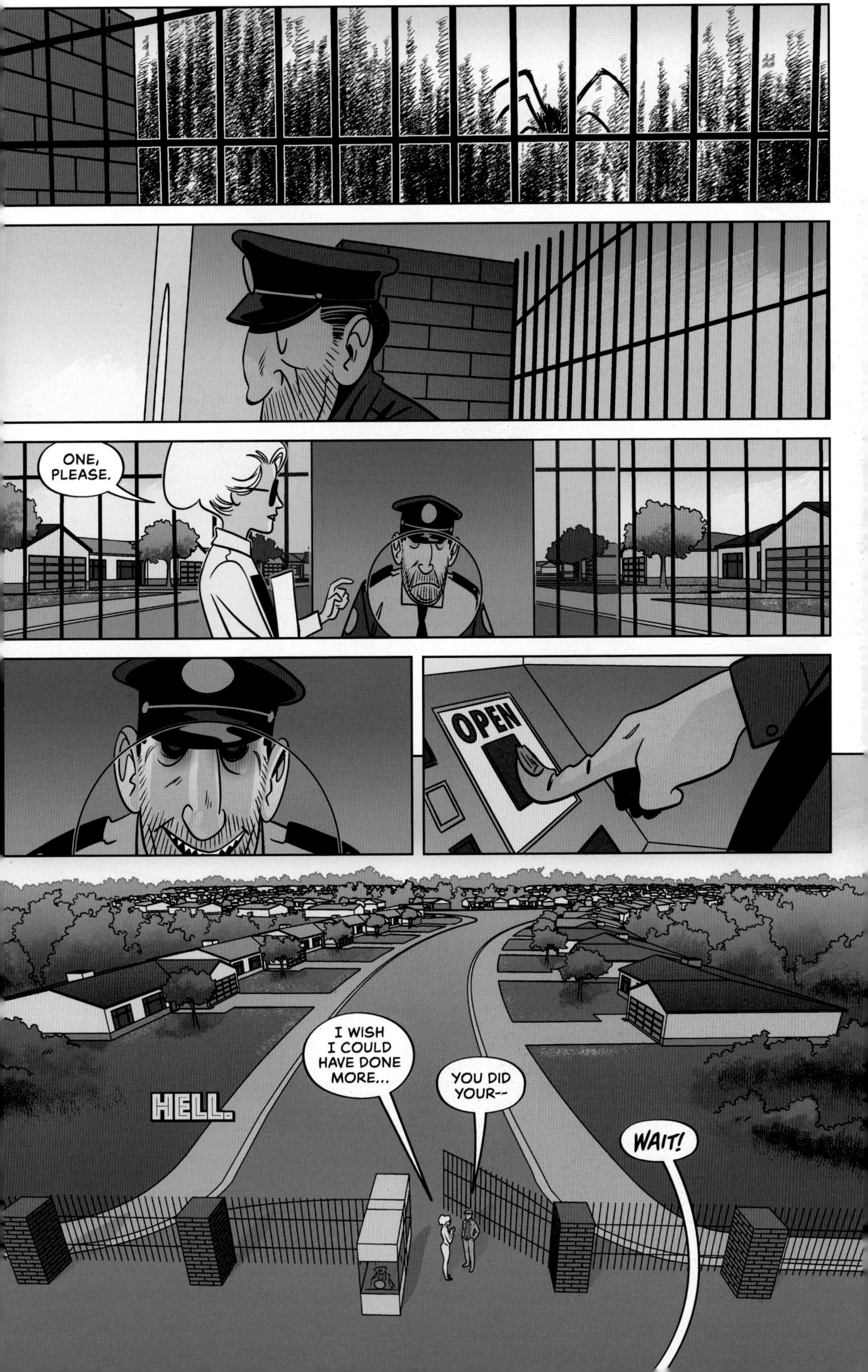
ONE, PLEASE.
OPEN
HELL.
I WISH I COULD HAVE DONE MORE...
YOU DID YOUR--
WAIT!

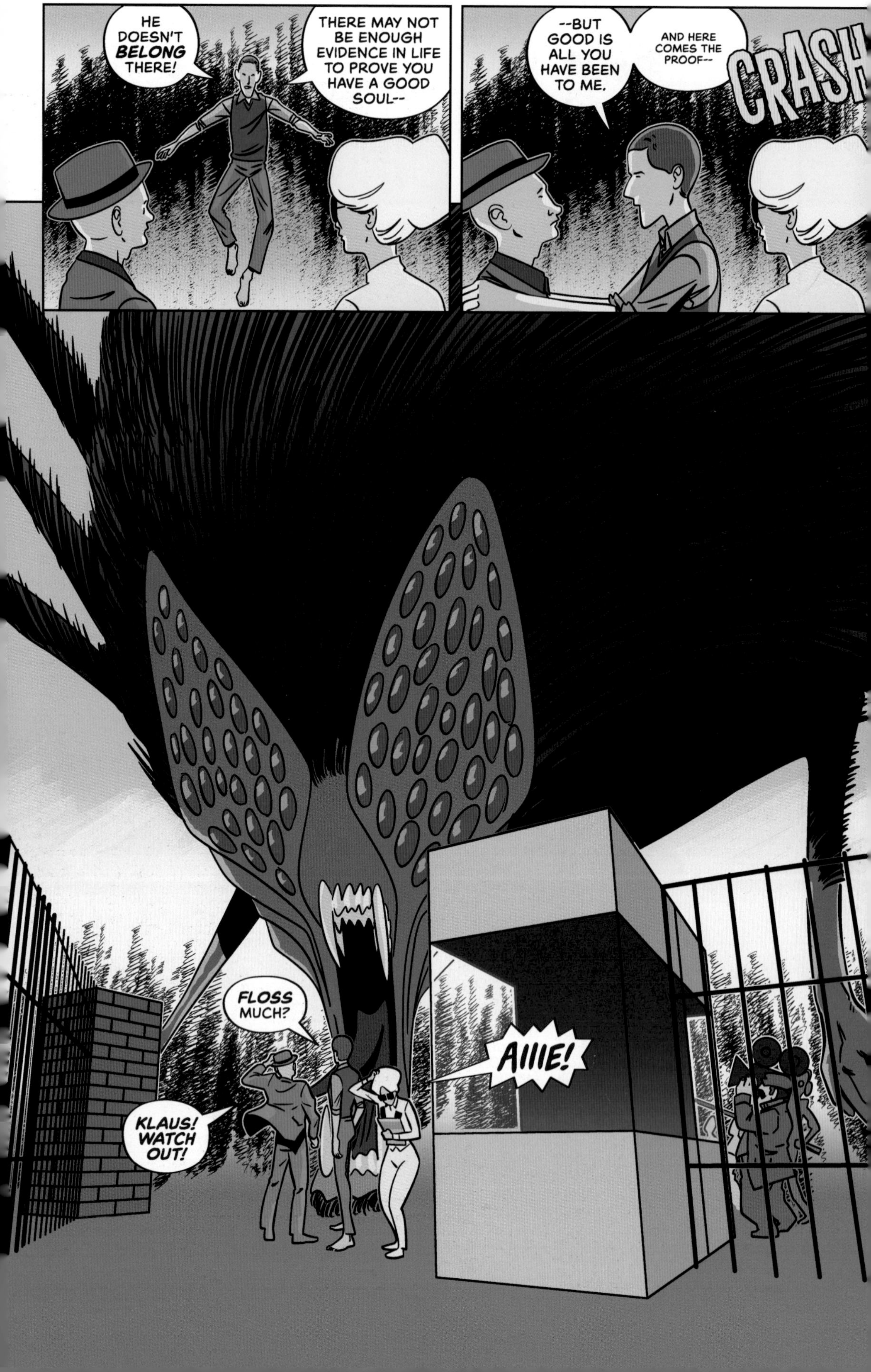
HE DOESN'T BELONG THERE!
THERE MAY NOT BE ENOUGH EVIDENCE IN LIFE TO PROVE YOU HAVE A GOOD SOUL--
--BUT GOOD IS ALL YOU HAVE BEEN TO ME.
AND HERE COMES THE PROOF--
CRASH
FLOSS MUCH?
AIIIE!
KLAUS! WATCH OUT!

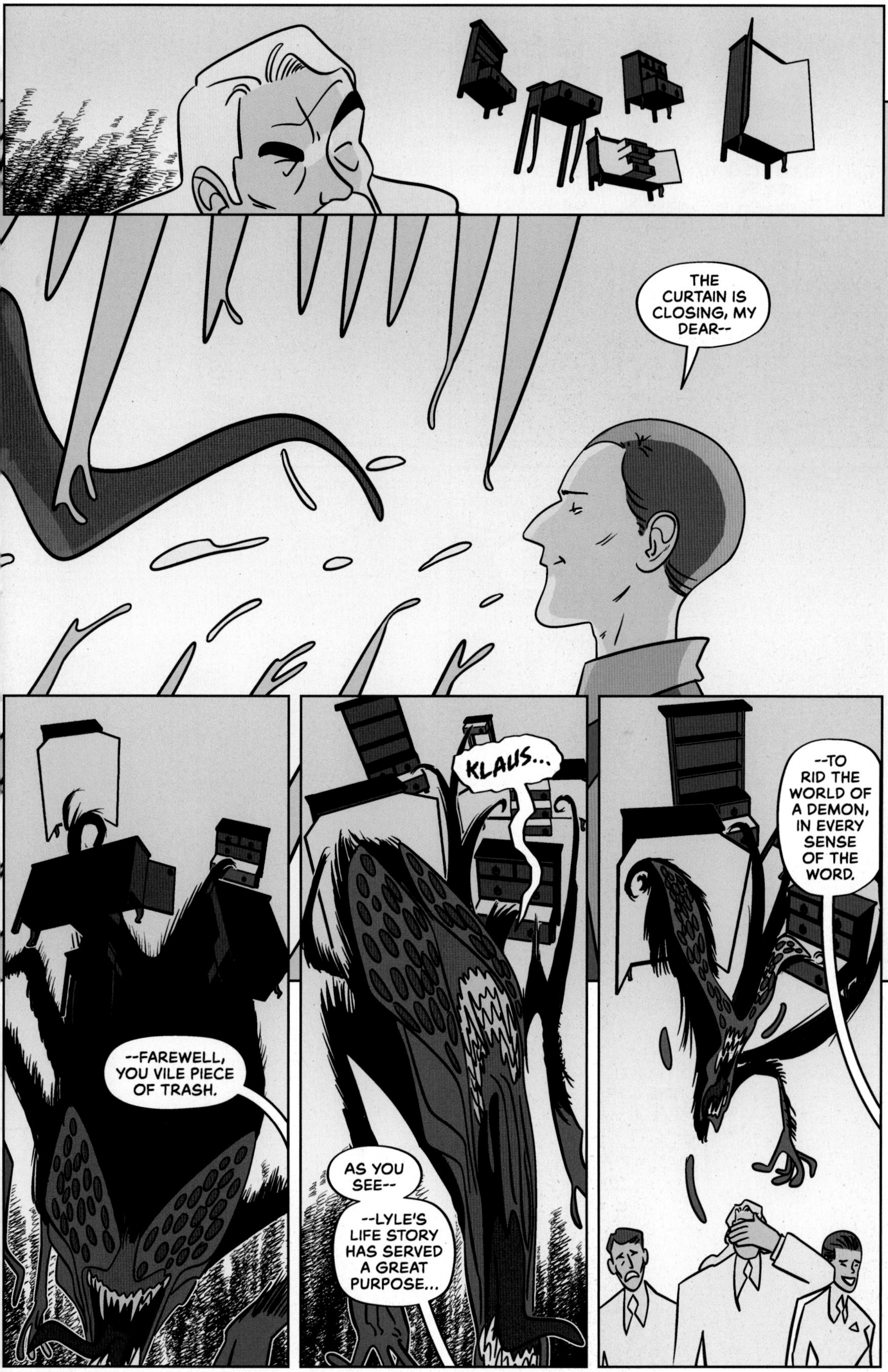
THE CURTAIN IS CLOSING, MY DEAR--
--FAREWELL, YOU VILE PIECE OF TRASH.
KLAUS...
AS YOU SEE--
--LYLE'S LIFE STORY HAS SERVED A GREAT PURPOSE...
--TO RID THE WORLD OF A DEMON, IN EVERY SENSE OF THE WORD.

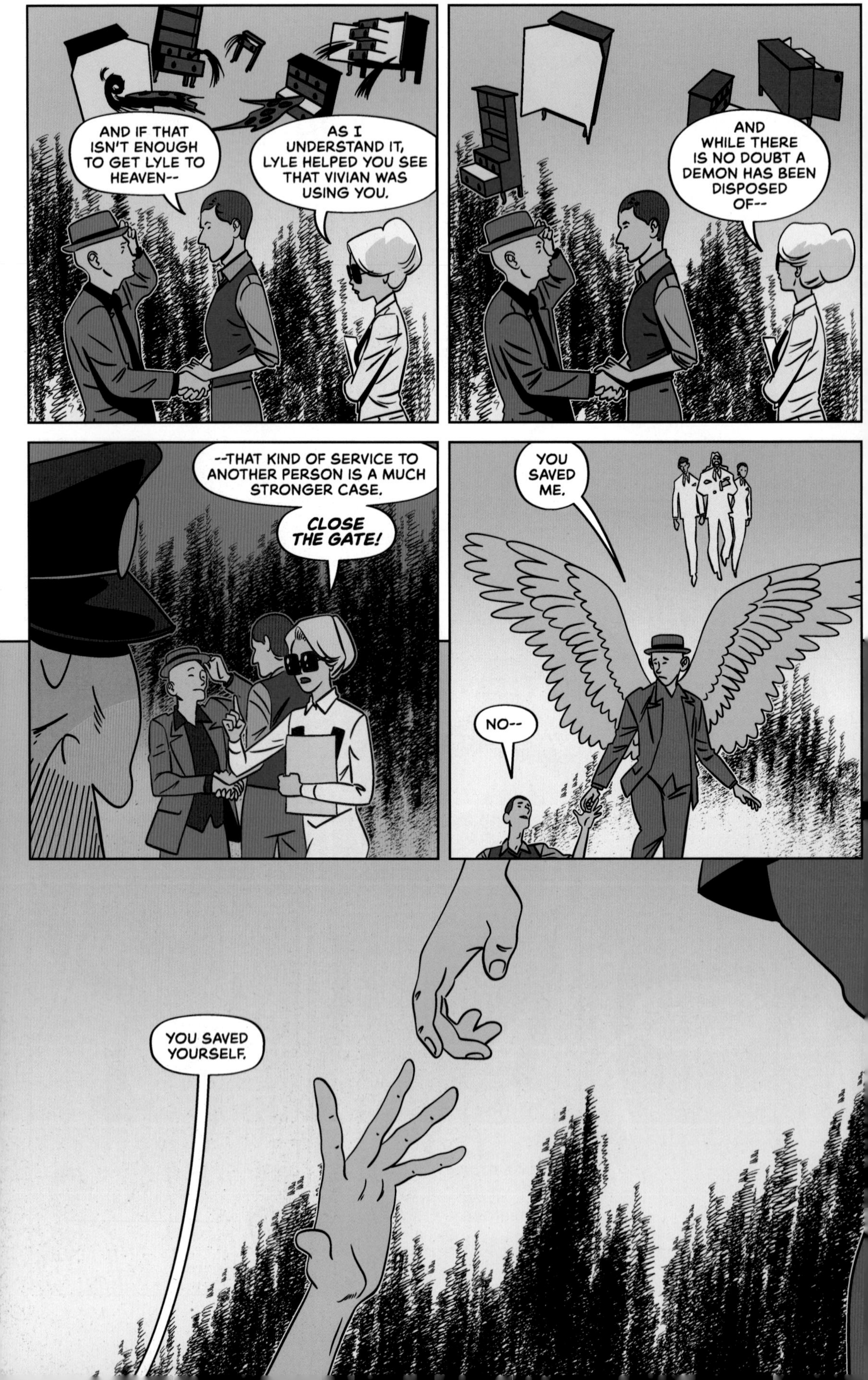
AND IF THAT ISN'T ENOUGH TO GET LYLE TO HEAVEN--
AS I UNDERSTAND IT, LYLE HELPED YOU SEE THAT VIVIAN WAS USING YOU.
AND WHILE THERE IS NO DOUBT A DEMON HAS BEEN DISPOSED OF--
--THAT KIND OF SERVICE TO ANOTHER PERSON IS A MUCH STRONGER CASE.
CLOSE THE GATE!
YOU SAVED ME.
NO--
YOU SAVED YOURSELF.

RIGHT, IT'S OKAY FOR *ME* TO SLOSH AROUND HERE, BUT--

TIME FOR A LOCATION CHANGE.

GODS, IF YOU WILL...

LIKE HELL--!

WHA--?

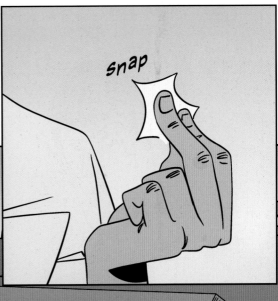

Snap

DOWNTOWN HOLLYWOOD.

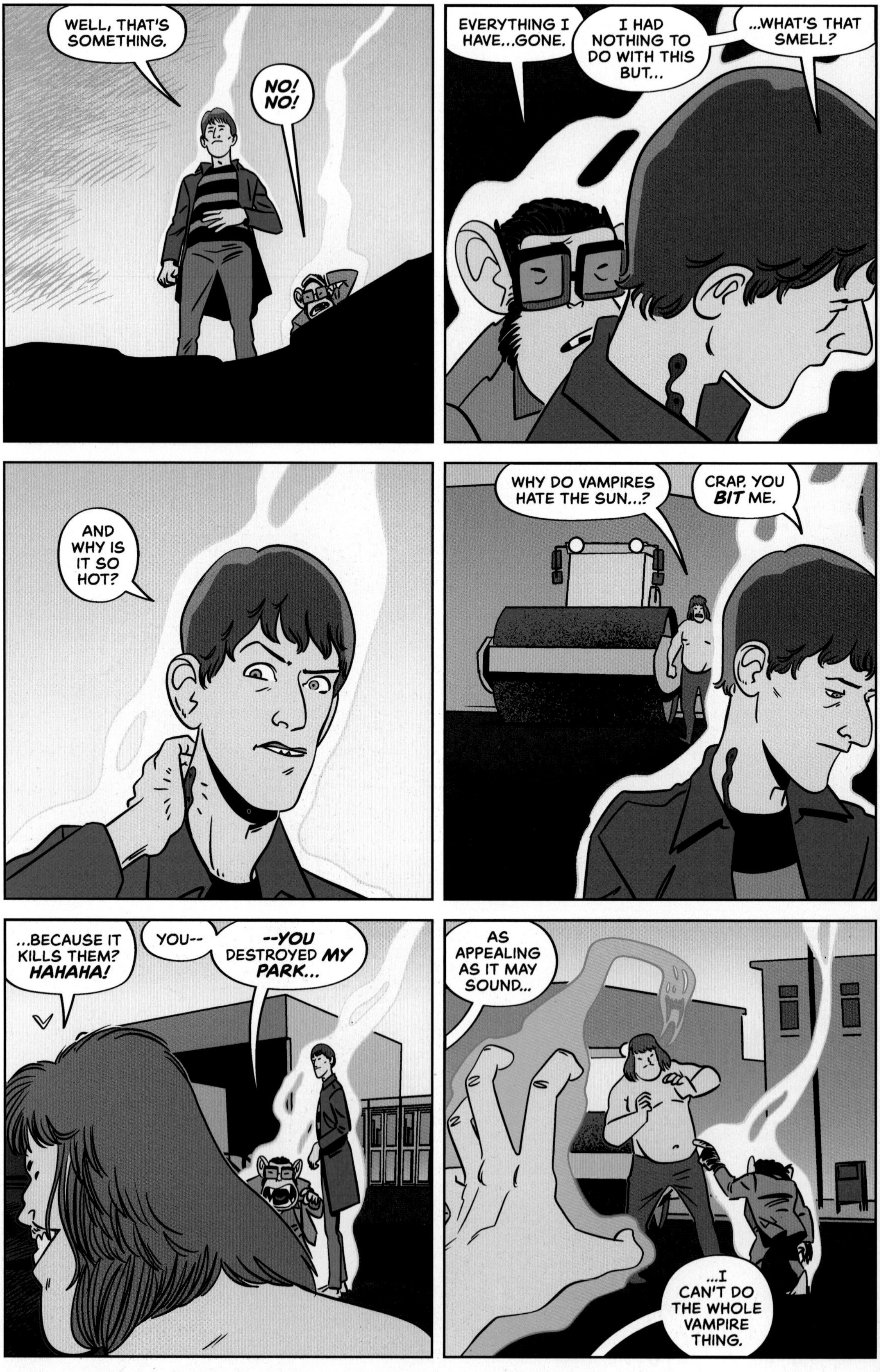
WELL, THAT'S SOMETHING.
NO! NO!
EVERYTHING I HAVE...GONE.
I HAD NOTHING TO DO WITH THIS BUT...
...WHAT'S THAT SMELL?
AND WHY IS IT SO HOT?
WHY DO VAMPIRES HATE THE SUN...?
CRAP. YOU BIT ME.
...BECAUSE IT KILLS THEM? HAHAHA!
YOU--
--YOU DESTROYED MY PARK...
AS APPEALING AS IT MAY SOUND...
...I CAN'T DO THE WHOLE VAMPIRE THING.

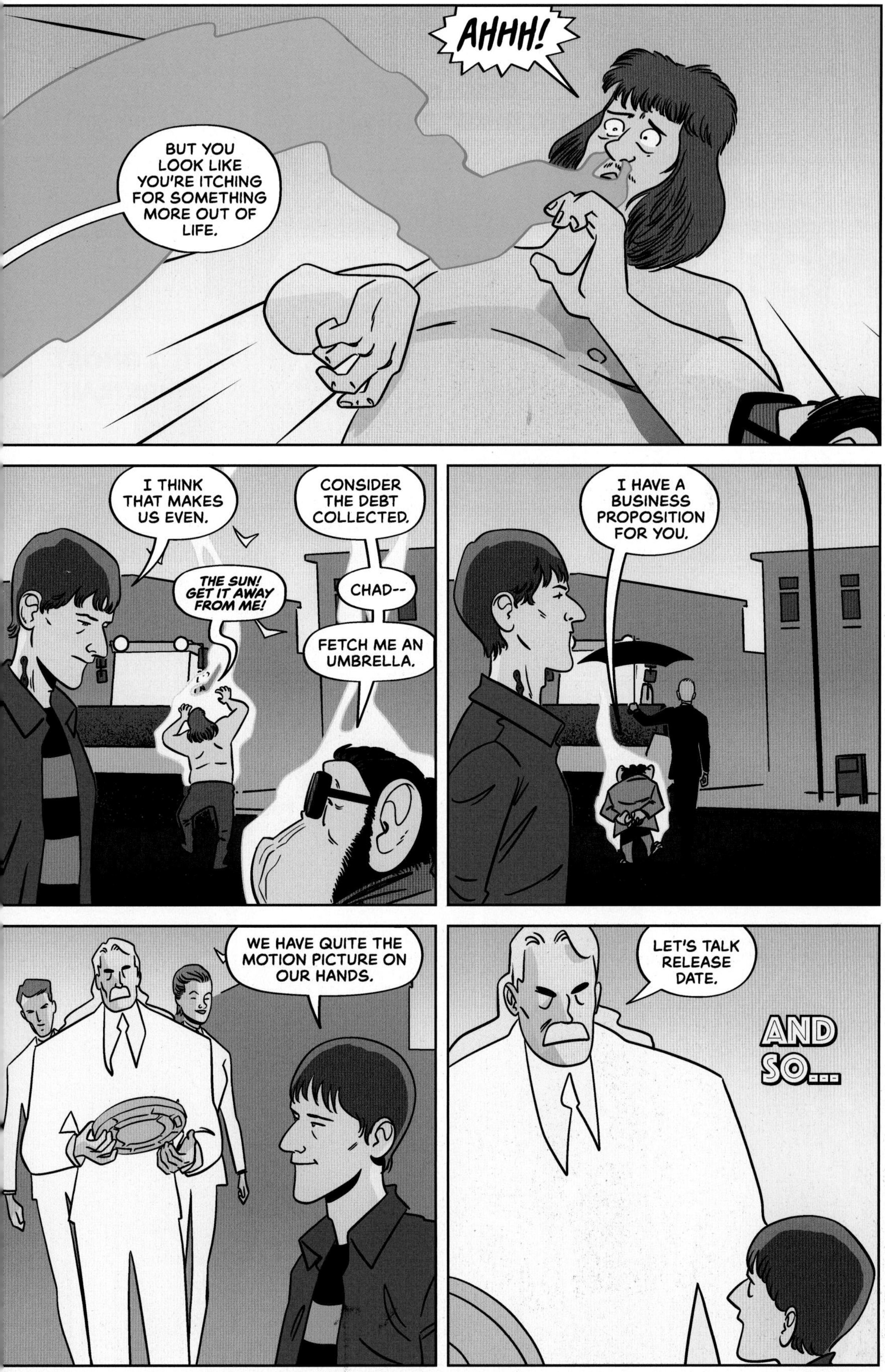
AHHH!
BUT YOU LOOK LIKE YOU'RE ITCHING FOR SOMETHING MORE OUT OF LIFE.
I THINK THAT MAKES US EVEN.
THE SUN! GET IT AWAY FROM ME!
CONSIDER THE DEBT COLLECTED.
CHAD--
FETCH ME AN UMBRELLA.
I HAVE A BUSINESS PROPOSITION FOR YOU.
WE HAVE QUITE THE MOTION PICTURE ON OUR HANDS.
LET'S TALK RELEASE DATE.
AND SO...

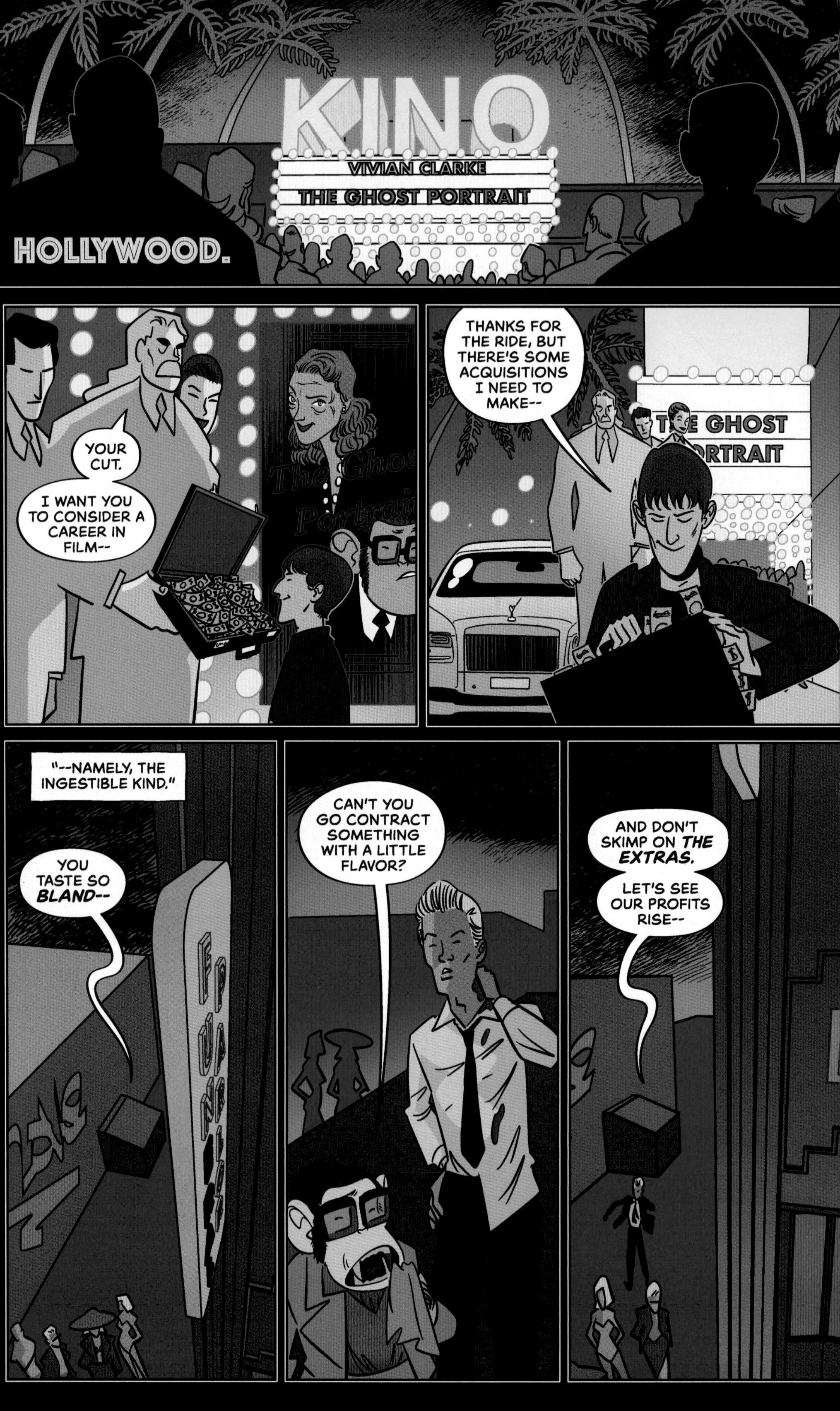
KINO
VIVIAN CLARKE
THE GHOST PORTRAIT
HOLLYWOOD.
YOUR CUT.
I WANT YOU TO CONSIDER A CAREER IN FILM--
THANKS FOR THE RIDE, BUT THERE'S SOME ACQUISITIONS I NEED TO MAKE--
"--NAMELY, THE INGESTIBLE KIND."
YOU TASTE SO BLAND--
CAN'T YOU GO CONTRACT SOMETHING WITH A LITTLE FLAVOR?
AND DON'T SKIMP ON THE EXTRAS.
LET'S SEE OUR PROFITS RISE--

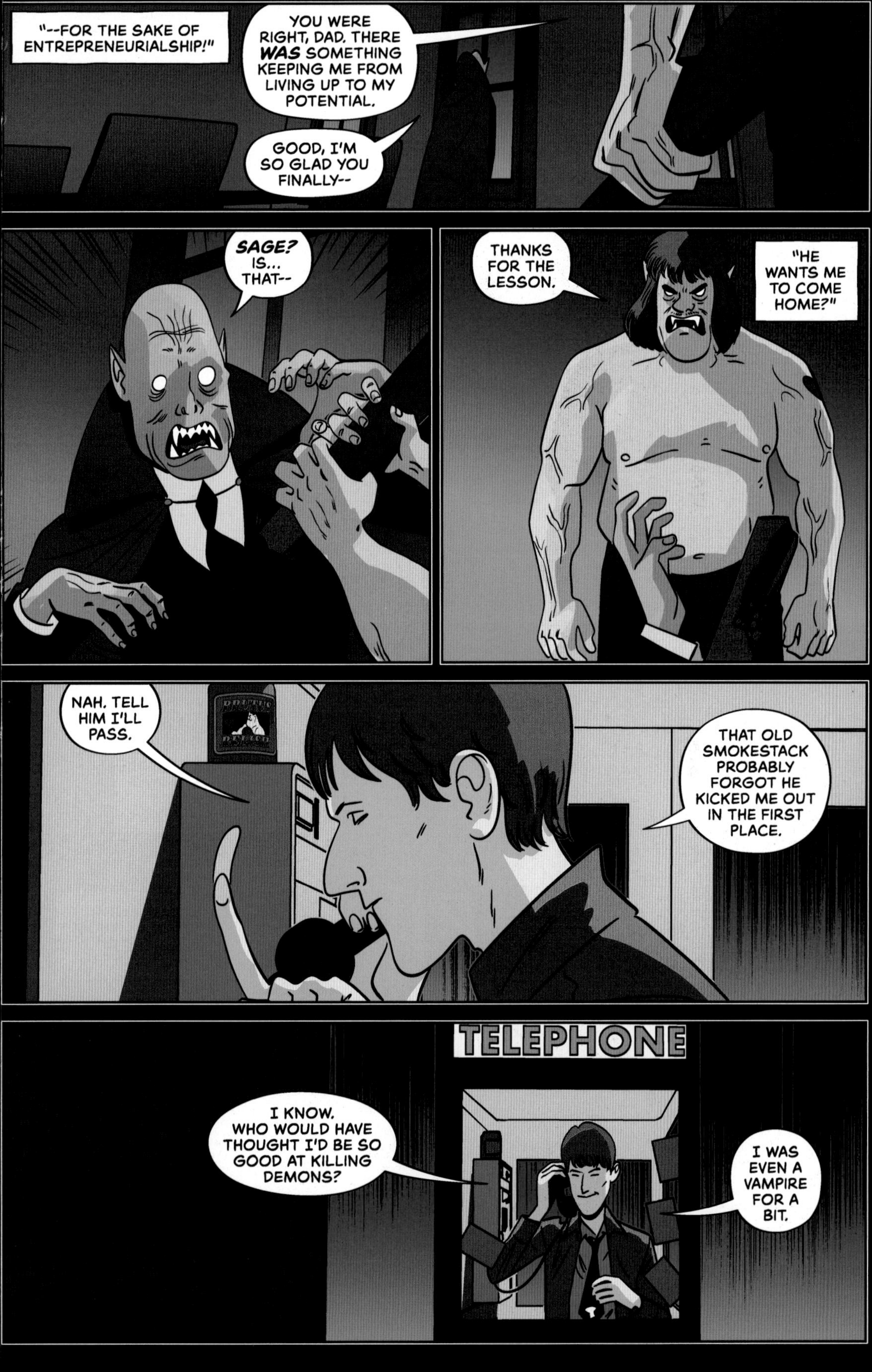
"--FOR THE SAKE OF ENTREPRENEURIALSHIP!"
YOU WERE RIGHT, DAD. THERE **WAS** SOMETHING KEEPING ME FROM LIVING UP TO MY POTENTIAL.
GOOD, I'M SO GLAD YOU FINALLY--
SAGE? IS... THAT--
THANKS FOR THE LESSON.
"HE WANTS ME TO COME HOME?"
NAH. TELL HIM I'LL PASS.
THAT OLD SMOKESTACK PROBABLY FORGOT HE KICKED ME OUT IN THE FIRST PLACE.
TELEPHONE
I KNOW. WHO WOULD HAVE THOUGHT I'D BE SO GOOD AT KILLING DEMONS?
I WAS EVEN A VAMPIRE FOR A BIT.

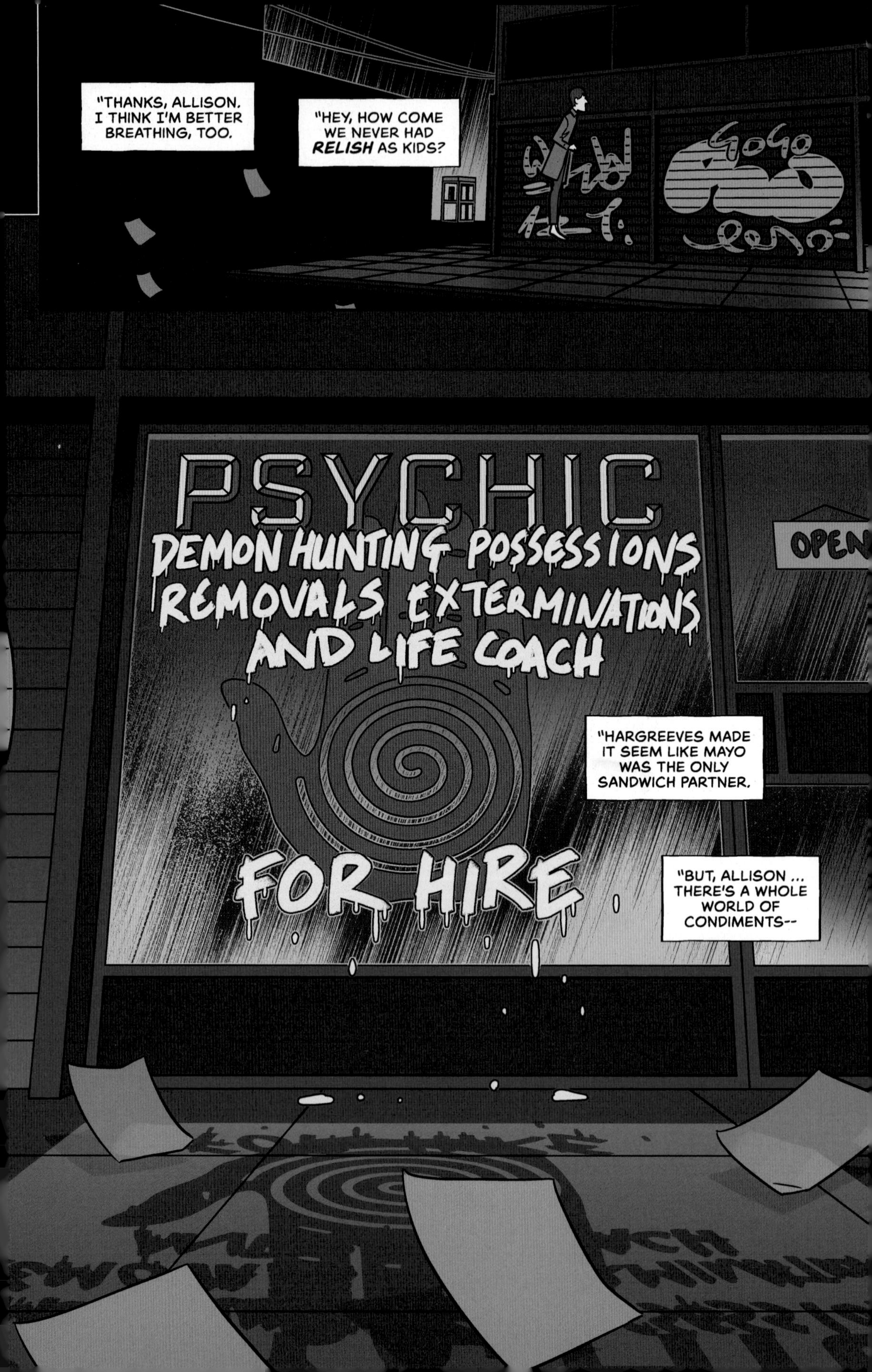
"THANKS, ALLISON. I THINK I'M BETTER BREATHING, TOO.
"HEY, HOW COME WE NEVER HAD RELISH AS KIDS?
PSYCHIC
DEMON HUNTING POSSESSIONS REMOVALS EXTERMINATIONS AND LIFE COACH
FOR HIRE
OPEN
"HARGREEVES MADE IT SEEM LIKE MAYO WAS THE ONLY SANDWICH PARTNER.
"BUT, ALLISON ... THERE'S A WHOLE WORLD OF CONDIMENTS--

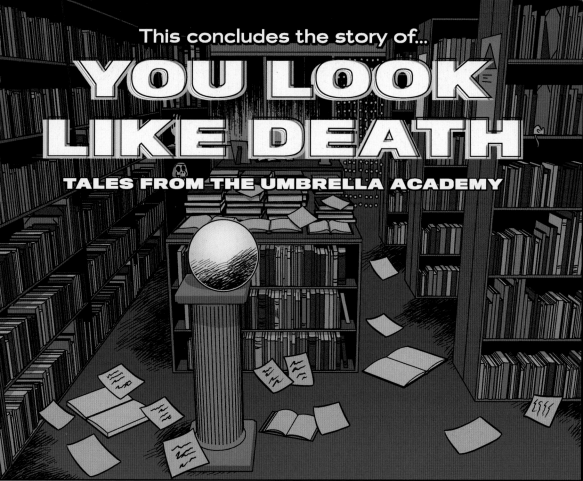

This concludes the story of...

YOU LOOK LIKE DEATH

TALES FROM THE UMBRELLA ACADEMY

"--AND MY MOUTH IS READY."

THE END

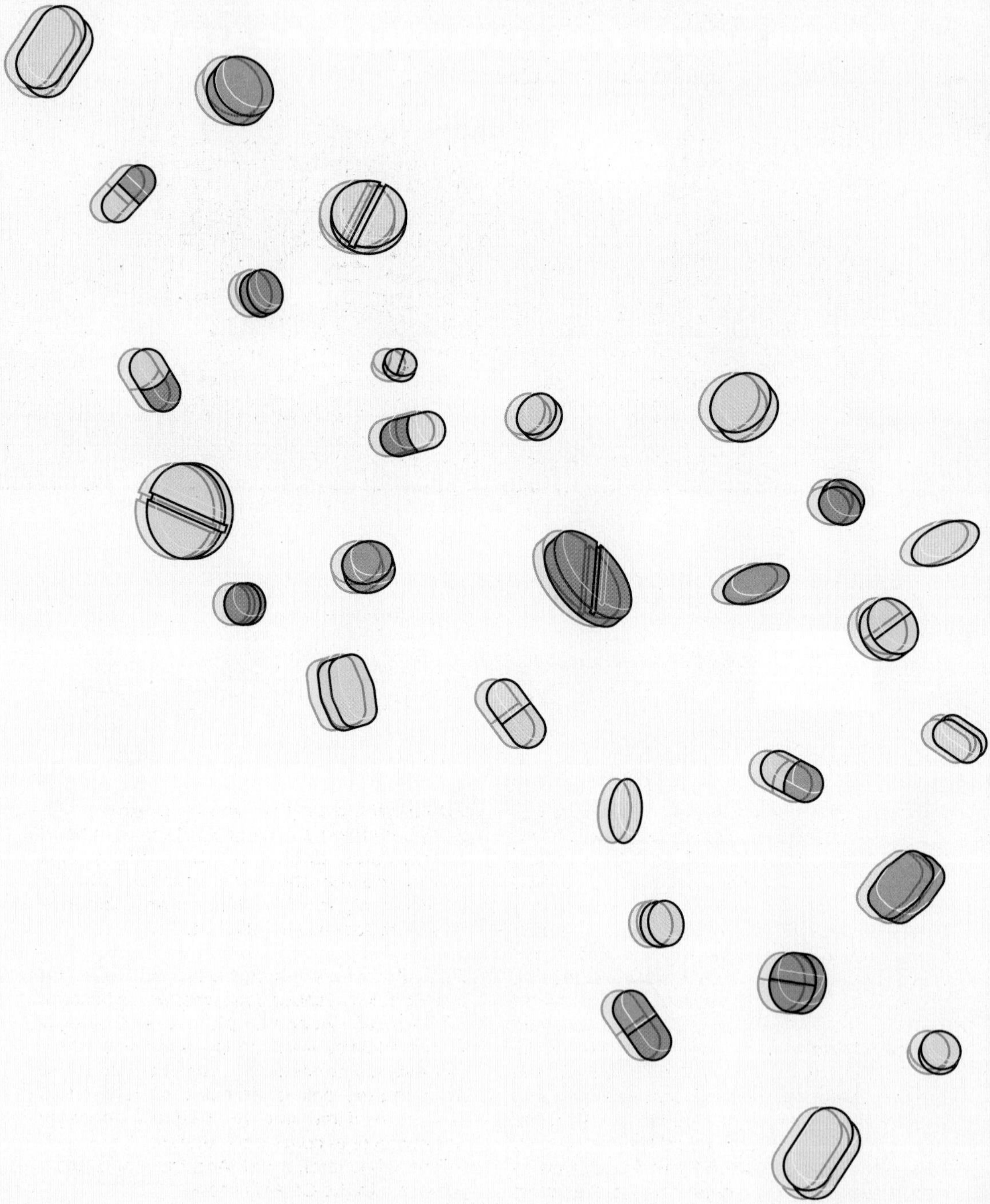

WELL, WHAT HAPPENED WAS . . .

BY SHAUN SIMON

It was probably sometime in winter of 2005 or 2006. I was sitting at Gerard's parents' kitchen table smoking cigarettes and drinking coffee, which everything always seemed to revolve around, when he pulled out a sketchbook. Now, I had known Gerard pretty well up to this point. We spent a few years together sharing a studio space in our separate bands which led to playing shows to a handfuls of kids in basements and VFW halls across North Jersey. I had then crashed on a bench in his van for a few more years while cities, states, and countries flew by outside the window. Throughout these adventures, a big part of what we did usually started with, "Well, what happened was . . ." and would be followed by wildly inaccurate stories of how a bridge came into existence or how a department store got its name or what the rotting tuna fish sandwich, that earned its own name and became a member of the crew, did when we went to sleep.

And yes, the Gerard that people were seeing on stage in places that were held together by allowance money and teenage angst was without

a doubt a big part of who he is—there was always another part to him I got to see in hotel rooms, cafés, ditches on the highway, and parking lots that those who snuck out of their homes at night, while their parents thought they were fast asleep, did not.

That all changed when he flipped open the sketchbook and showed me what would become the *Umbrella Academy* pitch. I remember it vividly because it hit me like a ton of bricks. I immediately connected to the characters, the story, and the look. It felt real. It felt lived in and fresh at the same time. The *Umbrella Academy* was my favorite comic book that didn't exist yet. A little while later, it did. And the world got a glimpse into the Gerard I knew.

Writing takes up a lot of head space and I have never had the desire to write mainstream comics for existing characters. I would rather put that energy into my own creations, or those of my friends and I. The only exception to that has always been *Umbrella Academy*. It's the only book that I have ever wanted to be part of. It's the only book that I felt I understood at its core and could add to. I don't think I ever told Gerard that, but I think he may have had the idea.

Just like those old days, Gerard and I have continued our, "Well, what happened was . . ." through our comics careers. It doesn't take place in the back of vans, hotel rooms, or at kitchen tables full of ashtrays and coffee cups anymore. Today, it's through texting and phone calls as we live on different sides of the country. We toss ideas around for stories and characters and feed off of each other in a creative whirlwind. I am not one who minds spoilers and have always dove in ear first when it came to hearing future *Umbrella Academy* stories.

A couple of years ago, around the time Gerard was getting back into the world of *Umbrella Academy* with "Hotel Oblivion", he called me up and asked if I would be interested in writing a spinoff with him. It would revolve around Klaus and would take place ten years before "Apocalypse Suite" started when Klaus ends up in Hollywood after Hargreeves kicked him out of the mansion. Obviously, I said yes. Out of all of the characters, Klaus always stood out to me. Behind the quick wit and carelessness, there is damage in him. Getting to explore that was going to make for a great story.

And then the ideas started. What if Klaus overdoses and ends up in a place called "The Void?" What if he loves it there so much that he keeps trying to get back because he meets a real friend? What if he's in debt to a vampire chimp drug-lord who chases him to Hollywood to get his money? What if this vampire chimp opens an amusement park for vampires in an old subway station? What if Klaus winds up with an aging actress who gives Klaus drugs in return for channeling old actresses into her so she can get her career back? What do we call the book?

This is how we work. It's a flurry of texts, e-mails, and phone calls. The whirlwind of ideas swirls around in our heads until the story takes shape around it. It's one of the best feelings in the world when it all comes together. I had my dream writing job at this point but there was still one question left: who would draw it?

Gabriel Bá is the *Umbrella Academy* artist. I was blown away from the the first time I had seen his initial pinup of Hargreeves and co. based on Gerard's pitch. From the way he draws the characters to the details he adds to this world; his style makes *Umbrella Academy* like no other comic book out there. It was hard for me to wrap my head around seeing this world through the art of anyone else. There was someone Gerard had his eye on for it, though—I.N.J. Culbard. Gerard's eye for visuals is like no one else and when he told me about I.N.J., it all clicked.

I.N.J. brings this book to life in ways that honors what Gabriel does in the regular *Umbrella Academy* series, but expands the world in amazing ways. It has been an absolute joy seeing his first designs for these characters, new and old, and getting his pages in. His colors round it all off and make this book as much of its own thing as it is part of the larger *Umbrella Academy* universe.

This book is the product of one of my oldest and best friends and me doing what we love together. There is little in this world that gives me more joy than that. As I sit here and wrap this afterword up, my phones dings. I haven't looked down at it yet, but there is a good chance it is Gerard texting to say, "Well, what happened was . . ."

SHAUN SIMON
AUGUST, 2020

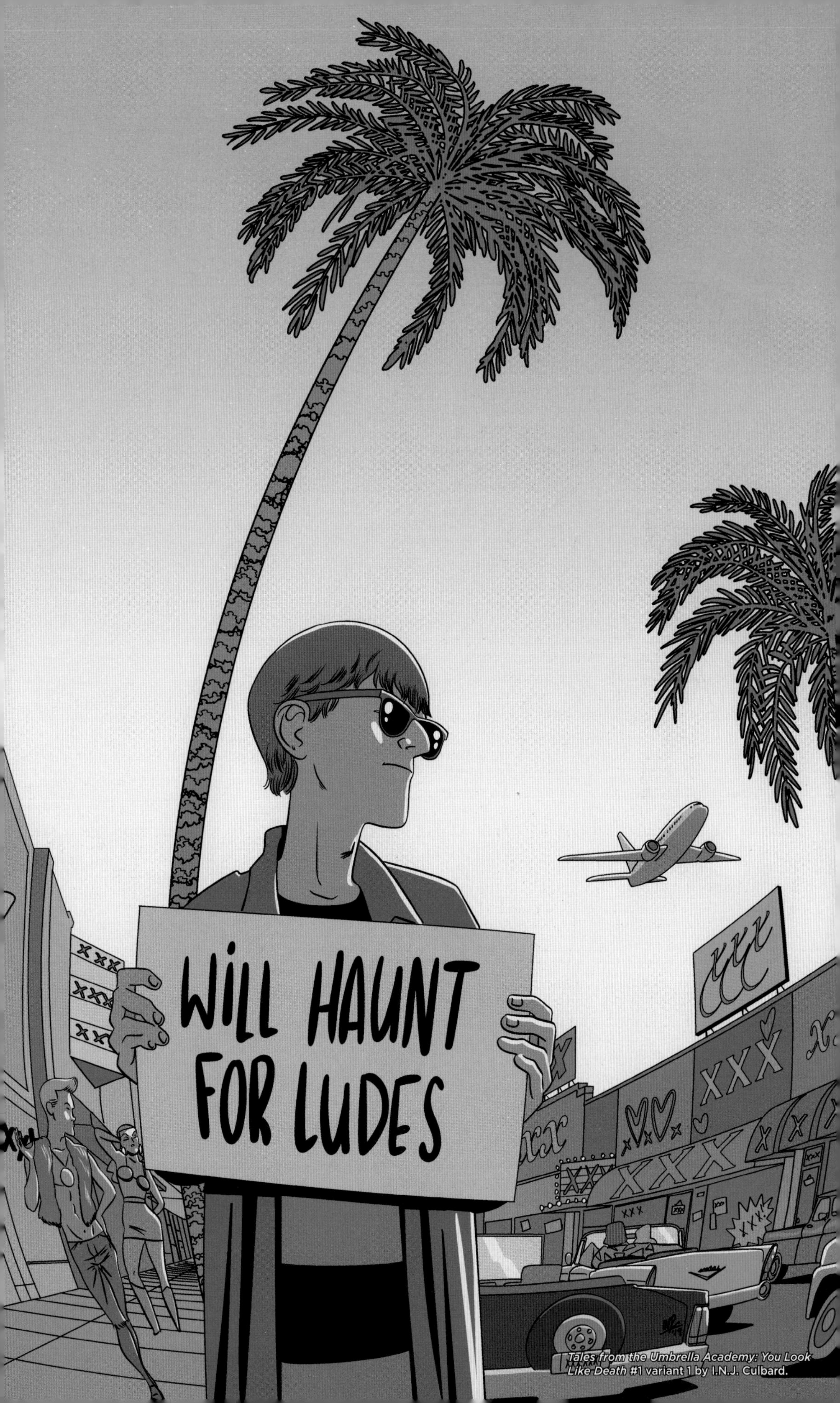
WILL HAUNT
FOR LUDES
Tales from the Umbrella Academy: You Look Like Death #1 variant 1 by I.N.J. Culbard.

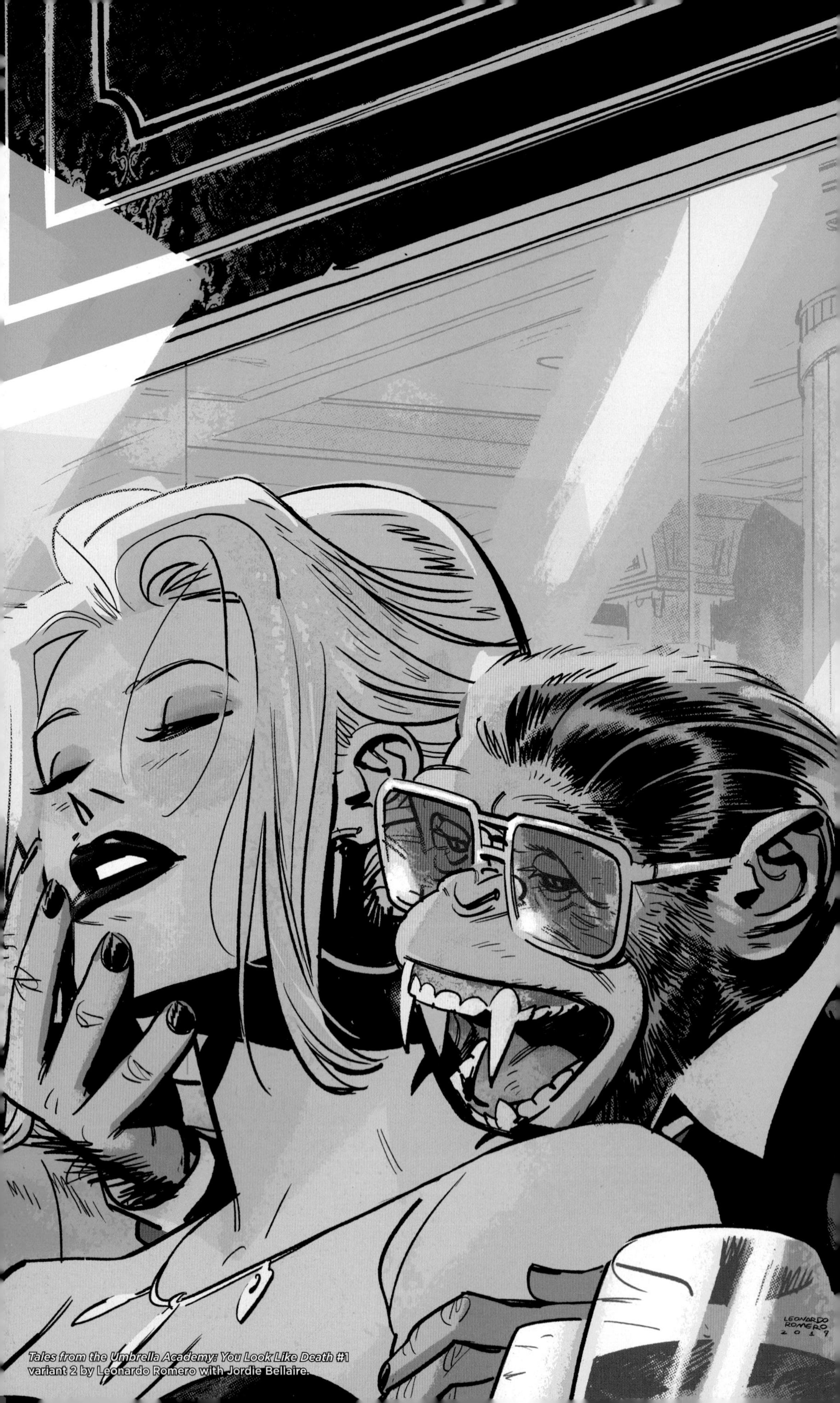
LEONARDO
ROMERO
2017

Tales from the Umbrella Academy: You Look Like Death #1
variant 2 by Leonardo Romero with Jordie Bellaire.

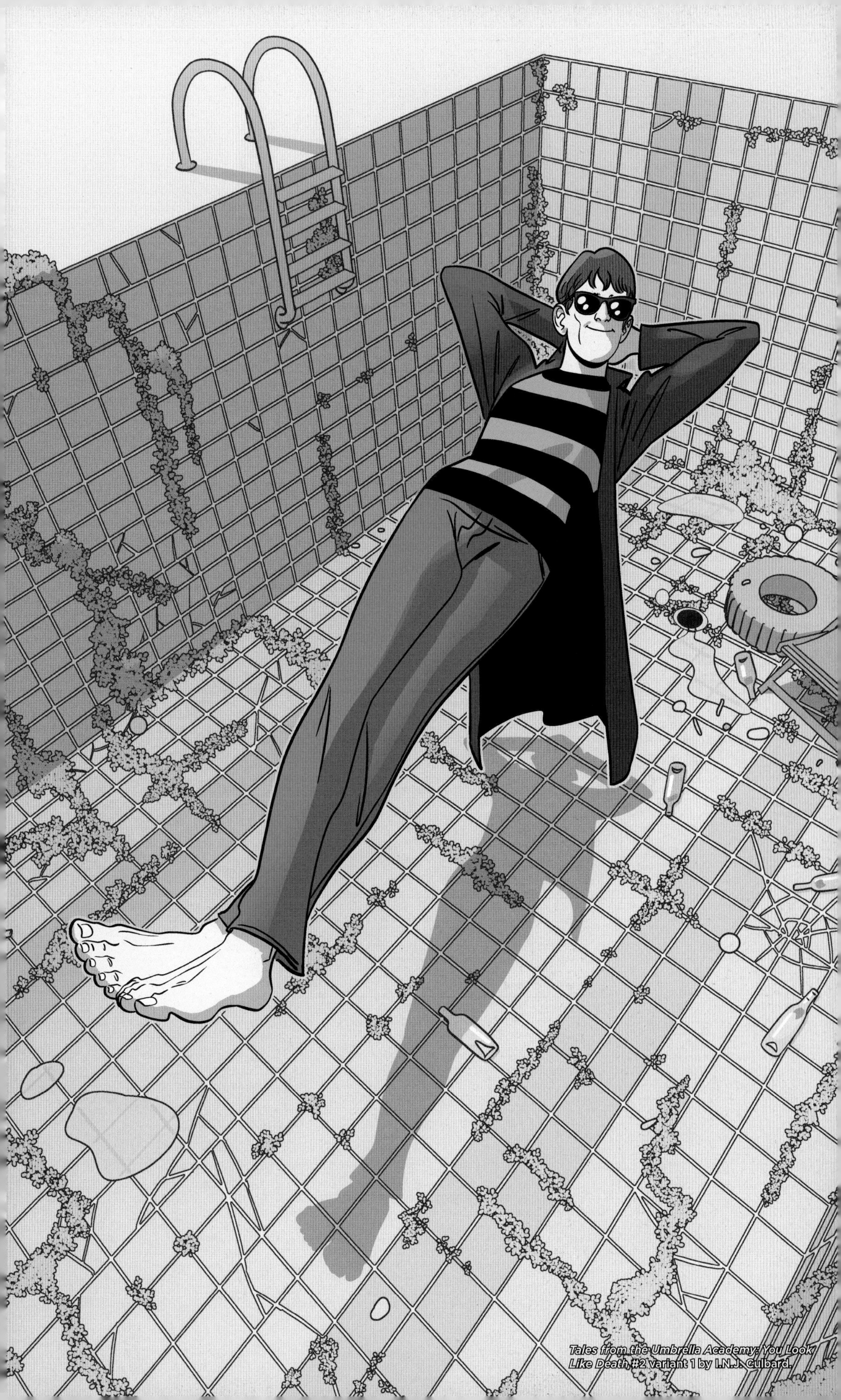

Tales from the Umbrella Academy: You Look Like Death #2 variant 1 by I.N.J. Culbard.

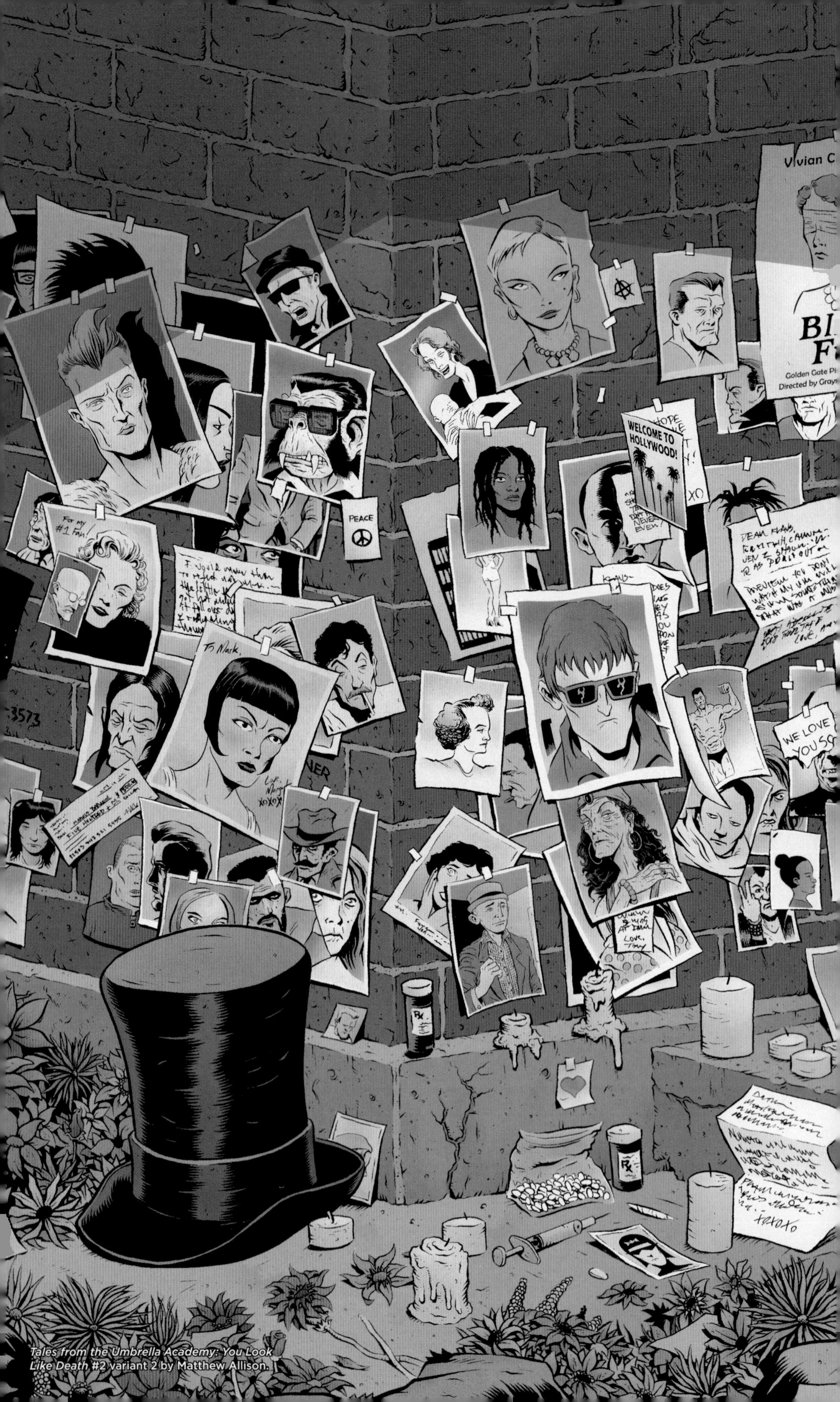
WELCOME TO HOLLYWOOD!
PEACE
For my #1 Fan!
To Mark,
Love, Tony

Tales from the Umbrella Academy: You Look Like Death #2 variant 2 by Matthew Allison.

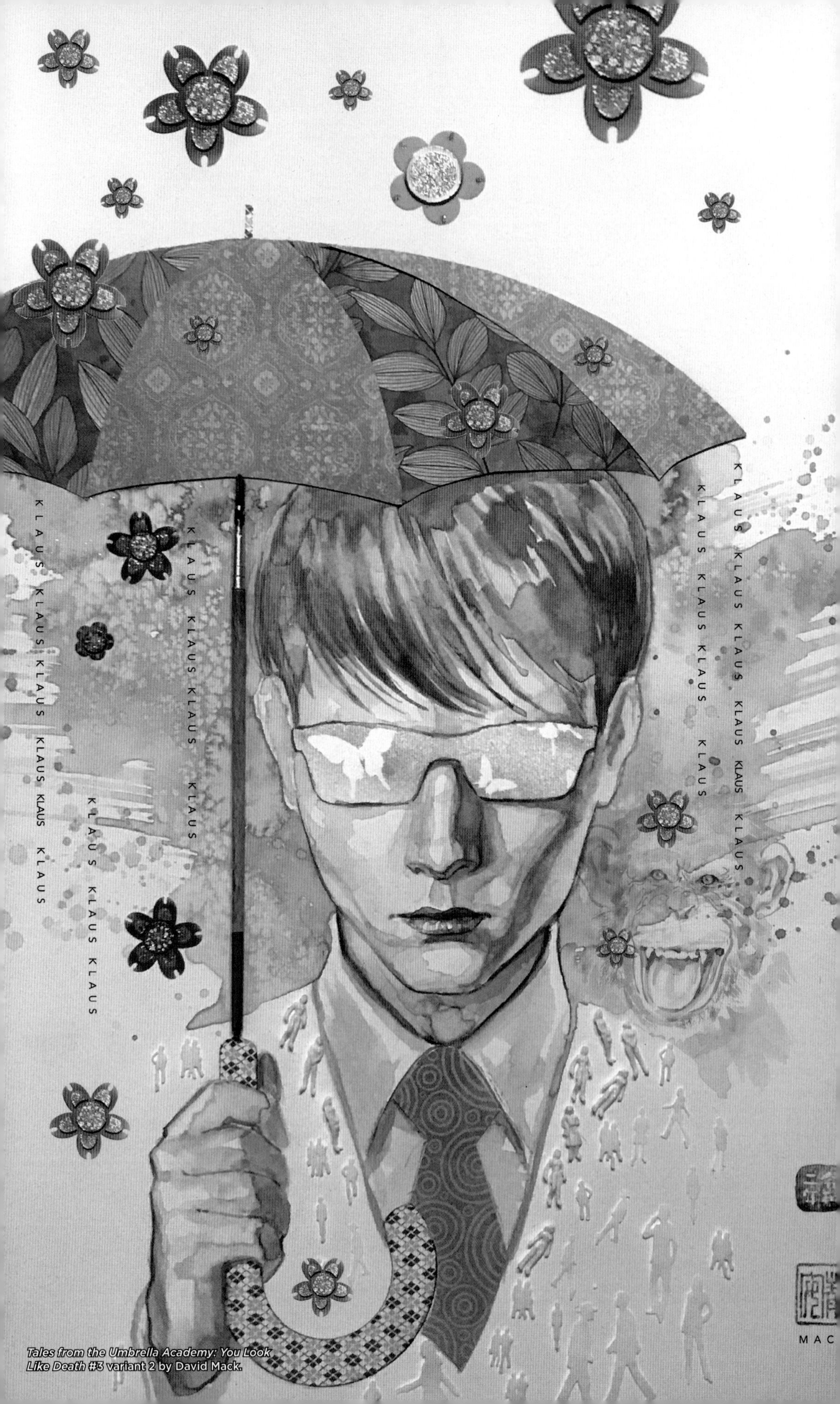
KLAUS KLAUS KLAUS KLAUS
KLAUS KLAUS KLAUS KLAUS
KLAUS KLAUS KLAUS
KLAUS KLAUS KLAUS KLAUS KLAUS
KLAUS KLAUS KLAUS KLAUS
MAC

Tales from the Umbrella Academy: You Look Like Death #3 variant 2 by David Mack.

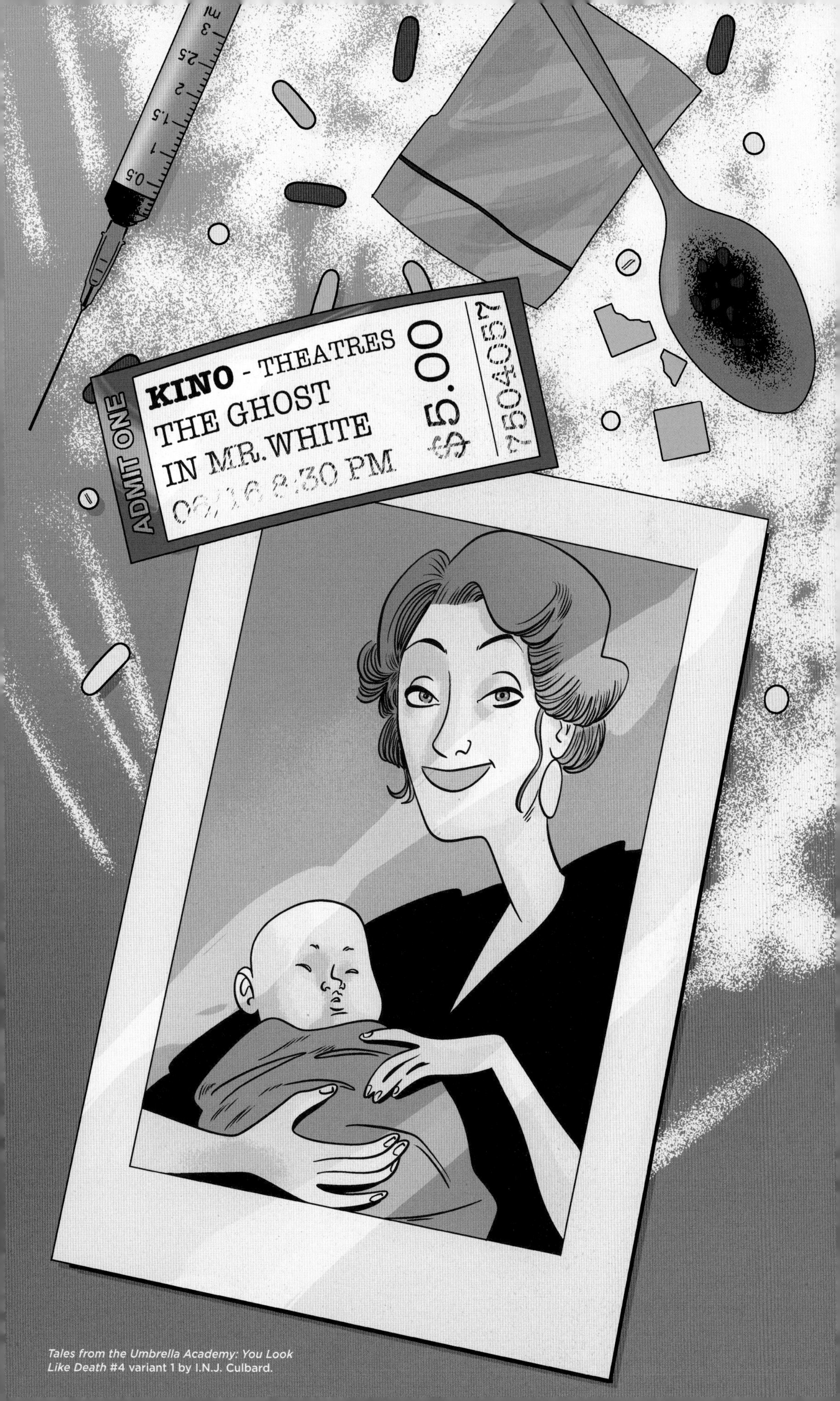
ADMIT ONE
KINO - THEATRES
THE GHOST
IN MR.WHITE
$5.00
7504057

Tales from the Umbrella Academy: You Look Like Death #4 variant 1 by I.N.J. Culbard.

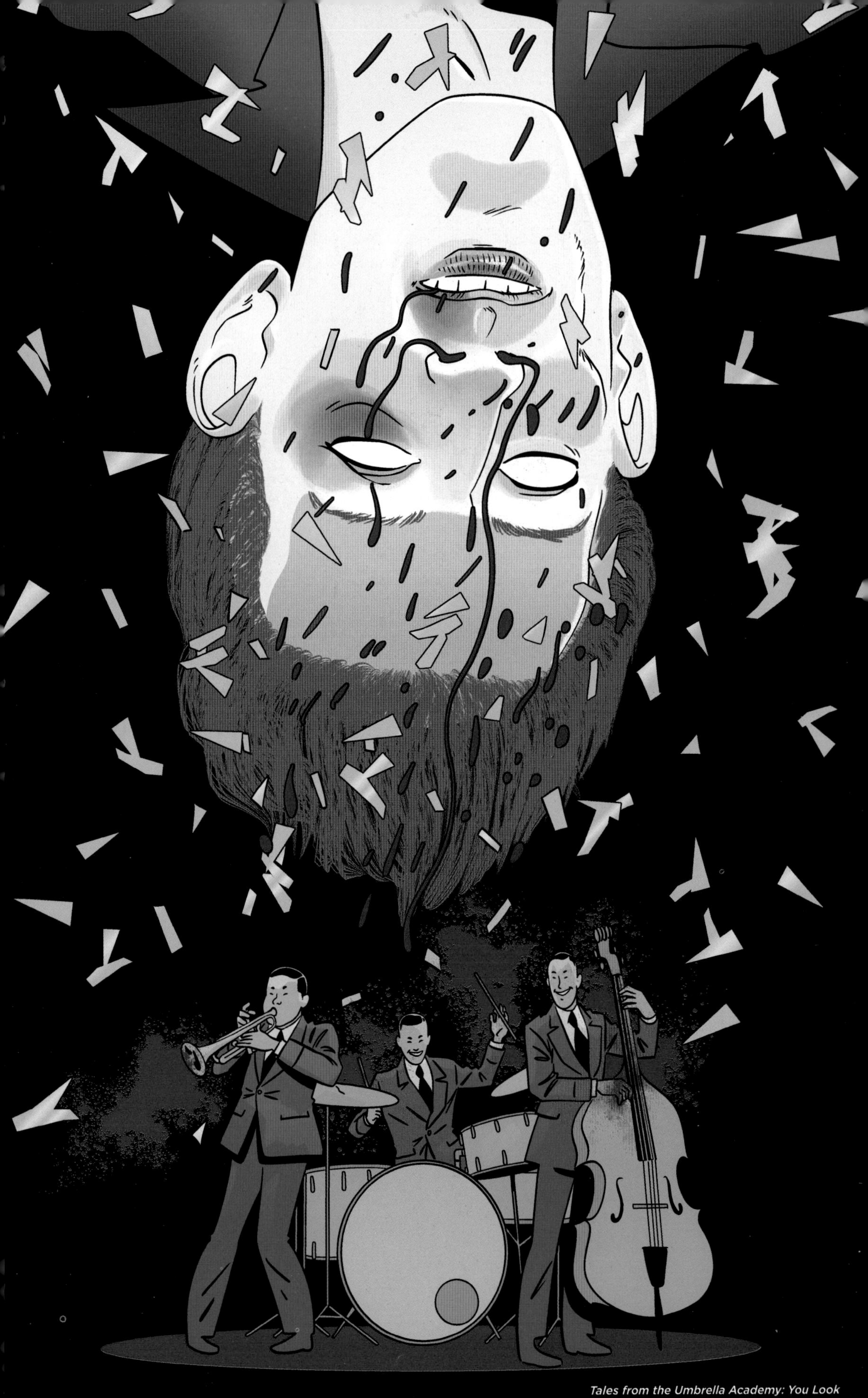

Tales from the Umbrella Academy: You Look Like Death #5 variant 1 by I.N.J. Culbard.

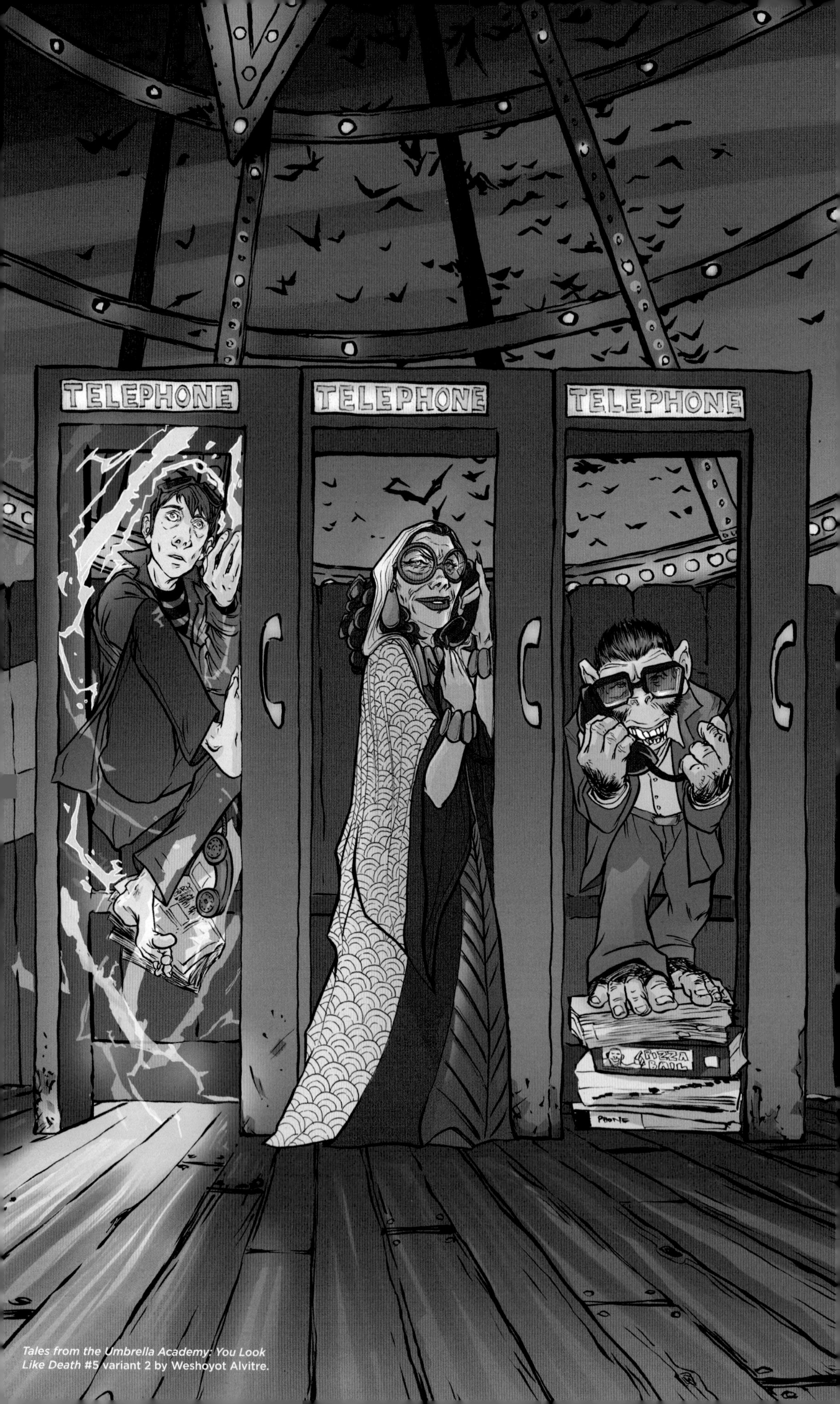
TELEPHONE
TELEPHONE
TELEPHONE

Tales from the Umbrella Academy: You Look Like Death #5 variant 2 by Weshoyot Alvitre.

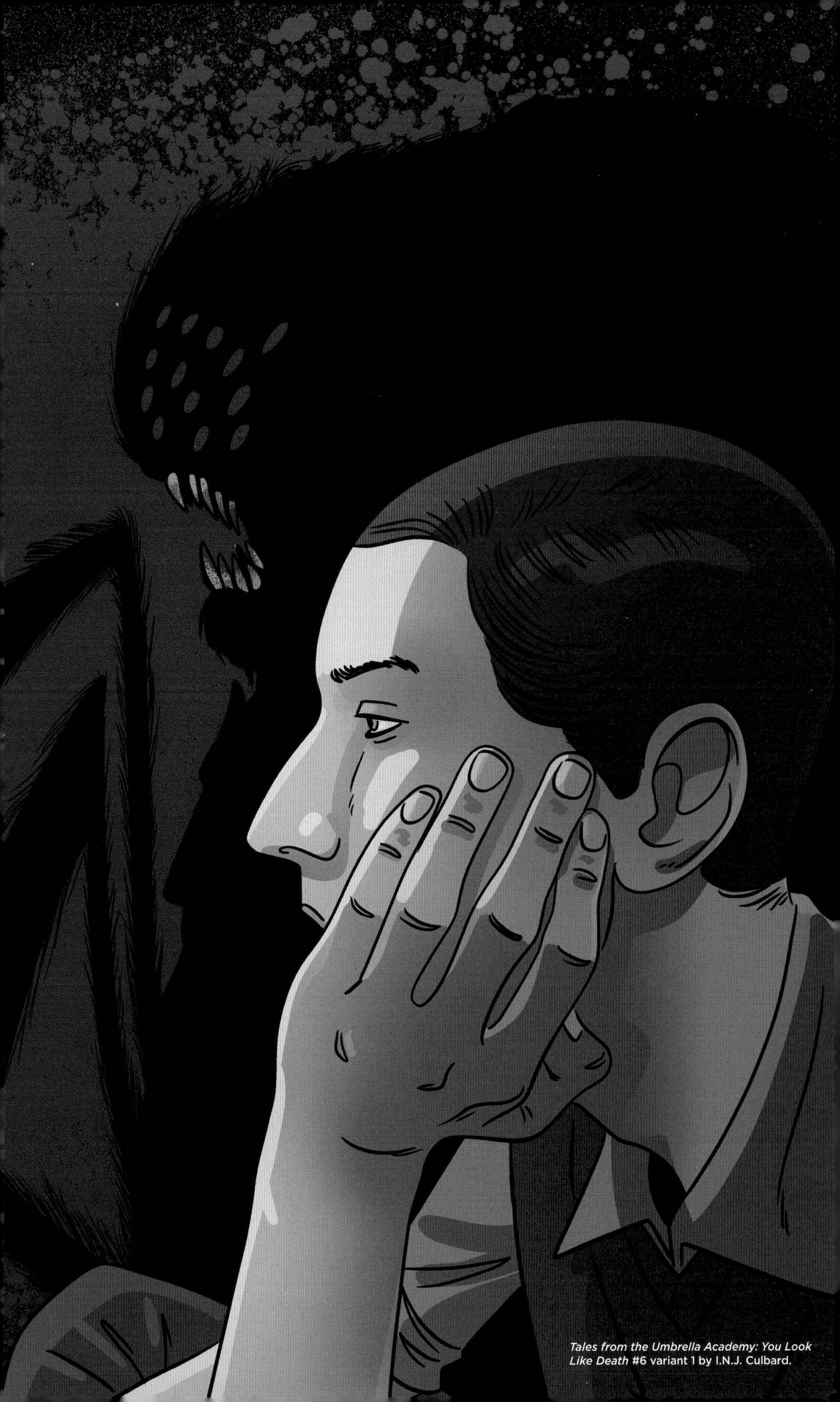

Tales from the Umbrella Academy: You Look Like Death #6 variant 1 by I.N.J. Culbard.

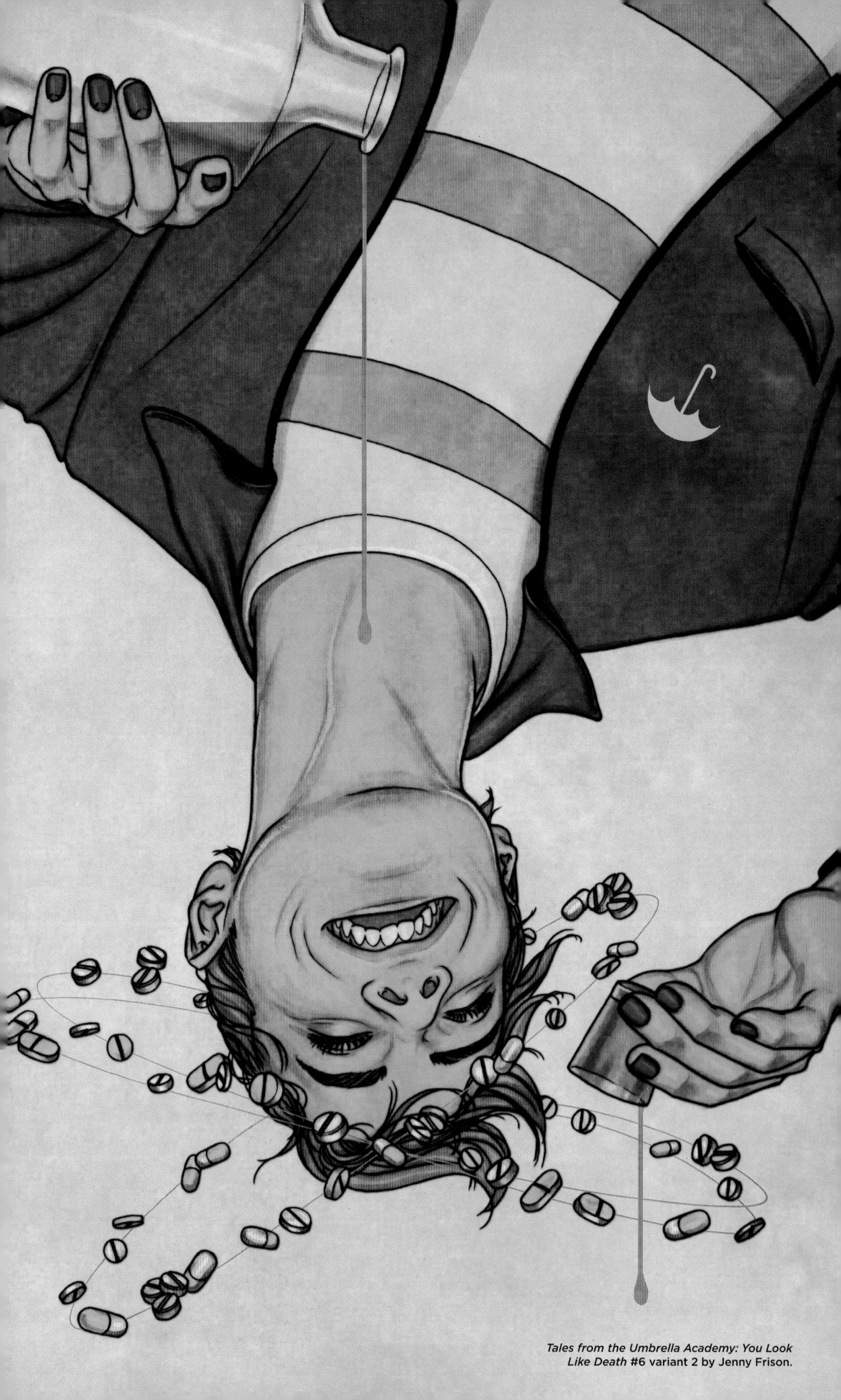

Tales from the Umbrella Academy: You Look Like Death #6 variant 2 by Jenny Frison.

YOU LOOK LIKE DEATH

TALES FROM THE UMBRELLA ACADEMY™

SKETCHBOOK NOTES BY I.N.J. CULBARD

This is the original costume design for Klaus for the series. Most of the elements here stuck, but the shirt and tie had to go in favor of a less formal striped T. He would eventually "level up" to wear the shirt and tie.

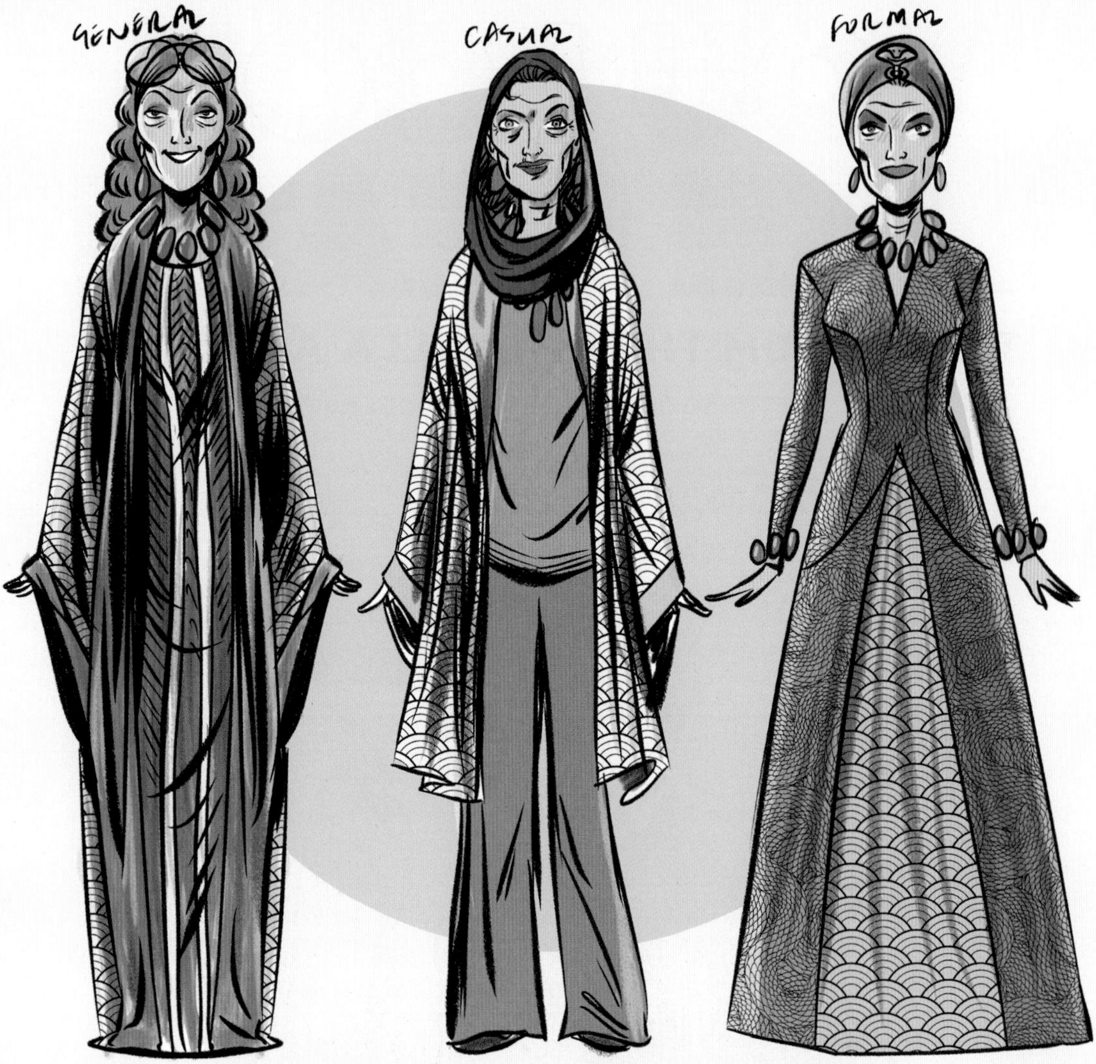
GENERAL
CASUAL
FORMAL

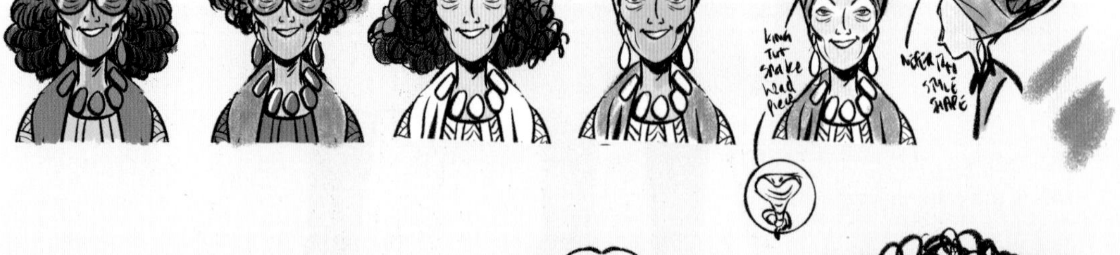
King Tut snake head piece

Viv needed to look old Hollywood, like Lauren Bacall or Bette Davis, so I focused on her eyes, giving them a distinctive size and shape. I think I managed to establish her facial features pretty swiftly. Her attire, on the other hand, took some time. Although she generally wears the same thing, issue to issue, her jewelry changes with each appearance.

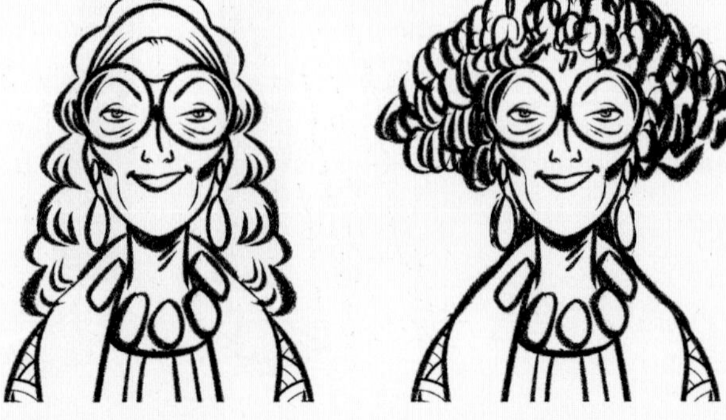

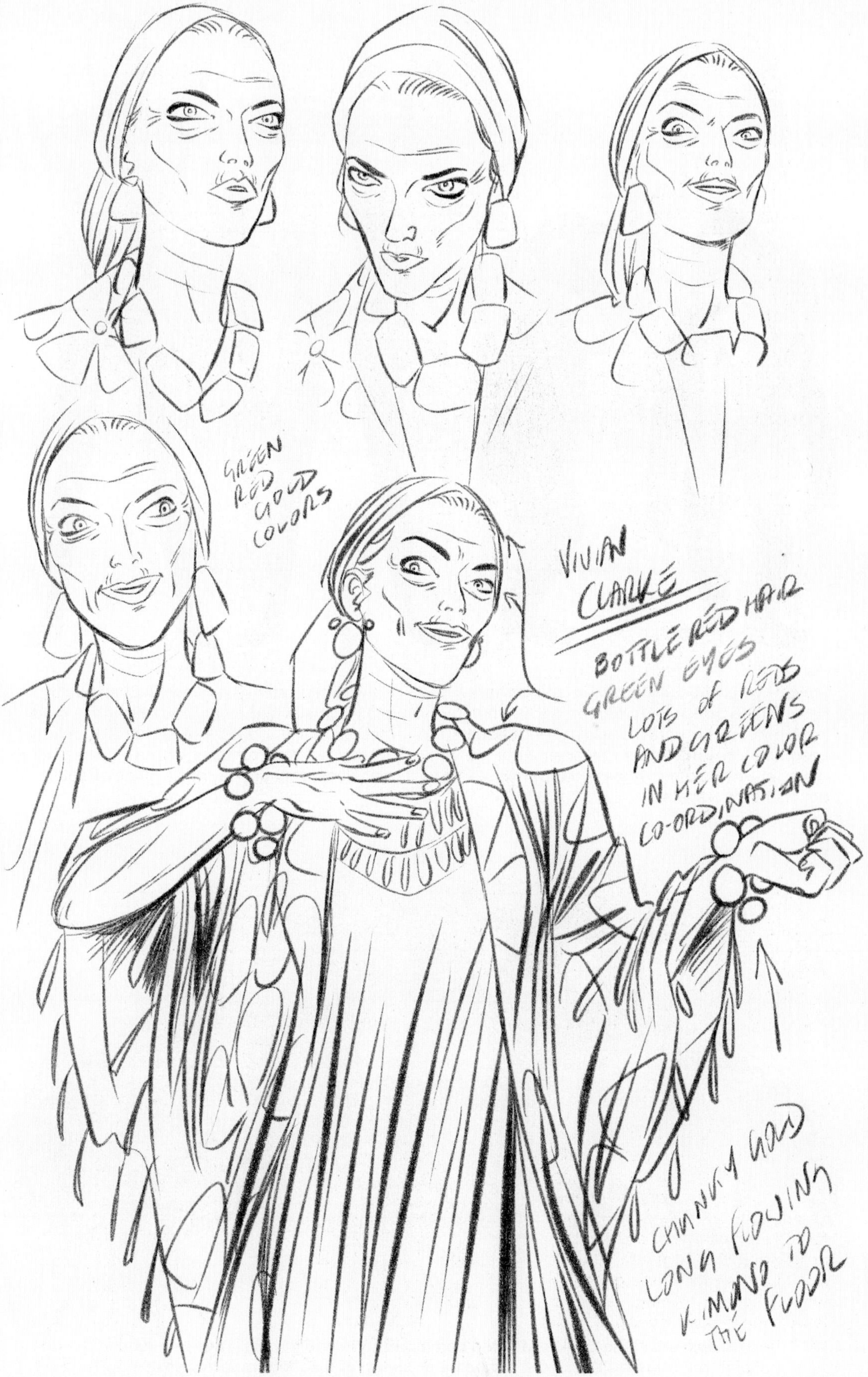
GREEN RED GOLD COLORS
VIVIAN CLARKE
BOTTLE RED HAIR
GREEN EYES
LOTS OF REDS AND GREENS IN HER COLOR CO-ORDINATION
CHUNKY GOLD
LONG FLOWING KIMONO TO THE FLOOR

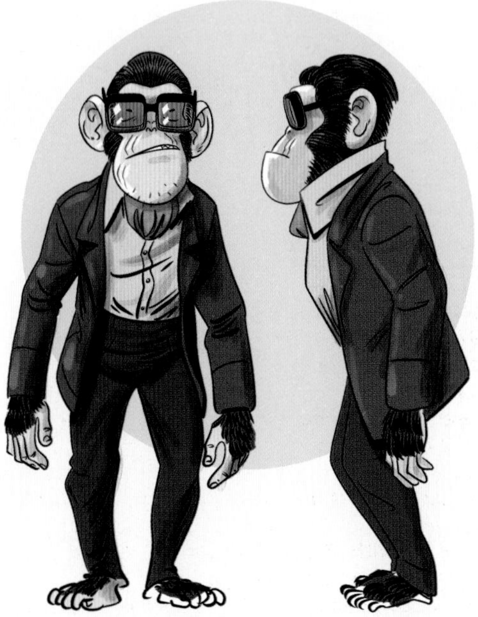

Shivers would loosen up a bit somewhere between this design and when we first see him in the book. His proportions would change once I had him alongside other characters, but his dress sense would not. Always dapper with a penchant for cravats.

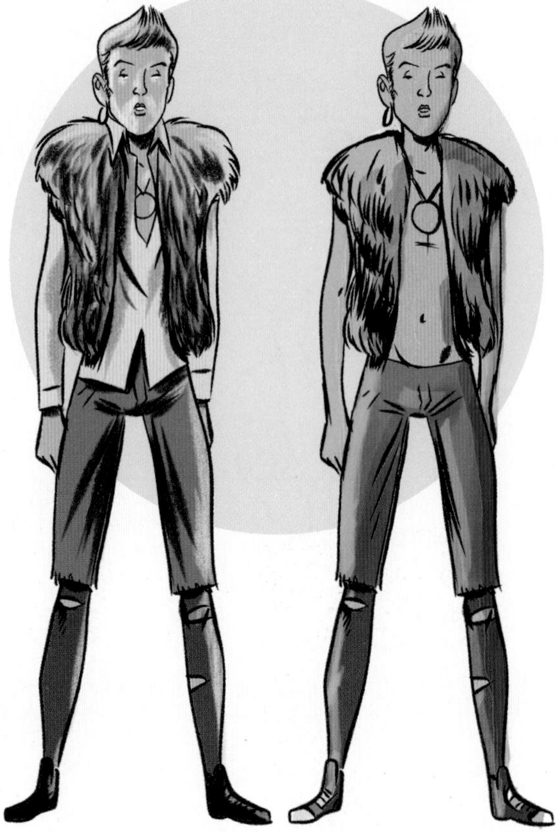

My very first attempt at drawing Chad had him in a white suit and flared trousers, with a gold medallion. He looked like he had too much money. All that remains of that idea is the medallion, very unlikely to be made of gold.

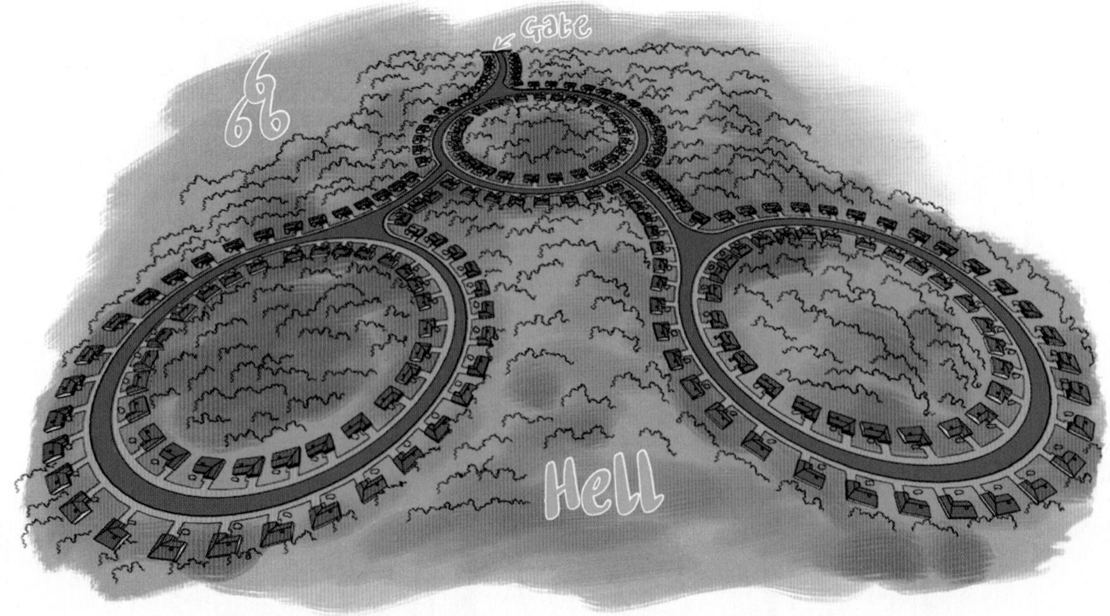
Gate
666
Hell

Hell appears in the book as a gated community. We don't actually see that much of it, but I figured the layout would be made up of a configuration of sixes.

GERARD WAY

Gerard Way began writing and drawing comics when his grandmother first put a pencil in his hand. Having developed a love of the arts, Way attended the School of Visual Arts in New York City, where he honored his skills as both writer and artist, before he made a career as a musician with My Chemical Romance. He continues to write comics to this day, including *True Lives of the Fabulous Killjoys* and *Doom Patrol*, and he enjoys it immensely. He lives in Southern California with his wife Lindsey and their daughter Bandit.
Photo by Jen Rosenstein

GABRIEL BÁ

Gabriel Bá is an Eisner and Harvey Award-winning Brazilian cartoonist, born in 1976, who has been creating comics for more than twenty years, mostly collaborating with his twin brother Fábio Moon. Together, they have published such graphic novels as the New York Times Bestseller *Daytripper* and *Two Brothers*, based on the acclaimed novel by Milton Hatoum, and *How to Talk to Girls at Parties*, based on the short story by Neil Gaiman. He also works with other writers on projects like super-spy-space-time-bending *Casanova* with Matt Fraction and *B.P.R.D.: 1947* and *B.P.R.D.: Vampire* with Mike Mignola. With *The Umbrella Academy*, he saw the opportunity to venture into the superhero genre, and to go bold with the crazy and bizarre storytelling possibilities of the medium, while still telling personal and deep character driven stories.
Photo by J.R. Duran

SHAUN SIMON

In the 8th grade, Shaun Simon won best looking male in a class consisting of five males. He has since tried to live that down by playing in bands and hanging out in alleyways, which has proved successful. Today, he writes comic books, some of which include *Neverboy*, *Art Ops*, *Wizard Beach*, *Collapser*, and *You Look Like Death: Tales of the Umbrella Academy*. He lives in the Northeast with his family and is mainly concerned with dinner.
Photo by Christine Simon

I.N.J. CULBARD

I.N.J. Culbard is an award-winning graphic novelist and has adapted legendary authors such as Arthur Conan Doyle, William Burroughs, Oscar Wilde, Robert W. Chambers, and H.P. Lovecraft for SelfMadeHero. He is an artist on original series such as *The New Deadwardians* (Vertigo), *Dark Ages* (Dark Horse Comics), *Wild's End* (Boom Studios), *Brink* (2000 AD), *Brass Sun* (2000 AD), and with Christopher Cantwell on *Everything* (Berger Books) and is the writer/artist of the original graphic novel *Celeste* (SelfMadeHero). His adaptation of Lovecraft's *At the Mountains of Madness* won the British Fantasy Award.
Photo by I.N.J. Culbard

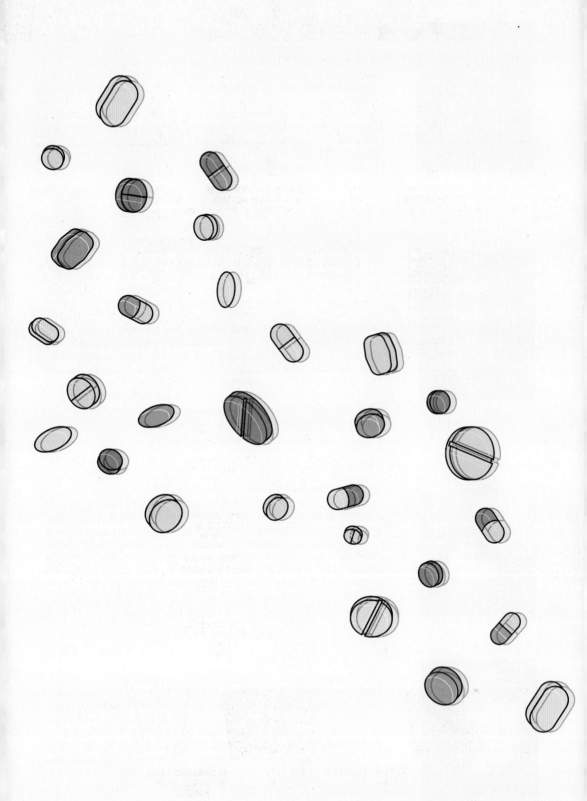

THE UMBRELLA ACADEMY™

Written by **GERARD WAY**
Art by **GABRIEL BÁ**
Featuring covers by **JAMES JEAN**

"...[F]lawless... stylish, imaginative..." —**NEWSARAMA**

"It's the X-Men for cool people." —**GRANT MORRISON (*ALL STAR SUPERMAN*)**

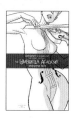

VOLUME 1: APOCALYPSE SUITE
ISBN 978-1-59307-978-9
$17.99

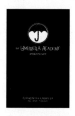

VOLUME 1: APOCALYPSE SUITE LIBRARY EDITION HARDCOVER
ISBN 978-1-50671-547-6
$39.99

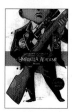

VOLUME 2: DALLAS
ISBN 978-1-59582-345-8
$17.99

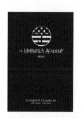

THE UMBRELLA ACADEMY: DALLAS LIBRARY EDITION HARDCOVER
ISBN 978-1-50671-548-3
$39.99

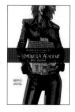

VOLUME 3: HOTEL OBLIVION
ISBN 978-1-50671-142-3
$17.99

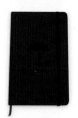

THE UMBRELLA ACADEMY JOURNAL
$19.99
NOV180283

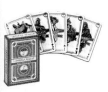

THE UMBRELLA ACADEMY PLAYING CARDS
$4.99
DEC180427

THE UMBRELLA ACADEMY MAGNET 4-PACK
$9.99
NOV180279

THE UMBRELLA ACADEMY "WHEN EVIL RAINS" MUG
NOV180282
$12.99

THE UMBRELLA ACADEMY HAZEL AND CHA CHA MUG
APR190333
$12.99

THE UMBRELLA ACADEMY ENAMEL PIN SET
$14.99
NOV180281

THE UMBRELLA ACADEMY COASTER SET
$9.99
NOV180280

THE UMBRELLA ACADEMY HAZEL AND CHA CHA MAGNET
$9.99
DEC190333

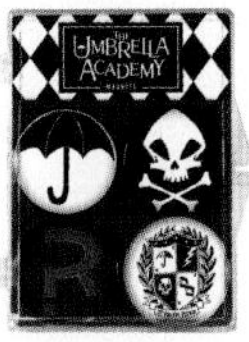

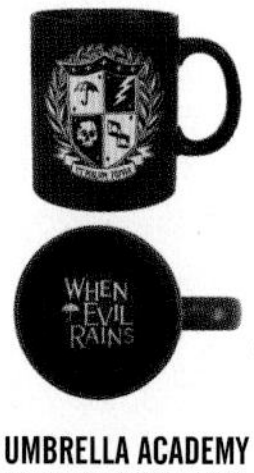

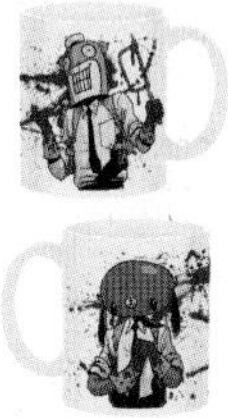

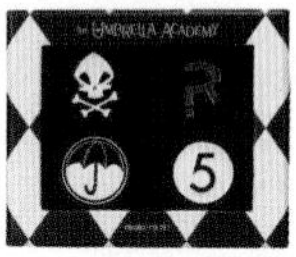

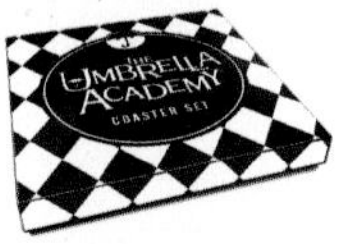

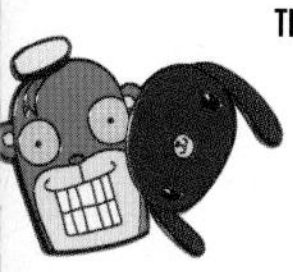

THE UMBRELLA ACADEMY CREST MAGNET
$9.99
DEC190330

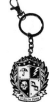

THE UMBRELLA ACADEMY CREST KEYCHAIN
$9.99
DEC190328

THE UMBRELLA ACADEMY UMBRELLA KEYCHAIN
$9.99
DEC190332

THE UMBRELLA ACADEMY HAZEL AND CHA CHA KEYCHAIN
$9.99
DEC190329

THE UMBRELLA ACADEMY HOTEL OBLIVION KEYCHAIN
$7.99
JUN190391

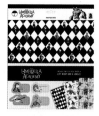

THE UMBRELLA ACADEMY UMBRELLA
JUL080073
$29.99

THE UMBRELLA ACADEMY COMPOSITION NOTEBOOK
$9.99
SEP190324

THE UMBRELLA ACADEMY UMBRELLA LOGO PATCH
$6.99
JUN190394

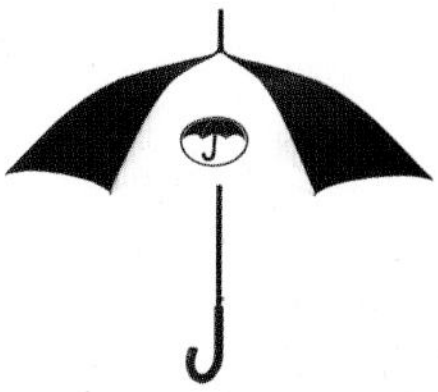

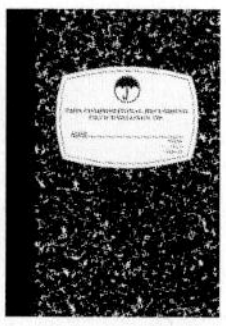

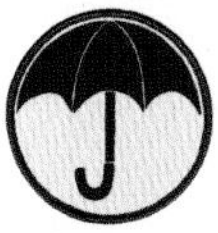

THE UMBRELLA ACADEMY CREST LOGO PATCH
$7.99
JUN190395

THE UMBRELLA ACADEMY THE RUMOR R LOGO PATCH
$6.99
JUN190393

THE UMBRELLA ACADEMY THE KRAKEN SKULL LOGO PATCH
$6.99
JUN190392

THE UMBRELLA ACADEMY WRAPPING PAPER
$9.99
AUG190333

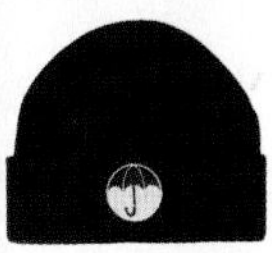

THE UMBRELLA ACADEMY KNIT HAT
$12.99
JUN190390

THE UMBRELLA ACADEMY HAZEL AND CHA CHA PINT GLASS SET
APR190334
$19.99

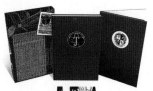

THE UMBRELLA ACADEMY: HOTEL OBLIVION DELUXE EDITION HARDCOVER
$79.99
ISBN 978-1-50671-645-9

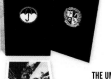

THE UMBRELLA ACADEMY: APOCALYPSE SUITE DELUXE EDITION HARDCOVER
$79.99
ISBN 978-1-50671-804-0

THE UMBRELLA ACADEMY: DALLAS DELUXE EDITION HARDCOVER
$79.99
ISBN 978-1-50671-805-7

DARK HORSE COMICS

AVAILABLE AT YOUR LOCAL COMICS SHOP OR BOOKSTORE

To find a comics shop in your area, visit comicshoplocator.com. For more information or to order direct, visit darkhorse.com.

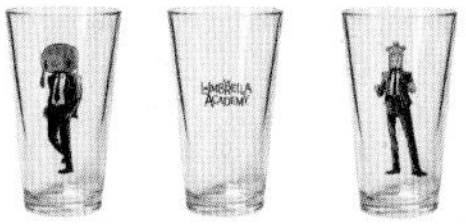

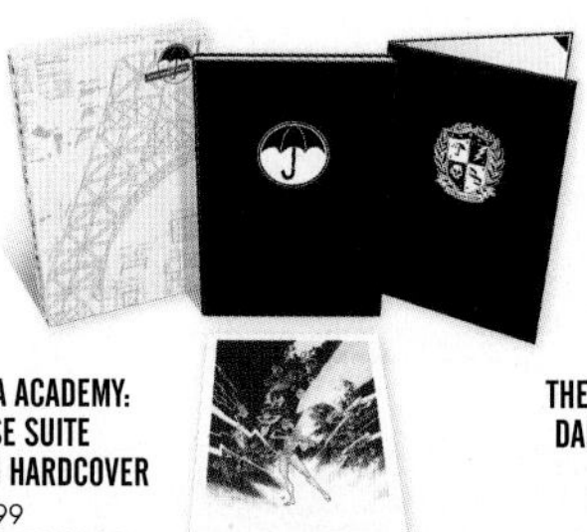

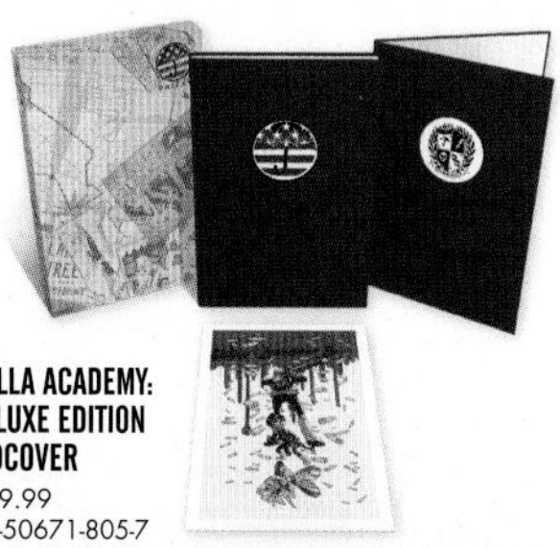

GABRIEL BÁ AND FÁBIO MOON!

"Twin Brazilian artists Fábio Moon and Gabriel Bá have made a huge mark on comics." —*Publishers Weekly*

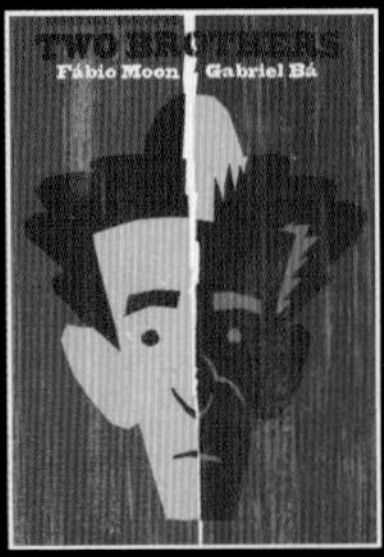
TWO BROTHERS
Fábio Moon
Gabriel Bá

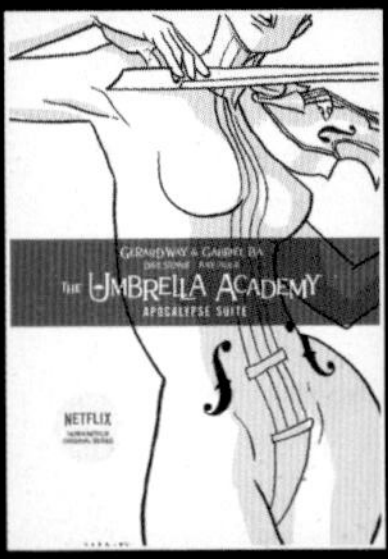
THE UMBRELLA ACADEMY
APOCALYPSE SUITE
NETFLIX

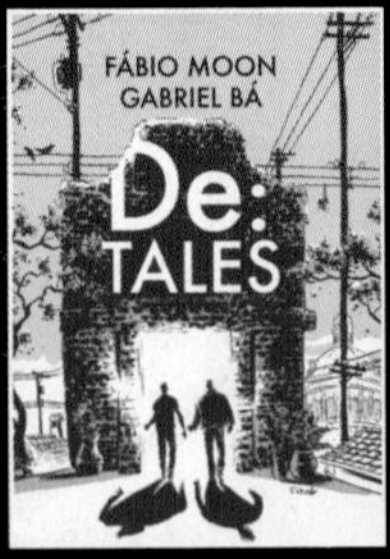
FÁBIO MOON
GABRIEL BÁ
De:
TALES

THE UMBRELLA ACADEMY: APOCALYPSE SUITE
Story by Gerard Way
Art by Gabriel Bá
TPB ISBN: 978-1-59307-978-9 | $17.99
Library Edition HC ISBN: 987-1-50671-547-6 | $39.99

THE UMBRELLA ACADEMY: DALLAS
Story by Gerard Way
Art by Gabriel Bá
TPB ISBN: 978-1-59582-345-8 | $17.99
Library Edition HC ISBN: 987-1-50671-548-3 | $39.99

THE UMBRELLA ACADEMY: HOTEL OBLIVION
Story by Gerard Way
Art by Gabriel Bá
TPB ISBN: 978-1-50671-142-3 | $19.99
Library Edition HC ISBN: 978-1-50671-646-6 | $39.99

PIXU: THE MARK OF EVIL
Story and art by Gabriel Bá, Becky Cloonan, Vasilis Lolos, and Fábio Moon
ISBN: 978-1-61655-813-0 | $14.99

B.P.R.D.: VAMPIRE
Story by Mike Mignola, Fábio Moon, and Gabriel Bá
Art by Fábio Moon and Gabriel Bá
ISBN: 978-1-61655-196-4 | $19.99

B.P.R.D.: 1946–1948
Story by Mike Mignola, Joshua Dysart, and John Arcudi
Art by Fábio Moon, Gabriel Bá, Paul Azaceta, and Max Fiumara
ISBN: 978-1-61655-646-4 | $34.99

NEIL GAIMAN'S HOW TO TALK TO GIRLS AT PARTIES
Story by Neil Gaiman
Art by Fábio Moon and Gabriel Bá
ISBN: 978-1-61655-955-7 | $17.99

TWO BROTHERS
Story and art by Gabriel Bá and Fábio Moon
ISBN: 978-1-61655-856-7 | $24.99

DE:TALES
Story and art by Gabriel Bá and Fábio Moon
ISBN: 978-1-59582-557-5 | $19.99

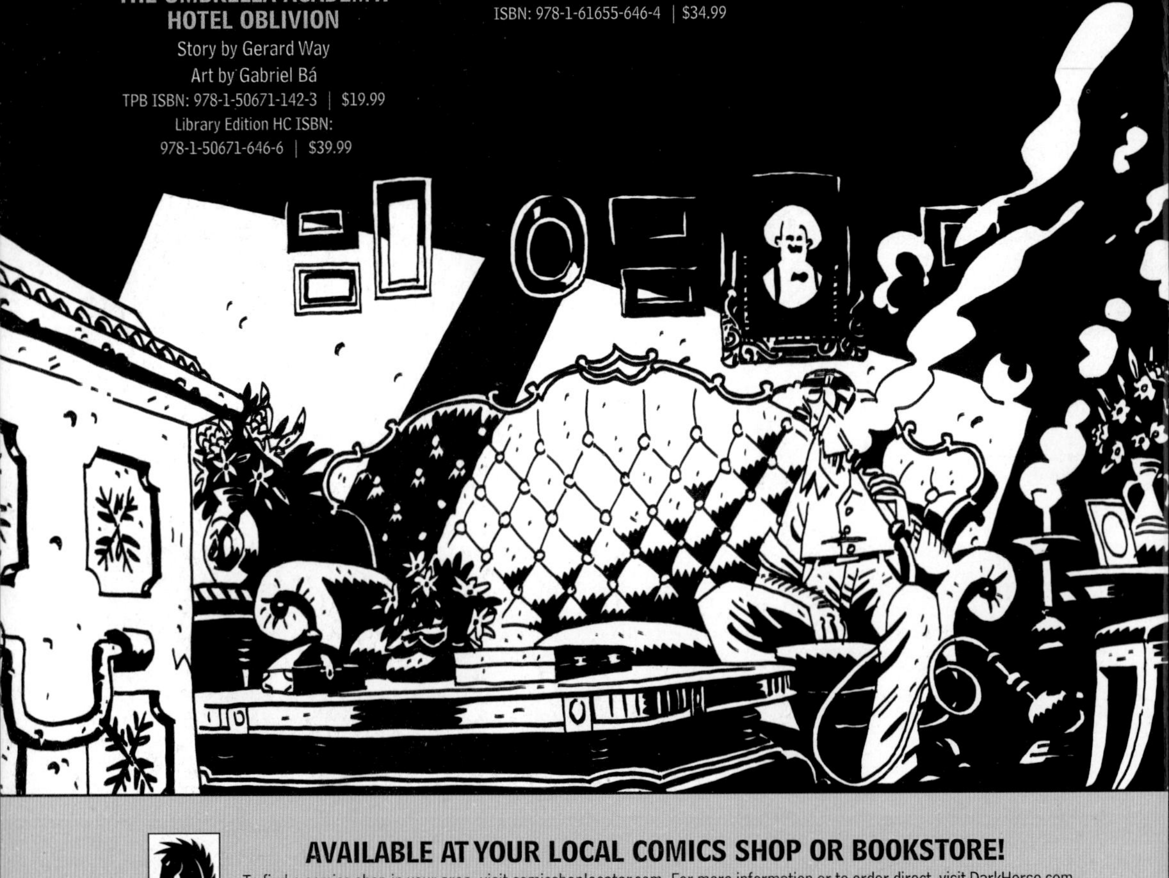

DARK HORSE BOOKS

AVAILABLE AT YOUR LOCAL COMICS SHOP OR BOOKSTORE!

To find a comics shop in your area, visit comicshoplocator.com. For more information or to order direct, visit DarkHorse.com